Starting an eBay® Business For Dummies®

Cheat Sheet

United States Tax Deadlines

Note: Please check with your state government offices for due dates on sales taxes and license fees.

15th of every month: Prior month payroll tax deposit date (if you're on the monthly deposit system)

January 15: Estimated taxes due

January 31: Last day to distribute 1099s and W2s to people you paid during the prior year

January 31: Payroll reports for quarterly period ending 12/31 due

February 28: Last day to send the government copies of your 1099s and W2s

March 15: Calendar year corporation tax due

April 15: Deadline for Individual or Partnership Annual Tax return or deadline to file an extension

April 15: Estimated taxes due

April 30: Payroll reports for period ending 3/31 due

June 15: Estimated taxes due

July 31: Payroll reports for quarterly period ending 6/30 due

September 15: Estimated taxes due

October 31: Payroll reports for quarterly period ending 9/30 due

If the due date falls on a weekend or a federal holiday, the due date is the first business day after that date.

See Chapter 15 for more official information.

When purchasing merchandise to sell:

- Try to pay the lowest possible price for your item — buy at wholesale or less whenever possible.
- If you're the handy fix-it-all type, find items in need of minor repair and put them up for sale "like new."
- Search for unique items that may be common in your geographic area, but hard to find in other places across the country.
- Attend estate sales — many a salable gem is hiding in someone's home.
- Visit closeout stores, liquidators, and auctions.

When Taking Auction Photos:

- Be sure that the item is clean, unwrinkled, and lint-free.
- Take the photo against a clear, undecorated background.
- Make sure that the picture is in focus.
- Be sure that you have enough lighting to show the details of your item.
- Take second and third images to show specific details, such as a signature or detail that better identifies your item.
- Don't use an image at a dpi over 72 for online purposes.
- Try to keep the *total* size of *all* your pictures under 50K for a smooth and swift download.

P9-CIW-557

For Dummies: Bestselling Book Series for Beginners

Starting an eBay®Business For Dummies®

Cheat Sheet

eBay Time Chart

You need to know what time your auctions will close all across the whole U.S. because you don't get top dollar for items that close while part of the country is asleep: Keep this page by your computer and refer to it every time you post an auction!

eBay	Pacific	Mountain	Central	Eastern
00:00	Midnight	1:00 a.m.	2:00 a.m.	3:00 a.m.
1:00	1:00 a.m.	2:00 a.m.	3:00 a.m.	4:00 a.m.
2:00	2:00 a.m.	3:00 a.m.	4:00 a.m.	5:00 a.m.
3:00	3:00 a.m.	4:00 a.m.	5:00 a.m.	6:00 a.m.
4:00	4:00 a.m.	5:00 a.m.	6:00 a.m.	7:00 a.m.
5:00	5:00 a.m.	6:00 a.m.	7:00 a.m.	8:00 a.m.
6:00	6:00 a.m.	7:00 a.m.	8:00 a.m.	9:00 a.m.
7:00	7:00 a.m.	8:00 a.m.	9:00 a.m.	10:00 a.m.
8:00	8:00 a.m.	9:00 a.m.	10:00 a.m.	11:00 a.m.
9:00	9:00 a.m.	10:00 a.m.	11:00 a.m.	Noon
10:00	10:00 a.m.	11:00 a.m.	Noon	1:00 p.m.
11:00	11:00 a.m.	Noon	1:00 p.m.	2:00 p.m.
12:00	Noon	1:00 p.m.	2:00 p.m.	3:00 p.m.
13:00	1:00 p.m.	2:00 p.m.	3:00 p.m.	4:00 p.m.
14:00	2:00 p.m.	3:00 p.m.	4:00 p.m.	5:00 p.m.
15:00	3:00 p.m.	4:00 p.m.	5:00 p.m.	6:00 p.m.
16:00	4:00 p.m.	5:00 p.m.	6:00 p.m.	7:00 p.m.
17:00	5:00 p.m.	6:00 p.m.	7:00 p.m.	8:00 p.m.
18:00	6:00 p.m.	7:00 p.m.	8:00 p.m.	9:00 p.m.
19:00	7:00 p.m.	8:00 p.m.	9:00 p.m.	10:00 p.m.
20:00	8:00 p.m.	9:00 p.m.	10:00 p.m.	11:00 p.m.
21:00	9:00 p.m.	10:00 p.m.	11:00 p.m.	Midnight
22:00	10:00 p.m.	10:00 p.m.	Midnight	1:00 a.m.
23:00	11:00 p.m.	Midnight	1:00 a.m.	2:00 a.m.

General Tips for Sellers

- Answer all e-mail questions from prospective bidders and buyers within 24 hours and check your e-mail hourly before the close of your auctions: Good customer service goes a long way in promoting your eBay business.

- When listing a new item, research your item and be sure that you know its value and the going price.

- Before listing, weigh your item and estimate the shipping cost. Be sure to list shipping and handling costs in your ad.

- Always see how many other sellers are selling your item and try not to have your auction close within a few hours of another.

- To encourage bidding, set the lowest possible starting bid for your item.

- Check the eBay guidelines to be sure that your item is permitted and that your listing doesn't violate any of the listing policies.

- Get to know the listing patterns of sellers who sell similar merchandise to yours and try to close your auctions at different times or days.

For Dummies: Bestselling Book Series for Beginners

™

References for the Rest of Us!®

BESTSELLING BOOK SERIES

Are you intimidated and confused by computers? Do you find that traditional manuals are overloaded with technical details you'll never use? Do your friends and family always call you to fix simple problems on their PCs? Then the For Dummies® computer book series from Wiley Publishing, Inc. is for you.

For Dummies books are written for those frustrated computer users who know they aren't really dumb but find that PC hardware, software, and indeed the unique vocabulary of computing make them feel helpless. For Dummies books use a lighthearted approach, a down-to-earth style, and even cartoons and humorous icons to dispel computer novices' fears and build their confidence. Lighthearted but not lightweight, these books are a perfect survival guide for anyone forced to use a computer.

"I like my copy so much I told friends; now they bought copies."
— *Irene C., Orwell, Ohio*

"Quick, concise, nontechnical, and humorous."
— *Jay A., Elburn, Illinois*

"Thanks, I needed this book. Now I can sleep at night."
— *Robin F., British Columbia, Canada*

Already, millions of satisfied readers agree. They have made For Dummies books the #1 introductory level computer book series and have written asking for more. So, if you're looking for the most fun and easy way to learn about computers, look to For Dummies books to give you a helping hand.

Wiley Publishing, Inc.

Starting an
eBay® Business
FOR
DUMMIES®

by Marsha Collier

Wiley Publishing, Inc.

Starting an eBay® Business For Dummies®

Published by
Wiley Publishing, Inc.
909 Third Avenue
New York, NY 10022
www.wiley.com

Copyright © 2002 Wiley Publishing, Inc., Indianapolis, Indiana

Published simultaneously in Canada

For general information on our other products and services or to obtain technical support, please contact our Customer Care Department within the U.S. at 800-762-2974, outside the U.S. at 317-572-3993, or fax 317-572-4002.

Wiley also publishes its books in a variety of electronic formats. Some content that appears in print may not be available in electronic books.

Library of Congress Cataloging-in-Publication Data:

Library of Congress Control Number: 2001093391

ISBN: 0-7645-1547-0

Manufactured in the United States of America

10 9 8 7 6 5

About the Author

Marsha Collier loves eBay. She loves the selling and buying, as well as meeting other users from around the world. As columnist for eBay Magazine, author of *eBay For Dummies,* and lecturer at eBay University, she shares her knowledge of eBay with millions of online users. As president of her own company, the Collier Company, she planned marketing and advertising for major companies for over fifteen years.

Originally, Marsha was Special Projects Manager for the Los Angeles *Daily News*. Upon the birth of her daughter, she wanted to start a business from home to spend more time with her daughter. In the days when very little respect was given to a home business, she left her job, put paneling on the walls of her garage, installed telephones and computers, and set up shop.

Entrepreneur Magazine featured the Collier Company in 1985 and, in 1990, Marsha's company received the "Small Business of the Year" award from her California State Assemblyman and the Northridge Chamber of Commerce. In *Starting an eBay Business For Dummies,* Marsha combines her knowledge of business, marketing, and eBay savvy to help you make a smooth and quick transition from part-time seller to full-time moneymaker.

Dedication

To the eBay entrepreneurs who have a zest for learning and the "stick-to-it-ive-ness" to follow through on their projects and stare success straight in the eye.

It's for those who are convinced that get-rich-quick schemes don't work, and that in the long run, only hard work and love of what you are doing get the job done and lead to financial achievement and contentment.

It's for you that this book is written. Good luck in all your endeavors. I hope this book will help you along the way.

Author's Acknowledgments

Lots of people made this book what it is: not just the editors, but a few of my friends. Thanks to my husband, Beryl Lockhart, for living with the fact that I'd be writing into the night, my daughter, Susan Dickman (the ultimate Tri-Delt) who would breeze through my office, bringing me up-to-date on all the exciting goings on in her life, and my mom, Claire Berg, who understood why I couldn't hang out too much. Thank you, Jillian Cline, for putting up with a part-time friend, reading my chapters, and helping me organize my thoughts — as well as helping take care of Brutus, the giant pumpkin. As a matter of fact, thanks to Brutus: He's second only to Wilson of *Castaway* fame in the Best Inanimate Object supporting role. Skippy and Blue sat patiently at my side, asking only for a scratch on the head now and then, not even minding the late nights in the office. Joni Lusk, you've been with me throughout the book, and I know you'll be with me forever.

The super folks at eBay help make the eBay community the special place that it is. Thank you for your friendship and support, George Koster and Walt Duflock. Abby Green and Ashleigh Liston, you guys have a great respect for the community and are real pros to work with. Jay Monahan and Rob Chesnut, you two are some of the sharpest tacks in the box.

Thanks also to the gang at Wiley Publishing: Andy Cummings, who first gave me the idea that I could *really* do this, Steven Hayes who put up with my annoying phone calls and hung in with moral support, and Linda Morris, my project editor, who was as cool as they come.

Publisher's Acknowledgments

We're proud of this book; please send us your comments through our online registration form located at www.dummies.com/register/.

Some of the people who helped bring this book to market include the following:

Acquisitions, Editorial, and Media Development

Project Editors: Linda Morris, Nicole A. Laux

Acquisitions Editor: Steven H. Hayes

Copy Editor: Nicole A. Laux

Technical Editor: Kerwin McKenzie

Editorial Manager: Constance Carlisle

Editorial Assistants: Amanda Foxworth, Jean Rogers

Production

Project Coordinator: Dale White

Layout and Graphics: Jackie Nicholas, Betty Schulte, Brian Torwelle, Julie Trippetti, Jeremey Unger

Proofreaders: Charles Spencer, TECHBOOKS Production Services

Indexer: TECHBOOKS Production Services

Special Help Teresa Artman

Publishing and Editorial for Technology Dummies
   Richard Swadley, Vice President and Executive Group Publisher
   Andy Cummings, Vice President and Publisher
   Mary C. Corder, Editorial Director

Publishing for Consumer Dummies
   Diane Graves Steele, Vice President and Publisher
   Joyce Pepple, Acquisitions Director

Composition Services
   Gerry Fahey, Vice President of Production Services
   Debbie Stailey, Director of Composition Services

Contents at a Glance

Introduction 1

Part I: Getting Serious at eBay 7
Chapter 1: Using eBay to Launch Your Business 9
Chapter 2: The Finer Points of eBay Auctions 31
Chapter 3: Cool eBay Tools 59
Chapter 4: Practicing Safe Selling 83
Chapter 5: Your Very Own eBay Store 105

Part II: Setting Up Shop 121
Chapter 6: Stocking the Store 123
Chapter 7: Know the Value of What You're Selling 141
Chapter 8: Establishing a Base of Operations: Your Web Site 153

Part III: Business Is Business — No Foolin' Around! 169
Chapter 9: Software Built for Online Auctions 171
Chapter 10: Dollars and Sense: Budgeting and Marketing Your Auctions 193
Chapter 11: Jazzing Up Your Auctions 207
Chapter 12: Providing Excellent Customer Service 223
Chapter 13: When the Money Comes Rolling In 231
Chapter 14: Getting It from Your Place to Theirs 255

Part IV: Your eBay Back Office 269
Chapter 15: Going Legit 271
Chapter 16: Practicing Safe and Smart Record-Keeping 279
Chapter 17: Building an eBay Back Office 297

Part V: The Part of Tens 309
Chapter 18: Ten (Or So) Successful eBay Sellers and Their Stories 311
Chapter 19: Ten Other Places to Move Merchandise 327

Part VI: Appendixes 335
Appendix A: Glossary of Auction and Accounting Terms 337
Appendix B: The Hows and Whys of a Home Network 341

Index 349

Cartoons at a Glance

By Rich Tennant

page 335

page 121

page 169

page 269

page 7

page 309

Cartoon Information:
Fax: 978-546-7747
E-Mail: richtennant@the5thwave.com
World Wide Web: www.the5thwave.com

Table of Contents

· ·

Introduction 1

   Success Awaits you 1
   Let's Start Now! 2
   My Silly, Foolish Assumptions 3
   How This Book Is Organized 3
      Part I: Getting Serious at eBay 3
      Part II: Setting Up Shop 3
      Part III: Business Is Business — No Foolin' Around! 4
      Part IV: Your eBay Back Office 4
      Part V: The Part of Tens 4
      Part VI: Appendixes 4
   Icons Used in This Book 5
   Where Do You Go from Here? 5

Part 1: Getting Serious at eBay 7

Chapter 1: Using eBay to Launch Your Business 9

   Getting Down to Bidness (er, Business) 9
      Budgeting your time: eBay as a
       part-time money maker 10
      Jumping in with both feet: Making eBay a full-time job 12
   Deciding What to Sell 13
      Turning your hobby into a business 14
      Including the whole family in the business 16
      Bringing your existing business to eBay 18
   Getting What It Takes to Sell 20
      Computer hardware 20
      Connecting to the Internet 20
      Choosing your eBay user ID 23
      Finding your eBay feedback 24
   Making Your Auctions Run More Smoothly 25
      Software you can use 25
      Collecting the cash 27
      Home base: Your Web site 28
      Setting up your shop 28

Chapter 2: The Finer Points of eBay Auctions 31

   Finding Where to Sell Your Stuff 31
      Automotive? Go eBay Motors 33
      eBay Premier 36

eBay Live auctions 37
Real Estate: Not quite an auction 38
Fixed Price Sales at eBay 40
eBay's half brother: Half.com 40
eBay Stores 44
Types of eBay Auctions 45
Traditional auctions 45
Dutch auctions 45
Reserve Price auctions 47
Restricted Access auctions 48
Private auctions 48
Running Your Auction 49
Starting the bidding 50
Auction timing 51
Marketing your auctions 52
Personal Offer 53
Listing Violations 54
Listing policies 54
Linking from your auctions 56
Linking from your About Me page 57

Chapter 3: Cool eBay Tools **59**

My eBay 60
Bidding/Watching 61
Selling 64
Favorites 67
Accounts 69
Preferences/Set-up 69
Your About Me Page 70
eBay Seller Services 72
Bidder-management tools 72
ID Verify 75
Feedback: Your permanent record 75
The eBay Power Sellers program 78
eBay auction software 79
Lloyd's of London insurance 79
eBay education 80

Chapter 4: Practicing Safe Selling **83**

Is What You Want to Sell Legal at eBay? 84
Prohibited items 85
Questionable items 86
Potentially infringing items 87
Trading Violations 89
When the competition doesn't play fair 90
Baaad bidders 93
Not knowing who's who 96

Taking Action: What to Do When Someone Breaks the Rules 97
    SquareTrade to the rescue 98
    eBay's SafeHarbor 103

Chapter 5: Your Very Own eBay Store 105

Online Stores Galore 105
Your eBay Store 107
    Setting up shop 107
    Listing your items 114
    Marketing your wares 116
    Making a sale 116

Part II: Setting Up Shop *121*

Chapter 6: Stocking the Store 123

Dollar Stores 124
Discount Club Stores 125
Garage Sales 127
Going-Out-of-Business Sales 128
Auctions 128
    Liquidation auctions 129
    Estate auctions 129
    Charity silent auctions 129
Goodwill, Salvation Army, and Resale Shops 130
Freebies 131
Salvage: Liquidation Items, Unclaimed Freight, and Returns 132
    Items by the pallet 134
    Job lots 135
Wholesale Merchandise by the Case 136
Resale Items at eBay 137
Consignment Selling 139

Chapter 7: Know the Value of What You're Selling 141

The Easy Way: eBay Search 142
    Advanced searching 143
    Smart Search 144
Useful Publications 148
Online Sources of Information 149
    Web sites 149
    Online appraisals 150
Authentication Services 151

Chapter 8: Establishing a Base of Operations: Your Web Site 153
  Free Web Space (A Good Place to Start) 154
  Paying for Your Web Space 157
    ReadyHosting.com 159
    Interland.com 160
    Microsoft bCentral 161
    Yahoo! Web site services 162
  What's in a Web Site Name: Naming Your Baby 163
  Registering Your Domain Name (Before Someone Else Takes It) 163
  Marketing Your Web Site (More Visitors = More Business) 164
    Banner ad exchanges 165
    Getting your URL into a search engine 166

Part III: Business Is Business — No Foolin' Around! 169

Chapter 9: Software Built for Online Auctions 171
  Considering Tasks for Automation 171
    Setting up images for automatic FTP upload 172
    Setting up your own auction photo gallery 173
    Sorting auction e-mail 175
    Automating end-of-auction e-mail 175
    Keeping inventory 175
    Generating HTML 176
    Posting or relisting auctions with one click 176
    Scheduling your listings for bulk upload 177
    Automating other tasks 177
  Managing Your Business with Online Resources and Software 179
    Online auction management sites 180
    Auction management software 186

**Chapter 10: Dollars and Sense: Budgeting and
Marketing Your Auctions** 193
  Listing Your Items 194
  eBay's Optional Listing Features 196
    Home page featured auctions 196
    Featured Plus! 198
    Highlight option 198
    Boldface option 199
    View counter 199
    The Gallery 200
    Buy It Now 202
  eBay's Cut of the Action 203
    Listing fees 203
    eBay Final Value Fees 205

Chapter 11: Jazzing Up Your Auctions **207**

Writing Winning Text 207
Your eBay Photo Studio 208
    Digital camera 209
    Other studio equipment 210
    Props 212
Taking Good Pictures 215
Using a Scanner 216
Image Editing Software 217
A Home for Your Images 218
    Free ISP space 218
    Auction management sites 219
    Paid image hosting 219
    eBay IPIX 219
HTML and You 220

Chapter 12: Providing Excellent Customer Service **223**

Meeting Your Customers 223
Communicating with Your Customers 225
    The initial inquiry 226
    The winner's notification letter 226
    The payment reminder 228
    The payment received/shipping notice 229

Chapter 13: When the Money Comes Rolling In **231**

It Doesn't Get Any Simpler: Money Orders 231
    7-Eleven 232
    United States Postal Service 233
    SendMoneyOrder.com 233
    BidPay.com 234
Pay Me When You Get This: Cash On Delivery 236
The Check's in the Mail: Personal Checks 236
    Paper checks 237
    Electronic checks 237
Hold This for Me: Tradeable Escrow Service 238
I Take Plastic: Credit Cards 240
    Credit card payment services 240
    Your very own merchant account 250
    Costco member's credit card processing 253
    The VeriSign Payflow link service 254

Chapter 14: Getting It from Your Place to Theirs **255**

Finding the Perfect Shipping Carrier: The Big Three ...255
    Federal Express 256
    United Parcel Service 259
    United States Postal Service 261

Getting Free Delivery Confirmation from Shippertools.com 263
Protecting Your Packages with Universal Parcel
    Insurance Coverage 265
        Stamp program 267
        Offline standard program 267

Part IV: Your eBay Back Office 269

Chapter 15: Going Legit 271
Types of Businesses 272
    Sole proprietorship 272
    Partnership 273
    Corporation 273
Taking Care of Regulatory Details 274
    Fictitious business name statement 275
    Business license or city tax certificate 275
    Sales tax number 277
    Don't withhold the withholding forms 278

Chapter 16: Practicing Safe and Smart Record-Keeping 279
Keeping the Books: Basics That Get You Started 280
Records Uncle Sam May Want to See 281
    Supporting information 282
    How long should you keep your records? 283
Bookkeeping Software 285
QuickBooks: Making Bookkeeping Uncomplicated 286
    QuickBooks Pro 2001 287
    QuickBooks EasyStep Interview 287
    QuickBooks chart of accounts 290
    QuickBooks on the Web 295

Chapter 17: Building an eBay Back Office 297
The Warehouse: Organizing Your Space 297
    Shelving your profits 298
    Box 'em or bag 'em? 298
Inventory: Keeping Track of What You've Got and
    Where You Keep It 299
The Shipping Department: Packin' It Up 300
    Pre-packaging clean up 300
    Packing materials 300
    Packaging — the heart of the matter 302
The Mail Room: Sendin' It Out 304
    Stamps.com 305
    Simply Postage 307

Part V: The Part of Tens 309

Chapter 18: Ten (Or So) Successful eBay Sellers and Their Stories 311

Ally-cat 312
BobMill 313
Bubblefast 314
CaliforniaMagic 316
Cardking4 317
CharmsandChains 319
CoinsByHucky.com 320
Dollectibles 321
Propigate@home.com 322
SallyJo 324
www.nelson.hm 325

Chapter 19: Ten Other Places to Move Merchandise 327

Donate to Charitable Organizations 328
    Classy gifting 328
    Online charities 328
Have a Garage Sale 329
Rent a Table at the Local Swap Meet 330
Consign Merchandise to the Local Antique Mall ...331
Take a Booth at a Community Event 331
Resell to Sellers at eBay 331
Visit a Local Auctioneer 332
Find Specialty Auction Sites 333
Run a Classified Liquidation Ad 334
Sell Everything at eBay for a $1 Opening Bid 334

Part VI: Appendixes 335

Appendix A: Glossary of Auction and Accounting Terms 337

Appendix B: The Hows and Whys of a Home Network 341

Home Phoneline Network 342
    Preparing to install your home phoneline network ...343
    Installing your home phoneline network 345
Internet Security and Your Home Network 347
    Firewall software 347
    Antivirus software 348

Index 349

Introduction

● ●

*T*hank you for opening this book. Stay awhile and read so that you can find out what it takes to set up your own business at eBay. I've written this book to serve as a manual to get you organized and get your eBay business off the ground. From handling your selling time at eBay more efficiently to stocking your store to the *real* way to set up your books and daily operations, I give you all the dirty details about running a successful eBay business. From my own years of experience and numerous interactions with hundreds of eBay sellers, I offer countless time- and money-saving tips — not to mention secret eBay hints — along the way.

I've made a successful living while working out of my home for the past 20 years, and I share my personal experiences with you to show you that you, too, can run a successful home business. I started my own marketing and advertising business so that I could be at home and near my pre-school daughter. She's in college now (don't start counting the years — it's not polite), and I still have my own business and also make some nice profits at eBay. Through perseverance and dedication, my small homegrown business financed my home, my daughter's upbringing, twelve years of private school, and now college.

One thing that I can't guarantee you is how much money you can earn selling at eBay. I've discovered — perhaps the hard way — that it takes a good deal of discipline to run a home business. The time you spend and the amount of devotion that you give your business will help you gauge your success.

Success Awaits you

If you've read *eBay For Dummies,* you know just how fun and profitable eBay can be. You've probably picked up this book because you've heard lots of stories about people making big money online, and you're interested in getting your piece of the pie. If you have a retail business, establishing an eBay Store can be a profitable extension of it. Is selling at eBay something that you'd like to do more of? Do you have a full-time job, but you'd like to sell at eBay part-time? eBay can easily supplement your income for the better things in life — like vacations or even private school for the kids. Perhaps you're looking to make a career change, and jumping into an eBay business with both feet first is just what you have in mind. If so, this is the book for you.

I've watched eBay change from a homey community of friendly collectors to a behemoth Web site of over 8,000 categories of items and over 30 million registered users. I'll bet you've been buying and selling with positive results and you can see the benefits of taking this a bit more seriously. What are you waiting for? There's no time like the present to get started on your new career. Thousands of people across the world are setting up businesses online, and now is your time to take the leap of faith to begin a profitable enterprise. eBay gives you the tools, the customers, and the venue to market your wares. So all you're going to need is a bit of direction.

Starting an eBay Business For Dummies picks up where *eBay For Dummies* leaves off. The tips I include give you the opportunity to improve your eBay money-making ability and just might turn an eBay novice into a professional running a booming eBay business. I also show the experienced user the prudent way to turn haphazard sales into an organized business. This book has it all! I've combined the fine points of eBay with real business and marketing tools to help you complete the journey from part-time seller to online entrepreneur.

Let's Start Now!

If you use this book the way you'd use a cookbook, jumping around from recipe to recipe (or chapter to chapter), you'll be able to find the answers to your particular questions all at once. Read the book from beginning to end if you'd like, and keep it handy to look up your questions in the future as they come to you. You don't have to memorize a thing; the information you need is at arm's length whenever you have a question.

In this book, you can find the answers to some important questions as I take you through the following tracks:

- ✔ Reviewing what you know and introducing some of the finer points of eBay auctions
- ✔ Sprucing up your auctions to attract more bidders
- ✔ Dealing with customers
- ✔ Setting up your business in a professional manner
- ✔ Deciding how to handle inventory (and where to find it)
- ✔ What you need to be in an eBay business . . . for ***real***

My Silly, Foolish Assumptions

If you've bought this book, I assume you're serious about selling at eBay, and want to find out the fine points of just how to do that. Or perhaps you want to know how much is involved in an eBay business so that you can make the decision whether to give it a go.

If I have you figured out and you've decided that it is time to get serious, here are some other foolish assumptions I've made about you:

- ✔ You have a computer and an Internet connection.
- ✔ You've bought and sold at eBay and are fairly familiar with how it works.
- ✔ You either have an existing small business or you'd like to start one.
- ✔ You feel that working from home in jeans and a sweatshirt is a great idea.

If you can say yes to my foolish assumptions, you're off and running! Take a few moments to read the following section to get a feel for how I've put this book together.

How This Book Is Organized

This book has six parts. The parts stand on their own, which means that you can read Chapter 12 after reading Chapter 8 and maybe skip Chapter 13 altogether (but I know you won't because that's where I discuss the money!).

Part 1: Getting Serious at eBay

Reviewing what you know is always a great place to start when you start anything. Considering the way eBay constantly changes, you'll probably find a little review worthwhile. So in this part, I delve into the finer points of eBay. Perhaps you'll discover a thing or two you didn't know — or perchance have forgotten.

Part II: Setting Up Shop

You need to decide what type of business you plan to run, and what type of inventory you'll sell. Here's where I discuss how to find merchandise and what's the best way to sell it. In this part, I also discuss the importance of your own Web site (and how to set one up) so that you're able to set up shop online.

Part III: Business Is Business — No Foolin' Around!

In Part III, I discuss exactly how to use available online and offline tools, how to implement auction management software, how to jazz up your auctions, and how to handle shipping efficiently and effectively. Working with customers and collecting payments is important, too, and here's where you'll find that information.

Part IV: Your eBay Back Office

Setting up your business as a real business entity involves some nasty paperwork and red tape. I try to fill in the blanks here, as well as show you how to set up your bookkeeping. This is the place where you'll find a checklist of the items you'll need to run your online business.

Part V: The Part of Tens

You can't write a Dummies book without including the traditional Part of Tens. So in an untraditional manner, I offer ten real stories of successful people selling at eBay and ten places to move your merchandise (if you want to sell elsewhere than eBay).

Part VI: Appendixes

I include a random collection of terms in Appendix A; you're probably already familiar with many of these, but others will be new to you. Refer to this glossary often as you peruse other parts of the book. In Appendix B, I briefly discuss the hows and whys of home networking, a perk you'll want to have as your eBay business grows.

Icons Used in This Book

If there's something I need to interject or I have a short time-saver to share, I indicate so by placing this tip icon in front of the paragraph. You'll know the tip to follow will be right on target!

Do you really know people who tie string around their fingers to remember something? Me neither; but this icon gives me the opportunity to give you a brief note that's worth taking note of. Kinda like a Post-it note.

I like this picture of a petard. Yep, that's what it's called; the round bomb device that Wile E. Coyote slam-dunks in the cartoons is called a petard. In that vein, if you don't heed the warning indicated by the small petard, you may be "hoisted by your own petard" or made a victim of your own foolishness.

Here I share some of the interesting thoughts I've picked up from eBay sellers over the years. Because I believe that knowledge is enhanced through learning from the mistakes of others, I include these little auction factoids so that you might gain some insight from them. After all, if someone else has learned from a unique trick, you can benefit by taking heed.

Where Do You Go from Here?

Time to hunker down and delve into the following pages. If you have time, just turn the page and start from scratch. If you're really anxious and already have some questions you want answered, check out the handy index at the end of the book and research your query.

My goal is to help all eBay members reach their goals. So please check out my Web site:

```
www.coolebaytools.com
```

Please e-mail me with any suggestions, additions, and comments. I want to hear from you and hope to update this book with your words of wisdom.

Part I
Getting Serious at eBay

The 5th Wave   By Rich Tennant

"I don't understand why no one at eBay is bidding on Junior's old baby clothes."

In this part . . .

*R*eviewing what you know is always a great place to start. Because eBay is constantly making changes, a little review is worthwhile in this case. eBay has made a lot of improvements, too, and some features are like hidden golden nuggets. So in this first part, I delve into the finer points of eBay with you; perhaps you'll discover a thing or two you didn't know, or perchance have forgotten.

Chapter 1

Using eBay to Launch Your Business

In This Chapter

▶ Getting serious about your business

▶ Making decisions about what to sell

▶ Taking your existing business online

▶ Having what it takes

So you've decided to get serious about your sales at eBay. Now you have to step up to the plate and decide just how much time you have to devote to your eBay business. In this book, I talk about all kinds of eBay businesses. Don't think that because you don't want to quit your day job (yet!) and start up at eBay full time that I think you're not serious. A large portion of sellers, even eBay power sellers (eBay sellers who gross over $2,000 a month in sales), works at eBay only part time.

eBay sellers come from all walks of life. A good number of stay-at-home moms are out there selling at eBay. So many retirees are finding eBay a great place to supplement their income that, in the future, I wouldn't be surprised if the AARP creates a special eBay arm. If, for one reason or another, you're pulled out of your normal work routine and faced with a new lifestyle, you can easily make the transition to selling at eBay. Selling at eBay can fit right in to a stay-at-home lifestyle.

Getting Down to Bidness (er, Business)

When you set out to launch a business, any business, you need to set your priorities. A business at home requires definite priority setting. You must apply some level of discipline to anything that you want to make a success of; your eBay business requires this discipline, too.

I won't bore you with the now legendary story of how Pierre Omidyar started eBay to help fulfill his girlfriend's Pez dispenser habit, blah, blah, blah. I will tell you that he did start his Auction Web with a laptop, a regular Internet Service Provider (ISP), and an old school desk. He and his buddy Jeff Skoll (a Stanford MBA) ran the twenty-four-hour-a-day, seven-day-a-week Auction Web all by themselves. Believe me, when I began using the service, I always had a lot of questions — I always got prompt, friendly answers to my e-mails. When the site started attracting more traffic, Pierre finally had to install a server in his apartment. To pay for the server, Pierre and Jeff began charging 25 cents to list an auction. Pierre was so busy running the site that the envelopes full of checks began to pile up — he didn't even have time to open the mail.

When Pierre incorporated eBay Auction Web in 1996 with his partner Jeff, they were each drawing a salary of $25,000. Their first office consisted of one room, and they had one part-time employee to handle the payments. They started small and grew.

In this chapter, I talk about budgeting *your* time and planning just how much time *you* will be able to devote to your eBay business. And you have to figure out what to sell. Your eBay business won't grow overnight, but with dedication and persistence, you may just form your own online empire.

Budgeting your time: eBay as a part-time money maker

A part-time eBay business can be very profitable. You can spend as little or as much time as you want at eBay, from a few hours a week to a full-time job. One thing that I stress in this book is that the more time and energy you spend on your eBay business, the more money you can make. That said, I now move on to the lowest possible level of time that you can devote to your business.

Maybe you enjoy finding miscellaneous items to sell at eBay. You find these items somehow in your day-to-day life. So you can figure that you spend at least a couple of hours (maybe three) a week at eBay. That's already in your schedule; now, you must figure in the time it takes to write up your auctions. If you're not selling the same thing every day, you need to allow approximately twenty minutes to write your auction, to take your picture or to scan your image, and of course, to upload it to a photo-hosting site.

How much time it takes to perform these tasks varies from person to person, and will improve according to your level of expertise. Regardless, every task in your eBay auction business takes time, and you must budget for that time. See the sidebar "Some handy eBay time-saving tips" elsewhere in this chapter for pointers.

TIP

Some handy eBay timesaving tips

Crunched for time? The following are some features that you're sure to find useful — and handy:

✔ **HTML templates:** In Chapter 11, I give you some tips to get basic HTML format templates for attractive auctions. These HTML templates cut your auction design time to a couple of minutes. Most experienced eBay sellers use preset templates to speed up the task of listing auctions, and this should be your goal.

✔ **Mister Lister program:** When you want to list a bunch of new auctions at once, I recommend using the eBay Mister Lister program. I estimate that Mister Lister enables you to put together and upload ten auctions in just fifteen minutes. In Chapter 9, I run

down the details on how to use this very cool tool.

✔ **Relisting feature:** When you sell the same item time after time, you can use the handy eBay relisting feature. When your auction ends at eBay, a link pops up offering to relist your auction. You can use this feature when you're in a hurry. If you want to run a different auction with a similar HTML format to the one that just ended, simply cut and paste the new title and description into the Sell Your Item page of your relisted auction.

✔ **Auction management software:** See the section "Software you can use" elsewhere in this chapter and Chapter 9, in which I detail various programs to integrate into your eBay business.

Only you can decide how much time you want to spend researching going rates for items at eBay and deciding when your item will sell for the highest price. You can take great photos and write brilliant descriptions, but cashmere sweaters won't go for as much in the heat of summer as they do in winter. Doing your research can take up a good deal of time when you're selling a varied group of items.

You also have to consider how much time it takes to shop for your merchandise. You may have to travel to dealers, go to auctions, or spend time online discovering new ways to find your auction merchandise. Many sellers set aside a full day each week for this undertaking. Your merchandise is what makes you money, so don't skimp on the time you spend identifying products. The time you spend on this comes back to you in higher profits.

Here's a list of various activities that you must perform when doing business at eBay:

✔ Setting up and photographing item

✔ Cleaning up and resizing image in photo editor

✔ Uploading image to host

✔ Weighing item and determining shipping cost

- ✔ Choosing auction title with keywords
- ✔ Writing a concise and creative description
- ✔ Listing your auction at eBay
- ✔ Answering bidder questions (average per day)
- ✔ Sending out EOA e-mails
- ✔ Banking
- ✔ Bookkeeping
- ✔ Packing
- ✔ Addressing labels and affixing postage
- ✔ Going to the post office

Take the time to perform each of the tasks; watch the clock and time yourself to see how long it takes you to accomplish each of them. The time varies when you list multiple items, so think of the figures that you come up with as your *baseline*, a minimum amount of time that you must set aside for these tasks. This information can help you decide how many hours in a month you need to devote to running your part-time eBay business.

Jumping in with both feet: Making eBay a full-time job

As you can see in the list in the previous section, the tasks required for your eBay business can be time consuming, but careful planning and scheduling can turn your business into an online empire. The best way to go full time at eBay is to first run your business part time for a while. In any business, ironing out the wrinkles takes time; an eBay business is no different.

After you become comfortable with eBay as a business, you're ready to make the transition to full-time seller. As a full-time seller at eBay, you'll probably become an eBay Power Seller. The minimum gross monthly sales for a Bronze level Power Seller is $2,000. If you plan your time efficiently, you can easily attain this goal. Head to Chapter 3 for more information on the Power Seller program.

Running a full-time business at eBay is the perfect option for the working mom who prefers staying at home with her children, a retiree looking for something to do, or someone who'd just rather do something else than work for his boss. Read some real life profiles of happy full-time sellers in Chapter 18.

See Figure 1-1 for a summer example of the eBay home page, the first stop for most buyers at eBay. Note how eBay makes an effort to reflect the seasonality to better market the items you put up for sale.

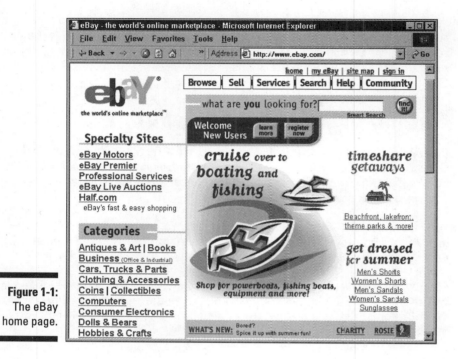

Figure 1-1:
The eBay
home page.

Deciding What to Sell

What should I sell? That is *the* million dollar question! In your quest for merchandise, you're bound to hear about soft goods or hard goods. These terms don't seem very useful at first, but when you buy in bulk, you must understand their meanings. *Soft* (or non-durable) goods are generally textile products, such as clothing, fabrics, and bedding. *Hard* goods are computer equipment, housewares, and anything else that's basically non-disposable.

When deciding what you're going to sell, the following are just a few points to consider:

- ✓ **Shipping costs:** Some differences exist between shipping hard and soft goods. Soft goods can fold up and be packed in standard box sizes, available from the USPS. Most hard goods come in their own boxes, which may or may not be individually shippable. You'll also need to use Styrofoam peanuts or bubble cushioning or to double package the item in an oddly sized box. See Chapter 17 for more shipping and packing information.

- ✓ **Possible storage problems** (for both hard and soft goods)**:** Do you have the room to store enough merchandise to keep you going? Soft goods can take up considerably less space.

- ✓ **Other shipping considerations:** Do you want to handle large boxes and deal with the hassles of shipping them?

You don't always have to buy in bulk to make money at eBay. The first things you sell might be things that you find in your garage or attic. To find out about some other fun ways to acquire goods to sell, check out the next section.

Turning your hobby into a business

C'mon, you've got a hobby; everyone does! Did you collect stamps and coins as a kid? Play with Barbie dolls? Maybe your hobby is cars? Did you inherit a bunch of antiques? eBay has a market for almost anything, so narrow your choices down to just a few.

You can't possibly be an expert on everything. You need to keep up on the market for your items, and following more than four or five basic item groups may divert your attention from actually selling.

Should you decide to major in miscellany and sell anything and everything, you should be prepared that you may not realize the highest possible prices for your items. This can be okay, too, if you have a source that permits you to buy items at dirt-cheap pricing.

Collectibles: Big business at eBay

Pierre Omidyar started eBay with the idea to trade collectible Pez dispensers; the site now lists sixteen main categories of collectibles (see Figure 1-2) that divide into hundreds of categories, sub categories, and sub-sub categories. Almost anything and everything that you'd want to collect is here: Everything from advertising memorabilia to Girl Scout pins to Zippo lighters! Nothing is missing.

If you have a collection of your own, eBay is a great way to find rare items. Because your collection is something dear to your heart and you've studied it on and off for years, you could probably call yourself an expert. Bingo — you're an expert at something! I recommend that you use your skills to find things in your area of expertise (you're liking this, aren't you?) at discount prices and then sell them at eBay for a profit. Who better than you? You've got connections with fellow collectors and even if you don't, I'd bet that you know where to get the goods. So start small and start with something you know.

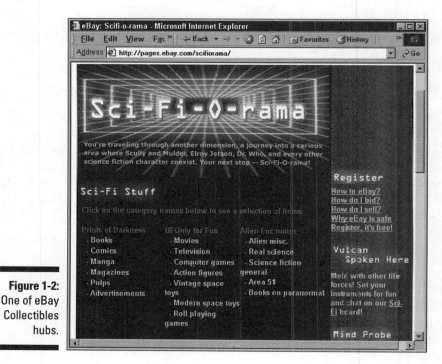

If there's one thing you know, it's fashion!

Ever since high school, you've known how to put together a great outfit. You can find bargains at Goodwill and, when you wear them, people think you've spent hundreds on your garb. I'd even bet that you're the kind that knows just where to get those in-season closeouts before anyone else does. Looks like you've found your market. Pick up as many of those stylish designer wrap dresses (you know whose at you know where) as you can and set them up on the mannequin you've bought to model your fashions for eBay photos (see Figure 1-3). (For more on setting up fashion photos at eBay, check out Chapter 11.) Within a week, you may be doubling your money — 'cause sweetie-darling, who knows fashion better than you?

If there's a ball, wheels, or competition involved — it's for you

I don't want to preach generalities, but I think I'm pretty safe in saying that most guys like sports. Guys like to watch sports, play sports, and look good while they're doing it. I see that as opening up venues for a profitable empire at eBay. I don't want to leave out all the women out there who excel and participate in many sports. Women may have even more discriminating needs for their sporting endeavors! (I know I do. My golf game stinks — but I do make a point to at least look good when I go out there, with respectable equipment and a great outfit.)

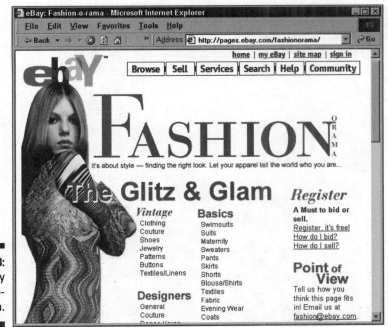

Figure 1-3:
eBay
fashion-o-
rama.

eBay has an amazing market going on right now for soccer equipment, and I don't even want to go into how much football and golf stuff is selling at eBay. And last time I looked, golf items (see Figure 1-4) totaled over 30,000 listings! That's just at eBay. Half.com (eBay's fixed price sales site) also has a sporting goods department where you can sell your items. What a bonanza! New stuff, used stuff — it's all selling at eBay. It's enough to put your local pro shop out of business — or perhaps put *you* in business.

Including the whole family in the business

Sometimes just the idea of a part-time business can throw you into a tizzy. After all, don't you have enough to do? School, work, soccer, kids glued to the TV — you might sometimes feel like you've no time for family time. The importance of family time is what brought me to eBay in the first place. I was working long hours in my own business and just felt too tired at the end of the day. My daughter Susan wanted to go shopping, perhaps for some Hello Kitty toys or a Barbie doll, and I just didn't have the strength.

Figure 1-4:
Golf central
at eBay,
including
Golf
Magazine's
monthly
equipment
report.

I'd heard about Auction Web from a friend, and had bought some things for my own collections online. (Okay, you got me; I collect Star Trek stuff — call me Geek with a capital G.) I'd also browsed around the site and found some popular toys selling for reasonable prices. So one evening I introduced Susan to eBay, and life has never been the same. We'd go to toy stores together when they first opened early in the morning, so we'd get first dibs on shipments of the hottest, newest toys. She would go to the dolls and I to the action figures. We'd buy several, go home, and post them for sale at eBay. We made money, yes, but the best part was our bi-weekly toy runs. They will always remain a special memory.

Susan is in college now (majoring in Business and Marketing) and calls home when she finds a hot CD, or has seen some closeouts of a top-selling item. We still purchase and list items together. The family that eBays together . . . always does.

My short trip down memory lane has a point: A family business can succeed and everyone can enjoy it. I was in charge of the financing and the packing while Susan looked up ZIP codes on the Internet and put pins in a 4' x 5' map showing every city that we bought or sold from. She learned some excellent lessons in marketing, advertising, and geography, all in one swoop.

Toys, books, and music — oh MY!

Having children in your home brings you closer to the latest trends than you could ever imagine. I remember sitting at a Starbucks a couple of years ago watching some dads and their sons pouring over notebooks full of Pokémon cards. (Actually, the kids were off playing somewhere and the dads were coveting the cards.)

And what about Star Wars? Star Trek? G.I. Joe? Can you say action figures? (If guys have them, they're not dolls — they're action figures.) If you have access to the latest and greatest toys, buy them up and sell them to those who can't find them in their neck of the woods.

If your home is like mine, books pile up by the tens! Old educational books that your children have outgrown (even college textbooks) can be turned into a profit. Remember that not every book is a classic that needs to be a part of your library forever. Let another family get the pleasure of sharing children's tales!

If anything piles up quicker than books, it has to be CDs and videos. Somehow the old lambada or macarena music doesn't hold the magic for you as it once did. Or maybe after a while, those zany kid comedies don't mesmerize you the way they used to. You can get rid of your own items and find plenty of stock at garage sales. Buy them cheap and make a couple of dollars.

Selling children's clothes

When I recently checked eBay for the total number of infant and children's clothes auctions in progress, I found more than 12,000 and the bidding was going hot and heavy. For stay-at-home moms, selling infant and children's clothing is a super way to pick up extra income.

If you've had a baby, you know all too well that friends and relatives shower moms with lots of cute outfits. If you're lucky, the baby gets to wear one or two of these (maybe only for a special picture) before outgrowing the item. These adorable portrait outfits can earn you a profit at eBay. Many mothers are out there with children a few steps behind yours, looking for bargain clothing at eBay — a profitable hand-me-down community. As your children grow up (and out of their old clothes), earn some money while helping another mother out.

Bringing your existing business to eBay

eBay isn't only a marketplace where you're able to unload slow or out-of-season merchandise. With the advent of eBay stores, you can set up your store right at eBay (see Figure 1-5). An eBay store allows you to list items at eBay at a reduced fee and keep them online for 30 days. When you run your regular auctions for special items, they will have a link to other items in your store.

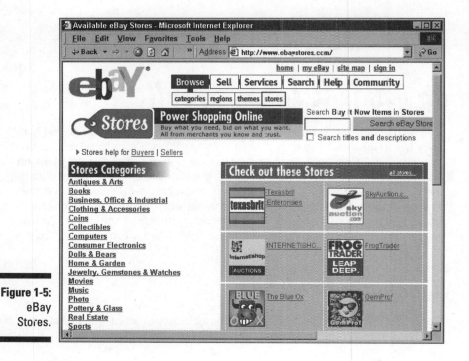

Figure 1-5:
eBay
Stores.

✔ **Opening a second store at eBay:** How many people run stores that sell every item, every time? If you're a retailer, you've probably made a buying mistake. Many times the item that isn't selling in your store is selling like hotcakes in similar stores elsewhere in the country. eBay gives you the tools to sell those extra items to make room for more of what sells at your home base.

Maybe you just need to raise some cash quickly. eBay has over 8,000 categories in which you can sell regular stock or specialty items. You are certainly not limited by what you can sell. Almost everything will sell at eBay. For a caveat on what's verboten, check out Chapter 4.

✔ **Selling by mail order:** If you've been selling by mail order, what's been holding you back from selling at eBay? It costs you far less to list your item at eBay than to run an ad in any publication. Plus, at eBay, you get built-in buyers from every walk of life. If your item sells through the mail, it will sell through eBay.

✔ **Licensed real estate agents:** Plenty of land, homes, and condos are selling at eBay right now. List your properties online so that you can draw from a nationwide audience. When you offer listings on the Web, you're bound to get more action. Give it a whirl and read more about selling real estate at eBay in Chapter 2.

You won't find a cheaper landlord than eBay. Jump over to Chapter 5 if you really can't wait for more information about how to set up your eBay store.

Getting What It Takes to Sell

I've heard many sellers-to-be say they want to start a business at eBay so that they can relax. Since when is running any business a way to relax? Granted, you don't need a whole lot of money to be a success at eBay and you won't have a boss breathing down your neck, but you know that nothing comes easy without working for it. To run a successful eBay business, you do need a few solid tools (aside from drive, determination, and your conscience to guide you), such as a computer, an Internet connection, and so on. In this section, I give you the lowdown on these things and more.

Computer hardware

First, you're gonna need a computer. In my basic assumptions about you (see the book's introduction), I figure you have one and you know how to use it. Your computer doesn't have to be the latest, fastest, and best available. It does help if your computer has a good deal of memory (perhaps 256MB or more) to process your Web browsing and image touch-ups. My eBay selling computer is an antique Pentium 333 MHz, an absolute turtle next to today's 1.4-gigahertz models. Combined with a speedy Internet connection, however, my little machine enables me to run many eBay auctions easily.

One thing to keep in mind is that hard drives are getting cheaper by the minute. The bigger your hard drive, the more space you'll have to store images for your auctions. (Individual pictures shouldn't take up much space because each should max at 50K.) A caveat: The bigger the hard drive, the more chance for making a mess of it by losing files. When you start with a 20GB hard drive (and bigger), be sure that you set up a sensible filing system by using folders and sub directories.

Check out Chapter 11, in which I talk more about the other stuff you need, such as scanners and digital cameras.

Connecting to the Internet

If you've been at eBay for any length of time, you know that your Internet connection becomes an extra appendage of your body. If your connection is down or you can't log on due to a power outage, you flounder around and can't function. I understand because I've been there myself. If you're selling in earnest, I recommend pulling the plug on your dial-up connection unless you absolutely have no choice.

Before investing in any broadband connection, visit www.dslreports.com (see Figure 1-6) and read the reviews for ISPs in your area. Users from around the country post their experiences with the many providers across the country and you can get a good idea of what's in store in your neighborhood in the connection arena. They also have more testing tools than you can imagine and will test the speed of your Internet connection at no charge.

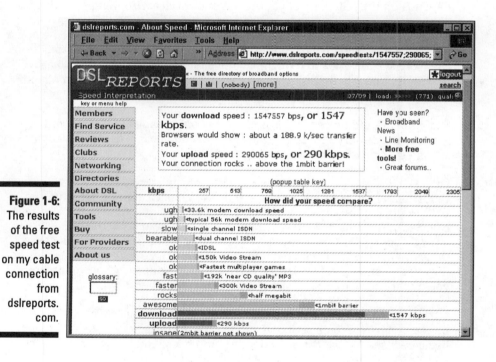

Figure 1-6:
The results of the free speed test on my cable connection from dslreports.com.

Dial-up connections

If you must use a dial-up connection, avail yourself of the many free trials that different Internet Service Providers (ISPs) offer to see which one gives your computer the fastest connection. After you find the fastest, be sure that it's reliable and has at least a 99 percent uptime rate. Visit www.ispmenu.com/ to get capsule reviews on dial-up ISPs in your area.

Most of the United States still logs on to the Internet with a dial-up connection. New users to the Web begin with a dial-up, so what can be so wrong? They are slow, painfully slow. An auction with more than one image can take minutes to load, and the average eBay user wants to browse many auctions and won't wait. For you to run your auctions and do your research, you need to be able to blast through the Internet with blazing speed. You need to be able to answer your e-mail, load your images to a server, and do your business without waiting around for connections. Although a modem is supposed to link up at 56K, the FCC regulations state that it cannot connect any faster than 53K. In practice, the highest connection I've ever experienced on a dial-up was 44K.

DSL

A confusing bunch of Digital Subscriber Line (DSL) flavors (ASDL, IDSL, SDSL, and more) are available these days, ranging from reasonably priced to way out of sight. DSL, when it works as advertised, is fast and reliable. A DSL line depends on the reliability of your telephone service: Dropping your dial-up connection or crackling lines can be a barrier to your using DSL. The main problem with a DSL connection is that your home or office needs to be no farther than 18,000 feet from your local telephone office. The service runs from $50 to $100 a month, and it might cost even more if you get DSL through a *booster* that boosts the signal to a location further away than the minimum 18,000-foot border.

Many homes and offices in this country fall out of range for DSL. If you can get it, true DSL service can give you a connection as fast as 1.5 megabytes per second download. (IDSL will only be 144K.)

I had DSL for about a year and was initially blown away by the speed. Unfortunately, every time it rained (it does rain occasionally in Southern California), my service went out. I had to call time after time to get a service call. Sadly, this is a well-known drawback of DSL. Your local telephone company (Telco in DSL-speak) owns your home or office phone lines. Because DSL goes over POTS (plain old telephone service), your DSL provider has to negotiate connection problems with the folks at your telephone company. As you might guess, one company often blames the other for your problems.

A friend of mine tried to get around this issue by getting DSL from the local phone company, which sounded great to me. It turned out to be not so great because it seems that the local phone companies tend to form companies to handle the high-speed connections. So even though the two companies are technically the same, the two will still argue about who's responsible for your problems. Broadband with this much difficulty can be too much trouble.

Digital cable

Eureka, I think I've found the motherlode of connections: cable. If you can get cable television, you can probably get a blazingly fast cable Internet connection. Your cable company is hopefully replacing old cable lines with newfangled digital fiber-optic lines. These new lines carry a crisp digital TV signal and an Internet connection as well. Actually these fancy new lines have plenty of room to carry even more stuff, and I'm sure it won't be long before cable companies have some hot new services to sell us.

At any rate, my digital cable Internet connection is generally fast and reliable. I just did a speed test on my line, and I'm downloading data at 2004 kilobauds per second. Compare that to the old-fashioned baud rate of dial-up measurement (2,004,895 baud per second — remember the old 300 baud modems?). So far, the service has been very reliable and I've experienced very little downtime. For $40 a month, I consider my cable connection well worth my investment.

As far as the myth about more users on the line degrading the speed — it's highly promoted by DSL service providers. A cable connection is more than capable of a 10mps transfer. That's already about 10 times faster than DSL. It would take a whole lot of degrading to noticeably slow down your connection. (Your computer still has to load the browser.)

Choosing your eBay user ID

"What's in a name?" I believe that's how the old quote goes. At eBay, there's a whole lot in your name! When you pick your eBay user ID, it becomes your name — your identity — to all those who transact with you online. They don't know who you are; they only know you by the name they read in the seller's or bidder's spot.

The lowdown on user IDs

When choosing your user ID, keep the following points in mind:

- Your ID must be at least two characters long.

- It doesn't matter if you want to use uppercase or not; eBay shows your ID in all lowercase letters.

- You may use letters, numbers, and symbols — except for @ and &.

- You can't use URLs as your ID.

- You can't use the word "eBay" in your user ID; that privilege is reserved for eBay employees.

- You can change your ID every 30 days if you want to. When you do, you get a small pair

of sunglasses next to your name, signifying that you're wearing shades with a new ID. Your feedback profile (permanent record) follows you to your new ID.

- Spaces aren't allowed, but if you want to use two words together, you can always separate the words by using the underscore key (press Shift+hyphen to type the underscore key). You may not use consecutive underscores.

- Do I have to tell you this? Don't use a name that's hateful or obscene; eBay (and the community) just won't permit it.

Ever wonder why you don't see many banks named Joe and Fred's Savings and Loan? Even if Joe and Fred are President and Chairman of the Board, the casual attitude portrayed by their given names doesn't instill much confidence in the stability of the bank. Joe and Fred might be a better name for a plumbing supply company; or, for that matter, Joe and Fred would be a great name for guys who sell plumbing tools at eBay! Joe and Fred strike me as the kind of friendly, trustworthy guys who might know something about plumbing.

Does your retail business have a name? If you don't have your own business (yet), have you always known what you'd call it if you did? Your opportunity to set up your business can start with a good, solid respectable sounding business name. If you don't like respectable (it's too staid for you), go for trendy. Who knew what a Verizon was? Or a Cingular? Or a Bubblefast, which is one of my favorite eBay shipping suppliers.

Are you selling flamingo-themed items? How about pink_flamingos for your selling identity? Be creative; you know what best describes your product.

Stay away from negative sounding names. If you really can't think up a good user ID, using your own name is fine.

You've no doubt seen a bunch of lousy user IDs out there; I had to go the distance to give you examples of what not to use. Here are a few: ISellJunk, trashforsale, mystuffisgarbage. Get the drift? Don't use these!

Your e-mail address works interchangeably at eBay with your user ID; they're one and the same. You can sign in with your fictional user ID or use your e-mail address; as long as you input your correct password, either will get you into the system.

If you decide to change your user ID, don't do it too often. Customers recognize you by name, and you may miss some repeat sales by changing your name.

Finding your eBay feedback

The number that eBay lists next to your name is your feedback rating; see Figure 1-7 for my rating. Anyone on the entire Internet has only to click this number to know how you do business at eBay — and what other eBay users think of you. That's quite a reputation to keep up and will reflect in your sales figures. At the top of every user's feedback page is an eBay ID card, an excellent snapshot of all your eBay transactions of the past six months. For the lowdown on feedback, go to Chapter 3.

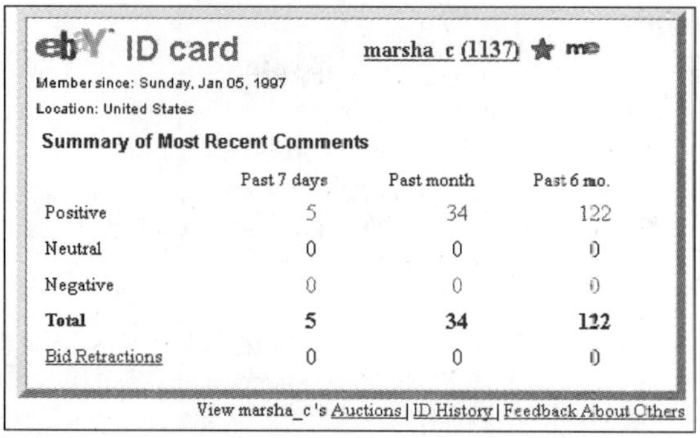

eb Y ID card   marsha_c (1137) ⭐ me

Member since: Sunday, Jan 05, 1997
Location: United States

Summary of Most Recent Comments

	Past 7 days	Past month	Past 6 mo.
Positive	5	34	122
Neutral	0	0	0
Negative	0	0	0
Total	**5**	**34**	**122**
Bid Retractions	0	0	0

View marsha_c's Auctions | ID History | Feedback About Others

Figure 1-7:
eBay
feedback ID
card.

If you're really serious about this business thing, and your feedback rating isn't as high as you'd like it to be, go online and buy some stuff. Even though eBay now distinguishes between Buyer and Seller feedback, the numbers will still grow. Feedback should always be posted for both buyers and sellers. Every positive feedback increases your rating by +1; a negative decreases it by -1. To get a high rating, you'd better be racking up those positives.

Making Your Auctions Run More Smoothly

In this section, I discuss a few more things that you'll need to round out your eBay home base. The following things are important, but you must decide which tools you'll use. Some people prefer a totally automated office while others prefer the old-fashioned way. One of my favorite eBay power sellers works with file folders, a hand-written ledger book, and hand-written labels. If it makes you happy, do it your way. I'm just going to suggest a few options to ease the pain of paperwork.

Software you can use

These days, software is available on this planet to accomplish just about anything. It would seem fitting that an all-encompassing software exists that can help you with your auction, right? Well, maybe. It depends on how much you want your software to do, and how much of your business you want to fully control. Throughout the following subsections, I go through some software examples that you might need and might actually find useful.

Auction management

Auction management software can be a very good thing. It can automate tasks and make your record keeping easy. You can keep track of inventory, launch auctions, and print labels all by using just one program. Unfortunately, most of these programs can be daunting when you first look at them (and even when you take a second look). But after you've mastered one, you'll more easily manage your auctions.

You have choices to make regarding software: How much are you willing to spend for the software, and do you want to keep your inventory and information online? Maintaining your inventory online enables you to run your business from anywhere; you just log on and see your inventory. Online management software is tempting and professional, and may be worth your time and money.

There are a good many sellers that prefer to keep their auction information on their own computers. It's very convenient and allows sellers to add a closer, more personal touch to their auctions and correspondence. Some folks say that keeping the information local, on your own computer, is more suited to the small-time seller. I really think it's a matter of personal preference.

In Chapter 9, I discuss the wide selection of management software available, including AuctionWorks.com, AuctionHelper.com, Auction Wizard, and the eBay-owned Seller's Assistant Pro.

HTML software

You may want to try some very basic HTML software to practice your ad layouts. I tell you where to find some templates in Chapter 11, but you'll want to preview your auctions before you launch them.

You can either check out our auctions in these templates with full-blown Web page software (such as FrontPage), or you may want to keep it simple. I use some software called CuteHTML all the time because it's about as simple as it can get. Go to www.globalscape.com where you can download a 30-day free trial. If you like it, buy it for only $19.95.

Spreadsheets and bookkeeping

Many sellers keep their information in a simple spreadsheet program such as Excel. It has all the functionality that permits inventory management and sales info.

For bookkeeping, I like Quickbooks, which is as complete as it gets. It's straightforward, but only if you have a basic knowledge of accounting. In Chapter 16, I discuss QuickBooks in some detail.

Collecting the cash

Credit cards are the way to go for the bulk of your auctions. Often, credit cards make the difference between a sale and a no sale. People are getting very savvy (and more comfortable) about using their credit cards online because they're becoming better informed about the security of online transactions and guarantees against fraud when certain credit cards are used for those transactions. So although you might truly love and adore money orders, you need to take credit cards as well. In this section, I discuss another decision you need to make: Do you want your own private merchant account or would you rather run your credit card sales through an online payment service? For more about these options read on.

Online payment services

Until you hit the big time, you may want to go with the services of eBay Billpoint or Paypal. They both offer excellent services and their rates are on a sliding scale, depending on your monthly dollar volume. Online payment services accept credit cards for you. They charge you a small fee and process the transaction with the credit card company. The auction payment will be deposited in an account for you. Unless your sales go into several thousand dollars a month, an online payment service can prove to be more economical for you than your own merchant account. For more about these services and accounts, see Chapter 13.

Your own merchant account

As you may or may not know (depending on the amount of spam in your e-mail), thousands of merchant credit card brokers are out there guaranteeing that they can set you up so that you can take credit cards yourself. These people are merely middlemen. You have to pay for their services, either in an application fee or as part of a hefty percentage for the processing software. Some of these brokers are dependable businesses and others are nothing more than hustlers. But if you have decent credit, you don't need these guys: You can go straight to your bank!

Your bank knows your financial standing and credit worthiness better than anybody. It's the best place to start to get your own *merchant account,* an account in which your business accepts credit cards directly from your buyers. You pay a small percentage to the bank, but it's considerably less than you pay to an online payment service. Some banks don't offer merchant accounts for Internet transactions because ultimately the bank is responsible for the merchandise related to the account if you fail to deliver the goods. Remember that your credit history and time with the bank play a part in whether or not you can get a merchant account.

The costs involved in opening a merchant account can vary, but you'll need between $300 and $2,000 to get started. Here are some of the possible costs you'll face:

- A monthly processing fee if you don't reach the monthly minimum set by your bank
- The discount rate (your bank's cut) of 15–30 cents per transaction
- An average of $700 for software that processes your transaction costs
- A monthly gateway fee of as much as $40

This is quite an investment in time and effort. In Chapter 13, I get into the details of a merchant account and explain exactly where all these costs go.

Home base: Your Web site

eBay offers you a free page — the About Me page — that's the most important link to your business at eBay; see Chapter 3 for more information. The About Me page is part of your eBay store if you have one. You can insert a link on your About Me page that takes bidders to your auctions. You can also link to your own Web site from the About Me page — if you have one. If you don't, I recommend that you get one, especially if you're serious about running an eBay business. Check out Chapter 8 where I provide some tips on finding a Web host and a simple way to put up your own Web site.

Your own Web site can have your complete inventory and information on your company. Relying on an eBay store to be your main base of operations isn't prudent. And you'll more than likely be selling items from your Web site as well. Remember that there's no listing or final value fee when you have repeat customers on your Web site. You can keep your complete inventory of items on your Web site and list them as auctions or in your eBay store as their selling season comes around.

Setting up your shop

Your office and storage space: the icing on the cake. Office and storage space are a must if you plan to get big. Many a business was started at the kitchen table (like Pierre started eBay), but to be serious with a business, you must draw definite lines between your home life and your online ventures. Concentrating when you've got a lot of noise in the background is difficult, so when I say draw a line, I don't just mean an environmental one but a physical one as well.

Your dedicated office

You must first separate the family from the hub of your business. Many eBay sellers use a spare bedroom. I started my home business in a small 10 x 12-foot room. But as time progresses and as your business grows, you're going to have to move. I chose to sacrifice my detached two-car garage. I guess I could have made it into a one-car garage, but I decided to take over the whole thing instead. Here's what I did:

Zoning laws in Southern California require me to have a garage, so I put a false office wall in the back so that the garage door could open normally. I used that area for extra storage. My garage had been wired (for some guy who was going to use big-time power tools, I suppose) and had its own breaker box. I hired an electrician to come in and place outlets around my office and had a large window cut into the wall overlooking my backyard (to remove the claustrophobic feeling and for ventilation). I now had a window and electricity.

The phone man came by and brought a line into the garage; a friend installed double jacks all around to accommodate the two phone lines. I picked out some reasonably priced paneling and hired workmen to install it and to drop a paneled ceiling with florescent lights. Finally, I bought furniture from my local Goodwill store. Presto-chango — I had successfully transformed what was once a dark garage into a bright, gleaming 18 x 20-foot *private* office. And here I successfully ran my advertising and marketing business for over ten years.

So you, too, have adjustments and decisions to make, just as I did, because you're going to need office space and storage space, too.

One power seller that I know moved all the junk out of his basement and set up shop there. He now has three computers and employs his wife and a part-time *lister* (who put his auctions up at eBay) to run the show. His basement office is networked and is as professional as any office. You've got to do this if you want to hit the big time.

Your eBay room

If you're able to set up an office similar to mine, you should have your storage space covered for a while. For a real business, a closet just won't do, even though most sellers begin their eBay careers with an eBay closet. You're going to have to seclude your stuff from your pets and family. Move it into another room. You'll also have to get shelving and plenty more supplies to organize things. I talk more about this in Chapter 17.

Chapter 2

The Finer Points of eBay Auctions

In This Chapter

▶ Finding the right category at eBay

▶ Figuring out fixed-price sales

▶ Selecting the auction type that works for you

▶ Pondering auction philosophies

▶ Breaking the rules: What you can't do at eBay

At first glance, eBay is this giant behemoth Web site that seems way too large for any novice to possibly master. In a superficial way, that's right. eBay is always growing and continually undergoing facelifts. Under all the cosmetic changes, however, you find the basics. eBay is still the same old trading site: a community of buyers and sellers who all follow the same rules and policies — which makes eBay a safe place to trade.

As anything gets larger, it must become compartmentalized to be manageable. The folks at eBay have done this most handily. The original basic eight categories now number close to 8,000. The category breakdown is clearer and more concise every day. When a new trend begins, the eBay tech gurus evaluate the sales and, when necessary, add new categories.

All this growth has forced eBay to expand. Aside from the traditional eBay auctions, you'll now find Dutch, Private, restricted, and even more. It can get confusing! In this chapter, I explain the new eBay features by reviewing how the site does business so that, armed with this knowledge, you can effectively do your business there.

Finding Where to Sell Your Stuff

The Internet seems crowded with auctions. Every major portal seems to now include auctions as part of its site. The bottom line is that most bidders and sellers go to eBay. Why? Because more computers and electronics are sold at eBay than at Buy.com; more used cars are sold at eBay than at Autotrader;

and more toys are probably sold at eBay than at KBKids. Even the United States Post Office has found a niche at eBay, selling the contents of undeliverable packages in odd lots.

Whether you're selling auto parts, toys, fine art, or land, you, too, must find your niche at eBay. Sounds easy enough. After all, deciding where to put your stuff for sale is pretty straightforward, right? Not necessarily. After taking a look at the eBay Category Overview page (see Figure 2-1), you can see that the inclusion of more than 8,000 categories complicates this task.

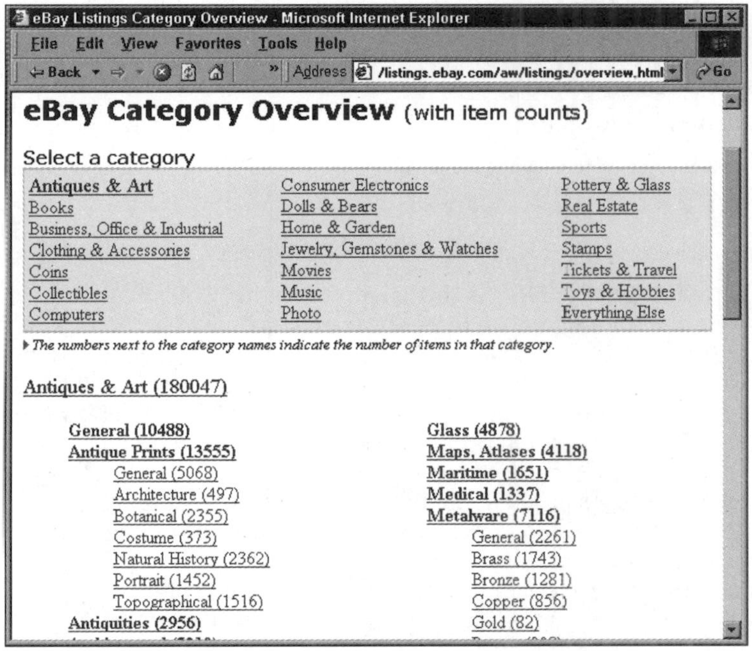

Figure 2-1: The eBay Category Overview page; numbers next to categories reflect active auction counts.

Consider the example of a Star Trek toy. Star Trek toys are becoming increasingly popular with the continuing saga in the new series and movies. The easy choice is to list the item under Toys, Bean Bag Plush: Action Figures: Star Trek. But what about the category Collectibles: Pop Culture: Science Fiction: Star Trek? This is the point where you must decide whether you want to list in two categories (and pay more) — see the review of extra charges in Chapter 10 — or count on the fact that your beautifully written Auction Title will drive those using the search engine directly to your item.

So you aren't into selling Star Trek toys? Suppose that you're selling a VHS of the movie *The Red Violin*. Would listing it in Movies: Movies: Videos: General, be the right choice? Or would you hit the proper audience of category browsers in Music: Musical Instruments: String: Violin, Viola? A book on 1960s fashion? Better in Books: Antiquarian, Rare: General, or Books:

Nonfiction: Collectibles? Actually I have my best luck going direct to the fans of 60s fashion in the category Collectibles: Vintage Clothing, Accessories: Clothing: Women: Other Women's Clothing.

Believe it or not, popularity of categories varies from time to time. Potential buyers may search one category more than others, and their preferences depend on which way the wind blows. News stories, the time of year, hot trends, or whether Katie Couric makes a comment about something all can change a particular category's popularity. Keeping up on these trends is sometimes tough, so you must do some research.

So how can you possibly know the best category for your item? You have to research. Research your items on a regular basis by using my favorite tool: the awesome eBay search engine. Visit Chapter 7 for more about using the search engine. After you've found the right category for the item you're listing, give it a try. But be sure to occasionally try alternatives as well. You may get surprising results in a category that may be hot at the moment because popularity of different areas of the site can come and go with time.

Even when you've been selling a particular item for a while — and doing well with it — you might be surprised to hear that changing to another related category can boost your sales. A little research now and then can go a long way to increasing your eBay sales.

Automotive? Go eBay Motors

Anything and everything automotive can go in the eBay Motors category (see Figure 2-2) and it will all sell like giant tires at a monster truck rally. Following are just a few of the car-related things that fit into this category.

Car parts

Got used car parts? There's an enormous market at eBay in used car parts. One seller I know goes to police impound sales and buys absolute wrecks — just to save some valuable parts that he can resell at eBay.

New car parts are in demand, too. If you catch a sale at your local auto parts store when it's blasting out door handles for a 1967 Corvette (a vehicle for which it's hard to find parts), it wouldn't hurt to pick up a few. Sooner or later, someone's bound to search eBay looking for them; if you're lucky enough to catch the trend, you'll make a nice profit.

Figure 2-2:
The eBay
Motors
home page.

Cars

Yes, you can sell cars at eBay. In fact, used car sales have skyrocketed online thanks to all the people who find eBay to be a trusted place to buy and sell used vehicles (check out Figure 2-3 for an example of a used car auction). Selling vehicles at eBay is a natural business for you if you have access to good used cars, work as a mechanic, or have a contact at a dealership who lets you sell cars at eBay for a commission or on a consignment basis. To get the ins and outs of consignment selling, check out Chapter 6.

eBay Motors and its partners offer useful tools to complete your sale. eBay Motors features an online Classic Car Insurance estimator at `http://pages. ebay.com/ebaymotors/services/hagerty-ccinsurance.html`, one-click access to Carfax reports, Department of Motor Vehicle and Escrow services, and vehicle shipping quotes from Dependable Auto Shippers. Access eBay Motors and its services from the eBay home page or go directly to `www.ebaymotors.com`.

Here are just a couple of things to keep in mind if you plan to sell cars at eBay:

✔ Selling a car at eBay Motors is a bit different from selling at regular eBay, mainly in the fees area. Take a look at Table 2-1 for significant differences. In Chapter 10, I include a chart of all the basic eBay fees for listings, options, and final values.

REMEMBER

✔ To sell a vehicle at eBay Motors, you must enter the Vehicle Identification Number (VIN) into the Sell Your Item page. This way, prospective buyers can always access a Carfax report to get an idea of the history of the car.

✔ Although many people who have found the vehicle of their dreams at eBay are more than happy to take a one-way flight to the vehicle location and drive it home, shipping a vehicle is a reasonably priced alternative. You can quickly and simply arrange to ship a car. In Table 2-2, I list some sample costs for shipping cars around the country from various sites.

TIP

✔ If your reserve isn't met in an eBay Motors auction, you may still offer the vehicle to the high bidder through the Personal Offer option. More information on that later in this chapter.

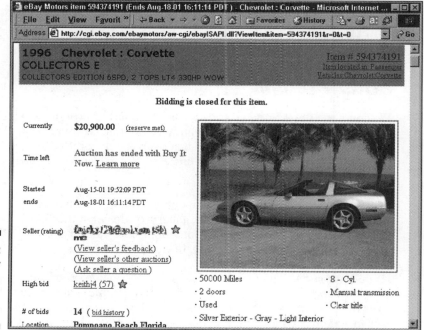

Figure 2-3: An eBay Motors auction for a used car.

Table 2-1	eBay Motors Vehicle-Specific Fees
Type of Fee	*Fee Amount*
Insertion (Listing) fee	$25
Reserve over $25 (refundable if the vehicle sells)	$1
Final value fee (if bidding reaches the reserve)	$25

Table 2-2	Estimated Costs for Shipping a Car to and from Various Sites	
From Here to There	*Terminal-to-Terminal Cost*	*Door-to-Door Cost*
Manhattan to Los Angeles	$715	$865
Los Angeles to Chicago	$775	$875
Newark to Dallas	$675	$755
Boston to Orlando	$660	$760
Phoenix to Houston	$595	$720

An item that you've listed at eBay Motors will appear in any search whether a potential buyer conducts a regular eBay search or executes a search in eBay Motors.

eBay Premier

Welcome to eBay's Rodeo Drive — eBay Premier (shown in Figure 2-4) — where you can reach a worldwide audience of fine art lovers. You'll find categories of Asian art; fine books and manuscripts; decorative arts; collectible and rare dolls; toys; memorabilia; fine arts; jewelry and time pieces; and native and tribal artwork.

Selling at eBay Premier comes with one big hitch. To sell at eBay Premier, you must be a qualified auction house, gallery, or dealer. If that's your business, you're in! Just fill out the application online and wait for approval. If you're not qualified, however, all is not lost.

If you have something to sell that falls into the venue of Premier, you may consign your item for sale to one of the eBay Premier sellers. After looking over the site, contact one of the authorized dealers on the site that specializes in a similar type of merchandise as the item you have for sale. Because dealers handle their businesses differently, study the different dealers and consider their backgrounds and terms before you consign your item to them.

Winners in eBay Premier auctions pay an additional 10 percent premium. As a seller, the final value fee will be 10 percent of the final bid amount *plus* the 10 percent Buyer's Premium. If you've consigned your merchandise to an auction house, you'll have to pay consignment fees, which may or may not include the eBay fee. Check out Table 2-3 for a quick-glance chart explaining these fees.

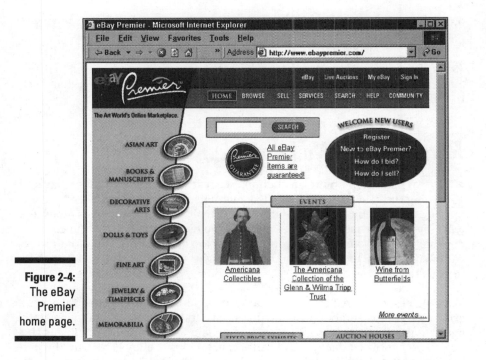

Figure 2-4:
The eBay
Premier
home page.

Table 2-3	eBay Premier-Specific Fees
Type of Fee	*Fee Amount*
Insertion (listing) fee	$10
Reserve	No charge
Featured auction	$10
Final value fee (if reserve is met; includes Buyer's Fee)	10%

eBay Live auctions

To sell at eBay Live Auctions, you must be a registered, licensed auction house. eBay Live Auctions supply non-stop, live auction action right on your desktop. Joining a live auction is a great deal of fun, and these auctions are places where you'll find rare and unusual items for sale. These auctions happen in real-time; you can see (and participate in) the bidding action on your screen as it's happening.

Licensed auction houses run the live auctions from their locations, which are broadcast worldwide through eBay. You have to register individually for each auction in which you want to participate, and there is also a Buyer's premium involved. More and more auctioneers are using this format to expand their customer bases.

As an eBay community member, you're able to bid on items featured in live auctions. It might be a good way to increase your own stock of merchandise to sell.

Real Estate: Not quite an auction

eBay Real Estate isn't quite an auction. Because of the wide variety of laws governing the sale of real estate, eBay auctions of real property aren't legally binding offers to buy and sell. Putting your real estate up at eBay is an excellent way to advertise and attract potential buyers. When the auction ends, however, neither party is obligated (as they are in other eBay auctions) to complete the real estate transaction. The buyer and seller must get together to consummate the deal.

Nonetheless, eBay real estate sales are very popular and the gross sales are growing by leaps and bounds. You don't have to be a professional real estate agent to use this category, although it may help when it comes to closing the deal. If you know land and your local real estate laws, eBay gives you the perfect venue to subdivide that 160 acres in Wyoming that Uncle Regis left you in his will.

For less than the cost of a newspaper ad, you can list your home, condo, land, or even your timeshare at eBay Real Estate (see Figure 2-5). On the Sell Your Item form, shown in Figure 2-6, you must specify special information about your piece of real estate.

In Table 2-4, I provide a listing of fees that you can expect to encounter at eBay Real Estate.

Table 2-4	eBay Real Estate-Specific Fees
Type of Fee	*Fee Amount*
Insertion (listing) fee	$50
Extend auction listing to 30 days	$50
Reserve over $25 (refundable if the reserve is met)	$1
Final value fee	None

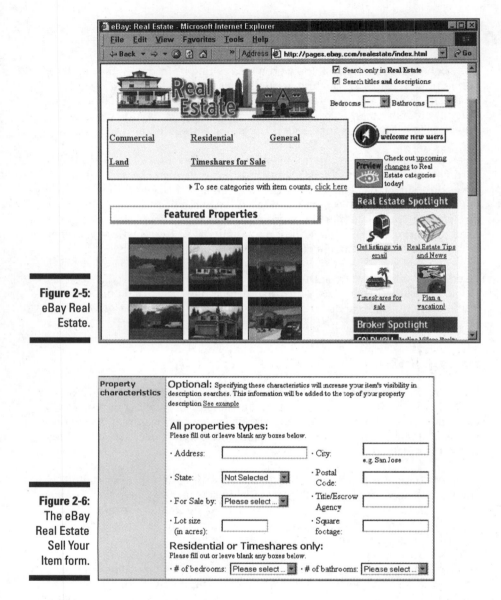

Figure 2-5:
eBay Real
Estate.

Figure 2-6:
The eBay
Real Estate
Sell Your
Item form.

If you're a licensed real estate agent, the real estate home page provides space — the Broker Spotlight — where you can place a clickable ad to your listings.

Fixed Price Sales at eBay

eBay is branching out (as if you weren't expecting it) into new arenas. To compete with Amazon.com and Yahoo!, eBay now includes *fixed price sales* on its site. Fixed price sales are an extension of the eBay Buy It Now feature. You put an item up for sale at a fixed price, and buyers pay the price that you're asking. Simple as that. Sellers are doing a great job at it too.

Fixed price sales at eBay are homed at the new eBay stores. Each eBay store is run by an eBay auction seller; eBay Stores has its own space at eBay — accessible through the navigation bar by clicking Browse and then Stores, by clicking the Visit eBay Stores link on the eBay home page, or by going straight to www.ebaystores.com from the Web. eBay users will soon get used to visiting the shops in addition to auctions, so here's where you need to set up an online shop; check out Chapter 5 for all the details.

Fixed price sales have been the cornerstone of the market in Half.com. Originally a site that sold used merchandise at half price, Half.com is now a home to the traditional eBay "gently used" products at any set price.

eBay's half brother: Half.com

Half.com, founded in July of 1999, was the brainchild of Half.com's President Joshua Kopelman. He observed the insufficiencies of retailing in the area of used mass-market merchandise and went to work on developing a new outlet for second-hand merchandise. Kopelman's site was so successful that eBay bought out Half.com after its first year of business.

Selling at Half.com is different from selling in your eBay (or other online) personal store because you're selling in a fixed price marketplace. Your item is listed head-to-head against more of the exact same item that other sellers are selling. Half.com isn't a home for your store; you might say that each item has its own store, complete with competing sellers.

You can sell many things at Half.com (see its home page in Figure 2-7), which presently ranks as one of the Internet's most visited sites. Half.com currently lists over 15 million items, including books, CDs, DVDs and VHS, video games, computers, electronics, sporting goods, and trading cards. Half.com is a separate site from eBay, and requires that you have a separate registration, password, and account. You even have to build up a new feedback rating, but it's definitely worth the trouble.

Figure 2-7:
The
Half.com
home page.

From a seller's point of view, the three best features of Half.com are

- The item listing is free.
- You can list your items from your telephone by using the Sellphone process.

If you don't want to bring all your books, CDs, movies, or games to your computer, you can list the books right from all over your house with your telephone by inputting the ISBN numbers and the item's condition. After you set up a Half.com account, sign up for a Sellphone account at www.half.com/account/account.cfm?function=sellphone. You'll get a PIN number and the number to call; after that, you're ready to list.

- The item stays on the site until the item is sold or until you take it down.

To list an item for sale at Half.com, you first need to locate the item's Universal Product Code (UPC) or a book's International Standard Book Number (ISBN). In case you're wondering what an ISBN is, turn this book over and find the bar code on the back. The number written below it is this book's ISBN number.

When someone searches for an item, a book for example, at Half.com, a listing of all sellers who are selling that book appears. The listings are classified by the condition of the book — categorized as Like New or Very Good — depending on what the seller entered. The list price of the book is included, as well as a comparison of selling prices throughout the Internet at various book dealers.

If you don't have an item's outer box with the UPC, search Half.com from any of its pages for your particular item (including its brand name). When your search comes up with the exact item, copy down the code number and use it with your listing.

You'll find that by using the UPC or ISBN in your listing, Half.com comes up with an image of your item, so you don't even have to take a picture for your sale. When an item is out-of-print, Half.com may not have an image to upload with the listing. In this case, the text, *Image not available,* appears in the area where the picture would appear. If your item doesn't have a code (outside of the books, music, movies, and games categories), you can upload your own photo and even add a 1,000-word description. Even in electronics, sports, and other categories, Half.com has an amazing database of items where you're sure to find the specs of any item you want to list.

When a prospective buyer searches and finds an item for books or coded items, a box appears in the corner of the listing with a price comparison of the item from various other online sales sites (see Figure 2-8).

Figure 2-8:
A book
listing at
Half.com.

When you list a coded item at Half.com, you have the opportunity to list a 70-character note describing the item's condition (see Table 2-5). Your selling price can be whatever you like, but keep it low enough to stay competitive with other sellers' items.

Table 2-5	Half.com Book Condition Rating
Term	*Meaning*
Like New	Shiny cover, no highlighting or writing, all pages undamaged, no missing pages; could be mistaken for new
Very Good	Doesn't look brand new; no noticeable damage to the cover or pages; no markings in the book, no visible damage
Good	Slight damage to cover, perhaps missing dust jacket, minimal underlining or highlighting, no missing pages, no writing on pages
Acceptable	Some damage to cover, perhaps writing in margins, and notes on pages; book is still complete and usable

When someone searches and decides to purchase your item, Half.com sends you an e-mail. You have 48 business hours to reply; after you reply, Half.com expects you to package the item appropriately and ship it within 24 hours. If you plan to be out of town, you can post a vacation notice so that your listing is removed from the site until you return.

Half.com pays you directly, either by direct deposit into your bank account or by sending you a paper check. Direct deposits are made twice a month (on the 15th and at the end of the month). Check payments are sent twice a month, depending on the total amount of your sales. When you register, you will be given the option of how you would like to receive your payments.

Half.com's cut of your sales is a flat 15 percent. Not too shabby a way to empty your bookshelves and unload some items at a discount.

When you list a book or other coded item for sale, you can also offer the option of shipping via media mail or Priority Mail. Half.com charges an additional flat fee to buyers for shipping when they make a purchase. As a seller, you are paid only for the amount of your sale (less Half.com's commission) and are credited a flat figure for shipping coded products.

For example, if you're selling a hardcover book for $37, here's what happens:

1. Buyer buys book that's priced at $37.

2. Half.com charges the buyer $2.99 for shipping and handling costs.

3. You pay Half.com a 15 percent commission, which is $5.55 on a $37 item.

4. You get a shipping reimbursement of $2.23.

    See Table 2-6 for Half.com shipping reimbursements.

5. Half.com sends you a net payment of $33.68.

There's no shipping credit for other, non-coded items although you may include a shipping charge in your item price.

Table 2-6	Half.com Shipping Reimbursements	
Shipping credits at Half.com	*Media Mail*	*Priority Mail*
For the first hardcover book	$2.23	$4.35
Each additional hardcover book	86 cents	1.75
Other books, movies, games, CDs	1.78	4.35
Other additional items	61 cents	1.25

eBay Stores

The new offering from the eBay stable is eBay Stores. eBay now gives you the chance to have your piece of the Web right at eBay. Potential buyers will be able to access your items from anywhere within the eBay site and the cost to you is *very* right. eBay Stores costs (see Table 2-7) compare favorably to any of the Web's megasite stores and are part of the eBay Stores Hub.

Table 2-7	eBay Store Fees
Type of Fee	*Fee Amount*
Monthly subscription fee	$9.95
Listing fees	None
Final value fees	1.25–5%

To get a complete overview on how to set up your own eBay Store, check out Chapter 5.

Types of eBay Auctions

An auction is an auction is an auction, right? Wrong! eBay has five different types of auctions for your selling pleasure. Most of the time you'll run traditional auctions, but other auctions have their place, too. After you've been selling at eBay for a while, you may find that one of the other types of auctions better suits your needs. Throughout this section, I take a moment to review these auctions so that you fully understand what they are and when to use each of them.

Traditional auctions

Traditional auctions are the bread and butter of eBay. You can run a Traditional auction for 3, 5, 7, or 10 days, and when the auction closes, the highest bidder wins. I'm sure you've bid on several and at least won a few. If you're reading this book, I'll bet you've made money running some of your own.

You begin the auction with an opening bid, and bidders (hopefully) will bid up your opening price into a healthy profit for you.

Dutch auctions

When you've purchased an odd lot of 500 kitchen knife sets or managed to (legally, of course) get your hands on a truckload of televisions that you want to sell as expeditiously as possible, the Dutch auction is what you'll want to use. In the *Dutch auction* (see Figure 2-9 for an example), which can run for 3, 5, 7, or 10 days, you can list as many items as you'd like and bidders can bid on as many items as they'd like. The final item price is set by the lowest successful bid at the time that the auction closes.

For example, suppose you want to sell five dolls at eBay in a Dutch auction. Your starting bid is $5 each. If five bidders each bid $5 for one doll, they each get a doll for $5. But, if the final bidding reveals that two people bid $5, one person bid $7.50, and another bid $8, all five bidders win the doll for the lowest final bid of $5.

In the following list, I highlight the details of the Dutch auction:

- The listing fee is based on your opening bid price (just like in a Traditional auction), but it's multiplied by the number of items in your auction to a maximum listing fee of $3.30.

- The final auction value fees are on the same scale as in Traditional auctions, but they're based on the total dollar amount of your completed auctions.

✔ When bidders bid on your Dutch auction, they can bid on one or more items at one bid price. (The bid is multiplied by the number of items.)

✔ If the bidding gets hot and heavy, rebids must be in a higher total dollar amount than the total of that bidder's past bids.

✔ Bidders may reduce the quantity of the items for which they're bidding in your auction, but the dollar amount of the total bid price must be higher.

✔ All winning bidders pay the same price for their items, no matter how much they bid.

✔ The lowest successful bid when the auction closes is the price for which your items in that auction will be sold.

✔ If your item gets more bids than you have items, the lowest bidders are knocked out one by one, with the earliest bidders remaining on board the longest.

✔ The earliest (by date and time) successful high bidders when the auction closes win their items.

✔ Higher bidders get the quantities they've asked for, and bidders can refuse partial quantities of the number of items in their bids.

For a large quantity of a particular item, your Dutch auction may benefit from some of the eBay featured auction options, which I detail in Chapter 10.

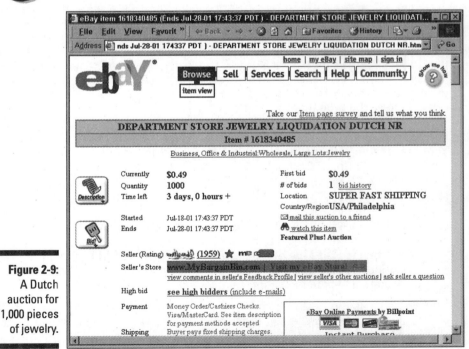

Figure 2-9:
A Dutch auction for 1,000 pieces of jewelry.

Reserve Price auctions

In a *Reserve Price auction,* you're able to set an undisclosed minimum price for which your item will sell, thereby giving yourself a safety net. Figure 2-10 shows an auction in which the reserve has not yet been met. Using a Reserve Price auction protects the investment you have in an item. If, at the end of the auction, no bidder has met your undisclosed reserve price, you aren't obligated to sell the item and the high bidder isn't required to purchase the item.

This seller has set a reserve price
that hasn't been met by bidders yet.

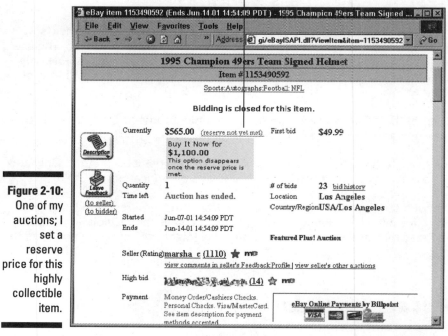

Figure 2-10:
One of my
auctions; I
set a
reserve
price for this
highly
collectible
item.

If, for example, you have a rare coin to auction, you can start the bidding at a low price to attract bidders to open up your auction and read your infomercial-like description. If you start your bidding at too high a price, you might dissuade prospective bidders from even looking at your auction and you won't tempt them to even bid. They may feel that the final selling price may go too high for their budgets.

Everyone at eBay is looking for a bargain or for a truly rare item. If you can combine the mystical force of both of these needs in one auction, you've got something special on your hands. The Reserve Price auction enables you to attempt — and hopefully achieve — this feat.

The fees for a Reserve Price auction are the same as for the traditional auction with one exception. eBay charges $1 for the privilege of running a Reserve Price auction. If your item sells, you get your dollar back.

The Reserve Price auction is a safety net for the seller, but often an uncomfortable guessing game for the prospective bidder. To alleviate buyer anxiety, many sellers put reserve prices in the item description, allowing bidders to decide whether the item will fit into their bidding budgets.

You can't use the reserve price option in a Dutch auction.

Restricted Access auctions

eBay won't allow certain items to be sold in non-restricted categories, so you must list them in the Adult Only area of eBay. eBay makes it easy for the user to find or avoid these types of auctions by making this area accessible only after the user enters a password and agrees to the terms and conditions of the area.

Items in the Adult Only area are not accessible through the regular eBay title search, nor are they listed in Hot Items or in the Newly Listed Items.

Anyone at eBay, whether bidder or seller, who participates in Adult Only auctions must have a credit card on file at eBay for verification.

Do not attempt to slip an Adult Only auction into a non-restricted category. eBay doesn't have a sense of humor when it comes to this violation of policy and may relocate or end your auction. eBay might even suspend you from its site.

Private auctions

Bidders' names are often kept private when dealing in the expensive fine art world. Likewise, to protect the innocent, eBay *Private auctions* don't place bidders' names on the auction listing. No one needs to know just how much you choose to pay for something, especially if the item is rare and you really want it.

As a seller, you have the option (at no extra charge) of listing your auction as a private auction.

The eBay search page features an area where you can conduct a Bidder search. You — and everyone else including your family — can find the items that you've bid on. One December my daughter told me that she didn't want a particular item — something I had just bid on at eBay — for Christmas. My creative daughter had been regularly perusing my bidding action at eBay to see what I was buying for the holidays! A Private auction would have kept my shopping secret.

The Private auction is a useful tool for sellers who are selling bulk lots to other sellers. It maintains the privacy of the bidders, and customers can't do a bidder search to find out what sellers are paying for the loot they then sell at eBay.

A great option for sales of items that are a bit racy or perhaps for purchases of items that may reveal something about the bidder, the Private auction can save you the potential embarrassment associated with buying a girdle or buying the tie that flips over to reveal a racy half-nude female on the back.

The Private auction, while a useful tool, may intimidate the novice user. If your customer base comes from experienced eBay users and you're selling an item that may benefit by being auctioned in secret, you might try this option.

Running Your Auction

The basic plan for running an auction is the same for everyone, except for decisions regarding the timing of the auction and the starting price. If you speak to 20 different eBay sellers, you'd probably get 20 different answers about effective starting bids and when to end your auction. Until you develop your own philosophy, I'd like to give you the tools to make a sound decision.

You can also successfully promote your auctions on and offline, and now you can legally offer your item to the next highest bidder if the auction winner doesn't come through with payment. I discuss a few of these ideas throughout this section.

Not quite adult enough . . .

I was surprised to see a Private auction listed on one of my favorite eBay seller's list. She usually doesn't sell items like "Fringe Black BRA 36B SEXY SEXY SEXY," so I looked through this seller's past auctions. I saw that she didn't get any bids when she listed the bra in the restricted (Adult Only) area of eBay in the category Everything Else: Mature Audiences: Clothing, Accessory. When she put the bra up for Private auction in the category Clothing & Accessories: Women's Clothing: Lingerie: Bras: General, she got five bidders and sold the item. I guess it wasn't sexy enough for the "adult" crowd!

Starting the bidding

The most generally accepted theory about starting bids is that setting the bidding too high scares away new bids. Also, as in the case of the Reserve Price auction, if the bidding begins too high, novices might be afraid that the bidding will go too high, and that they'll never win the auction.

Some sellers begin the bidding at the price they paid for the item, thereby protecting their investment. This is a good tactic, especially if you've gotten the item at a price far below the current going rate at eBay.

To determine the current going value for your item, I recommend using the completed auctions search, which I explain in Chapter 7. If you know that the item is selling at eBay for a certain price and that there is a demand for it, starting your bidding at a reasonably low level can be a great way to increase bidding and to attract prospective bidders to read your auction.

Years of advertising experience can't be wrong. If your item is in demand and people are actively buying, start the bidding low. Retail stores have done this for years with ads that feature prices starting at $9.99 or $14.98. Even television commercials advertising automobiles quote a low starting price. To get the car as shown in the ad, you may end up paying twice the quoted price.

When sellers know that they have an item that will sell, they begin their bidding as low as $1 or even a penny. Because of the eBay *proxy bidding system* (which maintains your highest bid as secret, increasing it incrementally when you're bid against), it takes more bids (due to the smaller bidding increments) to bring the item up to the final selling price.

You can benefit from this when a large number of bids (30 or more) forces your item into the *hot item* stage. When an auction is deemed as hot, eBay inserts a lit matchstick icon next to your auction on the listing page. This flaming match, which shows up in searches as well, indicates that the auction features a desirable piece of goods. The downside is that new bidders who aren't familiar with the system may bid only the minimum required increment each time they bid. This can be frustrating and they may quit bidding because it might take them several bids to top the current bid placed by someone who's familiar with the proxy bid system.

Very few of us know the proxy increments by heart, so as a refresher, I give you the goods in Table 2-8.

Table 2-8	Proxy Bidding Increments
Current High Bid	*Bid Increment*
1–99 cents	5 cents
$1–4.99	25 cents
$5–24.99	50 cents
$25–99.99	$1
$100–249.99	$2.50
$250–499.99	$5

Auction timing

Another debatable philosophy of eBay is the auction timing. People are continually asking me how long to run auctions and what's the best day to end an auction. You have to evaluate your item and decide the best plan:

- **Three-day auction:** If, as in the heyday of Beanie Babies, the item's price will shoot up right after you post it and someone will immediately buy it, a three-day auction works just fine. And it's great for those last minute holiday shoppers looking for hard-to-find items.

  With the eBay Buy It Now feature, you can pretty much accomplish the same thing. When you list your item for sale, you can set a price at which you will sell the item. This price can be any amount, and if someone is willing to pay, it sells. As long as eBay offers Buy It Now for free, you can run your auctions longer and depend on Buy It Now to close your auctions at a comfortable profit. But keep in mind that you're putting a cap on your profits. If eBay ever charges for the service, however, a three-day auction will again be appropriate for trendy, fast-selling items.

- **Five-day auction:** Five days will give you two days more than three and two days less than seven. That's about the size of it. If you just want an extended weekend auction, or if your item is a hot one, use it. Five-day auctions are useful during holiday rushes, when gifting is the main reason for bidding.

- **Seven-day auction:** Tried and true advertising theory says that the longer you advertise your item, the more people will see it. At eBay, this means that you have more opportunity for people to bid on it. The seven-day auction is a staple for the bulk of eBay vendors. Seven days is long enough to cover weekend browsers, and short enough to keep the auction interesting.

✔ **Ten-day auction:** Many veteran eBay sellers swear by the ten-day auction. Sure, eBay charges you an extra dime for the privilege, but the extra three days of exposure (it can encompass two weekends) can easily net you more than 10 cents in profits.

At eBay, your auction closes exactly three, five, seven, or ten days — *to the minute* — after you start the auction. Be careful not to begin your auctions when you're up late at night and can't sleep: You don't want your auction to end at two in the morning when no one else is awake to bid on it. If you can't sleep, use the time and the Mister Lister program to prepare your auctions and upload them for future launching when the world is ready to shop.

The specific day you close your auction can also be important. eBay is full of weekend browsers, so including a weekend of browsing in your auction time is a definite plus. Often, the auctions that close late Sunday afternoon through Monday close with high bids.

You'll need to do some research to determine the best times to run your auctions and for how long. In Chapter 10, I show you how to combine your search engine research with a special kind of statistical counter to help you identify the best closing time for your items. (See Chapter 7 for the details about using the search engine as a valuable research tool.) The best person to figure out the closing information for your auctions is you. Use the tools and over time you'll work out a pattern that works best for you.

A definite time *not* to close your auctions? Real-life experience has taught many sellers never to close an auction on a national holiday. Memorial Day, the 4th of July, and Veteran's Day may be bonanza sales days for retail shops, but eBay auction items closing on these days go at bargain prices. I guess everyone is out shopping the brick and mortars.

Marketing your auctions

How do you let people know about your auctions? What do you do if all 30 million users at eBay happen to not be on the site the week that your items are up for sale? You advertise.

Many mailing lists and newsgroups permit self-promotion. Find a group that features your type of items and post a bit of promotion. This works best if you have your own Web site. Your Web site, which should be the hub for your sales, can give you an identity and level of professionalism that makes your business more official in the eyes of buyers. In Chapter 8, I detail the ins and outs of business sites on the Web.

eBay supplies some nice link buttons (see Figure 2-11) that you can use on your Web site; visit `http://pages.ebay.com/services/buyandsell/link-buttons.html` to add these links to your site's home page.

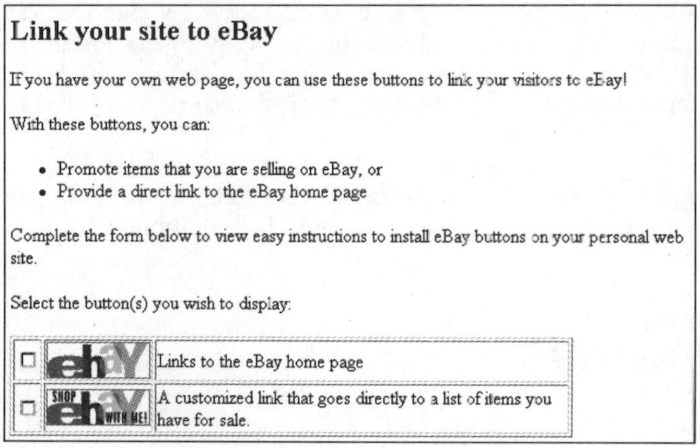

Link your site to eBay

If you have your own web page, you can use these buttons to link your visitors to eBay!

With these buttons, you can:

- Promote items that you are selling on eBay, or
- Provide a direct link to the eBay home page

Complete the form below to view easy instructions to install eBay buttons on your personal web site.

Select the button(s) you wish to display:

☐		Links to the eBay home page
☐		A customized link that goes directly to a list of items you have for sale.

Figure 2-11:
The Shop
eBay With
Me link
buttons.

I'm guessing that you already know all about your About Me page, a handy tool when it comes to marketing your auctions. You can — and should — link to your Web site from your little home page at eBay. In Chapter 3, I discuss the values of the About Me page.

Here's a great way to market your future auctions: When you're sending out items after making a sale at eBay, include a list of items that you'll be selling in the near future (along with your thank you note of course) — especially ones that may appeal to that customer. AuctionHelper.com, an auction management site, can even get your actual auction numbers ahead of time for use in this sort of promotion. (See Chapter 9 for more information about AuctionHelper.)

Do not link your auction to your Web site. It's against eBay policy to possibly divert any sales away from the auction site. See the section "Linking from your auctions" later in this chapter to find out just what you can and cannot link to and from.

Personal Offer

This new feature at eBay helps sellers to legitimize something that previously went on behind closed doors and in violation of eBay policy. When a winner doesn't complete a sale, the Personal Offer feature allows sellers to offer the item to the next highest bidder.

You must still go through the proper channels and file your non-paying bidder notice with eBay. After doing that, you can then send a Personal Offer to any under bidder no more than 60 days after the end of the auction. Your final value fee is then based on the actual price you receive when the offer is accepted.

In the Personal Offer scenario, the seller can leave two feedbacks: one for the winner (non-paying bidder) and one for the person who bought the item through the Personal Offer transaction. The bidder to whom you proffered your Personal Offer is covered by the eBay insurance and fraud protection program.

This feature is also available for eBay Motors vehicle auctions when the reserve price isn't met. It does not apply to Dutch auctions.

Listing Violations

eBay does not sell merchandise. eBay is merely a venue that provides the location where others can put on a giant, e-commerce party (in other words, sell stuff). To provide a safe and profitable venue for its sellers, eBay must govern auctions that take place on its site. eBay makes the rules; you and I follow the rules. I like to think of eBay as the place that lets you hold your senior prom in its gym. When I was in school, my classmates and I had to follow the rules or see our prom cancelled. Likewise, eBay has its rules and it punishes violators. You must understand and agree to follow eBay rules. Otherwise, a safe and trusted community can't exist at eBay.

Listing policies

eBay has some hard and fast rules about listing your items. Of course, you must list your item in the appropriate category (that only makes sense), but I highlight here a few other rules that you should keep in mind when listing. What I discuss in this section isn't a definitive list of eBay listing policies and rules. Take time to familiarize yourself with the User Agreement (which details all eBay policies and rules) at `http://pages.ebay.com/help/ community/png-user.html`. I recommend regularly checking the eBay User Agreement for any policy changes.

Choice auctions

Your auction must be for one item only: the item that you specifically list in your auction. It's against the rules to give the bidder a choice of items, sizes, or colors. eBay protects you with its insurance policy, which covers all online eBay transactions. When you give your bidders a choice, they must choose off of the eBay system. Anything that's negotiated off the eBay system can lead to either misrepresentation or fraud. You really don't want to be caught up in that sort of grief and misery.

If eBay catches you with a Choice auction, eBay will end the auction and credit the insertion fee to your account.

Duplicate auctions

Remember the old supply and demand theory from your economics class? When people list the same items repeatedly, they drive down the item's going price while ruining all the other sellers' opportunities to sell the item during the time frame that their auctions close.

eBay only allows you ten identical listings at any time. If you're going to list an item that many times, be sure to list them in different categories; it happens to be a rule, but it also makes sense. Nothing drives down the price of an item faster than closing identical auctions, one after another, in the same category. eBay also requires that you list your auction in a category that's relevant to your item.

If you have multiple copies of something, a better solution is to run a Dutch auction for the total number of items you have for sale, or perhaps two Dutch auctions in different (but appropriate) categories.

If you're caught with more than ten identical auctions, eBay may end the additional auctions (any over ten). eBay will credit the insertion fees.

Pre-sale listings

eBay doesn't like it when you try to sell something that's not in your hands (known as a *pre-sale listing*), which is a dangerous game to play anyway. In many situations, being the first seller to put a very popular item up for sale can get you some pretty high bids. And if you can guarantee in your auction description that the item will be available to ship within 30 days of the auction closing or purchase, you can do it. I don't recommend, however, even attempting a pre-sale listing if you're not completely sure that you'll have the item in time.

Pre-selling: Not worth the hassle

A seller I once knew pre-sold Beanie Babies at eBay. She had a regular source that supplied her when the new toys came out, so she fell into a complacent attitude about listing pre-sales. Then her supplier didn't get the shipment. Motivated by the need to protect her feedback rating (and by the fear that she'd be accused of fraud), she ran all over town desperately trying to get the beanies she needed to fill her orders. The Beanies were so rare that she ended up spending several hundred dollars more than what she had originally sold the toys for just to keep her customers happy.

If you know that you will have the item to ship — and it won't be lost on its way to you — you may list the item with the following requirement: You must state in your auction description that the item is a pre-sale and that the item will be shipped by the 30th day from the end of the listing or purchase. You will also have to use a little HTML here because the text must be coded to appear in a minimum of HTML font size 3.

Before you set up such an auction, check out the Federal Trade Commission rule covering these matters, which you can find at www.ftc.gov/bcp/conline/pubs/buspubs/mailordr/index.htm.

Bonuses, giveaways, raffles, or prizes

Because eBay is a site that sells to every state in the United States, it must follow explicit laws governing giveaways and prizes. Each state has its own set of rules and regulations, so eBay doesn't allow individual sellers to come up with their own promotions.

An auction that violates this rule may result in eBay ending it and refunding your listing fee.

Keyword spamming

Keyword spamming is when you add words, usually brand names, to your auction description that don't actually describe what you're selling (for example, describing that little black dress as Givenchy-style when Givenchy has nothing to do with it). Sellers use keyword spamming to pull viewers to their auctions after viewers have searched for the brand name.

Keyword spamming actually causes your auction to fall under potentially infringing items for sale at eBay. Keyword spamming is a listing violation and I mention it here because it affects all listings. The wording you choose when you run this kind of auction manipulates the eBay search engine and prospective bidders. For a complete discussion of keyword spamming and its complexities as an item that is an infringement of eBay's policies, see Chapter 4.

Linking from your auctions

Few issues set sellers to arguing more than the rules on linking. eBay, of course, has some hard and fast rules that govern linking, which I describe in this section.

In your auction item description, you *can* use the following links:

- One link to an additional page that gives further information about the item you're selling.
- A link that opens an e-mail window on the prospective buyer's browser to send you an e-mail.

✔ Links to more photo images of the items that you're selling.

✔ Links to your other auctions at eBay, your eBay Store, and Half.com listings.

✔ One link to your About Me page, besides the link next to your user ID that eBay provides.

✔ Links to vendors' sites that help you with your auctions. eBay considers listing services, software, and payment services to be third-party vendors. You can legally link to them as long as the HTML font is no larger than size 3; if you're using a logo, it must be no larger than 88 x 33 pixels.

Most third-party vendors are well aware of these restrictions and they don't want their credits pulled from eBay, so the information they supply as a link generally falls within eBay parameters.

In your auction description, you *cannot* link to the following:

✔ A page that offers to sell, trade, or purchase merchandise outside of the eBay site.

✔ Any area on the Internet that offers merchandise considered illegal at eBay. See Chapter 4 for information on illegal items.

✔ Any site that encourages eBay bidders to place their bids outside of eBay.

✔ Sites that solicit eBay user IDs and passwords.

Linking from your About Me page

eBay rules are pretty much the same when it comes to your About Me page. Because eBay gives you this page for self-promotion, you may link to your Web site from it. Be sure not to link to other trading sites or to sites that offer the same merchandise for the same or lower price. Read more about the About Me page do's and don'ts in Chapter 3.

Charity auctions at eBay

Over $6,000,000 has been raised at eBay for charitable organizations. If you represent a legitimate charity, you may run auctions at eBay to raise funds; just follow these simple steps:

1. Register the charity as an eBay member.

2. Prepare an About Me page describing your charity. Explain what it is, what it does, where the money goes, and so on. Set up the page to "Show no feedback" and indicate for the page to "Show all items." eBay will link this page to the Charity Auctions area.

3. Next, e-mail all the following information to eBay at charity@eBay.com:

   ✓ User ID and e-mail address that you registered with at eBay

   ✓ The completed About Me page

   ✓ Your 501c3/EIN number for your non-profit organization

   ✓ The time frame in which you expect to run your auction

   ✓ A brief description of your organization

   ✓ Examples of the items you'd like to list

   ✓ Name, e-mail address, and telephone number of the organization's main contact person

   ✓ The Web site address for your organization (if it has one)

You'll hear back from eBay when your charity has been approved. Your charity will then appear on the Charity Fundraising page, and you can start planning your charity auctions.

Chapter 3

Cool eBay Tools

• •

In This Chapter

▶ Making My eBay your home page

▶ Taking advantage of your About Me page

▶ Managing the business of your auction: eBay seller services

• •

*e*Bay offers you an amazing variety of tools. Unfortunately, very few of us know where they are, how to find them, or how to use them. I must admit that I fall victim to the "Oh, I didn't know I could do that" syndrome. I'll often be poking around eBay and find a cool tool or a neat shortcut that I didn't previously know about; it's always an eye-opener! The most important short-cut I can give you is to remind you to sign in, and check the box that says "Keep me signed in on this computer unless I sign out" before you attempt to do anything at eBay. This will permit you to do all your business at eBay without being bugged for your password at every turn.

If you have more than one user ID, or share a computer with other people, be sure to sign out when you're finished. The cookie system has been changed on eBay and now, as on other Web sites, your computer will hold your sign-in information until you sign out. For your protection, you will still have to type in your password for actions involving financial information. You can specify which tasks you want eBay to remember your sign-in information for in the Preferences area of the My eBay page.

Other eBay users frequently share with me some nugget of information that helps them along the way. And now I'll share these nuggets with you. eBay has developed some features that I find useful (such as My eBay, which allows me to customize eBay for my personal home page) that I discuss throughout this chapter. The About Me page enables me to tell the story of my business to the world — it also allows me to find out about the people I plan on buying from, and eBay offers too many helpful seller services to list them all here. To get the lowdown on the world of cool eBay tools, read on.

My eBay

My very own home at eBay pops up on my screen every morning with a cheery, My eBay - Hello, marsha_c. My eBay is no longer a step-by-step list of what you're bidding on and selling, but a veritable Swiss Army Knife of eBay tools.

Access the My eBay page by clicking the My eBay link above the eBay navigation bar (shown in Figure 3-1) that appears at the top of every eBay page. You can also click Services and then the My eBay block. Why? I don't really know why anyone would take two steps instead of one, but it's there and you can.

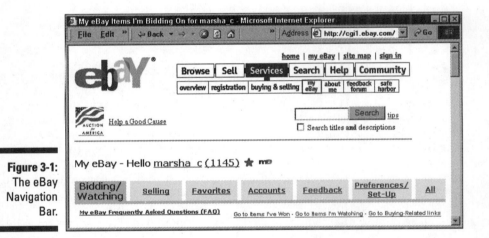

Figure 3-1: The eBay Navigation Bar.

On the bottom of each of the My eBay pages are convenient links to questions or services you may need while at eBay. The links are different from page to page with buying-related links on the Bidding/Watching page, selling-related links on the Selling page, account-related links on the Accounts page, and feedback-related links on the Feedback page. When you need them, you'll find these links very handy.

My eBay is divided into six pages (Bidding/Watching, Selling, Favorites, Accounts, Feedback, and Preferences/Set-up), which you select by clicking tabs. There's actually a seventh tab labeled All that shows you all of your My eBay pages on one page. I recommend that you use the individual tabs rather than the All tab because the pages load faster when you're looking at just one subject at a time and you have less scrolling to do.

How to view more than two days when you open your My eBay page

People often ask me how to reset the default of only showing two days of history on the My eBay page. The My eBay page is capable of showing as many as 30 days past history; keeping at least a week or two of history on the page would be useful. To reset the default, just follow these steps:

1. Sign in and go to your My eBay page.

   When the page is open in your browser, look at the top of your browser in the area that indicates the address.

2. Click within the address space.

   It reverses color from black text on white to white text on solid blue or black. Find &dayssince=2& in the URL shown in the following figure.

Address	=N&sellerSort=3&bidderSort=3&watchSort=3&dayssince=2&p1=0&p2=0&p3=0&p4=0&p5=0

3. If necessary, click again quickly to turn the color bar into a cursor and use your keyboard's arrow keys to scroll right until you see &dayssince=2&.

4. Highlight the number 2 and type in the amount of days that you'd like to reference on your My eBay page as a default (maximum 30); press Return.

   The number of days that you just typed in now appears on your My eBay page.

5. To save this new number as your default, do one of the following two things:

   ✔ *Put a shortcut on your desktop to this page:* Go to the top of your browser and choose File⇨Send⇨Shortcut to Desktop. A shortcut will appear on your desktop; simply click this shortcut to access your My eBay page (with your desired defaults).

   ✔ *Make this your home page:* Go to the top of your browser and choose Tools⇨ Internet Options. In the home page that appears, click Use Current and then OK so that your My eBay page shows up each time you open Internet Explorer.

Bidding/Watching

Here it is: the hub for keeping track of your bids, your wins, and any items you're watching. Although you plan to sell more than buy at eBay, I'm sure you'll occasionally find something to buy if only to turn around and resell it. I've often found a bargain item at eBay that I've re-sold immediately. Plus, I purchase most of my shipping supplies at eBay. In Chapter 17, I reference a few sources at eBay for great prices and fast shipping.

Items I've Bid On

When you place a bid at eBay, it automatically registers onto the table shown in Figure 3-2.

By using the Items I've Bid On page as your daily stop at eBay, you can see the status of your bids:

- Bid information that appears in green indicates that you're the high bid in the auction.

- The column My Max Bid reminds you of the amount of your highest bid; if you see a bid that surpasses your own, you'll know it's time to throw in another bid.

- Auction information appearing in red indicates that your bid is losing. If you decide to up your bid, simply click the auction title to go to the auction.

- The current dollar amount you're spending on pending auctions appears at the very bottom of the Bidding/Watching page. You'll see the total amount you've bid and a separate total representing auctions you're winning.

- As you win auctions, you can remove them from the Bidding/Watching page by clicking the Delete Selected Ended Items button. This is a good way to save space on the page.

- After you've won an auction, your win moves from Items I've Bid On to Items I've Won; see the following section.

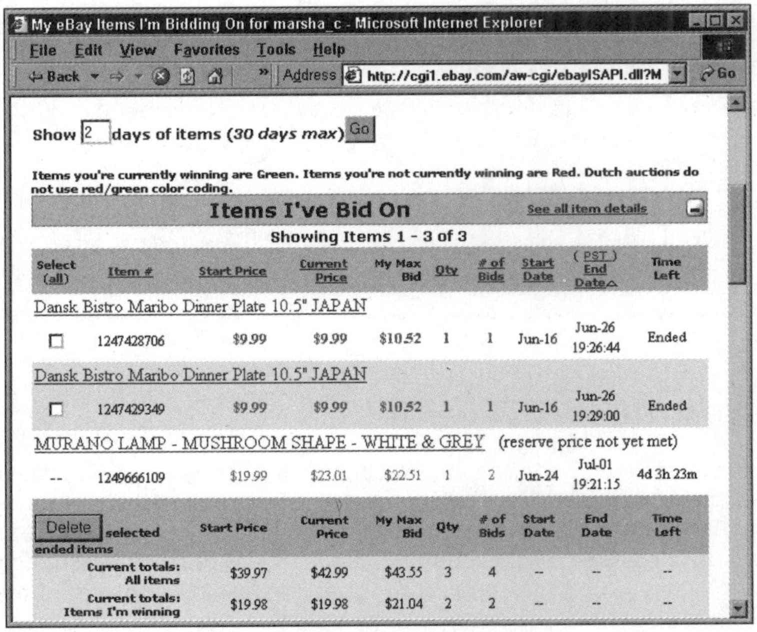

Figure 3-2:
Keeping track of your bidding at My eBay.

Dutch auctions appear in neither red nor green but in black. To determine whether you retain High Bidder status in a Dutch auction, you have to go to the actual auction.

Items I've Won

Depending on the amount of days you've set your show items, you'll see all auctions you've won in that many days. The Items I've Won area is a great place to keep track of items that you're waiting to receive from the seller. It's also a convenient, temporary way to keep track of your expenditures, should you be buying for resale.

The Items I've Won page is a one-stop management spot for your buying needs. Helpful features on this page include:

- **Item Number:** The auction number for your records.
- **Auction Title:** A link to the actual auction. I always use this when an item arrives so that I can be sure that the item I received is exactly as advertised.
- **Auction End Date:** Convenient way to see if your item is slow in shipping. After a week, it doesn't hurt to drop the seller an e-mail to check on the shipping status.
- **End Price and Quantity:** Helps you keep track of the money you've spent. Works in conjunction with the totals at the bottom.
- **Pay with eBay Payments:** An awesome feature that allows you to pay for the item directly from this page through eBay Payments.
- **Seller's Name:** It always helps to remember the seller's name, and this link allows you to send e-mail to the seller.
- **Leave Feedback:** After you've received the item and are satisfied that it's what you ordered, click here to directly leave feedback on that transaction.

As you receive items and leave feedback, click the Delete Selected Items button to remove completed transactions from view.

Items I'm Watching

Have you ever seen an auction that made you think, "I don't want to bid on this just now, but I'd like to buy it if it's a bargain"? The Items I'm Watching page (see Figure 3-3), one of the most powerful features of the My eBay page, is just the tool to help you. With this tool, you can observe an auction for bidding (or an auction's progress without ever bidding on it). This page lists each auction with a countdown timer, so you have an exact idea of when the auction will close. When an auction on your watch list gets close to ending, you can swoop down and make the kill — if the price is right.

My eBay Items I'm Bidding On for marsha_c - Microsoft Internet Explorer

File   Edit   View   Favorites   Tools   Help

⇦ Back ▾ ⇨ ▾ ⊗ ⊠ ⌂   »   Address ⚑ ate=0&nitem=0&rows=25&pagebid=&pagewon=   ⬩ Go

Items I'm Watching   Learn more

Select (all)	Item #	Item Title	Current Price	# of Bids	Time Left△	Bid on this item
☐	1437039890	Paul Revere Raiders Miami Beach 1965	--	--	Ended	--
☐	1440614341	CHEF PAUL PRUDHOMME'S CAJUN MAGIC COOKBOOK	--	--	Ended	--
☐	1248230292	New J. A. Henckels Pro "S" 4" Paring Knife	--	--	Ended	--
☐	1248562107	Corning Ware Sidekick Trays (2)	$10.50	2	0d 2h 27m	Bid Now!
☐	1609364802	CARTIER TANK LADIES WATCH W/STRAP VINTAGE	$460.00	7	0d 3h 6m	Bid Now!
☐	1248750837	HENCKELS FORGED 8-PC. STEAK KNIFE SET-NEW!	--	--	0d 20h 45m	Bid Now!
☐	1249871154	Henckels Pro S 8" Carbon Steel Chef's Knife	$27.00	5	0d 23h 0m	Bid Now!
☐	1249879739	Henckels International 7-Piece Knife Set	$35.00	1	0d 23h 34m	Bid Now!
☐	1250246650	Williams Sonoma Henckels Steak Knives (4)	$20.00	1	2d 3h 27m	Bid Now!
☐	1249191062	FLOKATI BATH MAT/RUG.....BLACK...NEW .2 x 3	--	--	2d 12h 23m	Bid Now!
☐	1249666109	MURANO LAMP - MUSHROOM SHAPE - WHITE & GREY	$23.01	2	4d 3h 20m	Bid Now!
☐	1249810206	new case kleenex (36) 2 ply	$18.50	8	4d 19h 8m	Bid Now!

Delete | selected items

Figure 3-3:
Sit back and
observe at
My eBay.

Also a handy marketing tool, Items I'm Watching allows you to store auctions from competitive sellers to see how they're going. This way, you can monitor the status of items similar to yours, and see whether the items are selling high or low, helping you to decide whether it is a good time to sell.

You've probably seen the tiny binoculars icon on each auction page that's accompanied by the phrase, `Watch This Item`. If you're watching items (eBay allows you to monitor 20 auctions at a time), you'll see a notation on the next page, once you click Watch This Item, indicating how many auctions you're currently watching.

My number one reason for using the Watch This Item function is that it allows me to keep my bargain hunting quiet. Everybody (including the competition) knows when you're bidding on an item; nobody knows when you're watching the deals like a hawk. When you're looking for bargains to buy and resell, you may not want to tip off the competition by letting them know you're bidding.

Selling

On your Selling page, eBay is giving out some smooth management tools. You can keep track of the items you currently have up for auction and also the items you've sold. It's a quick way to get a snapshot of the status of your auctions. It's a visual record of the dollar value of your auctions, as they proceed.

Although this isn't as good for marketing information (detailed counters are best — see Chapter 9), it's a pretty good way to tell at a glance how your items are faring.

Items I'm Selling

With this tool, you can keep an eye on your auctions and their bidding without jumping around the site. You can see how many bids your auctions have, if your reserves have been met, and, through a countdown timer, how long before the auction will close. By clicking an auction title, you can visit your auctions to double-check that your pictures are appearing or to check your counter.

If you want to check on the bidder's name or other items, click the See all item details link (see Figure 3-4) — a great feature *if* you want to see details on *all* your auctions. Usually, however, clicking one auction title and going directly to that auction is easier and faster.

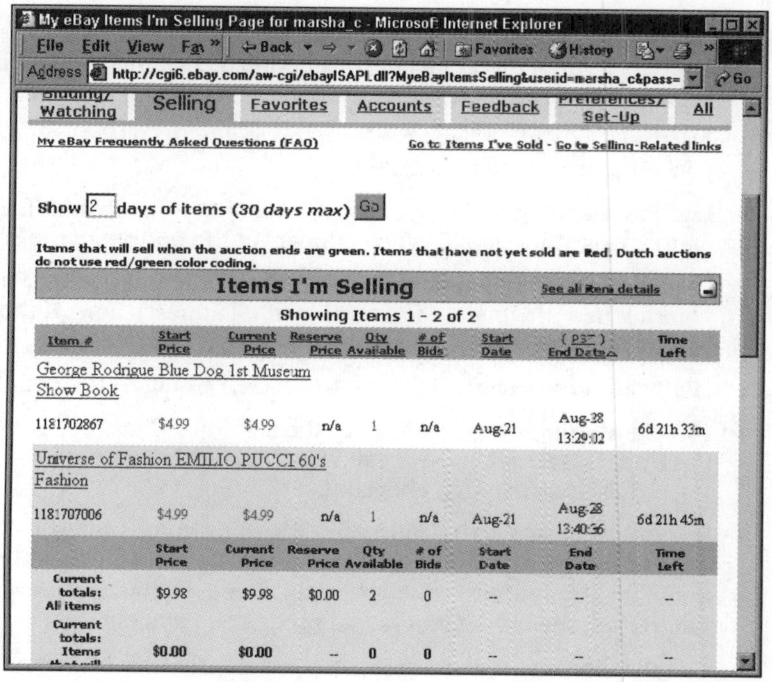

Figure 3-4:
Items I'm
Selling at
My eBay.

As in the Bidding area, auctions that appear in green have met any reserves you've set and will sell when the auction is over. Auctions in red haven't received any bids or the set reserve price hasn't been met. Dutch auctions aren't color coded and appear in black.

At the bottom of the Items I'm Selling area, eBay automatically totals all items by Start Price and Current Price, including bidding on items that haven't met your reserve. The total dollar amount of the items that will sell when the auction is over appears beneath these totals.

Items I've Sold

As you scroll down the Selling page, you come to the Items I've Sold area, which keeps your sales in a concise area. I use it, and many other sellers use it, in lieu of using fancy auction management software. If you're not selling hundreds of items a week, you can turn on your computer and go to this page to see all your information in front of you. If you are selling hundreds of items, your list will probably be too long to monitor individual auctions — but you'll have the benefit of viewing the total Current Price of the Items that Will Sell.

In Items I've Sold, eBay gives you the following features, which I'm sure you'll find helpful in completing your transactions:

- **Item Number:** The auction number for your records.

- **Auction Title:** A direct link to the auction. I click this link to check on my auction.

- **Auction End Date:** Keep an eye on the end date so that you can be sure you get your payment as agreed.

- **End Price and Quantity:** A running total of how much in dollars and how many items you've sold, which appears at the bottom of the section.

- **Paid via eBay Payments:** If you've offered Billpoint Instant Payment for your auction, the Instant Payment symbol appears here. If the bidder has paid through eBay Payments, this area is marked paid.

- **High Bidder's Name:** Click here to send an e-mail to the high bidder.

- **Checkout:** Here you have links to the auction's Checkout Summary or the Update page where you can view the particulars of the sale after the buyer has gone through checkout.

- **Payment Reminder:** If you haven't heard from the bidder within three days of the auction's end, you can have eBay send a perfectly charming and official sounding reminder e-mail. I've used this feature when I've heard from the bidder, but haven't received payment.

  Use the Payment Reminder feature judiciously because eBay sends out only one reminder.

- **Leave Feedback:** After you know that the item has arrived safely, and that your customer is happy, click here to leave feedback. For more information on leaving feedback, check out the section "Feedback: Your permanent record," later in this chapter.

Favorites

If you sell and have an interest in a few categories, look no further than the My eBay Favorites page, which gives you some quick links to check out what's hot and what's not. I recommend specializing in a few categories of items, so that you can track their popularity, and also sell what you know. When your specialization narrows to four categories, these are the ones you should watch here. This page helps you track trends and find some bargains to resell at eBay.

Favorite Categories

eBay allows you to store hot links for four categories. Because you'll probably narrow your sales to a few categories, these links give you the chance to check out the competition.

Before you list some auctions on a popular item, estimate the date and hour that other auctions selling that item will close. Then go into the category and check to be sure that your auction won't be closing during a flood of auctions for the same item. Nothing kills profits more than closing an auction in the middle of a series of five auctions selling the same thing. You can watch the final values drop one at a time, and you don't want your auction to be one of them.

Favorite Searches

Another tool that comes in handy for sellers as well as buyers is the My eBay Favorite Searches (see Figure 3-5). You can list as many as 15 of your favorite searches; when you want to check one out, simply click the <u>Search</u> link next to the item. You can view your saved searches, change them, delete them, or indicate that you'd like to receive e-mail notification when a new item is listed. To add an item to the list, run a search from any search bar on any eBay page and click the <u>Save this search</u> link that appears at the bottom of the search. The next time you reload your My eBay Favorites page, your new favorite is listed.

Keeping track of favorite searches is a valuable tool when you're looking for particular items to resell, and you want to find them at bargain-basement prices. Be sure to take advantage of asterisks (wild cards) and alternate spellings, so as to catch the items with misspellings in the title. These are your best bets for low prices. (See Chapter 7 for the lowdown on the search engine and how it can help your sales.) You'll change your favorite searches on a regular basis because you'll be looking for different items depending on the season.

If you choose to receive e-mail when your search locates a new listing, your request lasts for 90 days. You're allowed to receive new listing e-mails on just three of your fifteen searches. This service has replaced the old Personal

Shopper that used to send similar e-mails. Just check the box in the far-right column (refer to Figure 3-5); eBay sends its robot to check listings each night, so you'll get notification of a new listing the next morning.

Favorite Sellers

Favorite Sellers is where I keep a list of sellers who sell items similar to what I sell. I can check up on them and see what they're selling, when they're selling it, and for how much. It's a helpful tool that has prevented me from listing an item right next to one of their auctions. Use it to see when your competition might decide to blow out an item — that you plan on selling — at a discounted price. If that's the case, hold off on your sales until they sell out of the item, when the price will most likely go back up — supply and demand, remember?

Also, you'll find quite a few quality wholesalers and liquidators at eBay. I keep them under my favorite sellers, too, and search for lots that I can resell at a profit. To add a seller to your Favorite Sellers list, click the link in the upper-left corner of the table, where it says Add New Seller. Then all you need to do is input the seller's user ID on the next page. It will be automatically added to your Favorite Sellers list. You may add a maximum of 15 sellers to your list.

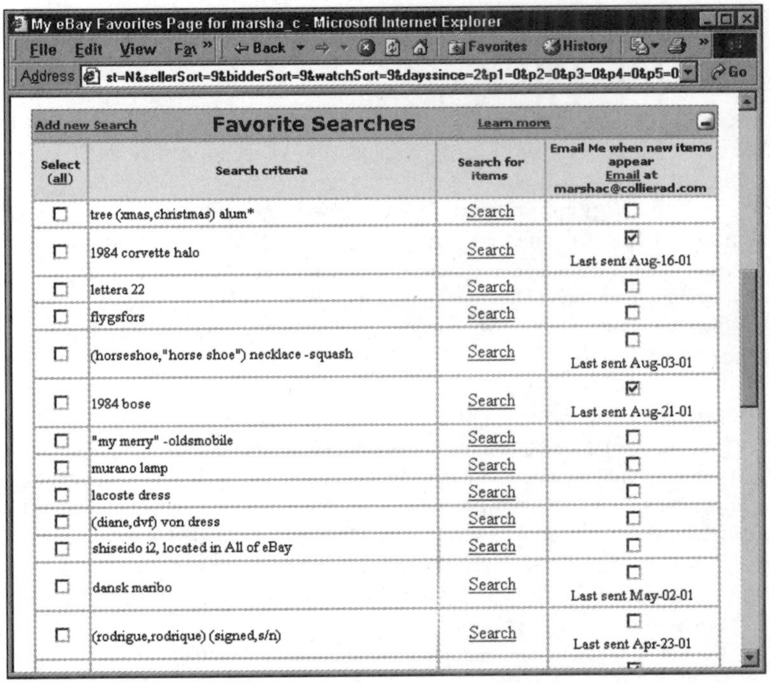

Select (all)	Search criteria	Search for items	Email Me when new items appear Email at marshac@collierad.com
☐	tree (xmas,christmas) alum*	Search	☐
☐	1984 corvette halo	Search	☑ Last sent Aug-16-01
☐	lettera 22	Search	☐
☐	flygsfors	Search	☐
☐	(horseshoe,"horse shoe") necklace -squash	Search	☐ Last sent Aug-03-01
☐	1984 bose	Search	☑ Last sent Aug-21-01
☐	"my merry" -oldsmobile	Search	☐
☐	murano lamp	Search	☐
☐	lacoste dress	Search	☐
☐	(diane,dvf) von dress	Search	☐
☐	shiseido i2, located in All of eBay	Search	☐
☐	dansk maribo	Search	☐ Last sent May-02-01
☐	(rodrigue,rodrique) (signed,s/n)	Search	☐ Last sent Apr-23-01

Figure 3-5: Some of my favorite searches (this month).

Accounts

Your eBay accounts page (see mine in Figure 3-6) lets you know how much you owe eBay, and how much they will charge your credit card that month. You can check your last invoice or your current account status. This is a quick and easy way to check on the status of credits, your account, and eBay payments (Billpoint); all the links are located in one area.

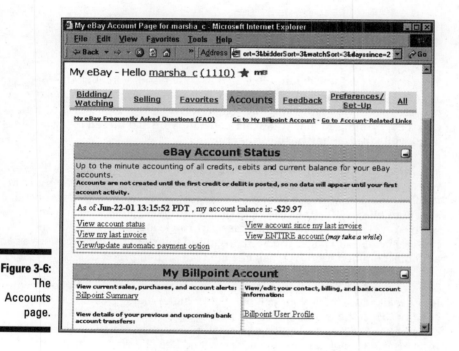

Figure 3-6:
The
Accounts
page.

You're able to access your eBay Payments account through this page. You can check to see when deposits were credited to your checking account. For a complete picture of how to sign up and use eBay Payments, visit Chapter 13.

Preferences/Set-up

Preferences/Set-up: the place that holds all the links to your personal information at eBay. Here you can change your e-mail address, your user ID, your password, and also create your About Me page. Also on this page, you're able to change or access any registration or credit card information that you have on file at eBay.

Another nifty feature of the Preferences/Set-up page is the opportunity to customize how you see your My eBay pages (see Figure 3-7). If you run many auctions, you can show as many as 200 items on these pages.

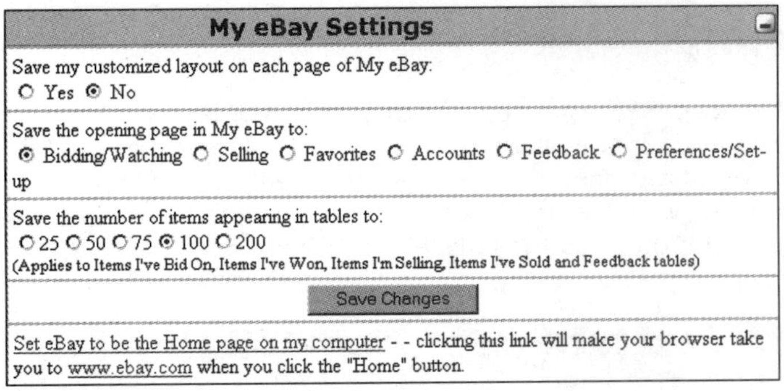

My eBay Settings

Save my customized layout on each page of My eBay:
○ Yes ◉ No

Save the opening page in My eBay to:
◉ Bidding/Watching ○ Selling ○ Favorites ○ Accounts ○ Feedback ○ Preferences/Set-up

Save the number of items appearing in tables to:
○ 25 ○ 50 ○ 75 ◉ 100 ○ 200
(Applies to Items I've Bid On, Items I've Won, Items I'm Selling, Items I've Sold and Feedback tables)

Save Changes

Set eBay to be the Home page on my computer - - clicking this link will make your browser take you to www.ebay.com when you click the "Home" button.

Figure 3-7:
Your My
eBay
customi-
zation links.

You can also customize your eBay Sign In activities. If you click the Modify your Sign In activities link, you're taken to a page where you can make your choices regarding what your eBay sign-in will do for you. You may as well check everything, so that you won't constantly be hammered for your password while transacting business at eBay.

The Microsoft Passport sign-in service may be available for signing in at eBay when you read this. This is an alternative way of signing in to eBay for community members who use Microsoft Passport. eBay users with Passport can sign in to eBay with either their Passports or their regular user IDs and password. You can request to use the Passport single sign-in service on the Preferences/Set-up page. You aren't required to use it; it's merely there as an added accommodation. You can change your sign-in preference at any time.

The Preferences/Set-up page also has a link that you can click to add a wireless e-mail address for your cell phone or Palm. What a great idea: eBay can send outbid notices and End of Auction notices right to your WAP-enabled cell phone. The trouble is, I've never gotten any such e-mail on my phone from eBay although it's had my address, and I've checked several times that it's the right one. I haven't heard any official word on it, other than the system is iffy. So don't count on it working.

Your About Me Page

If you're at eBay, you *need* an About Me page. I hate to harp on this, but eBay is a community and all eBay members are members of that community. Checking out the About Me pages of those you transact business with at eBay gives you an opportunity to get to know them. Because eBay is a cyberspace market, you have no other way to let prospective bidders know that you're a real person. Don't you shop at some stores because you like the owners or people who work there? The About Me page takes a first step toward establishing a professional and trusted identity at eBay. The About Me page enables you to personalize your business to prospective bidders. (See Figure 3-8 for an example.)

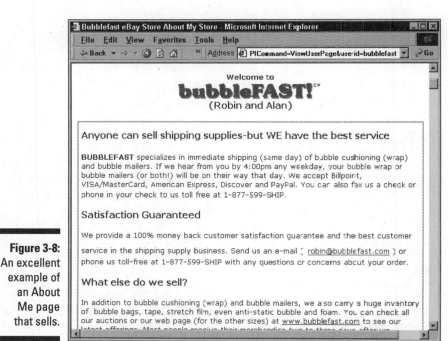

Figure 3-8:
An excellent
example of
an About
Me page
that sells.

Your About Me page also becomes your About the Store page if you have an eBay store. Plenty of sellers out there may not stock enough merchandise to have an eBay store or may only be part-time eBay sellers. Whether or not you have an eBay store, you need an About Me page to establish your eBay image.

It also benefits you when you buy. Sellers usually like to know about their bidders to build confidence in their trading partners. If you've put up an About Me page, you're halfway there.

If you don't have an About Me page, put this book down and set one up immediately. It doesn't have to be a work of art, just get something up there to tell the rest of the community who you are. You can always go back later and add to it or redesign it. When you plan your About Me page, consider adding the following:

- Who you are and where you live.

- Your hobbies; if you collect things, here's where to let the world know.

- Whether you run your eBay business full time or part time, and whether you have another career. This is more integral information about you; let the world know.

- The type of merchandise that your business revolves around. Promote it here; tell the reader why your merchandise and service is the best!

- Your most recent feedback and a list of your current auctions.

To create your page, click the Me icon next to any user's name, scroll to the bottom of the About Me page that appears, and click the <u>click here</u> link next to the words To Create Your Own About Me Page or go to `http://members.ebay.com/aw-cgi/eBayISAPI.dll?AboutMeLogin`. Just follow the simple pre-formatted template for your first page and work from there.

eBay Seller Services

eBay has more seller-specific services than I'll bet most eBay users know. It's more of what falls into the "wow, that's cool" category. I've dug deep into the eBay pond and dug up a few excellent tools to help you in your business online.

Even if you've used some of these before, eBay has implemented quite a few changes during the past year. eBay is always trying to come up with new features that will help its sellers along their way. The only problem is that sometimes sellers are so involved with their auctions that they don't see the new helper tools. So take heed of the tools I describe here and, in the future, keep your eyes peeled for changes.

Bidder-management tools

Did you know that you don't have to accept bids from just anyone? Although many sellers type notices in their auction descriptions attempting to qualify the bidders ahead of time, this doesn't always prevent them from bidding on your auction. Alas, part of the business is watching your bidders. With these tools, you can save yourself a good deal of grief.

Canceling bids

Any number of reasons can determine whether you want to cancel someone's bid on your auction. Perhaps an international bidder has bid on an auction in which you clearly state you don't ship overseas.

For whatever reason you're canceling someone's bid, you must first e-mail that person and clearly explain why you're doing so. After you cancel a bid, your bid cancellation appears in the auction's bidding history and becomes part of the auction's Official Record. For that reason, I recommend that you leave a concise, unemotional, one-line explanation as to why you've cancelled the bid.

A few more legitimate reasons:

✔ Bidder contacts you to back out of the bid; choosing to be a nice guy, you let him out of the deal.

✔ Your bidder has several negative feedbacks and hasn't gone through with other transactions that she has won.

✔ After trying via e-mail or phone, you're unable to verify the bidder's identity.

✔ You need to cancel the auction (see following tip).

I don't recommend canceling an auction unless you absolutely have to because it's just bad business. People rely on your auctions being up for the stated amount of time. They may be planning to bid at the last minute, or may just want to watch the action for a while. You may lose potential buyers by ending your listing early.

The link for the bid cancellation form:

```
http://pages.ebay.com/services/buyandsell/
        seller-cancel-bid.html
```

Canceling your auction

You may decide to end an auction early for any number of reasons. If any bids are on your auction when you close it, you are duty bound to sell to the highest bidder. So before ending an auction early, you must e-mail everyone in your bidder list on the auction's Bidding History, explaining why you're canceling bids and closing the auction. If an egregious error in the item's description is forcing you to this action, let your bidders know if you're planning to relist the item with the correct information.

After you've e-mailed all the bidders, you must then cancel their bids by using the bid cancellation form; for the link to this form, see the preceding section "Canceling bids."

Only after canceling all bids should you go ahead and close your auction. To close your auction, go to:

```
http://cgi3.ebay.com/aw-cgi/eBayISAPI.dll?EndingMyAuction
```

Following are some legitimate reasons for closing your auction:

✔ **You no longer want to sell the item.** Your account may also be subject to a "Non-Selling Seller" warning unless you really have a good reason. (See Chapter 4 for more details.)

✔ **An error occurred in the minimum bid or Reserve amount.** Your wife said that she really loved that lamp and you'd better get some good money for it, but you started the auction at $1.00.

✔ **The listing has a major error in it.** You misspelled a critical keyword in the title.

✔ **The item was somehow lost or broken.** Your dog ate it.

Blocking bidders

If you don't want certain bidders bidding in your auctions, you can remove their capability to do so. Setting up a list of bidders that you don't want to do business with is legal at eBay. If someone that you've blocked tries to bid on your auction, the bid won't go through.

You can block as many as 1,000 users from bidding on your auctions. However, I recommend that you use this option only when absolutely necessary. Situations change — even people change – and hopefully, you're able to clear up problems with particular bidders. Reinstate bidders at any time by deleting User IDs from your Blocked Bidders box. You can find the Bidder Blocking box at:

```
http://pages.ebay.com/services/buyandsell/biddermanagement.
          html
```

Preapproving bidders

Suppose that you're selling a big-ticket item and want to pre-qualify your bidders. If the bidder has taken advantage of the ID Verify feature, which I explain later in this chapter, you can be sure that your bidder is a real person. You can also scroll over a bidder's bidding history to see the amounts they've successfully bid in previous auctions and see whether the feedback on those transactions is A-Okay. Although eBay gives you the tools, you still have to do the bidder research to determine whether you deem particular bidders trustworthy enough to bid on your special auction.

In your auction, state that bidders must send you an e-mail claiming the intent to bid to pre-qualify for the auction. As you receive e-mails and approve of bidders' intentions, you can then build your Pre-Approved Bidder List.

Your Pre-Approved Bidder List is applicable on an auction-by-auction basis only. Using preapproved bidders doesn't mean that all bidders in all your auctions need to be preapproved. To use this feature, you must supply eBay with a particular auction number. You can add approved bidders right up to the close of the auction. Access the form at:

```
http://cgi3.ebay.com/aw-cgi/eBayISAPI.dll?PreApproveBidders
```

If someone who isn't preapproved tries to bid on your auction, eBay asks that bidder to contact you by e-mail before placing a bid. After you've investigated the bidder to your satisfaction, or even called the bidder, and you're comfortable with that bidder bidding on your auction, you can add the name to your Pre-Approved Bidder list for that auction.

ID Verify

ID Verify establishes proof that you are who you say you are. It also enables you to perform specialized eBay functions if you choose not to supply eBay with a credit card when you register. There is a one-time charge of $5, and Equifax (one of the nation's largest credit security companies) conducts the verification. It is not a credit check. Your personal information is checked alongside consumer and business databases for consistency so that Equifax can verify that you are who you say you are. If you aren't quite ready to get the SquareTrade seal (see Chapter 4) for your auctions, or if you find the monthly fees involved in the seal currently prohibitive, ID Verify is the next best thing.

The extra functions you can perform without supplying your credit card are:

- Buying an item through the eBay Buy it Now feature
- Placing a bid above $15,000
- Bidding on eBay Premier auctions
- Selling items in the eBay Mature Audiences category

Feedback: Your permanent record

Just like your high school permanent record, your eBay feedback follows you forever at eBay. If you change your User ID, it's there. If you change your e-mail address, it's there. Every user's eBay ID card (see Figure 3-9) is shown when someone clicks the feedback number next to a User's ID. The information it shows will tell you a lot about your bidder.

The most obvious tip-off to someone's feedback is the star that you see next to the user ID. The stars of different colors are awarded as folks reach milestones in their feedback ratings (click a star to find a list of the milestones). Your feedback means a great deal to people who visit your auctions. At first glance at your feedback page, they can see

- Whether you're an experienced eBay user
- Your eBay history
- When you started at eBay
- How many bid retractions you've had in the past six months

This is valuable information for both the buyer and the seller because it helps to evaluate whether you're the type of person who would make a responsible trading partner.

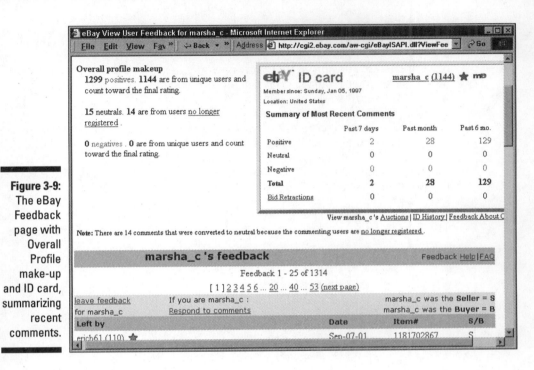

Figure 3-9:
The eBay
Feedback
page with
Overall
Profile
make-up
and ID card,
summarizing
recent
comments.

 Worried about negative feedback? There is one possible way that you can get negative feedback expunged from your record. You can file for mediation with SquareTrade (see Chapter 4 on how to do this). If the feedback poster (through mediation) agrees to remove the feedback, eBay will remove it.

Leaving feedback

Everyone in the eBay community is honor-bound to leave feedback. Sometimes when you've had a truly dreadful experience, you hate to leave negative or neutral feedback, but if you don't, you're not helping anyone. The point of feedback is not to show what a great person you are, but to show future sellers or bidders where the rotten apples lie. So be truthful and unemotional, and state just the facts when leaving feedback.

Feedback is important, so you should be sure to leave some for every transaction you're a part of. When a week has passed since you've shipped the item, and you haven't heard from the bidder or seen any new feedback, drop that bidder an e-mail. Write "Thanks for your purchase. Are you happy with the item?" Also emphasize that you'll be glad to leave positive feedback after you've heard a reply and ask for the same in return.

 Never leave feedback on a sale until you're absolutely, positively sure that the buyer has received the product and is happy with the deal. Many inexperienced sellers leave feedback the minute they get their money, but experience can teach them that it ain't over 'till it's over. A package can get lost or damaged, or the bidder may be unhappy for some reason. A bidder may also want to return an item for no good reason, turning a seemingly smooth transaction into a nightmare. You only get *one* feedback per transaction so use it wisely; you can't go back and say that the buyer damaged the product and then tried to return it. Forewarned is forearmed.

eBay provides so many different links to leave feedback that I could probably write an entire chapter on it. But I don't want you to fall asleep while reading, so I just go through the most convenient methods. You can leave feedback by

- Going to your auction page and clicking the <u>Leave Feedback</u> link at the left

- Clicking the number (in parentheses) next to the other user's name and, when you're on that user's feedback page, then clicking the <u>Leave Feedback</u> link

- Clicking the <u>Leave Feedback</u> link next to the completed auction on your My eBay page

- Visiting the feedback forum (this link shows up on the bottom of every page) and clicking the link that will show you all pending feedback for the past 90 days; when you've fallen behind in leaving feedback, this is a super-fast way to catch up.

Responding to feedback

You may occasionally get feedback that you feel compelled to respond to; did you know that you could? If the feedback is neutral or negative, I recommend that you cover yourself by explaining the situation for future bidders to see.

If you receive a negative feedback rating, a well-meaning Mea Culpa (admission of guilt) would work. You could say something like, "Unfortunately, shipping was delayed and I regret the situation." Prospective bidders will see that you've addressed the problem instead of just letting it go.

To respond to feedback, follow these steps:

1. **In your My eBay, go to the feedback page, find the feedback-related links at the bottom of the page, and click the** <u>Review and respond to feedback about me</u> **link.**

   The link carries you to the Review and Respond to Feedback Comments Left for You page, shown in Figure 3-10.

2. **Scroll to find the feedback comment that you want to respond to and click the link that says** <u>Respond</u>**.**

   The next page that appears is where you actually respond to the feedback.

3. **Type your response and then click the Leave Response button.**

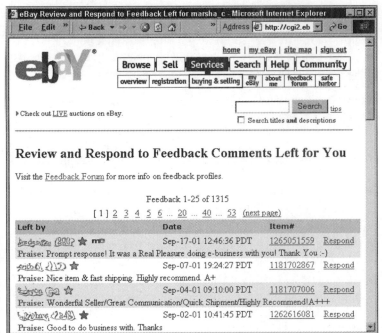

Figure 3-10:
Review and
respond to
your
feedbacks.

The eBay Power Sellers program

I'm sure you've seen that big, giant power seller logo on auctions that you browse. eBay power sellers represent the largest gross sales users at eBay. You can be a power seller, too, if you qualify. The requirements:

- A gross monthly dollar volume of $2,000 (Bronze level); $3,000 (Silver level); $10,000 (Gold level); $25,000 (Platinum); and $150,000.

   To remain a power seller, you must maintain your level's minimum gross sales for two out of three months, and of course, you have to keep current with all the other requirements. To advance on the power seller food chain, you must reach and maintain the next level of gross sales for a minimum of two out of three months.

   If you miss your minimum gross sales for two out of three months, eBay gives you a three-month grace period. After that time, if you don't meet the minimum gross figures for your level, you may be moved down to the prior level or be removed from the Power Seller program.

- At least 100 feedback comments, 98 percent positive.

   To calculate your feedback percentage, divide your number of positive feedbacks by your number of total feedbacks (negatives plus positives).

- A Satisfaction Guarantee offer.

The eBay Power Seller Satisfaction Guarantee is widely misunderstood at eBay. It does *not* mean that you have to have a 100 percent return policy. It does mean that you must stand by your clear and accurate item descriptions and that you will contact successful high bidders within three days. Sellers and buyers are responsible for resolving any differences that involve refunds or exchanges. You don't have to accept returns as long as you run your eBay auctions with a high level of professionalism.

Power sellers enjoy many benefits (see Figure 3-11), but the best thing about being a power seller is the incredibly awesome level of customer service you receive. When a power seller dashes off an e-mail to a special customer service department, a reply comes back in light speed.

Figure 3-11:
eBay Power
Seller
Benefits by
level.

Benefits	Bronze	Silver	Gold
PowerSellers Logo	X	X	X
Dedicated Email Customer Support (24 hours a day, 7 days a week)	X	X	X
PowerSeller Success Stories	X	X	X
Invitation to Special Events	X	X	X
Account Specialist Customer Phone Support (business hours)		X	X
Dedicated Account Manager			X
24-Hour Customer Support Hotline			X

Somehow, the bidder's perception of the Power Seller logo varies. Some Power Sellers don't include the logo in their auctions because they'd rather be perceived as regular folks at eBay. eBay doesn't require you to show the Power Seller logo in your descriptions when you attain that level.

eBay auction software

eBay has developed a fantastic software called Mister Lister, which is free and downloadable from the site. They also have a Seller's Assistant software to manage your auctions. For a complete breakdown of these software products and others to ease the seller's burden, skip to Chapter 9.

Lloyd's of London insurance

The minute an auction payment hits the mailbox, or the moment that a winner pays with an online payment service, eBay covers the buyer with its Fraud Protection Program. The program is insured with the world famous Lloyd's of London and covers the bidder for $200 of the final auction price. There is a $25 deductible.

The insurance doesn't cover packages that are lost or damaged by the shipper; this is fraud insurance only. The United States Postal Service offers insurance as an option, so I guess this means that if your package isn't insured, the bidder is out of luck. The eBay Fraud Protection Program policy only covers eBay buyers when they are defrauded, when the item is never shipped, or when the item is significantly different from the auction description. The policy does *not* cover sellers for anything — so don't ship that item until you're darn sure the check has cleared!

When you get down to the nuts and bolts of the program, there are a lot of ifs. Buyers can apply only *if* they did not pay with cash. Bidders, if they paid by credit card, need to first apply to their credit card companies to see whether they're covered through them. The insurance will not cover the bidder *if* the seller has a negative feedback rating. The bidder also cannot file any more than three claims within a six-month period.

eBay education

eBay offers many forms of training and education. No matter how advanced you are, it never hurts to go back to school, to eBay University, and take a refresher course on the basics. You can also find some very cool online interactive tutorials as you make your way through eBay. Take a moment when you can and watch them because you might just see one or two new features that you didn't know about.

More information about eBay education is available at http://pages.ebay.com/education/index.html.

eBay University

The eBay traveling tent show goes across the country, spreading the eBay word to the masses. It's quite an eye-opening event and you'll really enjoy yourself if you go. You may be an advanced seller, but you can still pick up a tip or trick at the advanced level class. You'll also have a chance to meet some really wonderful people who work for eBay and who enjoy answering questions. eBay University follows these tracks:

- **Browsing and Buying:** A fun course that'll educate anyone in how to find the gems at eBay, and how to use the search engine.

- **Basic Selling:** A beginning class for new sellers that lays out the basics so they can progress from there.

- **Improving Your Listing with Photos and HTML:** If you want to learn HTML, this is a fun class, often taught by eBay's Uncle Griff, Jim Griffith. You'll enjoy a clear and concise description of HTML and you'll walk away with enough knowledge to doll up your auction descriptions.

- ✔ **Advanced Selling Tips:** An interesting class that offers some of the newest ins and outs of eBay selling.

- ✔ **Seller Assistant Pro Software:** If you're going to use this software, there's nothing like a live class to make things clearer. An expert of the software teaches the class, and you'll gain a good understanding of the software and how it works.

Online seminars

eBay has ongoing online seminars that permit you to participate during the class via a chat screen. eBay experts give the one-hour classes online. You follow along on your computer while you hear the audio through your telephone line. Many interesting classes are recorded and archived on the eBay education area, so you can see the classes after they premiere.

Chapter 4

Practicing Safe Selling

· ·

In This Chapter

▶ Understanding the rules

▶ Watching out for violations

▶ Protecting yourself — and helping make eBay a safe place to trade

· ·

*T*here are a lot of *"shoulds"* in this world. You *should* do this and you *should* do that. I don't know who's in charge of the *shoulds*, but there are certain things that just make life work better. You may or may not take any of the advice on these pages, but they undoubtedly will make your eBay business thrive with a minimum of anguish. If you've ever had an auction pulled by eBay, for any reason, you know what anguish truly feels like.

In the real world, we have to take responsibility for our own actions. If we see a guy in the street, selling television sets out of the back of a truck for $25 and we buy one, who do we have to blame when we take it home and it doesn't work? We can whine and moan, but the upshot of this situation is that we know better than to expect something for nothing. You get what you pay for, and you have no consumer protection from the seller of the possibly "hot" TVs. Responsible consumerism is every buyer's job. Lawsuit upon lawsuit gets filed when someone feels they've gotten ripped off, and they're sometimes won, but my best advice is that if you stay clean in your auction business, you'll keep clean.

eBay is a community, and eBay believes in five basic values:

- ✔ We believe people are basically good.
- ✔ We believe everyone has something to contribute.
- ✔ We believe that an honest, open environment can bring out the best in people.
- ✔ We recognize and respect everyone as a unique individual.
- ✔ We encourage you to treat others the way that you want to be treated.

eBay is committed to these values, and it says so right on the Web site. We ought to all try to hold ourselves to these standards. eBay also believes that community members should also "honor these values — whether buying, selling, or chatting." So *should* we all.

Is What You Want to Sell Legal at eBay?

Although eBay is based in California and therefore must abide by California law, sellers do business all over the United States, and so items sold at eBay must be governed by the laws of every other state as well. As a seller, you're ultimately responsible for the legality of the items you sell and the way that you transact business at eBay. Yes, you're able to sell thousands of different items at eBay. But do you know what you aren't allowed to sell at eBay?

The eBay User Agreement outlines all eBay Rules and Regulations regarding what you can and can't sell as well as all aspects of doing business at eBay. If you haven't read it in a while, do so; you can find it at the following address:

http://pages.ebay.com/help/community/png-user.html

From time to time, eBay may make changes in its policies. As an active seller, you need to be aware of any changes. eBay will send out notifications of changes, but only if you request them. To request that you be notified when eBay makes such changes to the User Agreement, as well as to control any correspondence you receive from eBay, follow these steps:

1. **Go to** http://pages.ebay.com/services/myebay/optin-login.html.

2. **Once there, sign in with your User ID and Password.**

   You're directed to the Change Your Preferences page, as shown in Figure 4-1.

3. **On this page, click either the Yes or No radio buttons next to each of the options.**

   To receive important information that may affect how you run your auctions, be sure that you select Yes next to both User Agreement Changes and Privacy Policy Changes (under Legal Notices).

By now, you should have a firm grasp on the eBay listing policies (if not, check out Chapter 2). So now you know all about the rules and regulations of listing auctions. But there's more to the rules than just the listing policies. You must consider the items themselves. Throughout this section, I detail the three categories of items to be wary of: prohibited, questionable, and infringing. Some are banned, period. Others fall under a gray area. You are responsible for what you sell, so you'd better know what's legal and what's not.

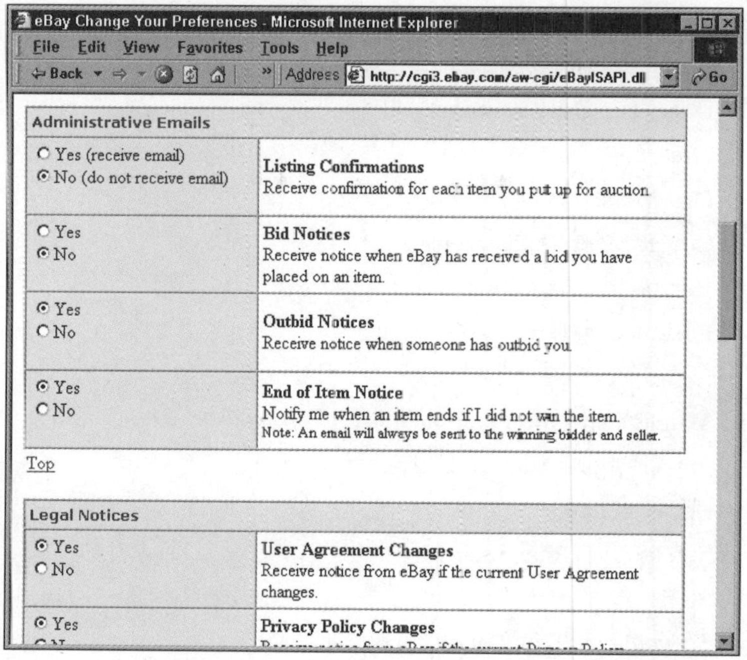

Figure 4-1:
The Change
Your Prefer-
ences form.

You may think that it's okay to give away a regulated or a banned item at eBay as a bonus item with your auction. Think again. Even giving away such items for free doesn't save you from potential legal responsibility.

Prohibited items

A *prohibited item* is one that's absolutely banned from sale at eBay. You cannot sell a prohibited item under any circumstance. Take a look at the following list. A little common sense tells you there's good reason for not selling these items (fake IDs are against the law, so you can't sell them at eBay), including real liability issues for the seller (what if you sold alcohol to a minor? — that's against the law, too).

The following is a list of items prohibited as of this writing, so don't try to sell 'em at eBay (check http://pages.ebay.com/help/community/png-items.html for updates):

Alcohol*

Animals and Wildlife Products

Catalogs (current issues)

Counterfeit Currency or Stamps

Counterfeit Items

Credit Cards

Drugs and Drug Paraphernalia

Firearms

Fireworks

Government IDs & Licenses

Human Parts and Remains**

Lockpicking Devices

Lottery Tickets

Mailing Lists and Personal Info

Prescription Drugs and Devices

Recalled Items

Stocks and Other Securities***

Stolen Property

Surveillance Equipment

Tobacco

TV Descramblers

United States Embargoed Goods from Prohibited Countries

*Alcohol may be allowed if the value of the item lies in the collectible container (bottle) that has a value exceeding the alcohol's retail price. It should not be currently available at a retail outlet. The auction should say that the container has not been opened and the seller should be sure that the buyer is over 21 years old.

**Skulls, skeletons, and items that may contain human hair are permissible — as long as they're used for educational purposes.

***Old or collectible stock certificates may be sold provided that they are cancelled or are from a company that no longer exists.

Questionable items

A *questionable item* is iffy — you know, determining whether or not you can sell it is tricky. Under certain circumstances, you may be able to list the item for sale at eBay. To fully understand when and if you can list a questionable item, visit the links that I highlight in Table 4-1. *Note:* All URLs listed in Table 4-1 begin with `http://pages.ebay.com/help/community`.

Table 4-1	Questionable Items and Where to Find the Rules Regulating Them
Can I Sell This?	*Go Here to Find Out*
Artifacts	/png-artifacts.html
Autographs	/png-autograph.html
Batteries	/png-batteries.html
Contracts and Tickets	/png-contracts.html
Event tickets	/png-tickets.html
Food	/png-food.html
Freon	/png-freon.html
Hazardous Materials	/png-hazardous.html
Mature Audiences	/png-mature.html
Offensive Material	/png-offensive.html
Police-related items	/png-badges.html
Scanners and Electronics equipment	/png-scanners.html
Used Clothing	/png-clothing.html
Used Medical Devices	/png-medical.html
Weapons & Knives	/png-weapons.html

Potentially infringing items

Potentially infringing items follow a slippery slope. If you list a potentially infringing item, you may infringe on existing copyrights, trademarks, registrations, or the like. Get the idea? It's for your own protection that these items may be prohibited from listing.

Items falling under the potentially infringing category are generally copyrighted or trademarked items, such as software, promotional items, and games. Even using a brand name in your auctions as part of a description (known as keyword spamming) may get you into trouble.

Keyword spamming manipulates the eBay search engine by listing the unrelated item in a search for the copyrighted or trademarked item, and then diverting bidders to an auction of other merchandise. This is frustrating to the person trying to use the search engine to find a particular item and also unfair to members who've properly listed their items.

The Chanel-style purse

I once listed at eBay a quilted leather women's purse that had a gold chain strap, which I described as a Chanel-style purse. Within two hours, I received an Informational alert from the eBay listing police. I described the item to the best of my ability, but found that it became a potentially infringing item. My use of the brand name Chanel caused my auction to come under the violation of keyword spamming (more on that in the section "Potentially Infringing items").

In its informational alert, eBay described my violation:

"Keyword spamming is the practice of adding words, including brand names, which do not directly describe the item you are selling. The addition of these words may not have been intentional, but including

them in this manner diverts members to your listing inappropriately."

Ooops! You can see how my ingenuous listing was actually a violation of policy. Think twice before you add names to your auction description. Thankfully, the eBay police judge each violation on a case-by-case basis. Because my record is clear, I merely got a reprimand. Had my violation been more deliberate, I'm sure that I might have been suspended.

To see the Chanel USA statement on violations, visit its About Me page. The violations apply to many items that may be listed at eBay.

```
http://members.ebay.com/aboutme
    /chanelusa/
```

Keyword spamming can take on many forms: Some are merely misleading the prospective bidder while others are legal infringements. A few of the most common are

- Superfluous brand names in title or item description
- Not Brand X, Not Brand Y
- Improper trademark usage
- Lists of "key" words
- Hidden text (white text on white background, or hidden text in HTML code). The white text still resides in the auction HTML, so it would show up in the search, but not be visible to the naked eye. Sneaky, eh?
- Drop-down boxes

To get the latest on the eBay keyword spamming policy, go to

```
http://pages.ebay.com/help/community/png-wordspam.html
```

Repeating various un-trademarked keywords can get you in trouble as well. eBay permits the use of as many as five synonyms when listing an item for sale. A permissible example of this might be: purse, handbag, pocketbook, satchel, and bag. Adding many un-trademarked keywords would cause the auction to come up in more searches.

Trading Violations

Both buyers and sellers can commit trading violations. Both buyers and sellers can participate in attempting to manipulate the outcome of an auction or sale. Many of the violations aren't necessarily buyer- or seller-exclusive, but apply to both. Regardless of the nature of a violation, such behavior violates everyone who's part of the eBay community. As a valued member of the community, it's partially your responsibility to look out for such violations — so that eBay continues to be a safe community in which to do business. Should you see a violation, report it immediately to SafeHarbor (see the section "eBay's SafeHarbor" later in this chapter). Throughout this section, I detail many common violations so that you can be on the outlook for them — and I'll just assume that you won't be committing any yourself.

The eBay Verified Rights Owners program

eBay can't possibly check every auction for authenticity issues. When it comes to trademarked items, it does care about these issues. Because of the breadth of items that eBay would have to cover, it formed the Legal Buddy program, now known as the Verified Rights Owners (VeRO) program.

Trademark and copyright owners expend large amounts of energy to develop and maintain control over the quality of their products. If you buy a "designer" purse from a guy on the street for $20, you can be sure that it's probably counterfeit, so don't go selling it at eBay.

eBay works with VeRO program members to educate the community about such items. They also work with verified owners of trademarks and copyrights to remove auctions that infringe on their products. If eBay doesn't close

a suspicious or blatantly infringing auction, both you and eBay are liable for the violation.

To become a member of the VeRO program, the owner of copyrights and trademarks needs to supply eBay with proof of ownership. To view the VeRO program information and to download the application for membership, go to

```
http://pages.ebay.com/help/
    community/
    notice-infringe2.pdf
```

Note: eBay also cooperates with law enforcement and may give your name and street address to a VeRO program member. The Nelson Brothers protect their family trademarks at eBay, as shown in the following figure. To view a list of other VeRO members' About Me pages, go to

```
http://pages.ebay.com/help/
    community/vero-aboutme.html
```

(continued)

(continued)

We need to be watchdogs because we need to protect the other users in our community. Don't feel squeamish about making a report because you don't want to be a squealer. It's just good business. Remember that it takes just one rotten apple to spoil the basket, so if you see a violation, do your duty and report it to Rules and Safety.

When the competition doesn't play fair

Unfortunately, you may sometimes encounter non-community minded sellers who interfere with your auctions or sales. This interference can take on several forms: sellers who illegally drive up bids, sellers who "steal" bidders, and the list goes on. Throughout this section, I touch on some of the biggies.

Again, should you fall victim to bad deeds, be sure to report the bad-deed doer's actions immediately (check out the section "Taking Action: What to Do When Someone Breaks the Rules" later in this chapter). eBay will take some sort of disciplinary action. Penalties range from indefinite suspensions to temporary suspensions or formal warnings. As in my case (see the sidebar "The Chanel-style purse," elsewhere in this chapter), eBay reviews each incident on a case-by-case basis before passing judgment.

Shill bidding

Shill bidding — the bane of every eBay user (whether buyer or seller) and something that truly undermines the community trust — is a felony. It is the practice of placing a bid on an item to artificially inflate the final value. Shill bidding is a violation of the Federal Wirefraud statute, which encompasses the practice of entering into interstate commerce to defraud — not something to be toyed with!

The practice of shill bidding has been a part of auctions from their beginnings. To prevent the suspicion of participating in shill bidding, people in the same family, those who share the same computer, and folks who work or live together should not bid on each other's items.

Should you ever even dream of participating in any sort of auction manipulation, I urge you to think twice. You might think you're smart by using another e-mail address and username, but that doesn't work. Every time you log onto your ISP, your connection carries a number, an IP address. So no matter what name or computer you use, your connection will identify you. eBay can use this number to track you through its site.

Shill bidders are fairly easy to recognize, even for the eBay user who isn't privy to things such as IP addresses and the like. By checking a bidder's auction history, you can easily determine a user's bidding pattern. A bidder who constantly bids up items and never wins is very suspicious.

Spurious sellers often employ shill bidding to increase the number of bids on an item to more quickly make it a hot item. A hot item is one that has received 30 or more bids; eBay gives hot items a flaming match icon, which then draws the attention of more bidders to the presumably hot auction. This doesn't mean that all hot auctions are products of shill bidding, it means that hot auctions are desirable and pull in lots of extra bids (due to the herd mentality). The rogues would like all their auctions to be hot, and may take any road to ensure that they are.

Transaction interference

Have you ever gotten an e-mail from an eBay seller offering you an item that you're currently bidding on for a lower price? Hopefully not. This is called *transaction interference* and, because it prevents sellers from gaining the highest bid possible, it hurts all sellers.

Transaction interference also occurs when a troublemaker who has it "in" for a particular seller e-mails bidders who are participating in the seller's current auctions to warn them away from completing the auction. Tales of woe and much bitterness usually accompany such e-mails. If a bidder has a problem with a seller, that bidder can — and should — file a report with eBay and leave negative feedback for that seller. This sort of e-mail barrage can potentially fall under the category of libel and isn't a safe thing to practice. If you receive an e-mail like this, ignore its message but report it to eBay.

Transaction interception

They say the criminal mind is complex; when it comes to transaction interception, it certainly is! *Transaction interception* occurs when an eBay scalawag keeps track of closing auctions and then, when the auction is finished, e-mails the winner as if the scalawag were the seller. The e-mail often looks official and is congratulatory, politely asking for payment. Interceptors usually use a post office box for such mischief. This behavior goes beyond being a trading violation — it's stealing. If people would use their creativity in productive ways, we wouldn't have to worry about so many things.

The best way to protect yourself from such miscreants is to accept payments through a payment service, such as eBay payments or PayPal, by using a Pay Now link. For more about setting up a payment service account, see Chapter 13.

Fee avoidance

Basically, *fee avoidance* is the practice of evading paying eBay fees by going around the eBay system. There are so many ways to commit fee avoidance — sometimes without even realizing it — that I can't count them all. Read this section carefully and don't fall into this violation by mistake.

You're guilty of fee avoidance if you

- ✔ Use information that you've gotten from an eBay member's contact information in an attempt to sell a listed item off the system

- ✔ Close your auction early because a user has e-mailed you offering to buy an item you're currently auctioning and you accept the offer

- ✔ End your auction before it legally closes, by canceling bids, to sell the item to someone who has e-mailed you with an offer of a higher price

- ✔ Use an eBay member's contact information to sell an item from one of your closed auctions in which the reserve wasn't met

- ✔ Offer duplicates of your item to the unsuccessful bidders in your auction

Take a look at the discussion on listing policies in Chapter 2 for listing violations that also might fall into this category.

Non-selling seller

Refusing to accept payment from the winning bidder and refusing to complete the transaction is simply wrong. Very, very, bad form! You are legally and morally bound to complete any transaction in which you enter at eBay.

Baaad bidders

Nothing can ruin a seller's day like a difficult bidder can: bidders who e-mail questions that are clearly laid out in your auction description; people who e-mail you asking to close the auction so that they can buy items offline; the list goes on. Sheesh — you'd think no one read the rules. From the non-paying bidder to the unwelcome and shady, you might encounter the buyers who I describe here and who can add bucketloads of anguish to your day.

Bid shielding

When two or more eBay members work together to defraud you out of real auction profits, they're guilty of *bid shielding*. One member places an early bid on your item, with a proxy bid. Immediately, his confederate places a very high Proxy bid to drive it to the max or beyond. The auction runs its course and, even if other legitimate bidders bid, all they accomplish is to ratchet up the second bidder's bid to higher levels, and they don't outbid the high bidder's Proxy. When the auction is coming to a close, the high bidder retracts his bid, thereby granting his buddy, the original low bidder, the winning bid. The ultimate point of bid shielding is that it increases the bid to such a high level that normal bidding by authentic bidders is discouraged.

This illegal bidding process is not only used to get bargained priced merchandise, but it can be used to drive bidders away from competitors' auctions by artificially inflating the high bid level, thereby sending genuine bidders to the only auction left with a low high bid.

Unwelcome bidder

In this business, you might think that you couldn't possibly regard anyone as an *unwelcome bidder* but, believe it or not, you just might. Remember how you painstakingly explain your terms in your auction description? That's lost on some people, who just don't take the time to read those descriptions — or who choose to simply ignore them. Consider the following points:

- You state in your description that you only ship within the United States, but you see a bidder with an e-mail address that ends in .jp (Japan), .au (Australia), .uk (Great Britain), or whatever. You should e-mail that bidder immediately to re-emphasize your domestic-only shipping policy.

- You state in your description that you don't want bidders who have a negative feedback rating or who have more than one negative in a six-month time span. You may wish to contact this bidder, as perhaps they are new to the eBay system and do not understand the legal connotations of making a bid.

- You decide to cancel a bid for one of the previous two reasons, but the bidder continues to bid on your auction.

- You've blocked a particular bidder (see Chapter 3) who's now using a secondary account to bid on your auctions.

If you encounter any of the previous situations, contact eBay immediately to report the unwelcome bidder; see the section "eBay's SafeHarbor" later in this chapter.

Non-paying bidders

If there's one thing that just ain't tolerated at eBay, it's a non-paying bidder (NPB). eBay reminds all bidders, before they place a bid, that "If you are the winning bidder, you will enter into a legally binding contract to purchase the item from the seller." You'd think that was clear enough, but sadly, many people out there think bidding at eBay is a game.

How often eBay sellers notice that buyers of ill-repute (those with many negative feedbacks on the bidding side of their transactions) bid depends on the seller and whether or not they pay attention to who's bidding on their auctions. If you see a high bidder on your auction who has a very low or negative feedback, dropping a line reiterating eBay policy never hurts.

How you, as a seller, communicate with the high bidder is also important. Staying on top of your winners is very important, as are congenial, businesslike communications. Many times a well-written e-mail can cajole the basically good person into sending payment. Your e-mails are your face to the outside world. It's the only way that a person in cyberspace can get an image of the kind of person that you are. A professional and yet caring letter can often turn the tide. To see some samples that get the job done, drop by Chapter 12 for a library of sample e-mail letters.

I've been selling and buying at eBay for more than five years. During that time, I've only had to file four non-paying bidder alerts (see the steps a bit later in this section). At less than one a year, that's not too bad. I think that non-paying bidders tend to bid on certain types of items. After you've seen some NPBs, you'll get an idea of which items to stay away from. My NPB items? A gas-powered scooter, a video game, and some Beanie Babies. Serious collector items have never been an issue.

To reduce the number of non-paying bidders, eBay has established that all eBay users are indefinitely suspended if they have three non-paying bidder alerts filed against them. An *indefinite suspension* is a suspension of members' privileges to use the eBay site for more than 60 days with no definite reinstatement date. If users attempt to re-register at eBay and use the system under new IDs, they risk being referred for criminal prosecution with the United States Attorney's Office for the Northern District of California.

To file a non-paying bidder alert, follow these steps:

1. **Contact the winner within three days of the auction's end time.**

2. **If you don't hear from the winner, send a payment reminder (go to the Items I've Sold area of your My eBay Selling page and click the payment reminder icon next to the pertinent auction).**

You may do this between 3 and 30 days after the auction closes.

If you still don't hear from or receive money from your high bidder, it's time to swing into action.

3. **File a non-paying bidder alert in order to get a Final Value Fee credit; go to**

```
http://cgi3.ebay.com/aw-cgi/
        eBayISAPI.dll?NPBComplaintForm
```

Even if you're permanently logged into eBay, this is one of the areas where you'll have to sign in again, for security reasons.

You must file the alert no earlier than 7 days after the auction has ended and no later than 45 days after the auction has ended.

4. **Seven days after you've filed your non-paying bidder alert, you may apply for your final value fee credit (see Figure 4-2) by going to**

```
http://cgi3.ebay.com/aw-cgi/eBayISAPI.dll?CreditRequest
```

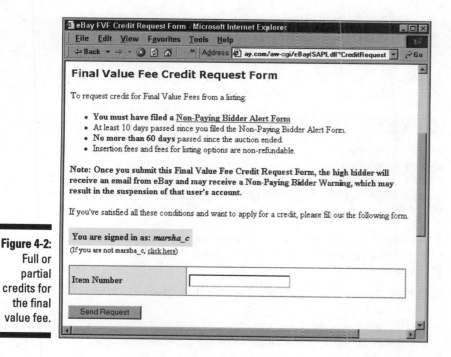

Figure 4-2:
Full or
partial
credits for
the final
value fee.

You may file for your final value fee credit anytime within 60 days of the auction's close.

When you file for the final value fee credit, you also have the option of blocking that bidder from your auctions.

5. **If you worked things out with the winner, you may remove the non-paying bidder alert within 90 days of the close of the auction; you'll find it at**

```
http://cgi3.ebay.com/aw-cgi/
        eBayISAPI.dll?RemoveNPBWarningShow
```

In the case of Dutch auctions, you may file a non-paying bidder alert only *once* per auction. You may file against as many bidders as necessary in that one alert, but you can't go back and file more alerts at a later date.

Not knowing who's who

Most eBay users choose to use User IDs rather than exposing their e-mail addresses for all to see. That's fine, but each of us must supply eBay with real contact information. When you register at eBay, its software immediately checks your primary phone number area code against your zip code to verify that the two numbers are from the same city. If you've supplied incompatible codes, the eBay servers will recognize that and ask you to reinput the correct codes.

An eBay member who's involved in a transaction with you can get your phone number by doing an eBay Member search at

```
http://cgi3.ebay.com/aw-cgi/eBayISAPI.dll?MemberSearchShow
```

When you arrive at the page, scroll to the form that requests Contact Info, as shown in Figure 4-3.

To be on the up-and-up at eBay (and to keep others honest, too), make sure that you

✔ **Have your current phone number on file at eBay:** If a bidder can't reach you, you're in violation of False Contact Information and you *can* be disciplined.

✔ **Have your current e-mail address on file:** If your bidder continually gets e-mail bounced back from your e-mail address, you could get in big trouble.

✔ **Report all underage bidders:** If you suspect that a bidder in one of your auctions is underage (eBay requires that all users be over 18), eBay may close the account. An underage bidder may be using Dad's credit card without permission for registration, or perhaps even a stolen card.

✔ **Verify e-mail purportedly coming from an eBay employee:** If someone e-mails you claiming to work for eBay, be sure to check it out before replying. When eBay employees conduct personal business on the site, company policy requires that they use a personal, non-company e-mail address for their user registration. If you suspect someone is impersonating an eBay employee for deleterious purposes, contact SafeHarbor Rules and Safety (see below).

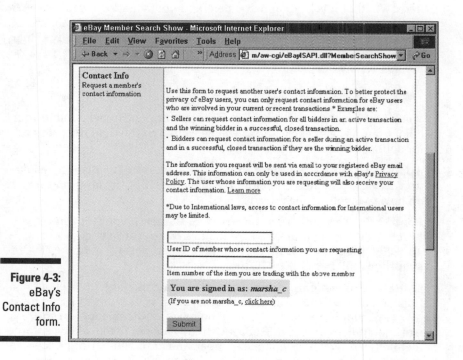

Figure 4-3:
eBay's
Contact Info
form.

Taking Action: What to Do When Someone Breaks the Rules

You need to take a business-like approach to problems at eBay, whatever those problems may be. Throughout the earlier sections of this chapter, I outline eBay's many rules, as well as the bad deeds and bad seeds you are, unfortunately, likely to encounter while doing business at eBay. As a member of the eBay community, you have the responsibility of knowing and abiding by the eBay rules and regulations; this includes notifying eBay when someone tries to sell an illegal item (see the section "Is What You Want to Sell Legal at eBay?" earlier in this chapter). This is an awesome responsibility, but integral to keeping eBay a safe and lucrative place to do business. So in this section, I discuss who to call when someone breaks the rules and what to do when a third-party is necessary.

Here are the basic steps you can follow:

- **Contact the buyer:** Get the buyer's contact information by using the link in the previous section "Not knowing who's who." Call the buyer to see if you can diplomatically resolve the situation.

- **Seek out SafeHarbor: Use SafeHarbor** any time you have a security issue at eBay. You should report any shady actions or possible fraud here. Whether it is a community member impersonating an employee or a suspicious auction, eBay has a first class way to report these infractions. Likened to the front desk at your local police station, eBay's Rules & Safety report form gets you action in a New York, okay, maybe a Texas minute. At any rate, go to

```
http://pages.ebay.com/help/basics/select-RS.html
```

You'll find an all purpose security form on this page to help you in your eBay transactions. These forms will be routed to the right department for action.

- **Apply for Online resolution:** SquareTrade offers online dispute resolution services and mediation for eBay members. See the following section on how to involve SquareTrade.

- **Contact the National Fraud Information Center:** If you feel you've become a victim of fraud, be sure to file a report through eBay channels. To really bring down wrath on your nemesis, report them to the NFIC; simply call toll-free: 1-800-876-7060.

- **Contact local law enforcement:** If you become the target of a check-bouncer, contact the local law enforcement in your bidder's home town. eBay will supply any information to help law enforcement clear the world of fraud. Just provide eBay with the name of the local law enforcement officer, agency, telephone number, and case number or police report number. Also include the offending user's ID and the auction item's number.

SquareTrade to the rescue

Threats of suing each other, filing fraud charges, and screaming back and forth doesn't really accomplish anything when you're in the middle of a dispute at eBay. Back in the olden days of eBay, when you weren't able to respond to feedback, users threw negative feedback back and forth willy-nilly, which resulted in some pretty vile flame wars.

These days you have SquareTrade, one of the best services that you can possibly use as a seller. When you're selling regularly at eBay, you will undoubtedly run into a disgruntled buyer or two. SquareTrade, a Web-based dispute resolution company, waits in the wings to pull you out of the most difficult situations.

Should you find yourself in an inexorably difficult situation with one of your bidders, and you'd like to take the situation up a notch, go to the following page, shown in Figure 4-4:

```
http://www.squaretrade.com/cnt/jsp/odr/overview_odr.
            jsp?vhostid=tomcat2&stmp=eBay
```

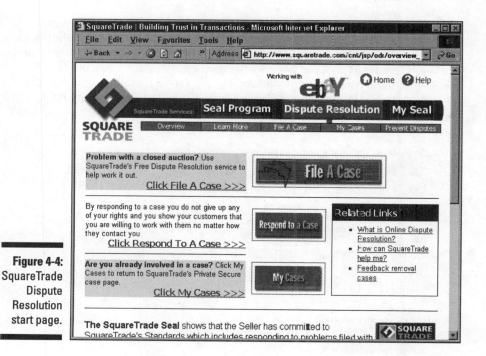

Figure 4-4: SquareTrade Dispute Resolution start page.

After you click the <u>File A Case</u> link on this page and answer a few specifics regarding the situation, SquareTrade automatically generates and sends an e-mail to the other party, giving instructions on how to respond. From this point, the case information and all related responses appear on a private, password-protected page on the SquareTrade site.

SquareTrade offers three main services to eBay members, which I discuss throughout this section:

- Online Dispute Resolution via direct negotiation
- Professional Mediation
- SquareTrade Seal

Online Dispute Resolution

This is a fast, private, and convenient way to resolve your auction disputes — and it's *free*. Both you and the buyer work together through the SquareTrade Web-based system. Online Dispute Resolution (ODR) will work whether your transaction is within the United States or in foreign countries. Every day, over 400 buyers file cases with the ODR service.

When you file a case (see Figure 4-5), the other party will hopefully respond. The SquareTrade Web-based negotiation tool is completely automated, and you both get to communicate with each other on neutral ground. When (and if) the buyer responds, the two of you can then hopefully work out the situation online and without human interaction. If you're unable to reach a solution, you'll need to move on to Professional Mediation (see the following section).

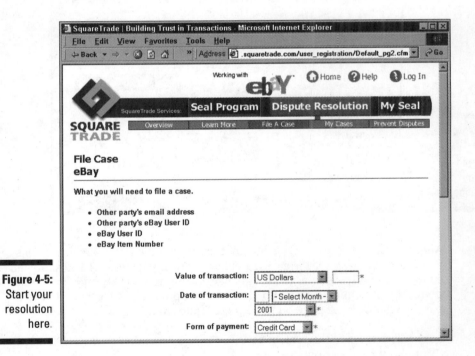

Figure 4-5:
Start your
resolution
here.

SquareTrade says that problems are usually solved within 10 to 14 days and that 85 percent of all cases are resolved without going to mediation. The process will run a quicker course if both people in the transaction are at their computers and answer e-mail during the day.

Participation in ODR is voluntary. If a buyer is set on defrauding you, that buyer probably isn't going to engage in a resolution process. If you get no response to your ODR, you should report your situation to Rules & Safety.

Professional Mediation

If push comes to shove, and in auction disputes it certainly may, you may have to resort to Professional Mediation, as shown in Figure 4-6. A *mediator,* neither a lawyer nor a judge but an impartial professional, works with both parties to bring the situation to a convivial conclusion. This service is available for a reasonable $15 per issue.

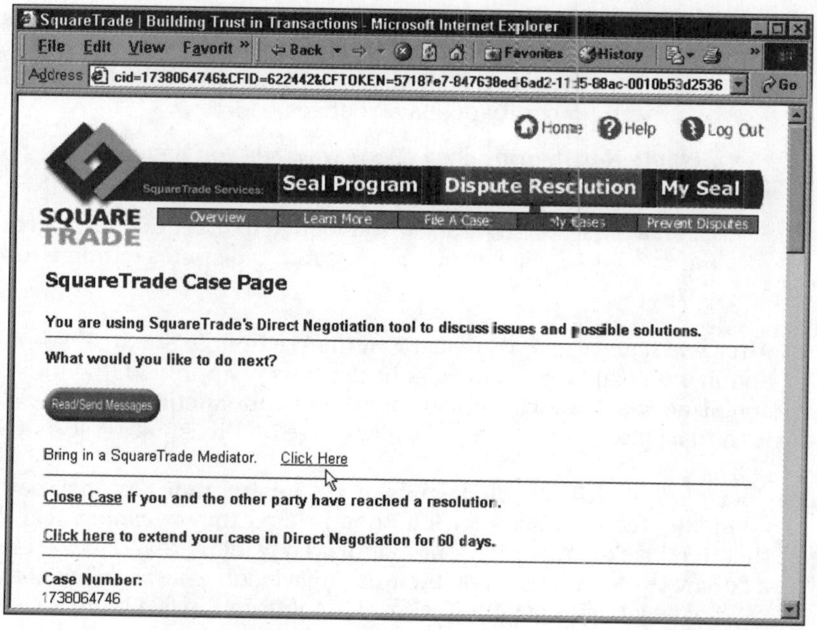

Figure 4-6:
The
Mediation
page.

If both parties participating in dispute resolution agree to mediation, each party communicates only with the assigned mediator, who communicates with both parties through the same case page. Your case page shows only your communications with the mediator. The mediator reviews both sides of the story to find a mutually acceptable solution to the problem. He or she tries to understand the interests, perspectives, and preferred solutions of both parties, and tries to help both parties understand the other's position.

The mediator is there to disperse highly charged emotions commonly associated with disputes and recommends a resolution only if both parties agree to have the mediator do so. By using the mediation service, you do not lose your right to go to court if things aren't worked out.

SquareTrade Seal

A SquareTrade Seal lets prospective bidders know that you deal with customers promptly and honestly. Should you choose to get a SquareTrade Seal, SquareTrade inserts it into your auctions automatically by using its patented technology from its secure server (and each seal icon contains a digital watermark with an encrypted expiration date). You can use the seal in your auctions only if SquareTrade approves you.

Your Square Trade Seal approval is based on several points:

- **Identity Verification.** Square Trade will verify your identity through the information you provide through a third party.
- **Superior Selling Record.** SquareTrade runs your eBay feedback history through five individual checks. It has an advanced system based on extensive experience of dispute resolution that allows it to evaluate the quality and quantity of eBay feedback.
- **Dispute Resolution.** They check whether you have a history of not resolving disputes.
- **Commitment to Standards.** You pledge to meet the SquareTrade standards on how you sell and to respond to disputes within two business days.

After you have a seal, you must continue to uphold SquareTrade standards and maintain an acceptable feedback rating. If approved, the nifty little personalized seal icon will appear on each of your auctions. Users can click the icon to access your own Seal Display page on the SquareTrade site.

Recently, SquareTrade did a study of 623 SquareTrade Seal members. They compared their feedback for four months after they became a seal member to their feedback in the prior four months. They found that once a seller became a SquareTrade Seal member, their negative feedback was reduced by 43%. The ratio of negative to positive feedback went from 1 in 60 before, to 1 in 280 after.

The SquareTrade Seal (shown in Figure 4-7), which currently costs around $7 per month — an affordable and good idea if you're in this business for the long run — tells prospective buyers that you care about good customer service and that you don't tolerate fraudulent activity. It also says that you abide by the SquareTrade selling and customer service standards, which dictate that you will

- Disclose contact information and credentials
- Provide clear and accurate descriptions of goods and services in your auctions
- Clearly disclose pricing, including all applicable fees
- List clear policies on after sales services, such as refunds and warranties
- Maintain privacy policies
- Transact only on secure sites
- Respond to any disputes filed against you within two business days

Figure 4-7:
The
SquareTrade
Seal.

eBay's SafeHarbor

SafeHarbor, also known as Rules and Safety, is the eBay version of the FBI. By rooting out evil deed-doers, SafeHarbor serves and protects — and puts up with an immense amount of e-mail from the users.

If you see an item at eBay that isn't allowed (see the section "Is What You Want to Sell Legal at eBay? earlier in this chapter), be sure to contact Rules and Safety to make them aware of the illegal auction. The Community Watch team will then take over and investigate the item and, when necessary, end the auction and warn the seller.

If you'd like to get SafeHarbor's attention quickly, don't send an e-mail. Instead, go to the following URL and fill out the step-by-step Customer Service report shown in Figure 4-8:

```
http://pages.ebay.Om/help/basics/select-RS.html
```

Figure 4-8:
Rules and
Safety
Investiga-
tions
reporting
form.

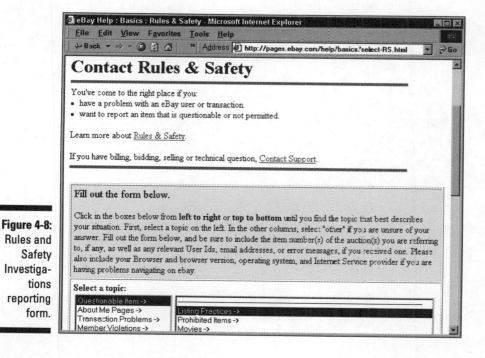

Chapter 5

Your Very Own eBay Store

In This Chapter

▶ Figuring out the lure of the online shop

▶ Boosting your sales with an eBay store

▶ Setting up an eBay store

▶ Closing your sales

*I*f you're doing well selling your items at eBay auctions, why open a store? Have you used the eBay Buy It Now feature? Did it work? In an eBay store, all items are set at a fixed price and listed for 30 days, so it's kind of like a giant collection of Buy It Now featured items. Get the idea?

When you're opening a store, you have just three main rules to remember and apply: location, location, location. If you were going to open a brick-and-mortar store, you could open it in the corner strip mall, a shopping center, or even somewhere downtown. You'd have to decide in what location your store would do best; that goes for an online store as well. You'll find tons of locations to open an online store, including online malls (when you can find them) and sites such as Amazon.com, Yahoo!, and, of course, eBay.

You have to pay rent for your online store, but opening and running an online store isn't nearly as expensive as a store in the real world (where you have to pay rent, electrical bills, maintenance bills, and the list goes on). Plus, the ratio of rent to sales makes an online store a much easier financial decision to make, and your exposure can be colossal.

Throughout this chapter, I show you step-by-step how to hang out your virtual shingle and get business booming by opening your own eBay store.

Online Stores Galore

Amazon.com, Yahoo!, and eBay make up the big three of online stores. They're the top locations and get the most visitors. In June 2001, according to Jupiter Media Metrix, these sites garnished an astounding number of *unique* visitors (that counts *all* of one person's visits to the sites just *once* a month):

✔ Yahoo!: 59,907,000 (it's a search engine; I must hit it ten times a day — but I rarely visit the auctions)

✔ eBay: 23,263,000

✔ Amazon.com: 19,972,000 (it sells books, CDs, DVDs, and lots of other merchandise, but how many of these people are going to the zShops?)

No doubt feeling competition from Yahoo! and Amazon.com, eBay decided to open its doors (in July 2001) to sellers who wanted to open their own stores. If eBay is to continue as the world's marketplace, the fixed price stores are a normal progression. And it makes sense: eBay Stores are a benefit to all current eBay sellers and open doors to new shoppers who don't want to deal with auctions.

eBay is the only online store that specializes in selling *your* stuff, not *theirs*. It doesn't stock a stick of merchandise and it isn't in competition with you. In addition to its staggering number of visitors, eBay offers you the most reasonable store rent. To see what I mean, check out the sample rents in Table 5-1.

Table 5-1	Online Store Monthly Costs		
	eBay	**Yahoo Shopping**	**Amazon zShops**
Basic rent	$9.95	$100*	$39.99
Listing fee	5 cents	N/A	After 40,000 items: 10 cents
High final value fee	5%	2% of sales over $5,000	5%

Yahoo charges $100 for a store with up to 50 items, $300 for up to 1,000 items, and $100 per month for each additional 1,000 items. A store with 6,000 items costs $800 per month.

For more information, go to the Gomez Associates Web site at `www.gomez.com/scorecards/index.asp?topcat_id=2`. This page keeps a quarterly scorecard of customer acceptance for the top ten auction sites. It's worth a visit now and again to see where the industry is going.

I don't think it's going to take a rocket scientist to convince you that having a space in eBay Stores (see Figure 5-1) is a way better bargain than setting up shop anywhere else. I know the stores aren't based on auctions, but Buy It Now items are as easy to handle as auctions, and people will visit your store regularly. To check prices and rules before opening your store, check the pages at `pages.ebay.com/storefronts/seller-landing.html`.

The Sellers link

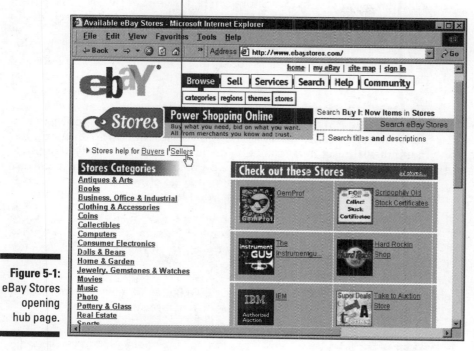

Figure 5-1:
eBay Stores
opening
hub page.

Your eBay Store

You've decided to take the plunge and open an eBay store. Do you have an eBay user ID? Have you thought of a good name for your store? Your store name doesn't have to match your eBay user ID. You can use your company name, business name, or a name that describes your business. I recommend that you use the same name for your eBay store that you plan to use in all of your online businesses. By doing so, you will begin to create an identity (or as the pros call it, a *brand*) that customers will come to recognize and trust.

Your online eBay store should not replace your Web site (see Chapter 8); it should be an extension of it. When people shop at your eBay store, you must take the opportunity to make them customers of your Web site through your About The Store page (which is also your About Me page at eBay). Good deal!

Setting up shop

It's time to get down to business. Go to the eBay Stores hub and click the Sellers link (refer to Figure 5-1). This takes you to the Seller's pages of eBay Stores (see Figure 5-2). If you click all the links you see here, you get the eBay company line about how good an eBay store can be for your business. You already know how good an eBay store can be for your business, so skip the propaganda and get right down to business (but don't forget to check for any policy changes that may affect your store's operations).

Before you click that link to open your store, I want you to ask yourself two questions:

- ✔ **Can I make a serious commitment to my eBay store?:** A store is a commitment. It won't work for you unless you work for it. You've got to have the merchandise to fill it, and you've got to have the discipline to continue listing store and auction items. Your store is a daily, monthly, and yearly obligation. When you go on vacation, you need someone else to ship your items or your customers may go elsewhere. You can close your store for a vacation, but eBay won't let you reopen it for 30 days.

- ✔ **Will I work for my eBay store even when I don't feel like it?:** You've got to be prepared that an order may come in for some of your merchandise when you don't feel like shipping, or even when you're sick. But you have to do it anyway; it's all part of the commitment.

eBay gives you the venue, but it's in your own hands to make your mercantile efforts a success. If you can handle these two responsibilities, read on!

Figure 5-2:
The Sellers welcome page to eBay Stores.

TIP

Mind your underscores and dashes

If you want to use your eBay user ID for your store name, you can — unless it contains a dash (-) or an underscore (_). Remember how eBay recommends that you break up words in your continual user ID with a dash or an underscore? Uh uh, that's no good for an eBay store name. I'm in that situation. My user ID is marsha_c; without the underscore, it translates into a user ID that someone else has already taken! Even though it hasn't been used since 1999, someone else has it, which means I can't use it. (marsha_c is probably a crummy name for a store anyway!)

A favorite seller of mine — mrswarren — realized that mrswarren isn't a good name for a store either. So she named her store *Pretty Girlie Things*, which suits her merchandise to a T.

Doing the "paperwork"

If you're serious and ready to move on, click the big blue Open Store Now button (refer to Figure 5-2). Because you're always signed in on your home computer, you're escorted to a page reminding you that eBay stores fall under the same User Agreement that you agreed to when you began selling at eBay. Click the Continue button to access the Store Content page (see Figure 5-3) and then follow the steps:

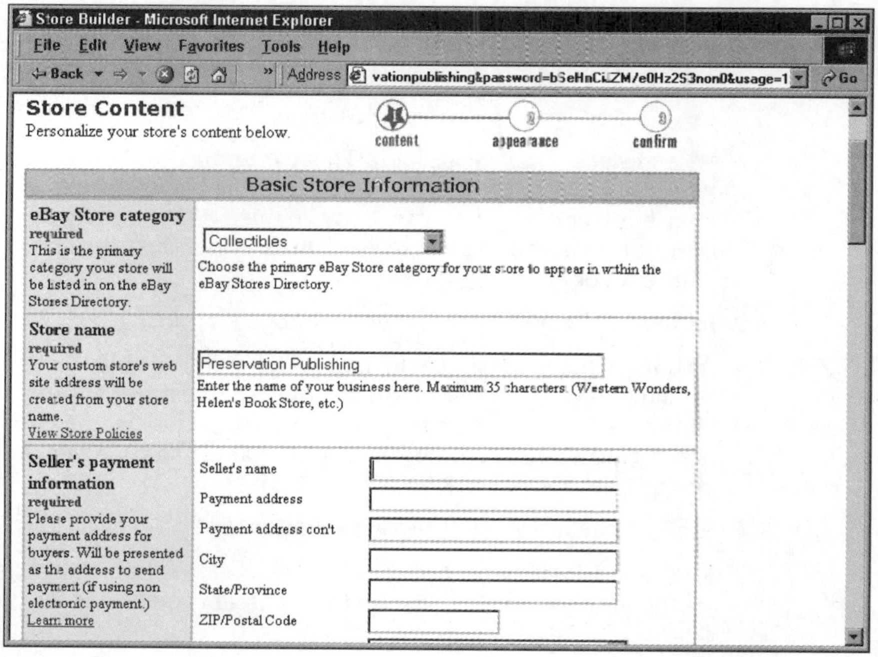

Figure 5-3: The eBay Store Content page.

1. **Choose your store category.**

   Choose from 14 main categories in which to classify your store. If you carry a wide variety of merchandise, choosing a category can be difficult. Doing searches of which categories auction items are listed in is always a good idea, but your eBay store items will come up in an eBay store search — so don't be afraid to pick the category you most use. And remember that you can always choose Everything Else. A large retail population has already settled into the Everything Else category, so why not give it a try? If you feel it isn't working for you after a while, simply change your category by clicking the Seller, manage store link on your completed store's home page.

2. **Type your store's name in the appropriate text box.**

   You've decided on a store name, right? Before you type it in, double-check that you aren't infringing on anyone else's copyrights or trademarks.

   You also can't use any permutation of the eBay trademarks in your store's name: eBay, Half.com, Butterfields, or Billpoint.

3. **Type in your payment information.**

   Your store's checkout system uses this information as the address to send any non-electronic payments, such as checks and money orders.

   After this point, eBay begins to limit the amount of characters you can use in the text boxes. I recommend writing your copy ahead of time in Word, where you can highlight the text and then choose Tools⇨Word Count. Word gives you the word count of the highlighted text, including a character count with spaces. That's what you want to check: the total characters and spaces, to be sure your text fits.

4. **Scroll down the page a bit to type a short description of your store in the allotted space (see Figure 5-4).**

   When I say short, I mean *short*. This paragraph is 311 characters and you only have *250* characters to give a whiz-bang, electric description of your store and merchandise. You can't use HTML coding to doll up the description, and you can't use any links either. Just the facts please, and a little bit of dazzle.

5. **Include store specialties, if you want.**

   Although this sounds like the place where you're able to put some brilliant copy about your store, it isn't. This text will appear on the top of your store Policies page, so you need to include some information about your store and how you want to handle sales. Again, keep it short; you've only got 200 characters this time.

6. **Include custom store categories (optional).**

   You can make up your own categories here. No eBay categories to limit your creativity. You may list up to 11 custom categories for your store.

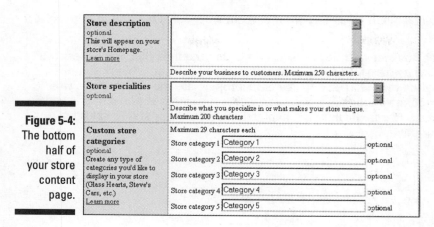

7. **Scroll down some more to specify your payment methods (see Figure 5-5).**

   In your eBay store, you must accept credit cards. You can accept credit cards through Billpoint, PayPal, Yahoo PayDirect, or a merchant account of your own. Select which credit cards you'll accept and Money order/Cashiers Check. If you haven't signed up to accept Billpoint, eBay will offer you registration down the line.

About Your Store

Store payment methods required Choose all that you will accept and enter any additional explanation, if needed.	☐ Money Order/Cashiers Check ☐ Personal Check ☐ Visa/MasterCard ☐ COD (cash on delivery) ☐ Discover ☐ American Express ☐ eBay Online Payments ☐ Other Additional payment explanation (optional): Maximum 200 characters

Store ship-to locations
required
	○ Will ship to United States only
	
	○ Will ship internationally (worldwide)
	
	○ I will ship to the United States and the following regions only:
	   ☐ Canada
	   ☐ Europe
	   ☐ Australasia
	   ☐ Asia
	   ☐ South America
	   ☐ Africa
	   ☐ Mexico and Central America
	   ☐ Middle East
	   ☐ Caribbean

8. **Indicate to what locations you'll ship.**

   Fill in this area just as you would when listing an eBay auction.

9. Scroll again to specify what percent store sales tax you plan to collect (see Figure 5-6).

Do you run your business in a state that requires that you collect sales tax? If your state doesn't require this, leave the area blank. If it does, select your state and indicate the proper sales tax. Most states won't require you to collect sales tax unless the sale is shipped to your home state. Check the links in Chapter 15 to verify your state's sales tax.

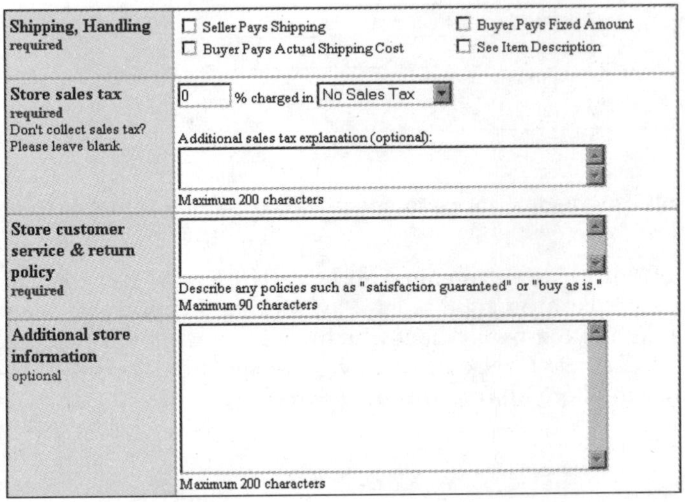

Figure 5-6: Specifying your sales tax, customer service policy, and additional information.

10. Establish your store customer service and return policy.

Fill in the information regarding how you handle refunds, exchanges, and so on. If you're a member of SquareTrade (see Chapter 4), mention here that you subscribe to its policies. Oh! — you only have 90 characters to do this.

11. Include whatever additional store information you think is pertinent.

eBay generously gives you an additional 200 characters to sell the world on your store.

12. Create an About Me page — if you haven't done so already.

Scroll past the additional information area where you'll be invited to create your About Me page. If you haven't already created an eBay About Me page, here's where you do it — and you should (see Chapter 3 regarding About Me pages). The folks at Preservation Publishing utilized the handy and easy-to-use eBay templates to put this page together, which took about ten minutes (see Figure 5-7).

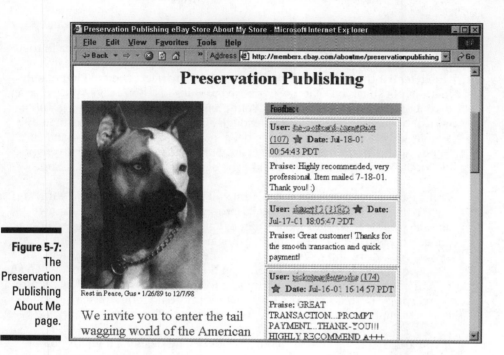

Figure 5-7:
The
Preservation
Publishing
About Me
page.

After you've filled out the entire Store Content page, pour a cup of coffee and take a deep breath. You've finished the hard part. Now you get to play with colors.

Selecting your color scheme

Pick out the one color scheme for your eBay store that you really like, but be prepared to change it after you've set up your store in case you don't like it. I'd like to show you the color schemes, but a black and white book is somewhat prohibitive in that regard. Don't select something overly bright and vibrant; you want something that's easy on the eyes, which is more conducive to a comfortable selling environment.

In all your eBay auctions, your seller name will be highlighted in colors that coordinate with your eBay store. Don't use too dark a color scheme or your seller's name will become nearly unreadable. After you've completed your store, click one of your auctions to check your color selection. On all your auctions, your store name appears under your eBay user ID and is accompanied by the <u>Visit my eBay Store!</u> link and the eBay Stores red tag. The red tag also appears next to your eBay user ID. If you don't like the way anything looks, go back and edit, er, manage your store.

After you've made your color selections, your next step is choosing graphics to jazz up the look of your store.

Choosing between pre-designed graphics and creating your own

If you want to temporarily put one of the pre-designed eBay graphics in the graphic space of your store, you must promise (hand over heart) that you won't keep it there for long. I'm not saying they're lame; they're kind of cute in a cartoony fashion. But these pre-fab graphics just don't give your store a distinctive look. People shopping your eBay store will see a line art graphic and know that you aren't serious enough about your business to design a simple and basic logo graphic. I've been in advertising for longer than I care to reveal and, in my opinion, using clip art in this way is a cop out — anybody can do it. Your store is special. Make the effort to make your store shine.

Perhaps you have a graphics program you've been playing around with, and have been waiting to use it for real. Here's your chance. Design your own simple graphic with your store's name that will appear on your store home page. Start with something simple; you can always change it later after you've set up your store and have more time to design. Save the image as a GIF or a JPG, and upload it to the site where you host your images (your own Web site or a hosting service). eBay won't host it for you. If you use the eBay picture service for your pictures, and don't have a photo hosting service, go to `www.myauctionphotos.com`. This site will host your eBay store logo for $1 a year!

If you aren't comfortable designing, have a friend design a logo for you or visit my Web site (`www.coolebaytools.com`) where I list references of people who can design one economically for you.

Now you're getting somewhere. At this point, your eBay store will look something like what you see in Figure 5-8. You have a storefront, but nothing up for sale yet. In the next section, I briefly discuss how you post items for sale.

Listing your items

You've all listed items at eBay, so I don't plan on boring you with a tutorial on how to list your items here (although I give you some listing and photo image tips in Chapter 11). The main differences between listing an item in your store (see Figure 5-9) and listing an auction at eBay are

✔ You have to assign your item to one of the pre-prescribed store categories that you designated while setting up your store. If your new item falls into a category that you haven't defined, you can always go back to your store and add a category (as many as eleven).

✔ You don't place a minimum bid or a reserve price on your store items because everything you list in your eBay store is a Buy It Now item that you list for 30 days.

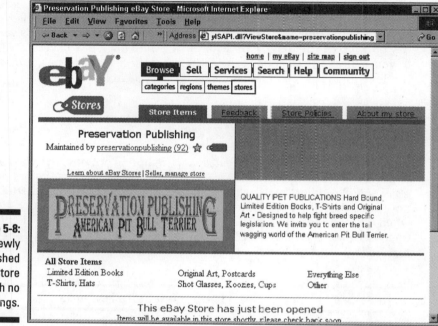

Figure 5-8:
The newly
published
eBay Store
with no
listings.

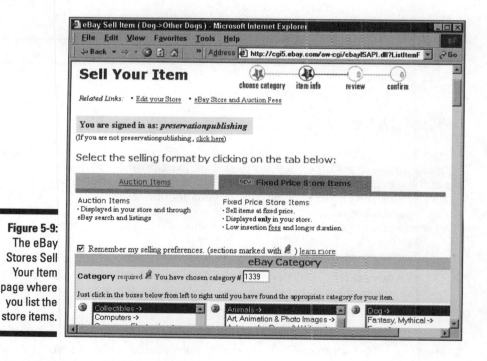

Figure 5-9:
The eBay
Stores Sell
Your Item
page where
you list the
store items.

The items you list in your eBay store *will not* appear in the regular eBay site title search. Your items *will* be seen if one of your buyers does a seller search. Your items will come up in an eBay Stores item (title) search. That's why you pay only 5 cents per listing for 30 days. You *must* put a link in your auctions to your eBay store — and tell the auction browsers that you've got more stuff for them that they "can't find in a regular eBay search."

Marketing your wares

Just like for your auctions, eBay has more tempting options that you can use to spruce up your store items. These options work exactly as the options that eBay offers for your auctions (see Chapter 10). When choosing whether or not to use these options, remember that your eBay store items only show up when someone searches within the eBay stores. eBay store items don't show up in a regular eBay search. Check out Table 5-2 for a rundown of optional feature fees.

Table 5-2	eBay Optional Store Features
Feature	*Price*
Feature item on top of search results page	$19.95
Highlight title	$5
Boldface title	$2

Making a sale

From the buyer's point of view, shopping at an eBay store is much different than winning an auction. eBay stores feature fixed price sales; the buyer will get the merchandise as soon as you can ship it (instead of waiting for the auction to run its course). Even though your auctions show up on your store home page, all regular listings in your eBay store are Buy It Now items. When a buyer makes a purchase from an eBay store, here's what happens:

1. **The buyer clicks the Buy It Now button (see Figure 5-10).**

   The Review Payments page appears (see Figure 5-11), where the buyer can review the purchase. This page contains the shipping amount that you specified when you listed the item.

2. **The buyer provides shipping information (required).**

   When eBay notifies you that a sale has been made, you have all the information you need — without scurrying around looking for the return address on the envelope (see Figure 5-12).

Buy It Now

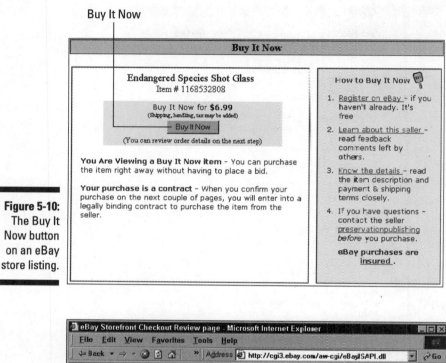

Figure 5-10:
The Buy It
Now button
on an eBay
store listing.

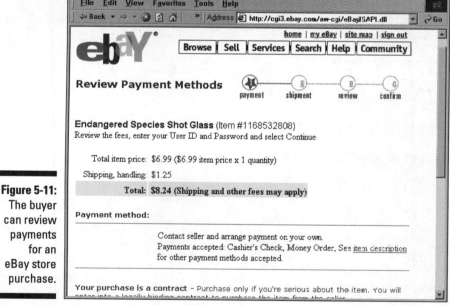

Figure 5-11:
The buyer
can review
payments
for an
eBay store
purchase.

3. **The buyer reviews the transaction and finally clicks the confirm button (upper-right corner in Figure 5-13).**

   The information about the sale is e-mailed to you, and the buyer receives confirmation of the sale (see Figure 5-14).

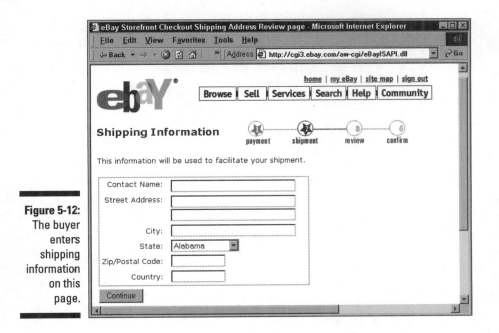

Figure 5-12:
The buyer
enters
shipping
information
on this
page.

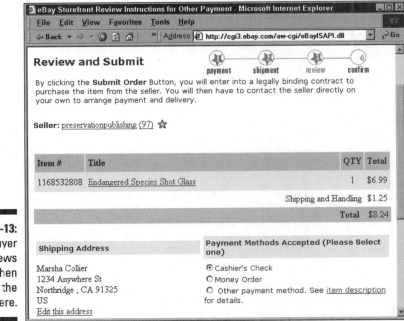

Figure 5-13:
The buyer
reviews
and then
submits the
order here.

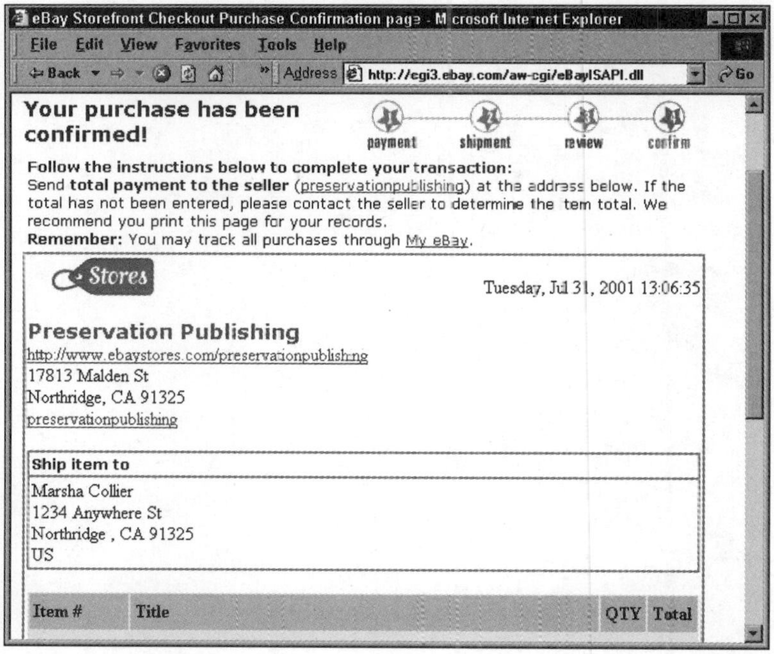

Figure 5-14: The order confirmation /invoice.

Part II
Setting Up Shop

The 5th Wave   By Rich Tennant

Did I mention that I ran across a balloon animal storefront on eBay recently?

In this part . . .

Your hobby is what you love, and I'm betting you've got a houseful of duplicate items — the perfect stuff to sell at eBay! Why not buy from other collectors locally and become a specialist at eBay? Perhaps you'd like to sell inventory from an existing business or from others on consignment. You can do whatever you choose; the options are countless. So in this part, I talk about how you find merchandise to sell, what's the best way to sell it, and your ever-important Web site.

Chapter 6

Stocking the Store

· ·

In This Chapter

▶ Timing your purchases

▶ Finding merchandise

· ·

*Y*ou're probably wondering just how you can possibly get enough merchandise to list as many as twenty items a day. You're thinking that there aren't possibly enough sources out there to fulfill that kind of volume. Success at eBay isn't easy. Many hours and a good deal of perspiration — along with loads of inspiration — are necessary to make a good living selling online. You *can* do it — if you apply the same amount of effort into acquiring your merchandise.

One of my mottoes is "Buy off-season, sell on-season." You can get great bargains on winter merchandise in the heat of summer. July's a great time to stock up on Christmas decorations, and the value of those trendy vintage aluminum trees doubles in November and December. Cashmere sweaters, too! In the winter, you can get great deals on closeout summer sports merchandise. Timing — it's all in the timing.

How are you going to acquire all the product that you need? I've spent hours, days, weeks, okay, even months trying to work out the best ways to stock an eBay business. Ultimately this depends on you, your personality, and the type of merchandise you plan to sell. But I've tried many of the tactics that I discuss throughout this chapter, as have some eBay sellers that I know, so here I pass on all the secrets and caveats that each of us learned along the way.

Dollar Stores

Dollar stores come in all shapes and sizes. They can be filled with junk or treasure, and it takes a practiced eye to separate the wheat from the chaff. You can always go in with a teenager, and see if she reacts to any of the items for sale. Sometimes only one in five visits works out, but you'll know when you see the item and at these prices you can afford to go deep! Stock at these stores doesn't stay on the shelf for too long; if you pass on an item, it may not be there when you return for it the next day. Maybe another savvy eBay seller picked up the values.

The crème de la crème of these stores on the West Coast are the 99¢ Only stores (see Figure 6-1). Forty-five percent of the items sold at 99¢ Only stores are closeouts or special opportunity buys. When a company changes its labels, it might sell all remaining stock with the old labels to 99¢ Only. I've found some profitable books, Olympics memorabilia, and pop culture items at this store. Because nothing sells for more than 99 cents, I feel comfortable starting auctions on items purchased here at just $1. The chain is expanding rapidly, so visit its Web site at www.99only.com to see if a store is coming near you. There are probably also other dollar stores in your area. Pull out the phone book (or bother the 411 operators) and see what you can find.

It's not unusual for dollar store warehouses to sell direct to a retailer (that's you!). Find out where the distribution warehouse is for your local dollar store chain and make contact. You can go a long way here by being nice. Befriend the office manager or warehouse manager, who might then call you when merchandise that matches your specialty comes in.

The Big Lots company

Another super selling chain is the Big Lots company, which encompasses the Pic N Save, Mac Frugal's, Big Lots, and Odd Lots stores. They may have items priced at more than a dollar, but they specialize in closeout merchandise. All their merchandise sells for well under most discounters and at deep discounts to retailers. This is a great place to find toys, household goods — almost anything. Troll their aisles at least once a month to find items that you can resell at eBay. The Big Lots company has stores in 46 states; check its Web site at www.cnstore.com for store locations near you.

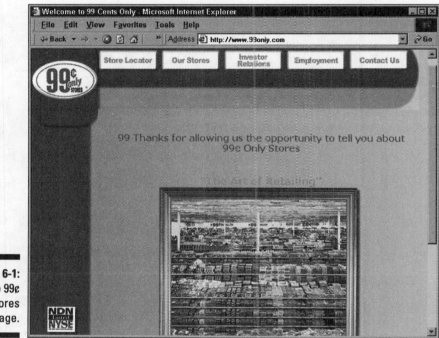

Figure 6-1:
The 99¢
Only stores
home page.

Discount Club Stores

Warehouse stores such as Sam's Club and Costco made their mark by selling
items in bulk to large families, clubs, and small businesses. In case you haven't
noticed, these stores have recently upscaled and sell just about anything that
you could want. Their shelves are brimming with current merchandise ripe for
the picking.

At www.samsclub.com, Sam's Club holds its own auctions (see Figure 6-2).
What a fantastic place to find merchandise to sell at eBay. The closeouts on
the auction site can close at retail or at a fraction of retail price. It's up to you
to check the auctions and furrow out the deals.

I recently checked the Costco Web site (see Figure 6-3), and the company was
running a special offer for a new *Snow White & the Seven Dwarfs* DVD. (You
can shop online and pick up at the store, but the deals are in the store's
trenches.) For $18.49, you pre-order the Snow White DVD, and get a second
Disney DVD for *FREE*. You can sell two items at eBay for the price of one.
With a little research, you can see which other Disney DVD sells well at eBay,
and you've got a good purchase for your business.

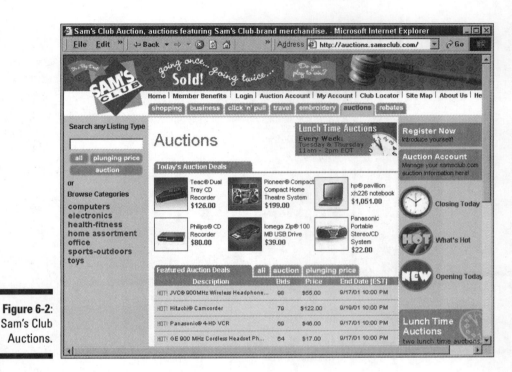

Figure 6-2:
Sam's Club
Auctions.

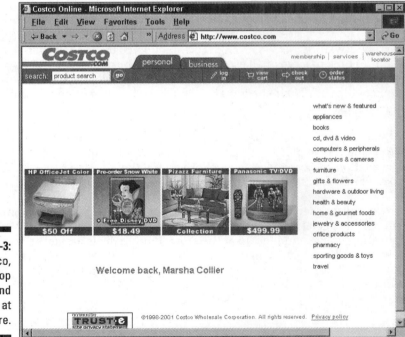

Figure 6-3:
At Costco,
you shop
online and
pick up at
the store.

Garage Sales

What can be better than getting up at 6 a.m. to troll the local garage sales? If you're motivated to find lots of good eBay merchandise and well prepared for the garage sales, I'd say nothing. Buy the newspaper or check your local newspaper's classified ads online (see Figure 6-4), and print out maps of the sale locations from MapQuest or Yahoo maps. You know the neighborhoods, so you can make a route from one to the next that makes sense — and figure in bathroom stops and coffee breaks.

Bring a friend, as oft-times neighbors take advantage of an advertised sale and put out some stuff of their own. You can cover more ground faster if two of you are attacking the sales.

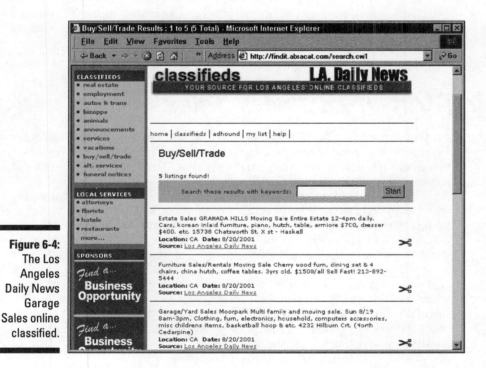

Figure 6-4:
The Los
Angeles
Daily News
Garage
Sales online
classified.

A few tips on shopping garage sales:

✔ Fancier neighborhoods have better stuff than poor or middle class ones. I know that sounds unfair, but I know for sure that the rich folks' trash is better than mine.

- ✔ Look for sales that say "Early Birds Welcome," and make them the first on your list, so you can get them out of the way. To read the ads, it seems like a universal bell goes off somewhere and all garage sales start at 8 a.m. *sharp!*

- ✔ The stuff you find at estate sales is often of a higher quality. These sales feature things that have been collected over many, many years.

- ✔ Keep an eye out for "moving to a smaller house" sales. These are usually people who have raised children, accumulated a houseful of garbage (collectibles? old toys? designer vintage clothes?), and want to shed it all so that they can move to a condo in Palm Springs.

   Any toys people like this are selling are usually good ones.

- ✔ I usually put sales that feature "kids' items and toys" on the end of my list, and I only go *if* I'm not too tired. These are generally young couples (with young children) who are trying to raise money or moving into a larger home. They're going to be keeping the good stuff, and are simply shedding the excess (more often than not).

Going-Out-of-Business Sales

Oh yeah, going-out-of-business sales are a bonanza, but be careful and don't be misled. Many states require businesses that are putting on a going-out-of business sale to purchase a special license that identifies the business as *really* going out of business. Some store ads may read "Going Out for Business" or some similar play on words, so you need to be sure that you're going to the real thing. When a retailer is liquidating its own stock, you're going to get the best buys. A retailer will often run the sale week by week, offering bigger discounts as time goes by. If it's really going out of business, don't be afraid to make an offer on a quantity of items.

A chain of children's wear went out of business here in southern California a while back; this chain carried a smattering of popular dolls. A seller I know made an offer for all remaining dolls, and subsequently purchased the dolls at a great price. Throughout the following year, she then sold them at eBay for three to four times what she had paid.

Auctions

Two types of auctions at which you can pick up some bargains are the liquidation and estate auctions (I also discuss charity auctions in this section, at which you may be able to find bargains while donating to a good cause). You'll find items that are perfectly salable and profitable at each, but each has its idiosyncrasies. Before you go to any auction, double-check payment terms and find out whether you must bring cash or can pay by credit card. Also, before you bid on anything, find out how much the *hammer fee* or *buyer's premium* is. These fees are a percentage that auction houses add to the winner's bids; the buyer has the responsibility of paying these fees.

Liquidation auctions

When a company gets into serious financial trouble, its debtors (the people to whom the company owes money) obtain a court order to liquidate the company to pay the bills. The liquidated company then sells its stock, fixtures, and even real estate. Items sell for just cents on the dollar, and you can easily resell many of these items at eBay. A special kind of auctioneer handles these auctions. Look in the phone book under Auctioneers: Liquidators and call local auctioneer's offices to get on mailing lists. This way, you'll always know when something good comes up for sale.

Estate auctions

Estate auctions are the higher level of estate garage sales. Here you can find fine art, antiques, paper ephemera, rare books, and collectibles of all kinds. Aside from the large estate auctions, most auction houses have monthly estate auctions in which it puts together groups of merchandise from various small estates. Find out when these auctions are being held and mark them on your calendar. These auctions are attended mostly by dealers, who are very savvy in the local going prices for the items they bid on. But because they're buying to sell in a retail environment, their high bids will generally be the wholesale price for your area. If a particular item is flooding your market, the high bid may be low. I've seen some incredible bargains at Butterfield's estate auctions here in Los Angeles. When you're in a room full of local dealers, they're buying what's hot to resell in your city — not what's going to sell across the country. That entire market will be yours.

Charity silent auctions

I'm sure you've been to your share of these. A school or organization will get everyone from major corporations to the local gift shop to donate items. The items are then auctioned off to the highest bidder, usually in a silent format.

You can find many a great item at these auctions. Aside from new merchandise, collectors may feel good about donating some collection overflow to a charity. I purchased the keystone of my Star Trek action figure collection at a charity auction: the very rare tri-fold Borg (one of perhaps only 50 in existence). This figure has sold as high as $1,000 at eBay and I paid just $60, all while donating to a charity.

Goodwill, Salvation Army, and Resale Shops

Donating to a charity like Goodwill or the Salvation Army is a powerful thing with many benefits. You don't have to worry about having a garage sale to get rid of unwanted stuff (no need to have strangers trodding all over the lawn, crunching the daisy borders while sniffing around at the stuff for sale), and you can pretty much write off many items as a charity tax deduction. And it's simple: You just load the goods into the car and take 'em to the store. It's a win-win-win situation. The extra win is you acquiring valuable pieces at bargain-basement prices.

At resale stores, such as Goodwill and the Salvation Army, you'll sometimes uncover treasures while other times you'll find only junk. For weeks, you might find nothing good and then one day something very special will come in. I recommend befriending the manager who sees the merchandise as it comes in, will know just what you're looking for (because you said so in a friendly conversation), and will call you before the items hit the floor. This type of relationship can save you from making fruitless trips.

Some stores receive merchandise from a central warehouse, where donations are first sent for minor rehabilitation and cleaning. Other, smaller operations process items in-house, with the store manager supervising. If your local charity store gets a truck, you should ask the manager (whom you've befriended) when it regularly comes in. The resale store is a business that runs things on a schedule. Being there when the truck arrives enables you to view the items before the general public.

A sharp seller that I know is always at his local Salvation Army when the trucks come in. One day as workers unloaded the truck, he saw a mounted baseball bat. Withholding his excitement, he picked it up and found that it was a signed Ty Cobb bat with a presentation plaque mounted with the bat. Although he didn't know exactly what it was, he took a gamble and brought it to the cash register, where he paid $33 minus the senior citizen discount. He took the bat to his office and made a few phone calls, later discovering that the bat is indeed a rare Louisville Slugger bat that had been presented to the Georgia Peach, Ty Cobb. But he'll never sell it because it's his good luck bat, which now hangs above the desk in his warehouse.

Goodwill Industries is definitely gearing to the 21st century. You can shop at its online auctions; just go to www.shopgoodwill.com (see Figure 6-5).

Figure 6-5:
ShopGood
will.com
online sales.

Freebies

Freebies come in all shapes and sizes and — best of all — they're free of course. Freebies are usually samples or promotion pieces that companies give away to introduce a new product, service, or, best of all, a media event. Even carefully trimmed ads from magazines can fetch high prices from collectors.

Remember the talking Taco Bell Chihuahua giveaway? Those cute little dogs were all the rage and sold for big money at eBay. It almost seems foolish to remind you of the McDonald's Teenie Beanie Baby giveaways; moms, dads, and dealers were all driving in circles through the drive-thru, purchasing as many of the Happy Meals that each store would allow. They'd then drive to the next McDonald's to purchase a different toy. In my house alone, we had frozen hamburgers for three months!

When *Return of the Jedi* was re-released in 1997, the first 100 people to enter each theater got a Special Edition Luke Skywalker figure. These figures are still highly prized by collectors and when the next part of the Star Wars saga is released, you can bet the prices on this figure will rise yet again.

In 1995, Paramount network premiered a new show, *Star Trek Voyager.* In selected markets, Paramount sent a promotional microwave popcorn packet as a Sunday newspaper insert. These are still selling well (when you can find them), although the value rises and falls according to current interest in Star Trek.

Before you pass by a freebie, reconsider its possible future value.

Salvage: Liquidation Items, Unclaimed Freight, and Returns

The easiest buys of all, *salvage merchandise* is retail merchandise that has been returned, exchanged, or shelf-pulled for some reason. Generally, this merchandise is sold as is/where is and may be in new condition. To buy this merchandise, you must have your resale (sales tax number) permit and be prepared to pay the shipping to your location. Unless you're buying it at eBay.

Available all over the country, the liquidation business has been thriving as a well-kept secret for years. As long as you have space to store it and a way to sell it, you can acquire salvage merchandise for as low as 10 cents on the dollar. When I say you need storage space, I mean lots of space. To buy this type of merchandise at bottom-of-the-barrel prices, you must be willing to accept truckloads — full 40–53 foot eighteen wheelers, loaded with approximately 22–24 4' x 4' x 6' (or 7') pallets — of merchandise at a time. Often these truckloads have manifests listing the retail and wholesale price of each item on the truck. If you have access to the over 10,000 square feet of warehouse that you'll need to unpack and process this amount of merchandise, you're in business.

There are several types of salvage merchandise:

- ✔ **Unclaimed freight:** When a trucking company delivers merchandise, a *manifest* (a document containing the contents of the shipment) accompanies the freight. If, for some reason, a portion of the shipment arrives incomplete, contains the wrong items, or is damaged, the entire shipment may be refused by the merchant. The trucking company is now stuck with as much as a truckload of freight. The original seller may not want to pay the freight charges to return the merchandise to his warehouse (or accept blame for an incorrect shipment), and so the freight becomes the trucker's problem. The trucking companies arrive at agreements with liquidators to buy this freight in the various areas that the liquidators serve. This way, truckers are never far from a location where they can dump, er, drop off merchandise.

✔ **Returns:** Did you know that after you buy something and decide that you don't want it and return it to the store or mail-order house, it can never be sold as new again (in most states anyway)? The merchandise is generally sent to a liquidator who agrees in advance to pay a flat percentage for goods. The liquidator must move the merchandise to someone else (hopefully at a profit). All major retailers liquidate returns, and much of this merchandise ends up at eBay or in closeout stores.

If you're handy at repairing electronics or computers, you'd probably do very well with a specialized lot. You may easily be able to revitalize damaged merchandise, often using parts from two unsalable items to come up with one that you can sell in like-new working condition.

✔ **Liquidation:** Similar to the liquidation auctions that I mention in the earlier section about auctions, these liquidators buy liquidation merchandise by truckloads and sell it in smaller lots. The merchandise comes from financially stressed or bankrupt companies who need to raise cash quickly.

✔ **Seasonal overstocks:** Remember my motto? "Buy off-season, sell on-season"? At the end of the season, a store may find its shelves overloaded with seasonal merchandise (swimsuits in August) and may need to get rid of it to make room for the fall and winter stock. These brand new items become salvage merchandise because they're seasonal overstocks.

✔ **Shelf-pulls:** Have you ever passed up one item in the store for the one behind it in the display because its box was in better condition? Sometimes the plastic bubble or the package is dented, and you'd rather have a nice clean pristine one. That box you just passed up may be destined to become a *shelf-pull*. The item inside may be in perfect condition, but it's cosmetically unsalable in the retail store environment.

I scoured the Internet and found tons of liquidators. The following is a list of some sites that stood out and offered a wide variety of deals:

www.merchandise4auctions.com

www.wholesalecentral.com

www.mywebwholesaler.com

www.auctionsection.com

www.salvagecloseouts.com/general.htm

www.amerisurplus.com

www.closeouts.digiscape.net

www.amlinc.com

www.tdwcloseouts.com

Some liquidators who specialize in selling to online auctioneers offer a *drop-ship service.* That means that you don't even have to take possession of the merchandise; you're given a photo and, after you sell the item, you give the liquidators the address of the buyer and they'll ship it for you. I think this is a great service, but it costs *you* more. If you're in business, your goal is to make as much money as you can. If you believe in a product, order a quantity, and have it shipped to your door. Don't pay for someone else's mark-up on shipping to your customers.

A proportion of liquidation items, unclaimed freight, and returns may not be salable for the reasons that I discuss throughout the rest of this section. While you'll acquire many gems that stand to bring you profit, you'll also be left with a varying percentage of useless items. Read on carefully.

Items by the pallet

Some suppliers take the risk and purchase salvaged merchandise by the truckload; they then break up each truckload and sell merchandise to you a pallet at a time. You'll probably find some local liquidators who offer this service, or you can go online to find one. Here's the rub: finding the right guy to sell to you.

As in any business, you'll find both good-guy liquidators and bad-guy liquidators. As you know, the world is full of e-mail scammers and multi-level marketers who are in business to take your money. No one trying to sell you merchandise can possibly *guarantee* that you'll make money, so beware of liquidators who offer this kind of guarantee. I don't care who they are or what they say. You need to carefully research whomever you choose to buy from. Use an Internet search engine and search for the words **salvage**, **liquidation**, **pallet merchandise**.

Some liquidation sellers sell their merchandise as it ships in, so what you get is a crapshoot. You may lose money on some items while making back the dollars on others. Other sellers who charge a bit more will remove the less desirable merchandise from the pallets. Some may even make up deluxe pallets with better quality merchandise. These loads cost more, but if they're filled with the type of merchandise that you're interested in selling, you'll probably write better descriptions and subsequently do a better job selling them.

Getting a pallet of merchandise shipped to you can cost a bundle, so finding a source for your liquidation merchandise that's close to your home base of operations is a good idea. You'll notice that many liquidation sites have several warehouses, which translates to lower shipping costs for the buyer (they can then also accept merchandise from places close to the various warehouses). You might see FOB (Freight on board) and a city name listed, which means that when you buy the merchandise, you own it in the city listed. You are responsible for whatever it costs to ship the merchandise to your door. Search around; you may have to go through many sources before you find the right one for you.

When you find a source from which you want to buy merchandise by the pallet, check out a few things before spending your hard-earned cash:

- ✔ Do they sell mostly to flea marketers (you might not want that kind of merchandise because you're looking for *quality* at a low price) or closeout stores (more retail-oriented)?

- ✔ Did you get a reply within 24 hours after calling or e-mailing?

- ✔ Does anyone you speak to appear to care about what you want to sell?

- ✔ Do the available lots run within your planned budget?

- ✔ Are the lots general or have they been sorted to include only the type of merchandise that you want to sell?

- ✔ How long has this liquidator been in business and where does its merchandise come from?

- ✔ Does the source guarantee that you *will* make money or that you *can* make money by buying the right merchandise? *Remember:* No one can guarantee that you'll make money.

- ✔ Does the supplier offer references on its Web site that you can contact to find out some real information on this seller's items and what the percentage is of unsalable goods in a box or pallet?

- ✔ Is there a hard sell involved? Or is it a matter-of-fact deal?

Job lots

Manufacturers often have to get rid of merchandise, too. Perhaps a particular manufacturer made five million bobbing head dolls and then sold only four million to retailers. It has to quickly unload this merchandise (known as *job lots*) so that it'll have the cash to invest in next season's array of items. Job lots often consist of hundreds or thousands of a single item. You'd best enjoy what you're selling because you'll be looking at the stuff for a while.

Remember supply and demand — don't ever flood the eBay market or your item will become valueless.

Many Web sites specialize in job lots, but you have to visit them often because the deals are constantly changing. Here are two that are worth checking out:

www.liquidation.com (see Figure 6-6)

www.isolve.com

Figure 6-6:
Liquidation.
com.

Wholesale Merchandise by the Case

Purchasing wholesale merchandise may require that you have your state's resale license, which identifies you as being in the business. Be sure that you have one before you try to purchase merchandise direct from another business. Also, when you purchase your merchandise from another business — known as business to business (B2B) transactions, your resale number says that you'll pay sales tax when you sell your item, so you probably won't be charged tax when you purchase your stock. Go to Chapter 15 to find out how to get that magic resale number.

When you have your resale number, you can go anywhere you want to buy merchandise. If you want to buy direct from a manufacturer, you can. Unfortunately, manufacturers often have a monetary minimum to the amount of your order, which may be more than you want to spend (and you'd get more of a particular item than you'd ever want at once). To remedy that, see if you can find some independent retailer who buys in quantity and who perhaps will let you in on some quantity buys with manufacturers.

TIP

Sometimes the liquidators that I discuss in the previous section get cases of perfectly salable goods in their loads. Pallets break up into many cases, and liquidators will often sell these cases individually at eBay. What a great way to acquire goods for your eBay business; I know of several eBay sellers who buy their merchandise this way. Figure 6-7 shows WholesaleCentral.com, a directory for wholesalers *and* liquidators.

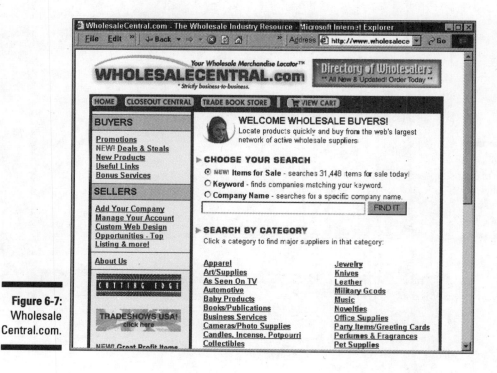

Figure 6-7:
Wholesale
Central.com.

Resale Items at eBay

I'll keep this short and sweet: Use the magic search engine! But be careful; many a get-rich-quick schemer will use the keywords I've bolded here in their auctions to attract your attention. Look only for good quality merchandise to resell. Remember that the only way to make a living at eBay is to sell quality items to happy customers so that they'll come back and buy from you again. Search eBay auction titles for the following keywords: **resale**, **resell**, **"case of"** (see Figure 6-8), **"case quantity"**, **"lot of"**, **"pallet of"** (see Figure 6-9), **closeout**, and **surplus**. Be sure to use the quotes anywhere that I've included them here because this forces the search engine to find the words in the exact order you write them inside the quotes.

Figure 6-8:
Results of a
"case of"
search
at eBay.

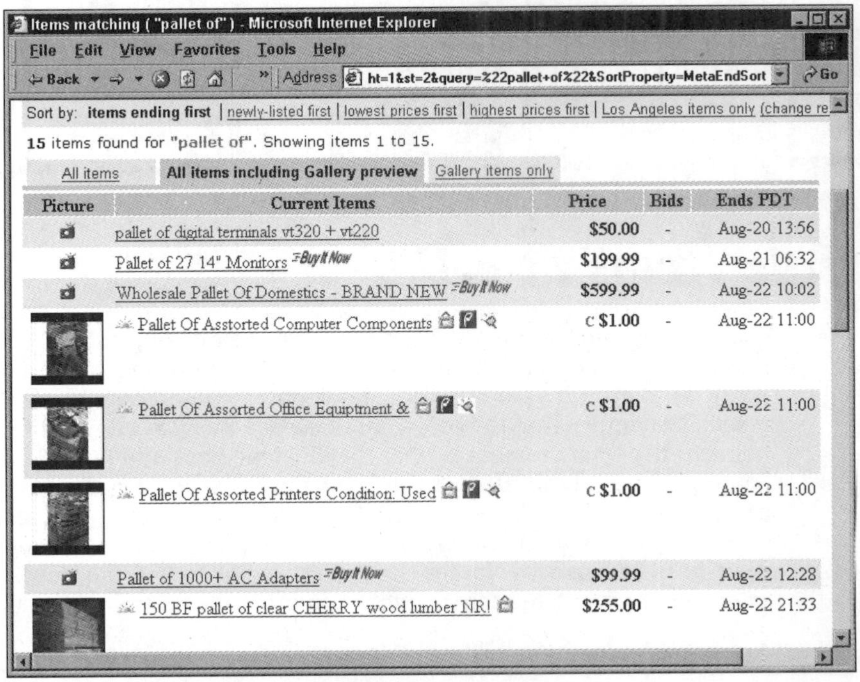

Figure 6-9:
Results of
"pallet of"
search.

Consignment Selling

Consignment sales are the up and coming way for you to help newbies by selling their items at eBay. You can just go to someone who still owns the merchandise, and make a percentage of the sale for your work. Plus, this gives you excellent experience for future auctions of your own merchandise. Consigning merchandise has probably been practiced for as long as things have been sold. You take property of the item from the owner and sell it at eBay for them. You're responsible for taking the photos and marketing the auction at eBay — for a fee.

To set up consignment sales, you should follow a few guidelines:

1. Design a consignment agreement (a contract), and send it to the owner of the merchandise before he sends you his item(s). Doing so ensures that all policies are set up in advance and that no questions will arise after the transaction has begun.

2. Have the owner sign and send the agreement to you (the consignor) along with the item.

3. Research the item based on past sales so that you can give the owner an estimated price range of what the item might sell for at eBay.

4. Photograph the item carefully (see Chapter 11 for some hints) and write a thoughtful, selling description.

5. Handle all e-mail inquiries as if the item were your own; after all, your fee is generally based on a percentage of the final sale.

What do you charge for all your work? I can't give you a stock answer for that one. Many sellers charge a flat fee for photographing, listing, and shipping, anywhere from $5–10, plus as much as a 30-percent commission on the final auction total (to absorb eBay fees). Other sellers base their fees solely on the final sale amount and charge on a sliding scale, beginning at 50 percent of the total sale, less eBay and payment service fees. You must decide how much you think you can make on an item.

Traditional auction houses handle consignment sales in a similar fashion.

Chapter 7

Know the Value of What You're Selling

In This Chapter

▶ Searching eBay

▶ Finding publications in your area of interest

▶ Using online appraisal services

▶ Authenticating your merchandise

*I*f you don't know what your item is worth, you absolutely will not get the highest prices in any market for your item. If you don't know how to make your item easy to find, your item may not be noticed by even the hardiest of collectors. If you don't know the facts or what to say, your well-written title and detailed description (combined with a fabulous picture) may still not be enough to get the highest price for your item.

Knowing your item is a crucial part of successful selling at eBay. This is why I suggest in Chapter 1 that you specialize in a small group of items so that you can stay on top of the ever-changing trends in marketability. An item may be appraised or listed in a book for a high value, but what you care about is how much that item will actually sell for. Imagine someone uncovering a secret hoard of your item and, not knowing the value of it, dumping all of them at eBay at a vicious pace with low Buy it Now prices; this unpredictable scenario will drive down the value of the item within a couple of weeks.

The values of collectibles go up and down over periods of time. Star Wars items are a perfect example; values skyrocketed during the release of the latest movie (1999), but now prices have settled to a considerably lower level. A published book of value listings is only valid for the *moment* the book is written. If you stay on top of your market in a few specialties, you'll be aware of these natural fluctuations in the market. I'd probably hold any special Star Wars items until the next film comes out — if you're looking for the highest price rather than just looking to liquidate excess inventory.

You no doubt *will* purchase the occasional (hopefully, more than occasional) gem and you *will* want to make the most money possible, so in this chapter I examine the different ways you can find out just how much something is really worth. I go step by step in this chapter, starting with the easiest and most accurate to the most laborious. Just hope you can get your answer the easy way.

The Easy Way: eBay Search

Who woulda thunk it? The best tool for evaluating your items is right under your nose. The eBay search tool is the best and quickest link to finding your pricing information. To see how items like yours have been selling, search the completed auctions. You can also search these results to see in which categories to list your item, and at what time of day the high bidders for your item jump in and win.

Every type of item has a different type of bidder. This makes sense, right? Would a person searching for collectible dolls have the same shopping habits as a coin collector? Probably not; coins tend to be more expensive than collectible dolls. Although generalities can be dangerous, *profiling* your item's buyer will be something you'll need to do. After you check out the completed auctions for items like yours, you'll be amazed at how the buying patterns of shoppers in different categories become crystal clear. After you arm yourself with this knowledge, you'll not only know how much your items should go for, but when's the best time to end the auction.

If you're selling a common item, it's also important to check to see how many other sellers are selling the same item — and when their auctions close. Nothing can kill your profits like being the second or third auction closing with the same piece of merchandise. You've got to space your auctions apart from the others, or the law of supply and demand will kick in — and kick you in the wallet.

The way the search system works has changed drastically over the years, so be sure that you know how to use this valuable tool. On almost every eBay page (even on the search page), eBay inserts a small box for searching. Initially you may find it easier to go to the search page, but if you know the search engine *syntax,* or shorthand, you can pinpoint your items with amazing accuracy.

Here are some pointers to help you get the most out of the eBay search engine:

- ✔ The search engine isn't case-sensitive, so you don't have to worry about using capitalization in your search.

- ✔ To find more needles in the haystack, be sure to select the check box that says `Search Titles` **and** `Descriptions`.

✔ If you're looking for a very popular item, don't search just auction titles and descriptions; search by category, too.

For example, say that you're searching for a Winnie the Pooh baby outfit. Go to the Clothing & Accessories: Infants: Clothing: 6-12 months category. Under the small universal search box in the upper-right corner of the page (see Figure 7-1) is a second option: Search only in Clothing: 6-12 months as well as Search titles and descriptions. Click both options and type **Pooh outfit** — I guarantee you'll find exactly what you're looking for.

✔ Don't use conjunctions (or, and) or articles (a, an, the) in your search; the search engine might misconstrue these *noise* words as part of your search.

Sellers may use the ampersand (&) in place of the word, and so if you include *and* in your search, you won't find the items by using the ampersand. Some sellers, due to the 45 character limit, may not place *the* in their title, even if it belongs; the same goes for *a*, *or*, and *and*.

Figure 7-1:
The eBay
search box.

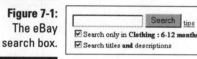

Advanced searching

If you need to find a particular item with pinpoint accuracy, or you just want to weed out bogus responses, you can try a variety of advanced searching methods. Table 7-1 is the advanced course in searching.

Table 7-1	Advanced Search Syntax	
Symbol	*Impact*	*Example*
Quotes (",")	Limits search to the exact phrase inside the quotes	**"American Staffordshire"** yields auctions only relating to this breed of dog
Asterisk (*)	Works like a wild card in poker	**196* fashion** brings up auctions that relate to 1960s fashion

(continued)

Table 7-1 (continued)

Symbol	Impact	Example
Parentheses (()) and comma (,)	Finds items related to either word	**(shipperke, schipperke)** will find items spelled both ways
Minus sign (-)	Excludes words	**watch -digital** gets you a lovely analog watch
Minus sign (-), parentheses (()), and comma (,)	Excludes more than one word	**Packard -(hewlett, bell)** will find those rare Packard auto collectibles
At (@) and number 1	Searches two out of three words	**@1 new purse shoes dress** will get you a nice new outfit

Now that you know how to finesse the search engine, head to the search page and see if you can work some magic.

Smart Search

The eBay Smart Search performs all the tasks of the universal search box and more. With the Smart Search, you can narrow your active auction search to check out the competition. In Smart Search (see Figure 7-2), you've also got a few extra options:

- ✔ **Price Range:** You can select a price range that you'd like to see the items in. For example, when I did a search for a particular software package, I came up with several hundreds of varied items. I soon realized that most of the lower prices were for books about the software. By narrowing down the price range, in this case for items over $70, I was able to narrow the search to just the software I was looking for.

- ✔ **View Results:** You can choose for your search to come up with the mini gallery thumbnails or not. While this may not ordinarily help when you're doing research, information is key; you might just see a variation of the item in other photos that you didn't know about. Maybe the item was commonly made in green and the one you want to sell is red — see, you've got a variation; perhaps it's worth more.

- ✔ **Payment:** You can isolate your search to only those sellers who accept eBay online payments. This may enlighten you as to whether buyers of this product pay higher prices if they have the option to pay with credit cards. (Although the Billpoint exclusion will not include PayPal or other methods of credit card payments, it still strongly speaks for credit card users.)

✔ **Search in Categories:** You can narrow your search to one of the 23 major categories at eBay. If your product is made for men, women, or children, you may get more efficient results by looking in the category that applies directly to your item. Strangely, when searching for a ladies watch, I found the following synonyms and abbreviations for lady's: ladys, lds, ladies, and femmes.

✔ **Item location:** If you're selling something big that you can't (or don't want to) ship, you want to deliver it or have the buyer pick it up. This option allows you to check out the competition only in your closest major metropolitan eBay trading area.

✔ **Sort by:** You can find items by auctions that end first (default), newly listed items first, lowest prices first, or highest prices first.

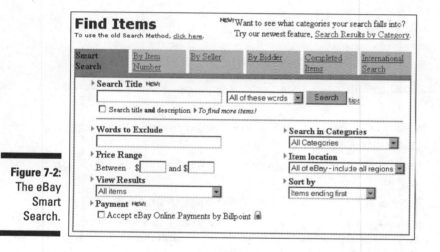

Figure 7-2:
The eBay
Smart
Search.

A new feature on the Smart Search page is the <u>Search Results by Category</u> link (see upper right corner in Figure 7-2). This feature is one of the best tools eBay has come up with in a long time. When you have a question about what category other people list items like yours, just click the link and perform the search.

So how can you search completed auctions to find out bidding patterns on items like yours? Here's a way to flesh out all the dirty little details that you need:

1. **Perform a Smart Search on the item you want information on.**

   When the results appear (see Figure 7-3), you'll see how many other sellers are selling your same item, and you can make the determination as to whether it's the right time to sell. (If all the active auctions for your items have high bids, it's time to sell — just be sure not to list your auction to end at the same time or after another one.)

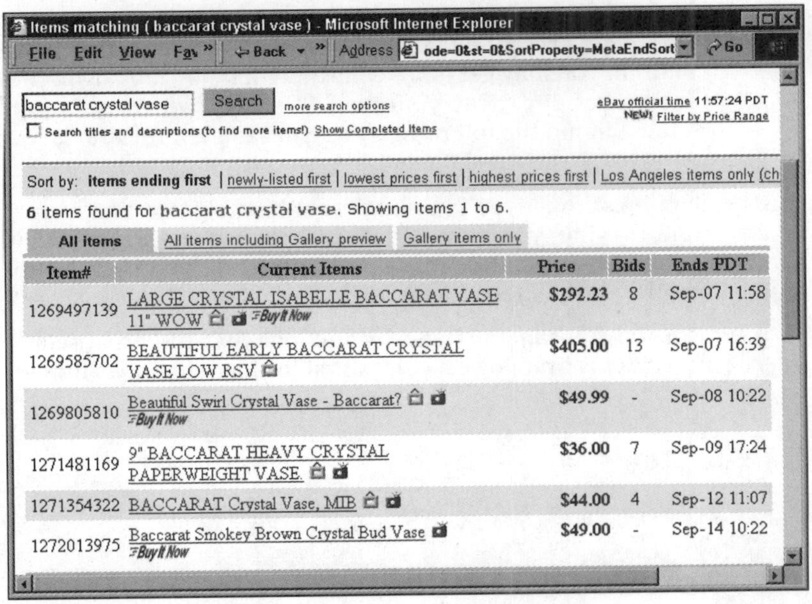

Figure 7-3:
Results of
a smart
search.

2. **Now that you've got your active auction results, click the <u>Show Completed Items</u> link.**

   The results of auctions of your particular item for the last 30 days appear.

3. **To re-sort by price, click the <u>highest prices first</u> link.**

   Now you're at the heart of the matter (see Figure 7-4). Pull out your calendar and make note of what days your item landed the highest bids. More often than not, you'll find that a pattern appears. Your item may see more action on Sunday or Monday or Thursday or whenever. After you figure out the days that your items get the highest bids, pull out a copy of the eBay time chart that appears on the Cheat Sheet and evaluate what time of day your high bidders like to bid.

There you have it: the method that will get you the most information that eBay can give you on the sales trends on your item. It's money in the bank. Use it!

If you can't find any auctions for your item, you've got a few more options. You're not gonna believe I'm saying this, but try searching on `auctions.yahoo.com` or go to `www.amazon.com`. Try searching for your items there — at least you'll see if someone else in the world is selling one. None of the cool search features that I previously discuss are going to work, buy hey, they ain't eBay.

Figure 7-4:
The
Completed
Auctions
search,
sorted by
highest
prices first.

eBay also has a superior tool for checking the competition's auctions. After a while, you will identify the sellers that frequently sell similar items to yours. Aside from keeping them in your Favorite Sellers list on your My eBay page, here's a way to check their auctions to see if they're currently selling an item that competes with yours (to add sellers to your My eBay Favorites, see Chapter 3):

1. To see if one of your competing sellers has an item like yours up for sale, go to the Find Items search area and click the By Seller tab.

2. Scroll down a bit to search Items by Title and by Sellers.

3. Type your keywords and the Seller's user ID in the boxes, as shown in Figure 7-5.

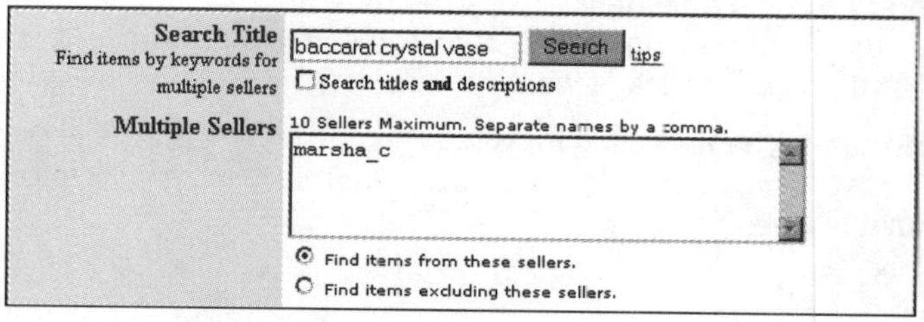

Figure 7-5:
Find items
by seller.

Useful Publications

So what if your item isn't up for sale at eBay and hasn't been for 30 days? Horrors! What's the first thing to do? Check out your local newsstand for one of the many publications devoted to collecting. Go over to Yahoo Yellow Pages at yp.yahoo.com. Type your zip code to limit the search to your part of the country and type in a search for **newsstand** and **news stand**. You can also search for **Magazines - Dealers** in your area. Let your fingers do the walking and call the news stands in your area and ask if they have publications in your area of interest. If no newsstands are listed in your area, visit the local Barnes and Noble or Borders Books. They don't have a complete selection, but it's better than nothing. When you decide where to go, get in the car and go out to the most complete local newsstand that you can find.

Here's a list of some very popular reference publications:

- **Action Figure Digest:** Find out who's hot in the action figure biz in this monthly magazine. Its Web site sells back issues; go to www.tomart.com/html/store.html.

- **Antique Trader:** This magazine has been the bible of the antique collecting industry for over 40 years. Visit its online home at www.krause.com/collectibles/at/ for more articles and other information.

- **Autograph Collector:** This magazine gives the lowdown on the autograph business and gives samples of many autographs for identification. Its Web site, www.autographcollector.com, features links to many price guides published by the company.

- **Collector Editions:** You'll find information on plates, figurines, glass, prints, cottages, ornaments, and dozens of other contemporary decorative collectibles in this monthly magazine. For a free issue, go to www.teddybearreview.com/cccpages/ceedit.html.

- **Disneyana:** A bi-monthly magazine that features what's new and hot for Disney collectors. You can purchase back issues at www.tomart.com/html/store.html.

- **Doll Reader:** The Ultimate Authority Doll Reader has been dishing out the scoop on collectible dolls of all sorts for over 26 years. It's the place to go to catch the trends on the latest in doll collecting. At www.dollreader.com, you'll get an idea of what's in the very informative magazine.

- **Goldmine:** The magazine for CD and record collecting. The Web site, www.krause.com/records/gm, has many sample articles and information from its issues.

- **Numismatic News:** Another old standard, Numismatic News has been around for more than 50 years. The first issue each month includes a pull-out guide to retail U.S. coin prices. Every three months, it also includes a U.S. paper money price guide. Check out Numismatic News on the Web at www.krause.com/coins/nn/.

- **Sports Cards Magazine and Price Guide:** An excellent source for all you need to know about trading cards from all sports. Check out its Web site at www.krause.com/sports/bc/.

- **Sports Collectors Digest:** Takes sports collectibles to the highest level. Visit its Web site at www.krause.com/sports and sign up for a free e-mail newsletter.

- **Stamp Collector:** I subscribed to this magazine when I was in grade school and it's still around. Actually it's been around a lot longer, since 1931. (Hey, I'm not that old!) They too have an informative Web site; go to www.krause.com/stamps.

- **Teddy Bear Review:** Since 1986, this review has offered pages of information on bear collecting. For a free sample issue, go to www.teddybearreview.com/cccpages/tbredit.html.

It seems that every leading magazine has its own Web site. In the next section, I mention some useful Web sites for pricing references.

Online Sources of Information

Because you're all so Internet savvy (what's better than getting the information you want at a millisecond's notice?), I assume you plan to visit the magazines' sites that I mention in the preceding section. In this section, I give you a few more fun sources where you can hopefully get more insight into your items.

Web sites

Many Web sites are devoted to different collectible areas and list prices realized at recently completed auctions. Recent prices realized at auction give you the best evaluation of items because these auctions are usually directed towards specialists in the specific collectible category. Most of the participants in these auctions *really* know their stuff.

You may have to poke around the following Web sites to find prices realized, but once you do, you'll have the holy grail of estimated values. Look for links that point to auction archives, and you'll find the recent prices realized of many items. Many of these sites will consign your item from you as well and sell it to their audience:

- General Collectible Auctions: www.collectors.com
- Antiques, art, all kinds of rare stuff: www.butterfields.com
- Art Auctions: www.artprice.com

  This site charges for its searches by artist, but has an immense database that's searchable by artist.
- Autographs: www.autographs.com
- Collectible glasses: www.glassnews.com (you've got to see this stuff!)
- United States Coin Price Guide: www.pcgs.com/prices/
- Currency Auctions: www.lynknight.com
- Rock and Roll Memorabilia (Home of the World's Rarest Records): www.goodrockintonight.com
- Rare Coins: www.bowersandmerena.com
- Sports Memorabilia and Cards: www.superiorsports.com

Online appraisals

I've had a bit of personal experience with online appraisals, which seem quite tempting at first glance. At a second glance, though, I realized that unless the person doing the appraisal could actually *see* and *feel* the item, an accurate appraisal couldn't be performed. Also, you have no guarantee that the person at the other end is really an expert in the field that relates to your item.

I had a few items *e-appraised* by a very prestigious (now defunct) online appraisal company, and the appraisals seemed a bit off. But, I figured, what do I know? I took one, a painting, to Butterfields in Los Angeles and found that the value of the painting was ten times what my e-appraisal read.

The bottom line here is that if it's an item of real value and it's really worth appraising, it's worth getting appraised in person. Most large cities are sure to have some auction houses. Most auction houses have monthly *consignment clinics* (a way for auction houses to get merchandise for their future auctions). If you bring an item to the auction house, you aren't legally bound to have it sell your item for you, but it may not be a bad idea. All you'll get is a free verbal appraisal; the auction house won't fill out any official paperwork or anything, but at least you'll get an idea of what your item is worth. Real appraisals are quite expensive, are done by licensed professionals, and come with a Formal Appraisal Document.

Authentication Services

Some companies provide the service of *authenticating* (verifying that it's the real deal) or authenticating and *grading* (determining a value based on the item's condition and legitimacy). To have these services performed on your items, you'll have to send them to the service, and for a fee, they'll examine the item.

A few excellent sites for getting your coins graded:

- Professional Coin Grading Service (PCGS): www.pcgs.com

- American Numismatic Association Certification Service (AMNACS) — but sold to Amos Press in 1990: www.anacs.com

- Numismatic Guaranty Corporation of America (NGCA): www.ngccoin.com/ebay_ngcvalue.cfm

  The site offers eBay users a discount rate and features a mail-in grading and certification service for your coins.

For comic books, Comics Guaranty, LLC (CGC) www.cgccomics.com/ebay_comic_ book_ grading.cfm will seal (enclose in plastic to preserve the quality) and grade at a discount for eBay users.

You can find the links to eBay users authentication discounts at pages.ebay.com/help/community/auth-overview.html.

Sports cards and sports memorabilia have a bunch of authentication services. If you got your autograph or memorabilia direct from the player or team, you can assure its authenticity. Having the item authenticated may or may not get you a higher price at eBay. Try these sites:

- **Professional Sports Authenticator (PSA):** Offers eBay users a discount at www.psacard.com/cobrands/submit.chtml?cobrandid=23.

- **Sportscard Guarantee (SCG):** Has an eBay discount on card authenticating at www.sgccard.com/ebay/ebay.html.

- **Online Authentics:** Reviews autographs by scans online or by physical review. Take a look at its services at www.onlineauthentics.com.

The best way to find a good authenticator in your field is to search the items at eBay and see who is the most prominent authenticator listed in the descriptions. For example, note in the coins area that certain grading services' coins get higher bids than other services.

You can also go to an Internet search engine and type in the keywords (for coins) **coin grading**. You'll come up with a host of choices; use your good sense to see which one suits your needs.

Remember that not all items need to be officially authenticated. Official authentication does add value to the item, but if you're an expert on your items, you can comfortably rate the items on your own in your auctions. People will know from your description whether or not you're a specialist. Your feedback will also work for you by letting the prospective bidder/buyer know that your merchandise from past sales has been top-drawer.

Chapter 8

Establishing a Base of Operations: Your Web Site

In This Chapter

▶ Finding free Web space
▶ Choosing a host
▶ Picking the perfect name
▶ Registering the perfect name
▶ Marketing your piece of the Web

*Y*our eBay store is very important to your business, but it doesn't replace a commerce Web site. Yes, eBay is a very important site (duh), but so is your business Web site. You should establish your own presence on the Web. And although you can — and should — link your site to eBay, don't miss out on the rest of the Internet population.

Don't have a Web site yet? The Web has so many sites with pictures of people's dogs and kids that I just assumed you had your own site, too. The space for a Web site comes free from your ISP (I even have an embarrassing one with family pictures). One of these sites can be the practice site for your business. Take down pictures of the baby, and post pictures of items you're selling.

Do you have a Web site? Have you taken a good look at it lately to see whether it's up to date? (I just looked at mine — ugh.) Does it link to your eBay auctions, eBay store, and the gallery that I discuss in Chapter 5?

Whether or not you have a Web site, this chapter has something for you. I detail a great deal about Web sites, from thinking up a name to choosing a host. If you don't have a site, I'll get you started on launching one. If you already have a site, I give you some pointers about finding the best host. For the serious-minded Web-based entrepreneur (that's you), I also include some ever-important marketing tips.

Free Web Space (A Good Place to Start)

Although I love the word free, in real life it seems like nothing is *really* free. Free generally means something won't cost you too much money — but may cost you a bit more in time. When your site is free, you aren't able to have your own direct URL (Universal Resource Locator) or domain name. Most likely, a free Web site has an address like `www.netcom.com/~marshac`, `home.socal.rr.com/marshac`, or `members.aol.com/membername`. At least having some kind of site gives you the experience in setting one up; when you're ready, you can always use your free site as an extension of your main business site.

In order to access the Internet, you had to sign on with an Internet Service Provider (ISP), which means you more than likely already have your own Web space. Most ISPs allow you to have more than one e-mail address per account. Each e-mail address is entitled to a certain amount of free Web space. Through the use of *hyperlinks* (small pieces of HTML code that, when clicked, route the clicker from one place to another on the page or other Web site; usually denoted with underline or other emphasis), you can combine all the free Web space from each e-mail address into one giant Web site. Take a look at Table 8-1, in which I include comparisons of some popular ISPs.

Table 8-1	ISP Providers Who Give You Free Web Space	
ISP	*# of E-Mail Addresses*	*Total Space per Account*
America Online (AOL)	7	2MB per e-mail address (14MB)
Earthlink/Mindspring	8	10MB
AT&T WorldNet	6	10MB per e-mail address (60MB)
RoadRunner	5	5MB/99 cents per extra MB per month
Pacific Bell DSL	3	3MB
MSN (using Explorer 6.1)	8	30MB
Yahoo GeoCities*	1	15MB
WebTV Plus (msn TV)	6	3MB

*Yahoo GeoCities isn't an ISP, but a reliable online community that gives each member online Web space. Extra megabyte space is available for purchase.

If America Online (AOL) is your Internet provider, you may already realize that AOL has some serious issues regarding its users getting e-mail from the rest of the Internet. You can't afford to run a business in an area that has e-mail issues. Your AOL account gives each of your seven screen names 2MB of online storage space (refer to Table 8-1). You can best utilize this space by storing images for eBay there, but not for running a business site. Each screen name, at 2MB, can store fifty 40K images. (For more information on how to use this space for your extra images, see Chapter 11.)

Poke around your ISP's home page for a <u>community</u> or <u>your web space</u> link. For example, in Figure 8-1, I located the Road Runner home page at www.rr.com. After poking around this page, I found and clicked the <u>Member Services</u> link, which led me to a page offering various options. I finally found a <u>Personal Home Page</u> link, which took me to a page that would walk me through setting up my own home page (Figure 8-2).

After agreeing to the Terms of Service, I can simply log on and set up my home page. Road Runner offered me the option of using Microsoft FrontPage, which is one of the best and easiest Web-building programs around. I highly recommend the FrontPage software, but if you want all the benefits of FrontPage, you'll need a site that uses FrontPage *extensions* (portions of the FrontPage program that reside on the server and enable all the HTML magic to happen automatically — and you don't have to write in the code). If you're interested, check out *FrontPage 2002 For Dummies,* by Asha Dornfest (published by Hungry Minds, Inc.).

Save FrontPage extensions for *hosted* Web sites (the ones you pay for) when you have a good deal of allotted space. Installing Microsoft FrontPage extensions on a small Web site like the one that Road Runner provides will take up too many of your precious megabytes (although Yahoo has them installed for the GeoCities sites, and does not count them as part of your allotted megabyte count).

Opt to use FTP (File Transfer Protocol) file transfer any time you can. You can still design pages in Microsoft FrontPage — just don't use the fancy features. FTP will upload your home page and your images easily. The ISP Road Runner supplies an FTP program for you. If your ISP doesn't, go to www.globalscape.com and download CuteFTP. Cute FTP is a small, simple program that'll help you get your pages and images to your site. You can also try the gold standard WS_FTP Pro from www.ipswitch.com. You can download either program free on a 30-day trial basis.

Your first Web pages may be simple, and that's okay. You'll have to get used to having a Web site before you can really use it for commerce. Put up a home page that links to a few product-related pages and your eBay auctions and voila, you're in business. If you're feeling more adventurous about your Web site, check out the next section, in which I describe a handful of Web site hosts and give you the details on choosing one.

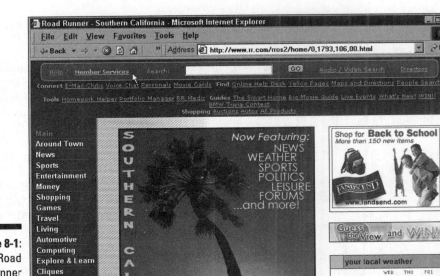

Figure 8-1:
The Road
Runner
Southern
California
home page.

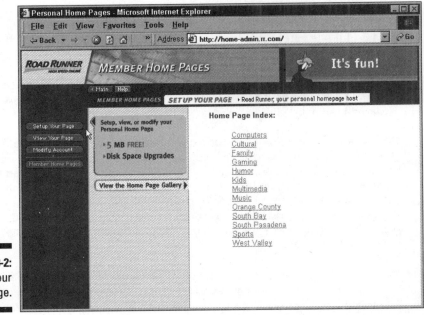

Figure 8-2:
Set up your
home page.

Why learn HTML when Web page editors can do it for you?

If you need some help designing those first pages (I *never* became proficient in HTML and still depend on FrontPage to design my site), try looking for inexpensive HTML Web software. I just checked eBay, and an older version of Corel Web Designer was selling for $9.99. Check again; I'm sure you're bound to find something because lots of Web page editors are out there. The key is to find one that's WYSIWYG (what you see is what you get), which includes a graphical interface that allows you to preview your pages as you design them. You can also use an older version of Microsoft FrontPage (without the extensions) to design simple Web pages.

Paying for Your Web Space

If you've been on the Internet for any length of time, you've been bombarded by hosting offers through your daily spam, some of which may come from people you've never even heard of. A Web hosting company is a company that houses your Web site code and electronically doles out your pages and images to Web page visitors.

Before deciding to spend good money on a Web hosting company, thoroughly check it out. Go to that company's site to find a list of features that the service offers. If you still have questions after perusing the Web site, look for an 800 number to call. You won't find any feedback ratings like you find at eBay, but the following are a few questions to ask (don't hang up until you're satisfied with the answers):

- **How long has it been in business?** You want a Web host that didn't go into business just a couple of months ago and is operating out of someone's basement. Dealing with someone who's been around the Internet for a while — and hence, knows what they're doing — is important. Is the Web site professional looking? Or does it look like your neighbor designed it? Does the company look like it has enough money to stay in business? You wouldn't want it disappearing mysteriously with your money.

- **Who are some of its other clients?** Poke around to see if you can find links to sites of other clients. Take a look at who else is doing business with it and analyze the sites. Visit several of its client sites. Do the pages and links come up quickly? Do all the images appear in a timely manner? Web sites that load quickly are a good sign.

✔ **What is its downtime/uptime ratio?** Does the Web host guarantee *uptime* (the span of time its servers stay operational without going down and denying access to your site)? Expecting a 99 percent uptime guarantee is not unreasonable; you're open for business — and your Web host needs to keep it that way.

✔ **How much Web space do I get for my money?** MSN (Microsoft Network Internet access service) gives you 30MB for free; you'd better be getting a whole lot more if you're paying for it!

✔ **What's the Data Transfer limit?** *Data Transfer* is a measurement of the amount of bytes that are transferred from your site on the server to the Internet. In July 2001, my site had 93,000 hits. Each hit transfers a certain amount of bytes (kilobytes, megabytes) from your host's servers to the viewer's computer. Perhaps I'm mistaken, but I'm sure that a whole lot of bytes transferred from my host's servers. I know that I'm nearing my service plan's 5GB monthly limit, so I'll probably have to soon switch to a more expensive level that provides a higher level of transfer.

✔ **Does it offer toll-free technical support?** When something goes wrong with your Web site, you need it fixed immediately. You must be able to reach tech support quickly without hanging around on the phone for hours. Does the Web host have a technical support area on its Web site where you can troubleshoot your own problems (in the middle of the night)?

Whenever you're deciding on any kind of provider for your business, take a moment to call its tech support team with a question about the services. Take note of how long you had to hold and how courteous the techs were. Before plunking down your hard-earned money, you should be sure that the provider's customer service claims aren't merely that — just claims.

✔ **What's the policy on shopping carts?** In time you're probably going to need a shopping cart interface on your site. Does your provider charge extra for that? If so, how much? In the beginning, you can just have your items on your site and set up a PayPal shopping cart, a convenient and professional-looking way to sell items on your site. When you're running your business full-time, a shopping cart to accept credit cards is a must.

✔ **What kind of statistics will I get?** Visitors who go to your Web site leave a little bread-crumb trail. Your host collects these statistics and you'll be able to know which are your most popular pages, and which pages people bail out of quickly. You can know how long people linger on each page, where they come from, and what browsers they're using. How your host will supply these stats to you is very important. One of the best reporting formats is from a company called WebTrends (www.webtrends.com).

✔ **Are there any hidden fees?** Is it charging exorbitant fees for set up? Charging extra for statistics? Imposing high charges if your bandwidth suddenly increases?

✔ **How often will the Web host back up my site?** No matter how redundant a host's servers are, a disaster may strike and you need to know that your Web site won't vaporize. *Redundancy* is the safety net for your site. You may be interested in how many power backups a company has for the main system. Perhaps it has generators (more than one is good) and more.

If you have a Web site and you're like me, you're always looking for other hosts that offer more bang for your buck. Finding the right host is of ultimate importance for your online business because it takes time to look behind the glitzy promotional statements and find out the facts behind each company. Take a look at Table 8-2 for a comparison of some host service costs.

Table 8-2	Comparing Basic Host Service Costs			
Feature	*ReadyHosting.com*	*Interland*	*Microsoft*	*Yahoo!*
Monthly plan cost	N/A	$27.95	$29.95	$14.95
Yearly discount rate	$99	$301.80	$259	N/A
Hard drive storage	500MB	150MB	40MB	100MB
Data transfer/ month	Unlimited	5GB	Unlimited	15GB
Toll-free tech support	Yes	Yes	N/A	N/A
E-mail aliases	Unlimited	30	Unlimited	Unlimited
Shopping cart	Yes	N/A	Yes	No

Table 8-2 lists some of the basics but doesn't answer all of the questions. Throughout the rest of this section, I fill you in with some details about ReadyHosting.com, Interland, Microsoft, and Yahoo!, but I always recommend checking out Web sites to get the most current information.

ReadyHosting.com

Here's a little guy who's doing it right: ReadyHosting.com (see Figure 8-3), hosting Web space since June 2000, is ranked in the cNet Top Five most popular Web services list, and over 100 new sites sign up with the service each day. Sites are hosted on servers running state-of-the-art Windows 2000, and each site comes with a Cart32 e-commerce Shopping Cart. Cart32 integrates directly into Microsoft FrontPage, holds inventory, validates credit cards, and more. For details, check out `www.readyhosting.com`.

Interland.com

Interland is a big company with big sophisticated equipment (one of its big investors is Microsoft), and it hosts a bunch of the big guys on their own private servers. They recently merged with Micron Electronics' HostPro division to become a strong force in the hosting business.

To little guys, Interland (see Figure 8-4) offers *shared hosting* and that's probably what you'll be using for quite a while. Shared hosting is where your site resides with others on a single server, sharing all resources. When your Internet sales gross several hundred thousand a year, you might have to look into some *dedicated hosting* of your own. When you have dedicated hosting, your site will be located on a server of its own, managed by the hosting company. One of the best features of this company is its 24/7 toll-free technical support: Its online support gives intensive advice on how to solve problems on your own. Check out this site at `www.interland.com` to see what you think.

Figure 8-3: The Ready Hosting.com home page.

Figure 8-4:
The
Interland.
com home
page.

Microsoft bCentral

If Interland is big, Microsoft is gargantuan; it's the leader in everything that's personal computing-related (as if you didn't know that . . .). To grab a piece of the e-commerce market, Microsoft is making a strong push with its new and improved bCentral with Business Web. bCentral (see Figure 8-5) has always been a home for business Internet utilities, and now it has come full circle to hosting Web sites and promoting e-commerce.

Availing yourself of bCentral Web hosting is an easy procedure. You can sign up on the site (`www.bcentral.com`) and choose from over 55 theme templates to design your site by adding your own text and graphics. After you've garnered the basics from the site, use FrontPage to make your site more robust.

Each site that bCentral hosts includes an integrated shopping cart featuring customer order tracking, and shipping calculation. Add real-time credit card processing for an additional $19.95 per month through Cardservice International (plus transaction fees). You don't have to subscribe to Cardservice to accept orders online.

Don't forget about the bCentral Commerce Manager I mention in Chapter 9. It's an up and coming application that you can apply to your bCentral or *any* FrontPage-enabled Web site.

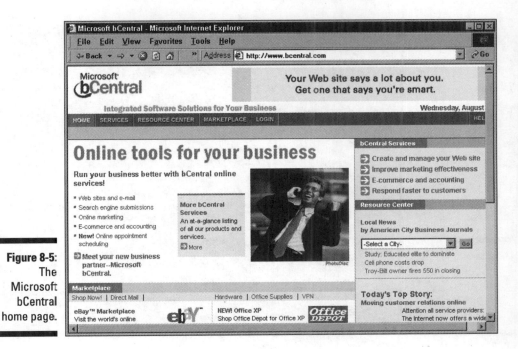

Figure 8-5:
The
Microsoft
bCentral
home page.

bCentral also has a program for advertising on Excite, MSN, and Baby Center. Campaign prices on its Adstore range from $50–$2,000. Rates rise as you target your advertising and specify where you want the ad to appear. See the section "Marketing Your Web Site (More Visitors = More Business)" later in this chapter for more about getting the word out about your Web site.

Yahoo! Web site services

Hey, it's Yahoo! It's trying to do a little bit of everything these days. I'm never sure which direction it's going. Yahoo! took over GeoCities (one of the original free Web site hosts) a few years back and so my family Web site became a Yahoo! site. Considering that I have a free site, I must admit that the services that Yahoo! offers have been top-drawer, disproving the notion that you get what you pay for. But then again, I'm not running a business from the site; it's just a bunch of family pictures.

Featuring a drag-and-drop application for building and editing your pages, Yahoo! allows you to customize your site as much as you want. Its PageBuilder allows you to be up and running with the basic site quickly and, thank goodness, you don't have to know any HTML to use it.

You have the option to create your online store through Yahoo! Store, but when you consider the cost ($100 a month for a 50-item store), you can see that you'd probably do better at eBay or with bCentral.

What's in a Web Site Name: Naming Your Baby

What to name the baby, er, Web site? It's almost as much of a dilemma as deciding on your eBay User ID or your eBay store name. If you don't have an existing company name that you want to use, why not use the same name as your eBay store? (Check out Chapter 5 for details about eBay stores.) Lock it up now so that you can keep your brand forever.

Name your site with a name that identifies what you do, what you sell, or who you are. And be sure you like it because once its yours and you begin operating under it and establishing a reputation, it'll be with you 20 years from now when you're still selling online! (I know, it should only happen!)

A few Web sites offer Wizards to help you decide your domain name. A particularly intuitive one can be found at www.namesarecheap.com/wizard.shtml. In a small, Web-based form, you input your primary business type and a short description of your business; the wizard comes up with a large number of options and also lets you know whether the options are available. Very convenient.

Before you attempt to register a name, you should check to be sure it isn't anyone else's trademark. To search an updated list of registered United States Trademarks, go to www.trademarksearchforfree.com to use its electronic trademark search system.

After a search, you may want to trademark your site name. NameProtect.com is an online service that can help you with that. It offers online trademark applications and also refers you to an attorney if you'd like to use one; just go to www.nameprotect.com/tm_protection.html.

Registering Your Domain Name (Before Someone Else Takes It)

Talk about your junk e-mail. I get daily e-mails advising me to Lose 40 pounds in 40 days, accept credit cards now, and of course REGISTER MY NAME NOW! These latter scams seem to be geared to obtaining my e-mail address for other junk mail lists rather than trying to help me register my Web site. Choosing a select *registrar* (the company that handles the registering of your site name) with care is as important as choosing the right Web host. You must remember that the Internet is still a little like the wild west, and that the James gang might be waiting to relieve you of your hard-earned cash. One of the ways to protect yourself is to understand how the *registry* works (knowledge *is* power), so read the next paragraphs.

In October of 1998, U.S. government officials decided to open up the Web domain registration business by breaking up the Network Solutions site (previously the only place that you could register your Web site). This opened up the WWW to all kinds of people selling domain names.

Before you decide on a registrar for your domain name, take a minute to see if it's accredited by ICANN (Internet Corporation for Assigned Names and Numbers), or if it's reselling for an official ICANN-accredited registrar. The Accredited Registrar Directory is constantly updated, so you can look up your registration service at www.internic.com/regist.html. For a comparison of registration fees, check out Table 8-3.

Table 8-3	Comparable .com Registration Fees (Per Year)	
Registrar	**Registration Fee**	**URL Forwarding**
e-names.org	$16.99	Free
inexpensivedomains.com	$15	$14.95
namesarecheap.com	$14	$15
networksolutions.com	$35	$12
registrars.com	$35	$25

If you're registering a new domain name but already have a site set up with your ISP, you need a feature called URL forwarding or Web address forwarding. This feature directs any hits to your new domain name from your existing long URL address. Some registrars offer this service, but watch out for hidden surprises — like a free offering of the service, which means it'll probably smack a big fat banner at the bottom of your home page. Your registrar should also have some available tech support. Trying to troubleshoot DNS issues is a job only for those who know what they're doing! Remember, sometimes you get what you pay for.

Marketing Your Web Site (More Visitors = More Business)

After you set up your Web site, it's time to let the world know about your Web site and your business. I've spent many years in the advertising business and I can tell you that I can spot businesses that *want* to fail. These businesses open their doors and expect the world to beat a path to them and make them rich. This doesn't happen — ever.

You must take a proactive approach to letting the world in on the goodies you've got for sale. This means spending a good deal of time promoting your site by running banner ads and getting your URL into a search engine. There are no shortcuts.

About a trillion people out there want to take your money for advertising your Web site. As with all transactions regarding your Web site, knowing who you're dealing with is key. If want to run your banner on someone else's site, don't spend money; ask to do an exchange. The more advertising that you can get for free, the better. If you decide that you want to pay for advertising, I recommend that you wait until after you've made a decent profit on your site.

Banner ad exchanges

The way banner ad exchange services work is simple. You design a banner ad in your graphics program to a pre-designated size following certain standards (see following list), and the service displays the banner on other sites. When Web surfers click your banner, they're taken to your site, where they'll see all the great stuff you have for sale. You can even target what type of sites that you want your banner to appear on as well. Remember that this is an *exchange.* Someone else's banner will appear on your pages in exchange for showing yours on other sites.

Here are the standard specs for a banner ad:

> 468 pixels wide by 60 pixels high
>
> GIF format (no JPEGs)
>
> Non-transparent
>
> Less than 10K in file size (10240 bytes)
>
> If animated, the animation stops at seven seconds and doesn't include loops

Banner design

If you think that designing an eye-catching banner ad (see one I used for my company in Figure 8-6) is beyond your graphic talents, you'll be happy to know that there are many excellent graphic artists on the Internet that can produce one for you. Type **banner design** into any search engine, and you'll come up with a ton of listings. Take a look at samples (and pricing) on their Web sites to find a designer who matches your needs.

TIP

On the eBay home page, click the <u>Professional Services</u> link under the heading `Specialty Sites`. On the Professional Services page that appears, click the <u>Banner Ads</u> link under Graphic Design. When I clicked <u>View all Providers</u>, I found 43 *pages* of banner ad designers; I'm sure you'll find one who meets your needs.

Figure 8-6:
My com-
pany's old
animated
banner ad.

I've set up a service on my site (www.coolebaytools.com) that automatically generates a basic banner for you for free. Others are available from a small library of banners (for as low as $19.99); you can easily customize these banners for your site by answering a few questions.

bCentral Banner Network

bCentral Banner Network is the new name for LinkExchange, the original banner ad exchange network on the Internet. LinkExchange takes your advertising banner and displays it on other Web sites. This is one of the largest and most effective networks on the Net. bCentral rotates your banner throughout its 300,000 sites and gives you great stats on how often your banner is viewed, your page visits, and your click-through ratio (how many times people click your banner and visit your site to the number of times your banner is displayed).

Getting your URL into a search engine

In order for people to find your site (and what you're selling), they must be able to locate you. A popular way that people do this is by searching on a search engine. So you must submit your site to search engines. Go to the search engines that interest you and look for a link or a help area that will enable you to submit your site. Be sure to follow any specific instructions on the site; some may limit the amount of keywords and/or the characters allowed in your description.

To submit your URL to search engines, you need to do a little work (nothing's easy, is it?). Write down 25–50 words or phrases that describe your Web site; these are your *keywords*. Now, using as many of the words you came up with, write a description of your site. With the remaining words, create a list of keywords, separating each word or short phrase by a comma. You can use these keywords to add *meta tags* to the header in your HTML document for your home page. Meta tags are identifiers used by search engine *spiders*, robots that troll the Internet looking for new sites to classify on search engines. Meta tags are used like this:

```
<META NAME = "insert your keywords here" CONTENT = "short
          description of your site">
```

Yahoo! GeoCities

If you have a problem coming up with keywords, Yahoo! GeoCities has a handy meta tag generator that you can use for free. Go to http://geocities. yahoo.com/v/res/meg.html to use this tool.

Incidentally, Yahoo! is one of the more difficult sites to list with although you *can* get a free listing if you fill out all the forms right and want to wait six to eight weeks. Instructions for the free listing are at http://docs.yahoo.com/info/suggest/.

If you pay Yahoo! $299, you'll be listed immediately (funny how that works). Go to http://smallbusiness.yahoo.com/business_solutions/ promote_your_business.html for more details. Yahoo! guarantees that you'll be reviewed in just seven days.

MSN LookSmart

MSN LookSmart network has a list-for-pay deal. As a matter of fact, the only Web sites it lists have paid to be listed. For a two-day turnaround, Microsoft charges $299; for an eight-week turnaround, the fee is only $149. Visit http:// submit.looksmart.com/info.jhtml?synd=zdc&chan=zddsearch for more information.

Submit It

Submit It (www.submitit.com; see Figure 8-7), now part of bCentral, handles your site submissions to over 400 different online search engines automatically, saving you the trouble of going from site to site. For $59 a year, you can set up its service, which submits and resubmits as many as five URLs as often as you'd like, and sends you a regular report. Going from engine to engine to submit your site is far more time consuming. This is $59 well spent.

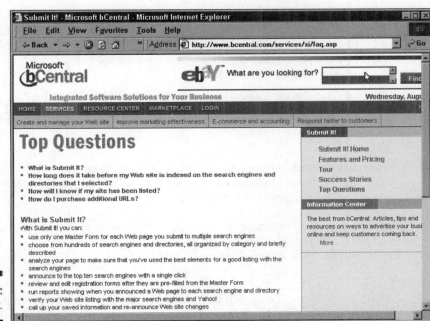

Figure 8-7:
Submit It.

Part III

Business Is Business — No Foolin' Around!

In this part . . .

Now it's time to delve into the dollars and sense of your auctions. In this part, I discuss automating your business by using online and offline tools, jazzing up your auctions, setting up your home photo studio, and handling shipping (the bane of most businesses). Working with customers and collecting payments is important, too, and this part is where I give you the lowdown.

Chapter 9

Software Built for Online Auctions

In This Chapter

▶ Figuring out what tasks you can automate

▶ Determining whether automation works for you

▶ Finding online auction management services

▶ Exploring auction management software

*N*ow that eBay has become a world marketplace, a single page auction or item listing is becoming an increasingly valuable piece of real estate. Millions view your sale, and the more auctions and fixed price items that you can list, the better your chance to make a good living. Time is money: You need to post your auctions quickly and accurately.

Auction posting, record keeping, inventory cataloging, photo managing, and statistic gathering are all tasks that you can automate. The more your business grows, the more confusing things can become. Automated tools can help you keep it all straight. But remember that the more tools you add, the more expense you may be adding to your business. Always keep your bottom line in mind when evaluating whether to use fee-based software and services.

In this chapter, I discuss how to automate which tasks, software that you can use to automate, and Web sites that offer services to make your daily chores considerably more bearable. After you read this chapter, you'll be well-equipped to decide whether or not you want to automate your business.

Considering Tasks for Automation

You'll have to perform certain office tasks, no matter how few or how many auctions you're running. Depending on your personal business style, you may want to perform any or all of the following tasks through automation. You may choose to use a single program, a manual method, or pick and choose some features from one program and some from others. If you aren't quite ready for the automated plunge, I offer you alternatives to automation as I go along. Where appropriate, I insert references guiding you to where in this chapter (or where in this book or on the Web) you can find more information about the automated services I discuss.

Setting up images for automatic FTP upload

You have several ways to store the display images in your auctions. If you're using an auction management service or software (such as Auctionworks.com or Auction Wizard, both of which I discuss later in this chapter), an *uploader* is usually included as a part of the software, but you'll have to set up your FTP information. Many online services merely fetch the photos from your hard drive without the need for additional FTP software. To accomplish this, you'll have to use a screen similar to the one from ManageAuctions.com (which I also discuss later) shown in Figure 9-1 (other sites are similar).

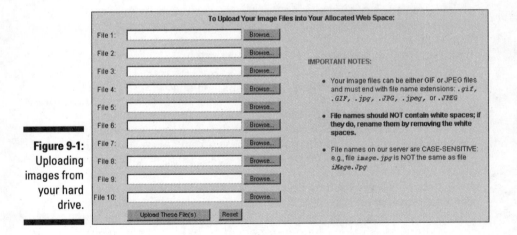

Figure 9-1: Uploading images from your hard drive.

With this format, you merely click the browse button to access the Open File window, and then find the location of the image on your hard drive. When you've located the images that you want to upload (one per line), just click the Upload button and the images are on their way to the service's servers.

If you choose to keep images on your own Web site (which makes the images available for your Web site, too), you'll have to use some sort of FTP software. You probably aren't using the total space that your hosting service allots to you for your Web site, making for plenty of room to store a separate folder of eBay images. ISPs often also give you several megabytes of storage space.

A straightforward standalone FTP software should be part of your auction arsenal, even if you use a service or other software (I always like to have a backup method of doing things). My personal favorite is CuteFTP Pro (see Figure 9-2) from GlobalSCAPE. CuteFTP Pro is so simple to use, I've never read the instructions. All I know is that to send files to a site, all you have to do is type in the location, your username, and password. Click connect and CuteFTP automatically connects to the site. From this point it's merely a drag and drop to move a file from the screen on the left (your hard drive) to the screen on the right (your Web site). A 30-day free trial is downloadable from www.globalscape.com. If you like it, you can register it for only $39.95.

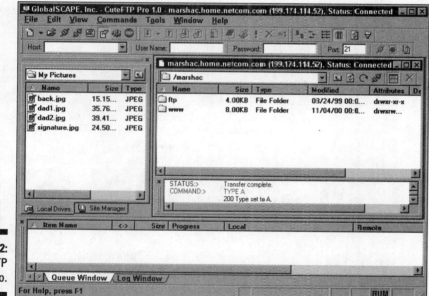

Figure 9-2: CuteFTP Pro.

Setting up your own auction photo gallery

Setting up a photo gallery is a great option — and I emphasize *option*. If your customers have a broadband connection, they're able to browse your auctions through photographs. Some auction management sites host your own gallery. Some charge for this service; others do not. The best part is that you can produce your own gallery without any fancy programs.

To make your own gallery at eBay, all you need to do is pay the additional 25 cents per auction and place eBay gallery photos for your listings. Use the following URL to set up your own gallery page, as shown in Figure 9-3. When using the URL, be sure to substitute your own user ID where indicated (in italics).

```
http://search-desc.ebay.com/search/search.dll?
        MfcISAPICommand=GetResult&query=youreBayuserID&ht=
        1&srchdesc=y&SortProperty=MetaEndSort&st=1
```

Insert the following HTML into your auction description to include a link to your gallery (see Figure 9-4). As you can see in the figure, this also inserts the custom eBay button. Be sure to put your User ID somewhere in the description. The code looks for this as the anchor

```
<a href="http://cgi6.ebay.com/aw-cgi/ebayISAPI.dll?
        ViewListedItemsLinkButtons&userid=youreBayuserID">
        <B>Click <I>here</I> to view my Gallery</B> <img
        src="http://pics.ebay.com/aw/pics/ebay_my_button.
        gif" alt="My Gallery on eBay"></a>
```

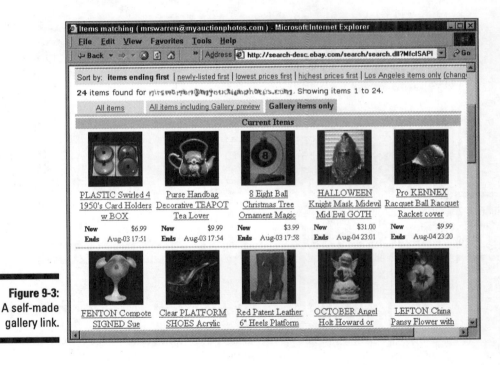

Figure 9-3:
A self-made
gallery link.

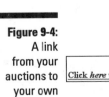

Figure 9-4:
A link
from your
auctions to
your own
gallery.

Sorting auction e-mail

Any auction software or system that you use must have the ability to send e-mail for you, but you must decide whether you want the program to receive e-mail as well. A vital function of any management program is the ability to customize and send e-mails to your winners. Many sellers use the default letters in these programs, which tend to be a bit — no, incredibly — impersonal and uncaring. (To see some examples of customer-friendly e-mails and tips on drafting your own, head to Chapter 12.)

The computer resident auction management programs, Auction Wizard and Auction Wizard 2000 from Standing Wave Software, Inc. and eBay's Seller's Assistant, have their own built-in e-mail software that functions as part of the program. When you download your winner information from eBay, it automatically generates invoices and congratulatory e-mails. See the section "Auction Wizard and Auction Wizard 2000" for more details. Ultimately, you must decide how to handle your auction-related e-mail. Although I use Auction Wizard 2000 to send auction related e-mails, I choose to receive auction e-mail through Outlook, using a separate folder titled Auctions that contains sub folders for eBay Buy and eBay Sell.

Automating end-of-auction e-mail

If you want to set up e-mails to be sent automatically after an auction ends, you must use a software application to do so. The software must download your final auction results, generate the e-mail, and let you preview the e-mail before sending it out. Many of the online sites that I discuss later in this chapter (see the section "Online auction management sites") send out winner confirmation e-mails automatically when an auction is over; be sure that you set your preferences to Preview if you want to use this option.

Keeping inventory

Many eBay power sellers depend on the old clipboard or notebook method — crossing off items as they sell them. If that works for you, great. Others prefer to use an Excel spreadsheet to keep track of inventory. Many modern automated ways are available to handle your inventory.

Most of the auction management packages that I detail later in this chapter (see the section "Auction management software") handle inventory for you. Some automatically deduct an item from inventory when you launch auctions. You have your choice of handling this directly on your computer or keeping your inventory online with a service that's accessible from any computer, wherever you are.

Generating HTML

Fancy auctions are nice, but fancy doesn't make the item sell any better. A clean listing with as many photos as necessary goes a long way to sell your product. Some of the software and services offer a large selection of templates to gussy up your auctions. But you must think of your customers; many of them are still logging on with dial-up connections, which are notoriously slow. The use of simple HTML doesn't slow the loading of your page, but the addition of miscellaneous images (decorative backgrounds and animations) definitely makes viewing your auction a chore for those dialing up. While I'm at it, forget the background music — it *really* slows things down!

Don't fret; you can make do by repeatedly incorporating two or three simple HTML templates, cutting and pasting new text as necessary. Most auction management programs (including Auction Wizard and Seller's Assistant; see the section "Auction management software") offer you several choices of templates. I recommend that you stick with a couple that are similar, giving a standardized look to your listings, just the way major companies give a standardized look to their advertising and identity. Your customers will get used to the look of your auctions, and reach a comfort level each time they open one.

If you're in a rush and need a quick and easy HTML generator, go to my Web site at www.coolebaytools.com and click where it says Click to JAZZ UP Your Auctions.

Posting or relisting auctions with one click

Using an auction software or service really speeds up the process of posting or relisting items. After you input your inventory into the software, posting and/or relisting your auctions are a mouse click away. All the auction management software packages that I detail later in this chapter include this feature.

If you buy your items in bulk, eBay offers a free relisting tool. By clicking the Relist this item link (see Figure 9-5) on any completed auction, you can automatically relist your items. If the item didn't sell the first time, and sells upon relisting, you won't pay a second listing fee. You can also relist through your MyeBay Selling page, by clicking the Relist link in the Items I've Sold area.

One of my favorite sellers uses the eBay relist feature even to post new auctions. She merely clicks the relist link, and then cuts and pastes her new information into the existing HTML. Her auctions all have the same feel and flavor to them, and that's why.

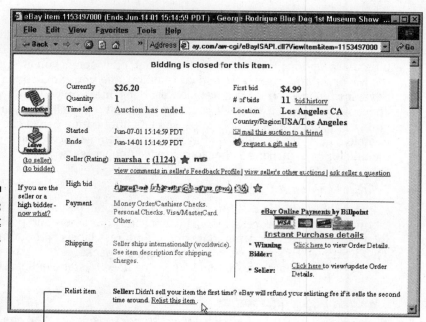

Figure 9-5:
The Relist
this item
link on a
completed
auction
page.

Click here to relist an unsold item.

Scheduling your listings for bulk upload

If you want to schedule the unattended launch of your auctions, you must use a software or online management service (check out the sections detailing these programs and services, later in this chapter). If you can be at your computer to do it, you can use the Mister Lister application (which I also detail later in this chapter) that eBay offers to you at no charge.

Automating other tasks

That's not all! There are a few more tasks that you can also automate. Having so many options is like being in a candy store: You may want them all, but they may not be good for you — in one way or another. If you use online postage, you may not want to print out your labels because that would be doubling your work. Take a serious look at the options you're offered and see if they fit into your particular work style. You don't have to use every option you're offered.

Checking out

eBay's checkout integrates directly with eBay Online Payments (Billpoint), so if that's all you want to use for your auctions, that's all you need. But if you offer many options when a buyer checks out, eBay sends you an e-mail with the buyer's shipping address and information, and you can arrange for payment. Online auction management services offer you your own private checkout area, which will cost you, and you must decide if this is an option you want to pursue. A personalized winner's notification e-mail can easily contain a link to your Billpoint, PayPal, or payment service (which you can include for free), making a checkout service unnecessary.

Printing shipping labels

Printing shipping labels without printing postage can be the beginning of a laborious two-step process. Stamps.com prints your labels and postage all in one step. Some sites print your winner's address labels without postage. That works well if you don't mind carrying your packages to the post office for postage. (Why would you do that? A burning need to stand in line, I guess!)

Tracking buyer information

Keeping track of your winners isn't exactly rocket science. You can do it in an Excel spreadsheet or in a Word document, which are exportable to almost any program for follow-up mailings promoting future sales. If you choose to have an online management service do this for you, be sure that you can download the information to your computer (in case you and the online service part ways someday).

Generating customized reports

Sales reports, ledgers, and tax information are all important reports that you should have in your business. Online services and software, such as those discussed below, supply different flavors of these reports.

PayPal allows you to download your sales data into a format compatible with Intuit QuickBooks, a highly respected and popular bookkeeping program. Billpoint, eBay's payment service, has a download area where you can download Excel spreadsheets (they also work in Microsoft Works) that are chock full of intensely detailed information about your sales and deposits. Putting this information in a standard accounting software makes your year-end calculations a bit easier to bear. (In Chapter 16, I detail what else you might need for this chore.)

Submitting feedback

If you're running a lot of auctions, leaving feedback can be a chore. One solution is to automate the submission of feedback. But, timing the automation of this task can be tricky. One thing to remember is never to leave feedback for an eBay transaction until after you've heard from the buyer that the purchase is satisfactory. Leaving positive feedback immediately after you've received payment from the buyer is too soon. After you receive an e-mail assuring you that the customer is satisfied, manually leaving feedback by going to the feedback forum can be just as easy — if not easier — as bulk-loading feedback.

Managing Your Business with Online Resources and Software

If you searched the Internet for auction management services and software, you'd come up with a bunch. For simplicity's sake, I've chosen to examine just a few of these services in this chapter. After speaking to many sellers, I've found online services that offer uptime reliability (uptime is key here; you don't want the server that holds your photos going down or mislaunching your auctions) and software that's continually updated to match eBay changes.

Using a site or software to run your auctions takes practice, so I suggest that you try any that appeal to you and that offer free preview trials. I can't possibly list each and every feature of these different applications. As I list and describe them, I include a current link so that you can check them out further. In Table 9-1, I compare the costs of the auction management software and online services that I discuss throughout the rest of this chapter.

Table 9-1	Cost Comparisons for Auction Management
Site or Software	*Cost*
AuctionHelper.com	1.5% of sales (15 cents–70 cents); $10/month (minimum)
Auction Wizard Software	$35 (one-time fee)
Auction Wizard 2000 Software	$75 (one-time fee)
AuctionWorks.com	2% of sales (10 cents–$3.00); $14.95/month (minimum)
ManageAuctions.com	5 cent listing fee; $4.95–$24.95/month
Microsoft bCentral Commerce Manager	$24.95/month
Seller's Assistant Software	$4.99/month
Seller's Assistant Pro	$15.99/month

Some software and services work on a monthly fee, whereas others work on a one-time purchase fee. For a one-time-purchase software application to truly benefit you, it must have the reputation for updating its software each time eBay makes a change in its system. The programs that I discuss throughout this chapter have been upgraded continually to date.

Online auction management sites

Auction management Web sites handle almost everything, from inventory management to label printing. Some sellers use every feature a site offers, whereas others select a bit from column A and a bit from column B, often doing some of the more personalized tasks manually. Read on to determine what service might best suit your needs.

Although there are quite a few excellent online services for automating sales, I only have room here to show you a few. Remember that by using an online service, your information resides on a server out there in cyberspace; if you're a control freak, it may be a bit much to bear. Many services are similar in format, so in the following sections, I point out some of the highlights of a couple of representative systems. That way at least you'll know what you're looking for.

Please remember that these two are certainly not the only two in the online auction management arena. Some other very popular ones are

> andale.com
>
> AuctionWatch.com
>
> ChannelAdvisor.com
>
> ManageAuctions.com
>
> Zoovy.com

Most services have a free trial period. Be sure that you don't spend a bunch of your precious time inputting your entire inventory, only to discover you don't like the way the service works. Input a few items to give the service a whirl to decide whether you like it without investing a heap of time.

AuctionHelper

AuctionHelper (www.auctionhelper.com) can make listing your eBay auctions an absolute pleasure. Currently, it has patents pending on 55 unique claims to proprietary tools and technology that can make your auction business run smoother.

Some high-volume eBay sellers looking for an easier way to handle their auctions started the company, making the site's system intuitive for the experienced eBay seller to navigate. The main highlights of AuctionHelper include

- ✔ **Item and inventory management:** Includes calendar- and time-based (dates and times for launching) auction scheduling, automated auction launching and relisting, the ability to import past or current auctions, and the ability to import auction data from a spreadsheet or database.

- ✔ **Templates:** The site offers more than 40 predefined templates that can give your auctions a professional look. Be careful here, as it may be tempting to use the "themed" templates. Stick to the more basic version so that you can give a universal look to your auctions.

- ✔ **Image hosting:** Offers unlimited space in which to store pictures. You have your choice to either upload bulk images from its Web site or FTP your images directly.

- ✔ **Auction reporting:** Generates current running auction statistics — the total number and dollars of current and past auctions (up to 30 days; as many as 5,000 auctions) — and an itemized report of each auction.

- ✔ **Post-auction management:** Allows you to send (manually or automatically) a variety of customized e-mails to winners and non-paying bidders. You're able to link directly to AuctionHelper to create an invoice or include links to PayPal and Billpoint. The site also provides a secure credit card entry form.

  The post-auction management features also include the ability to send automatic feedback and to create mailing labels for each sale. So that feedback isn't posted until you're sure the transaction is successfully completed, you have the option of disabling the automatic feedback feature.

Two unique features that set AuctionHelper apart from other auction management sites are

- ✔ **AuctionLynxx:** A patent-pending, Java-based tool, AuctionLynxx (see Figure 9-6) cross-advertises your auction items both within your auctions or through global Internet advertising. eBay has given this technology its approval and doesn't consider it keyword spamming. (See Chapter 4.) It automatically updates itself as you post auctions to provide accurate listings for all your auctions within one concise area.

- ✔ **Front Runner:** The proprietary way of retrieving auction numbers for your items *prior* to you listing them, this amazing tool allows you to reserve and print out item numbers ahead of time to prepare items for shipping, or to use the auction numbers in advertising and/or promotions. Use this feature to print out thank you notes to include in shipments and to draw customers to upcoming auctions.

Figure 9-6:
AuctionLynxx
placed in
your auction
can cross-
reference
to all your
other
auctions
from one
auction
page.

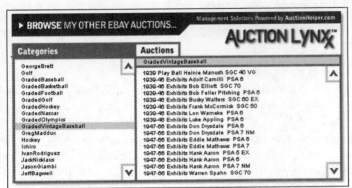

AuctionHelper offers a 30-day free trial to new users and is offering an additional $20 credit to the cost of its services for readers of this book. For more information, go to www.AuctionHelper.com/ebayfordummies.html.

Auctionworks

A group of collectors who saw the need for power tools for power sellers developed this highly graphic site (www.auctionworks.com). I think they've succeeded. The site touts a high percentage of eBay power sellers who use it. That's great for the power sellers, but I want to know what Auctionworks can do for you and me.

The site offers help links at every turn, a first-rate online tutorial, free toll-free support (that's a free phone call and free support), and free interactive training classes for registered users. The site integration is broad, featuring

- **Item and Inventory management:** Features the ClickLaunch Single Step Launcher, which launches individual items to auction while simultaneously adding them to inventory. (The site also has a bulk item launching capability.) You can import existing auctions from eBay and import files from Mister Lister, Seller's Assistant Basic and Pro, Excel, and MS Access. Auctionworks integrates your items throughout its system and into your Auctionworks gallery and storefront. You can use its simple but effective basic templates in your choice of over 60 different color schemes.

- **Image hosting:** Enables you to bulk upload 15 images at a time to its servers. The basic account allows 100MB of storage. If your images average 30K each, you should be able to upload almost 3,500 images into the 100MB image hosting space. If you need legroom for your images, your monthly minimum fee increases as follows: 250MB, $24.95; 500MB, $49.95; and 1GB, $99.95.

- ✔ **Auction reporting:** Generates accounts receivable, item history, and post-sales reports from the Reports area. Auctionworks has its own Traction System for sales and item tracking.

- ✔ **Templates and Listing:** Auctionworks uses their own trademarked Ballista template listing system. You can use their predefined color templates or use their macros with your own predefined HTML template, substituting the macros for stock areas in your template. Auctionworks has developed a very unique method of letting you make the choice of how your template looks. By using their custom ad template option and their very well-thought-out macros, you can take your own HTML and make an Auctionworks template.

- ✔ **Bulk importing utilities:** If you keep your current inventory in Microsoft Excel or Access, you will be able to import your current data seamlessly into their site. They even offer sample spreadsheets so that you'll know how to identify the cells. If you are currently using Seller's Assistant (Basic or Pro) or even eBay's Mister Lister, you'll be able to import your data directly. For Mister Lister, they use their own utility, Mr. Lister Twister. You download this small program onto your own computer and run it. Then open Mister Lister and submit batches to eBay. The catch? Mr. Lister Twister intercepts the batches and imports the data directly into your Auctionworks inventory. Anyone who uses eBay's listing program has plenty of backups of their old inventory items — this importing utility will save a great deal of time.

- ✔ **Post-auction management:** Sends out automated e-mail to your winners, linking them back to its proprietary ClickOut checkout system. If customers want to pay with Billpoint or Paypal, they have to link from there. Auctionworks combines multiple wins for shipping and invoicing.

  You have the option to set six different feedback notices, which you choose at the time of posting.

Auctionworks features Auctionworks Gallery, which links directly to your current eBay auctions. The Gallery is part of each member's Auctionworks StoreFront (see Figure 9-7). When you load items into inventory, you have the choice of immediately listing them in your StoreFront. All your items are seamlessly integrated.

You pay no additional charge to set up a StoreFront or Gallery. If an item sells from your StoreFront, you pay the usual two percent commission. Your StoreFront has its own URL: www.auctionworks.com/awstore/ yourauctionworksuserid.

To get current information and sign up for a free two-week trial, go to http://www.auctionworks.com/freetrial.asp.

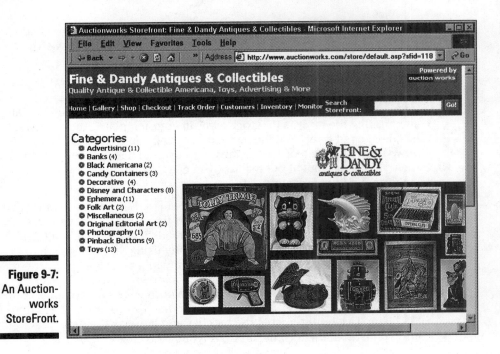

Figure 9-7:
An Auction-
works
StoreFront.

ManageAuctions.com

Some highly educated, really smart people got together and founded ManageAuctions.com (www.manageauctions.com), making magic with their code and offering many features that the big guys also offer. Although you might have to study the site a bit to get up and running, its online tutorials should guide you through the intricacies of the software.

To use ManageAuctions.com, you pay a minimum $4.95/month. At no extra charge, you're able to take advantage of its enhanced counter statistics, automated feedback posting to your downloaded eBay auctions, and photo hosting. Its counter statistics are unlike any other you'll find: The counter gives you total hits broken down hour by hour, day by day (see Figure 9-8). You pay a five-cent listing fee and no percentage on gross sales, so this site may be an excellent choice for using selected features.

ManageAuctions.com will also host your Web site for as low as $9.95/month and integrate a gallery from your eBay auctions. (See Chapter 8 for more information about your Web site.)

Don't be put off by the site's lack of graphic beauty; it makes up for it with robust features:

✔ **Item and inventory management:** Provides tools that launch auctions automatically, with or without a time delay. Import your auctions from eBay to inventory items for future launching from the ManageAuctions.com site. It offers three basic templates that should do for most auctions. You can also use your own HTML to design auction descriptions.

✔ **Post-auction management:** Merges your winning auction information and generates customized e-mail to your auction winners. Choose to send e-mails automatically or manually and post feedback from one of 11 feedback phrases that you personally design.

Figure 9-8:
A completed auction's statistics at Manage-Auctions.com.

Auction Site: eBay.com;   Seller ID: marsha_c;   Item #: 1153497000
George Rodrigue Blue Dog 1st Museum Show Book

Day\Hour	00	01	02	03	04	05	06	07	08	09	10	11	12	13	14	15	16	17	18	19	20	21	22	23
06/08/2001			1	1		1		1	1			1				1		1						
06/09/2001							2		1		1	1									2	1		
06/10/2001						1		1				2					1		1		1			
06/11/2001		1						1	2					3		1	1	4					1	
06/12/2001			1				1	2		1	1			2	2	1	3		1					
06/13/2001		1			1				1		1			1	3	2							1	
06/14/2001		1								1	1		2	4										
06/15/2001																2		1						
Totals	0	3	1	2	1	1	4	1	6	2	4	4	1	4	11	6	7	1	7	2	2	0	2	

> **TIP**
>
> Take the ManageAuctions.com tour at `auction1.inetu.net/cgi-bin/show_page?p=tour` to find out about its free 45-day trial period.

The Microsoft bCentral commerce manager

Surprise! Microsoft is getting into the e-commerce management arena. Who'd a thunk it? Microsoft is offering a commerce manager through bCentral (see Figure 9-9). An amazing tool that you can use to transform your inventory into an online catalog and sell in marketplaces all over the Internet, bCentral gives you the ability to sell products on *any* FrontPage-based Web site.

The bCentral Commerce Manager is a subscription-based add-in that even allows you to create templates for your product pages, shopping cart, and order processing features (including optional credit card processing). It notifies you of purchases via e-mail and keeps track of open orders and payments. Here are a few of the standard features:

✔ **Inventory and item management:** You have a central dashboard that automates sales and inventory management. Use this tool to push your product lists to Web sites, participating marketplaces, and even eBay.

✔ **Sales reporting:** They provide sales history reposts for your item sales.

For new features and information, visit `www.bcentral.com/services/cm/default.asp`.

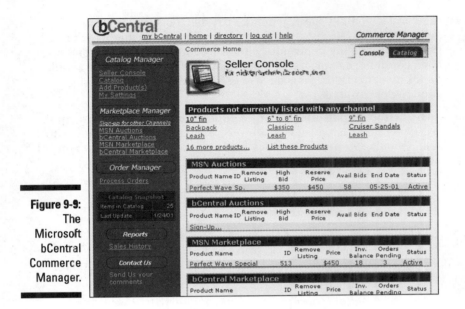

Figure 9-9:
The
Microsoft
bCentral
Commerce
Manager.

Auction management software

Many sellers prefer to run their auction businesses from their own desktops. I happen to like the option of being able to reference my old auctions on my backups. Luckily, some valuable auction software programs are available to perform all the same tasks you get from the online services.

To those who would rather have the software at home, there are quite a few solid choices other than the ones I examine below. You might also want to visit the following sites for their auction management software:

> Auctiontools.net
>
> Auctiva.com
>
> foodogsoftware.com

You can accomplish almost all the same tasks on your own computer as you can with online services — except online auction checkout (you can always use eBay's checkout as your final stop or include a link in your end of auction e-mails). If you want, you can always set up a checkout page on your own Web site that gathers your auction information.

Unfortunately, some of the auction management software packages require that you use their strange, off-size (ever see an eBay auction that forces you to scroll to the right to see the entire thing?) and off-color templates. Remember that the photos of your items will all be in different colors and if you choose a template with set colors, the template may seriously clash with photos of your items. Whenever you can, stay with neutral (black, gray, and white) templates, and only add complementary colors to your headlines. I suggest you examine a program's templates carefully before you decide which one to use.

Auction Wizard and Auction Wizard 2000

Way back in 1999, Standing Wave Software developed a product that would handle large inventories and that would meet the needs of the growing eBay population. Enter Auction Wizard. In 2000, the company introduced a more robust version, Auction Wizard 2000, while still maintaining and updating the more basic Auction Wizard software for users who don't need all the bells and whistles. Standing Wave Software has been updating the software continually to meet the challenges presented by the changes at eBay.

The basic edition, Auction Wizard, is for the sporadic seller, and the Auction Wizard 2000 is a major management program for your home computer. To check out which program is for you, visit the page www.auctionwizard2000.com/Compare.htm.

This software is a tour-de-force of auction management whose pieces are integrated into one program, including tools for

- Maintaining inventory (cost and item location in your warehouse/office)
- Preparing and listing auctions (see Figure 9-10)
- Managing e-mail
- Updating auctions
- Automating feedback
- Incorporating HTML templates
- Utilizing the Web Wizard
- Tracking income and expenses

Auction Wizard generates invoices and e-mails, helps you post your feedback, and enables you to generate 37 reports on your auctions, including reports for shipping, finance, and more. The program interface is pretty straightforward. I always plunge into new programs without reading the instructions, and I was able to use the program right off the bat. I'm still not a whiz at it, but that's probably because Auction Wizard 2000 has so many features that I haven't had the time to study it all.

Auction Wizard imports up to 11 image formats, converts them into the JPG format for use at eBay and your Web site, and crops, rotates or resizes the images for your auctions. It has its own built-in FTP software (so that you can upload your pictures while you're working on your auctions), eliminating the need for another piece of auction business software.

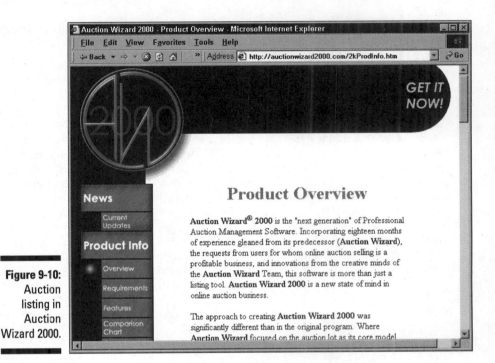

Figure 9-10:
Auction
listing in
Auction
Wizard 2000.

To begin using the Auction Wizard software, simply download your current eBay auctions directly into the program. When your auctions close, send out customized e-mails (the program fills in all the auction information into pre-defined fields) and manage all your end-of-auction business. Some sellers launch their auctions by using Mister Lister (see the section "Mister Lister" at the end of this chapter), and then retrieve them and handle the end-of-auction management with Auction Wizard.

Auction Wizard 2000 builds upon the original program by offering more features: support for eBay stores, automatic listing and relisting, auction description spell checking (to save you from embarrassing typos), image editing, auction fee tracking, and Seller's Assistant Pro data import. Believe it or not, there's more to it, so visit www.standingwavesoftware.com to compare programs and to take advantage of the free software trial (30 days for Auction Wizard and 60 days for Auction Wizard 2000) to determine if this is just what you need.

Since 1999, this program has been building fans in the eBay seller's community. Fans of the program recently set up an internet discussion board at http://pub83.ezboard.com/bauctionwizarddiscussionboard. Aside from the technical support given by Auction Wizard, users get together here to discuss new features and how to use them.

Seller's Assistant Basic and Pro

Of the two versions of Seller's Assistant, Basic and Pro, the professional version of Seller's Assistant is what you're really going to need to use for your eBay business. Because the software is owned by eBay, it is the first to have the latest updates to eBay's latest changes.

The program is available on a monthly subscription fee from eBay, and it is charged to your regular eBay bill. The set-up, as with other management programs, takes a while. With this program, you have the option of using IPIX for your photos if your Web site goes down for any reason.

eBay's Seller's Assistant Basic is a solid listing program, offering a variety of templates (known as *themes;* it comes with 20 and you can download more online — as many as 170). Seller's Assistant automatically inputs your standard shipping information and auction messages into your auctions so you don't have to retype them every time. Customize your e-mail correspondence: Seller's Assistant generates standard e-mail messages after retrieving your completed auction information from the site. The program is available on a monthly subscription fee from eBay, which is charged to your regular eBay bill.

The Pro version (which supports multiple user IDs) takes things up a notch, handling your auction listings as well as automating bulk listing and end-of-auction business. The Pro version will

- ✔ Spell check your auction listings
- ✔ Schedule your auction launches for a later posting (see following tip)
- ✔ Keep track of your inventory
- ✔ Launch items directly from stock at hand

Automating bulk-feedback posting, printing shipping labels, and creating sales reports are all more options you'll enjoy with Seller's Assistant Pro, shown in Figure 9-11.

AAPro's Template studio can be a bit of a challenge until you're used to it. Seller's Assistant Pro comes with a gaggle (yes, a gaggle) of various "themes." The good thing about the themes is that you can put your picture anywhere you want in the description. The bad part is you have no control of the spacing of the lines of text. Also, you need to go through each and every theme to find one you like. The names aren't very descriptive. Can you figure out what "The Real Thing" looks like? (Yep, its red.) Or how about "Abby's Room"? (Pink, of course!) Most of the themes are a bit busy, and you won't see colors or typefaces like these on professional Web sites. Luckily, they're all editable, so you can customize a look for your auctions.

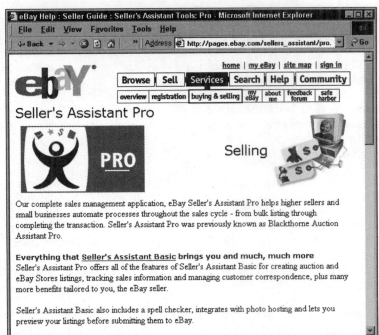

Figure 9-11:
Go to the
Seller's
Assistant
page on
eBay for
the free
downloads.

One of the finer points of the Pro edition is that you can schedule your auction listings for a particular time and space out your auctions (within a group of items to be listed) by a set number of minutes. This is valuable because so many bidders bid during the last few minutes of the auction, when the highest bidding takes place.

To check out the latest changes and upgrades, and to compare the two program versions, visit `pages.ebay.com/sellers_assistant/compare.html`.

Mister Lister

I like Mister Lister because it's simple and easy to use. When I plan to be away from my home computer, I can input a few auctions before I leave town, and then review and launch them from another computer with Mister Lister. When the auctions are over, I download the final results to a management program at home. You can use Mister Lister to bulk launch a bunch of auctions without fuss or muss.

Using Mister Lister is as simple and straightforward as posting a Sell Your Item form. But to use the free eBay Mister Lister application, you must first fulfill the following requirements:

✔ Have a credit card registered with eBay

✔ Have a feedback rating of 10 or more

✔ Be an eBay member for at least 60 days

Mister Lister allows you to prepare auctions while offline and group them for launching at eBay. Using the program is a two-step process. First, you must download the application from eBay `http://pages.ebay.com/services/buyandsell/composer-info.html`.

After you've installed Mister Lister on your computer, you can list auctions on the easy to use form (see Figure 9-12) and send them all to eBay in a group. After sending the auctions to eBay, you have two weeks to launch them. When you're ready to get the auctions or store listings online, go to the Mister Lister reviewer, preview and edit the auctions as necessary, and then when you're happy with everything, launch the entire batch at once. What could be simpler?

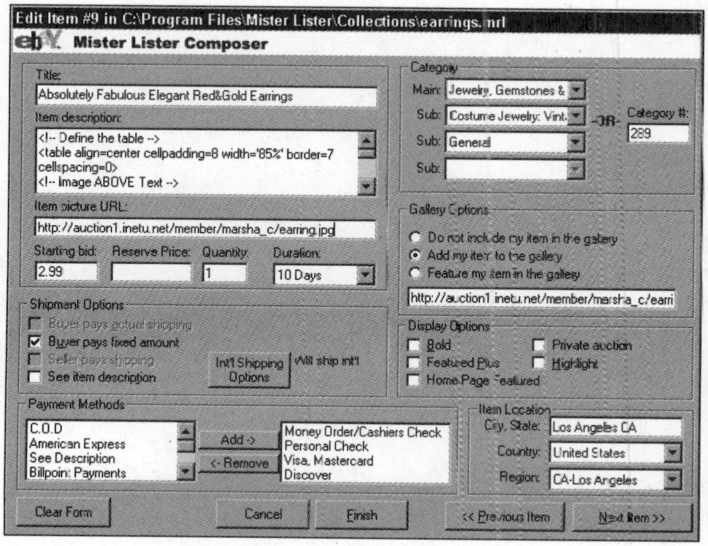

Figure 9-12: A Mister Lister-composed listing on your home computer.

Mac users, rejoice!

Yes, Mac users, there's finally a software that you can use to list your auctions at eBay. Pre-Lister 3 by Black Magik Software is a full powered offline listing software that allows you the freedom to write up auctions on your own time. Pre-Lister 3 can interface with Mister Lister (see the section "Mister Lister" elsewhere in this chapter) so that after you've written your auctions on your computer, you can send the data directly to the Mister Lister hub and launch your auctions all at once. Pretty cool! Download this softwarefrom www.blackmagik.com/gavelware.html for just $35; it's updated regularly to conform to any changes in eBay listing procedures.

Chapter 10

Dollars and Sense: Budgeting and Marketing Your Auctions

In This Chapter

▶ Marketing your listings by choosing the right category

▶ Using promotional options to your advantage

▶ Paying eBay: The lowdown on basic fees

*Y*our entire online business is just that: a business. In every business, decisions are made regarding how much money is spent for each division of the company. Because you're the head of your company, you must make these decisions. Even if you're running auctions on a part-time basis, you still have to consider budget concerns. The one area that you don't have to set aside money for is shipping and fulfillment because, gratefully, the eBay model allows that the buyer pays your shipping and handling costs (see Chapter 14 for more on shipping).

When you list an item for sale at eBay, you must consider what the item will sell for, in what category to list it, and whether to add any of the eBay listing options. Even if you've managed to purchase an item at an incredible price, you don't have to cut your own profits to market it (see Chapter 7 where I discuss knowing the value of your items). Establish a minimum percentage that you assign as your profit so that you can determine how much to spend on your advertising budget.

Although millions visit eBay each day to view and possibly buy any of the items up for sale there, you still must consider making your item stand out — you must advertise it. If your item has a considerable amount of competition in its category, you may want to add some of the options eBay offers to make folks notice it and want to buy it. The cost of these options (or advertising) needs to fit into your established advertising budget for the particular item.

In this chapter, I give you a preview of the various options eBay offers its users, highlighting the cost of these options along the way. I also detail the basic eBay fees. When you're done with this chapter, you should be well on your way to establishing a working budget and have a handle on marketing your items.

Listing Your Items

With over 8,000 categories, finding the right place for your item can be daunting. (For more on eBay categories, see Chapter 2.) Placement in a category may seem obvious, but you need to apply some marketing techniques when deciding where to place your auctions. You should also be thinking about your budget; you can list an item in two separate categories, but you have to pay double for that. Does your budget allow for it?

To find where other sellers have listed items that are the same as or similar to yours, go to the Find Items search page and click the <u>Search Results by Category</u> link in the upper right corner. This takes you to the page shown in Figure 10-1. Now type your item keywords in the Search Title box (see Figures 10-1 and 10-2). You may find that your item is listed successfully in more than one category. If you see that you aren't one of the few selling the item but one of about forty or fifty, you need to get creative as to where to list your item. The key is evaluating the item and its potential buyers. In what categories would someone shopping for your item search?

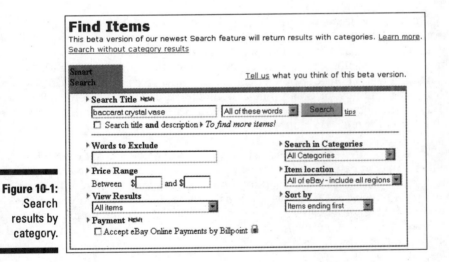

Figure 10-1:
Search
results by
category.

Suppose you've found not one but two perfect categories in which to list your item. eBay does allow you to list an item in two categories (see Figure 10-3), but does that mean it's the best marketing decision for your auction? That depends. When you list an item in two categories, you must pay two listing fees. Depending on the time, season, availability of your item, and how much you paid for it, you may or may not have the money to budget for listing an item twice. Many eBay buyers are becoming quite savvy in using the search engine. They may search for your item via the search engine rather than by browsing the categories, which may possibly make your listing the item in two categories a needless expense.

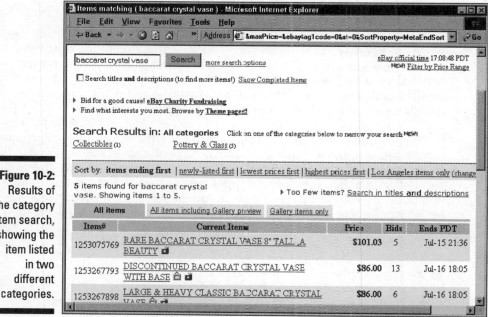

Figure 10-2: Results of the category item search, showing the item listed in two different categories.

You can always change your category mid-auction, starting it in one category and ending it in another. If you list the item in one category and it doesn't sell, you can always use the relisting feature to run the auction again in another category.

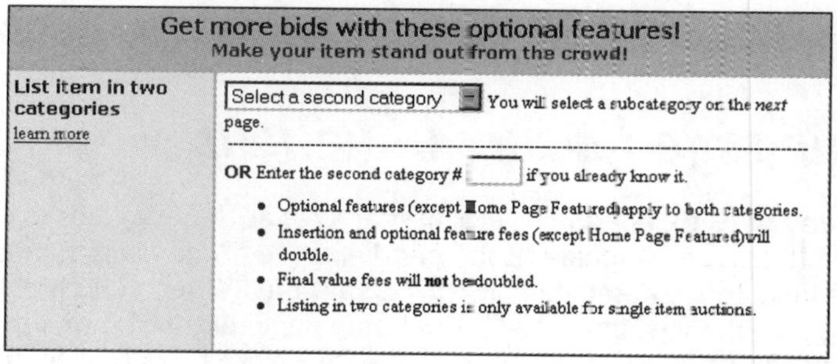

Figure 10-3: List your item in two categories.

eBay's Optional Listing Features

When you come to the point in listing your item that brings you to eBay's optional listing features, you see the headline, "Get more bids with these optional features! Make your item stand out from the crowd!" Sounds pretty good, doesn't it? But getting carried away by these options is easy and can lead to spending all your expected profits before you earn them.

In the eBay University Advanced Selling class, instructors quote auction conversion rates for the features, but in the real life of your business, it really varies from auction to auction and category to category. If you take the bold-face option and then your auction appears in a category full of boldface auction titles, the bold just doesn't have the punch you paid for. Your auction would stand out more without the bold option. It's the same with highlighting. Certain categories are loaded with sellers that go overboard in the use of this feature — all the auction titles appear in a big yellow blur.

As you consider the options, you must weigh the pros and cons in terms of how these options affect your eBay business. Will spending a little extra money enhance your item enough to justify the cost? Will you be able to make the money back in auction profits? You must have a good understanding of what the options are and when and how you can use them to their fullest advantage.

In every auction you run, you have to pay an insertion fee for listing your auction, a final value fee (I discuss these two fees in the section "eBay's Cut of the Action" later in this chapter), and a fee to the payment service for accepting a credit card. After estimating your expenses from these basics, you can then consider spending money for advertising by using the options that I highlight in the following sections.

Home page featured auctions

A user who goes to www.eBay.com first arrives at the eBay home page. A Featured Items area appears in the middle of the home page; beneath this area are links to six home page featured auctions. When you click the all featured items link (see Figure 10-4), the home page featured items page appears (see Figure 10-5). Most of these items are Dutch auctions that feature hundreds of items at a time. Many also feature items that list for over $1,000.

Figure 10-4:
The <u>All</u>
<u>Featured</u>
<u>Items</u> link on
the eBay
home page.

Featured Items   *all items...*
- The Black Cauldron Original Production Cel
- Lose 75lbs In 1month? Guaranteed Weight Loss
- Photo Paper War! Try Finding A Lower Price!
- Lose 80 Lbs By Sept!? Best Diet Pill! $9.95!
- Syringe Of Blood or Red Ink Pen? Dr's Luv em!
- "chinese Cash" 1979 by O.D. Cresswell 120 Pgs
- *all featured items...*

The home page featured auction option will set you back $99.95. If you've got hundreds of widgets or a big ticket item to sell, you've found the perfect location to draw an audience that may easily earn back your $99.95. People who are new to eBay come in through the front page; this is prime real estate. The six auctions that are actually featured on the home page rotate at random throughout the day.

Another benefit of this option is that if someone searches your keywords or browses through your category, the front page featured auctions appear at the top of the page (along with the Featured Plus! auctions, which I describe in the following section). But you must keep in mind how much you're paying for this feature. Unless your auction is going to bring you more than a few hundred dollars, this feature probably isn't worth the extra overhead.

Figure 10-5:
The Home
Page
Featured
Items page.

Status	Featured Items - Current	Price	Bids	Ends PDT
🔒📷	4102 Tokay PGClos St Urbain Rangen deThann 89 🔍	$1000.00	-	Jul-21 21:00
🔒📷	CYLINDRICAL VASE, decorated with the New Mk 🔍	GBP 90.00	-	Jul-21 15:30
🔒📷	ALLEN JONES (b. 1937) Chest 1968 Fibreglass 🔍	GBP 2,400.00	-	Jul-18 23:00
🔒📷	CARVED GILDED WOODEN FRAME 60 plus year old 🔍	$30.00	-	Jul-18 02:30
🔒📷	EBAY'S #1 DIET PILL! FREE SHIPPING!	$12.95	-	Jul-25 14:22
🔒📷	~ STERLING TWO CARAT STUD EARRING SET ! ~	$4.99	-	Jul-18 14:17
🔒📷	BUILD & REPAIR COMPUTERS LIKE A PRO- On Sale!	$7.95	-	Jul-22 14:12
📷	#1 Diet Pill @eBay! Get FREE Samples Here! 📷	$0.05	-	Jul-25 14:02
🔒📷	WORLD'S #1 DIET PILLS GUARANTEED FAST RESULTS 📷	$12.95	-	Jul-25 13:36
🔒📷	WORLD'S #1 DIET PILLS GUARANTEED FAST RESULTS 📷	$12.95	-	Jul-25 13:34
📷	AIRCRAFT TOOL CLECO PLIERS +10 FASTNERS NoRes	$17.95	-	Jul-22 13:07
📷	XYRON 850 Laminator STICKERMAKER w/75' supply	$1.00	-	Jul-25 12:58
🔒	GREAT WOOL AUBUSSON 5'x8' AREA RUG 📷	$159.99	-	Jul-25 12:53

Featured Plus!

Featured Plus is an option that I've actually used with much success. When you choose the Featured Plus option, your auction will be listed at the top of the page when a shopper searches for keywords or browses category listings. Although your auction doesn't appear on the eBay home page (see the previous section), it will appear at the top of your selected *category* home page (see Figure 10-6).

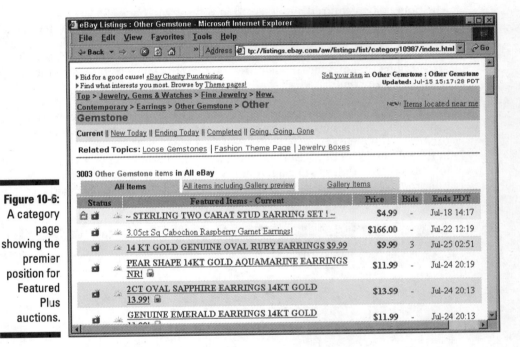

Figure 10-6:
A category page showing the premier position for Featured Plus auctions.

For just $19.95, you get extra exposure, but you still must consider your auction budget. How much do you expect your item to sell for? Will the $19.95 expense benefit your auction enough to justify the expenditure? Be sure that your item will bring you more than a couple of hundred dollars before choosing this option.

Highlight option

I was very excited when eBay announced this option. I'm a big fan of highlighting books, reports, and the like. Ever since college, I can't read a book without my trusty neon-yellow highlighter. Highlighting makes anything stand out on a white page of text. This works just as well at eBay as it does on paper.

Unfortunately, as with anything in life, less is more. If you choose to list your auction in a category where all the sellers decide to use this option, the only listings that will stand out will be the ones *without* the highlighting.

The highlighting feature will set you back just $5. Does your budget allow for that? To give your auction title a punch for a smaller amount of money, consider the bold option that I highlight in the following section.

Boldface option

This is my favorite, and probably the most used option in the eBay stable. An auction title in boldface type will definitely stand out in a crowd, unless . . . you got it, unless it's in a category loaded with boldface auction titles. Odds are if the $2 that eBay charges for this benefit is in your auction budget, it will get you a good deal more views than if you didn't use it. Boldface is an exceptional buy; I suggest going for it whenever you can.

To recap your title option costs, see Table 10-2 in the section "Listing fees" later in this chapter.

View counter

Counters have become a popular free option in the online world. Placed on your auction by an outside service at your request, the numeric view counter ticks up each time someone loads your page from eBay. This can add up to some very impressive numbers — impressing bidders (convincing them they're viewing a hot deal) or impressing other sellers to run out and sell the identical item at eBay.

A counter is a terrific tool for marketing your auctions — sometimes. If you have an auction with no bids and a counter that reads a high number, newbie bidders may be dissuaded from taking a flyer and bidding on your auction. Their thinking is if that many people looked at this auction and didn't bid, something must be wrong with the item. They'll tend to doubt their own instincts as to what's a good deal and what isn't. In a situation such as this, however, what really might be going on is that savvy bidders are just watching your auction, waiting to bid at the last minute.

A *private counter* shields the actual numbers from the eyes of casual lookie-loos. The actual figures are available to only you through a password protected login page. Private counters come in different flavors. Some of the most helpful private counters are available from ManageAuctions.com (see Figure 10-7), which offers a breakdown of visitors hour-by-hour. It offers counters for free, and also gives you 5MB (for free) of image hosting just for signing up. More on the ManageAuctions.com services in Chapter 9.

Auction Site: eBay.com;			Seller ID: marsha_c;				Item #: 580920588																
NWT $220 Diane Von Furstenberg Silk Dress 8																							
Day\Hour	00	01	02	03	04	05	06	07	08	09	10	11	12	13	14	15	16	17	18	19	20	21	22	23
04/18/2001											2		3	2	3	1	3	4	4	2	1	1	2	
04/19/2001						1			3	2		1	2		1	2			2		2	1		
04/20/2001					1	1	2	1		1	3	1	3	1	2	3	1	2	2			3	1	
04/21/2001	1					1	2			1	3	1	1				2		1					3
04/22/2001	1			1				1			3	1			1	4	4	1	2	2				
04/23/2001	2		2			1	1	3		4	6	2	1	1		2	2	2	2	1	2	1		
04/24/2001	4		2			3	1	6	2	1	3	3	10	7	10	9		1		1		1		

Figure 10-7:
A Manage-Auctions.com private counter.

eBay offers you a free counter, but you must sign up with Honesty.com (a branch of ándale.com) to get it. I don't think it's a good idea to sign up on too many Web sites; it's the key to receiving more and more e-mail that you don't want to read because they sell your name from one to the other. If you want to get a counter, I recommend that you sign up where you can get other free benefits as well. You can apply a counter from almost any auction management Web site; it doesn't have to be from Honesty.com.

The Gallery

eBay bills the gallery as its "miniature picture showcase," and indeed it is. In the gallery, a thumbnail image (96 x 96 pixel size) of your item appears next to your listing in the category, which can reap you many benefits. When someone runs an auction search, eBay defaults to showing all items, and that includes a gallery preview (see Figure 10-8). Users have to select the listings only option on the search results page if they want to see only listings. This makes choosing the 25-cent option a worthwhile expenditure. If your item is only going to sell for $10, however, I recommend that you reconsider the extra charge.

Don't get carried away with the idea that a large percentage of bidders are going to view their search results in the Gallery Items Only mode, which results in pages featuring gallery photos and titles only. Those who know what they're doing — and who are searching for a deal — aren't going to dismiss auctions without gallery photos. The newbies — or anyone for that matter — with dial-up connections may not have the patience to wade through pages of slow-loading images.

eBay also offers to feature your gallery photo on the top of gallery-only pages for $19.95. These photos run three across the top of the page (see Figure 10-9), rather than the five across for the regular gallery pictures. These featured gallery pictures are larger (140 x 140 pixels) than the regular gallery pictures.

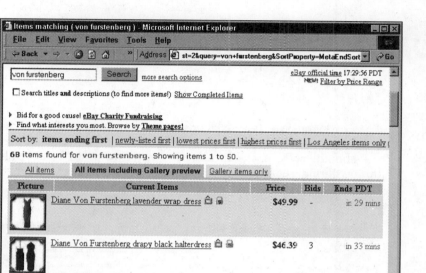

Figure 10-8:
An eBay
search; note
the gallery
photos.

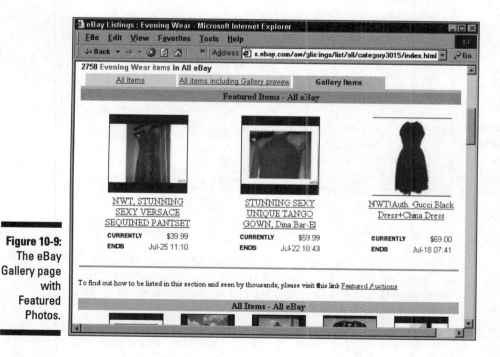

Figure 10-9:
The eBay
Gallery page
with
Featured
Photos.

TIP

If you take advantage of the Gallery, be sure to crop your photo tight to the subject. For more help with your images, see Chapter 11.

Buy It Now

The *Buy It Now* feature (see Figure 10-10) has a couple of significant benefits. If the item you're listing is one that you have a predetermined idea of what you should get for it, make that your Buy It Now price. You can also use this option during frenzied holiday shopping times. Try posting a slightly higher than normal price and perhaps you'll get a bite, er, sale.

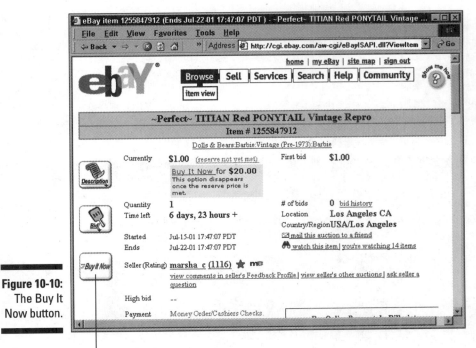

Figure 10-10:
The Buy It Now button.

Buy It Now

This feature will disappear when a bid is placed on the item. If you've placed a reserve on the auction, the Buy It Now button doesn't disappear until a bidder meets your reserve price. Combine this with the eBay Instant Purchase feature, which I detail in Chapter 13.

As of the day I'm writing this book, this feature adds nothing to the cost of your listing. eBay currently says it's free during the promotional period, which is currently almost a year old. eBay may begin to charge for the Buy It Now feature by the time this book is out. In that case, remember my golden rule and before paying for this feature, ask yourself: "Is it in my budget?"

To use this feature, you must have a feedback rating of at least 10, or be ID Verified. (ID Verify is eBay's secondary form of identification on the site, permitting you to participate in the site without submitting a credit card, see Chapter 3 for more info.) You also cannot use Buy It Now with a Dutch auction.

eBay's Cut of the Action

Although becoming complacent and blithely ignoring your eBay costs as you list items for sale is easy to do, it isn't a good idea. As a person in business for yourself, you must always take into account outgoing costs as well as incoming profits. The cost of your initial listing is the beginning of your advertising budget for that item. Your final value fee is what you pay eBay. For fees regarding your eBay store, check out Chapter 5. In this section, I review the costs for listing an auction at eBay.

The fees I'm detailing here aren't the end of your fees. If you use a credit card payment service, it will also charge you a fee. In Chapter 13, I examine the costs of the most popular credit card payment services.

Listing fees

Your listing fee is based on the highest dollar amount from two things: your minimum opening bid or the dollar amount of your reserve price. So if you start your auction at $1 and set an undisclosed reserve price of $50, your auction will cost $2.20 to post. (If you start the bidding at $1 and have no reserve, the listing fee is 30 cents; see Table 10-1.)

If your item doesn't sell, don't think you can get your insertion fees back. They are non-refundable. You do have the option of relisting your unsuccessful auction without being charged a second listing fee, but *only* if your item sells with the second listing. If it doesn't sell, you *will* be charged again. Writing a better title, starting with a lower opening bid, or adding a snappier description will definitely help in selling the item. Maybe you should think about changing the category as well.

In Table 10-1, I summarize listing fees for you.

Table 10-1	eBay Listing Fees
Opening Bid or Reserve Price	*Insertion Fee*
1 cent–$9.99	30 cents
$10–$24.99	55 cents
$25–$49.99	$1 10
$50–$199.99	$2 20
$200 and more	$3.30

Whether you're listing one item with a starting bid of $1,000 or 100 items for $5 each in a Dutch auction, your insertion cost per auction is never more than $3.30.

I recap the cost of the various eBay listing options in Table 10-2.

Table 10-2	eBay Listing Option Fees
Option	*Listing Fee*
Home Page Featured	$99.95
Featured Plus!	$19.95
Highlight	$5
Bold	$2
Gallery	25 cents
Gallery featured	$19.95
List in two categories	Double listing fee
Ten-day auction	10 cents added to your listing fee

eBay Final Value Fees

eBay's version of the Hollywood back-end deal is the final value fee. Big stars get a bonus when their movies do well at the box office; eBay gets a cut when your auction sells. After your auction ends, eBay charges the final value fee to your account in a matter of minutes. We all know that the fee exists, but even a rocket scientist would have trouble figuring out exactly how much eBay receives at the end of your auction. To help you calculate how much you'll owe eBay, see Table 10-3.

Table 10-3	Final Value Fees
If Your Item Sells Between	*You Pay a Final Value Fee Of*
1 cent–$25	5% of the selling price
$25.01–$1,000	5% on the first $25 plus 2.5% on selling prices of $25–$1,000
$1,000 and up	5% on the first $25 plus 2.5% on selling prices of $25.01–$1,000 plus yet another 1.25% on selling prices over $1,000

An auction in the Real Estate category is *not* charged a final value fee. Successful auctions in the eBay Motors category, however, are charged a flat $25 final value fee.

The editors of *eBay For Dummies* and the people who proofed the book spent days confirming the figures in Table 10-4. I must repeat them here because these figures and calculations may prove useful to you and also because I may never be able to figure them out again.

Table 10-4	Sample Prices and Commissions	
Closing Bid	*Price Percentage*	*What You Owe eBay*
$10	5% of $10	50 cents
$256	5% of $25 plus 2.5% of $231	$7.02
$1,284	5% of $25 plus 2.5% of $974.99 plus 1.25% of $248	$28.72
$1,000,000	5% of $25 plus 2.5% of $974.99 plus 1.5% of $999,000	$15,010.62
$1,000,000	5% of $25 plus 2.5% of $974.99 plus 1.5% of $999,000	$15,010.62

Chapter 11

Jazzing Up Your Auctions

● ●

In This Chapter

▶ First things first: Writing a great description

▶ Setting up a photo studio

▶ Shooting great pics: It's a snap!

▶ Scanning your items

▶ Kicking it up with imaging software

▶ Hosting your pics

▶ Finding HTML templates

● ●

Rule #1: A good photograph and a concisely written description should be the goal for all of your auctions. My years of advertising experience have proved this to me over and over again in almost every type of media. Bright and cheery colors are fun but often overdone. If you're trying to fetch the highest possible bid for an item, you must keep your auction listings simple and professional: no dancing clowns (unless you're selling clowns), no overdone graphics, and no difficult-to-read typefaces. Less is more.

To make this clear, I devote this entire chapter to writing eye-catching descriptions and improving the visual elements of your auction listings. After reading this chapter, you should have a pretty good idea of what you need to do to doll up your auctions. From there, you can make decisions regarding what you want to do and how to best accomplish your goals.

Writing Winning Text

When you write the descriptions for your auctions, be sure that you describe your items clearly and completely. Mention everything about the article; be honest and even mention flaws or damage. When you're honest up front, you'll have a happy bidder. Remember to include your terms of sale and specify what type of payments and credit cards you accept. Be sure to include your shipping charges, too. Following is a checklist of things to mention:

- ✔ Size, style, color

- ✔ Condition (used, new, gently used, well-worn)

- ✔ Manufacturer's name

- ✔ Year of manufacture (if important to the item)

- ✔ Fabric/material the item is made of (if fabric/material is an issue)

- ✔ Any and all damage to the item

- ✔ Any special features that apply to the item

- ✔ That you've stored it in a clean, dry place (if you have)

After you list all the facts, get a little flowery in your description. Think infomercial! Think Shopping Channel! They make things sound so good that you feel that you *must* have whatever item they're selling. You can do the same, if you just take the time. In Chapter 12, I give you some more pointers on writing the best auction descriptions possible.

Your eBay Photo Studio

Taking pictures? No problem! You've got a digital camera, and you know how to use it. Just snap away and upload that picture, right? Sorry, but no. There's a good way and a bad way to take photos for eBay and, believe it or not, the professional way isn't necessarily the most expensive way. I recommend that you set up a mini photo studio in which you take your eBay auction pictures, so you don't have to clean off your kitchen counter every time you want to take pictures. By setting up a photo studio, you'll have everything in one place, always set up and ready for you to take any photos that you'll need. Remember that last time when you got a real find at a garage sale and ran into the house to take a picture so that you could list the item as soon as possible, and then you had to spend 20 minutes setting things up? No more; you're going to have a small photo studio in your eBay office.

You need several things in your photo studio; what extras you need will be based on the type of merchandise that you're selling. An eBay *generalist,* someone who'll sell almost anything online — like me! — should have quite a few extras for taking quality photos. Check out my home photo studio in Figure 11-1. You may not be making a living as a photographer, but your photographs can help sell your merchandise. You need to start taking this portion of your business seriously.

What you find throughout this section might be more than you thought you'd need to take good pictures. Of course, if you only sell one type of item, you won't need such a varied selection of stuff, but you should have the basic photo setup. Go into it slowly, spending only as much as is prudent for the time, and check my Web site (www.coolebaytools.com) for more ideas.

eBay Seller's Photo Lighting Kit

Tired of your auctions having fuzzy pictures? The answer is to use this professional photo light kit, designed for online images. It consists of two 10" reflectors with zinc die-cast stand adapters. Each reflector has an integrated ceramic socket for bulbs as high as 250 watts, with wood handling knobs. Two 6 foot all metal adjustable stands complete the kit. The kit comes with a short image tutorial by the author of "eBay for Dummies".

Bid with confidence and win this set at close to wholesale price as it is selling with NO RESERVE! Winning bidder to pay shipping & handling of $9, and must submit payment within a week of winning the auction. Credit cards are accepted through Billpoint and PayPal. Good luck!

GOOD LUCK, HAPPY BIDDING!

Click below to...
View my other auctions - Win more than one and $AVE on shipping!

Figure 11-1: My eBay photo studio, which I'm featuring here in an eBay auction.

Digital camera

Digital cameras are mysterious things. You may hear a lot about *mega pixels* (a million pixels) and know that more is supposed to be better, but that doesn't apply to eBay applications or to Web images. Mega pixels measure the image resolution that the camera is capable of recording. For your use, a 1.5 mega pixel camera is the high end. All you need from a camera is 640 x 480 pixels because computer monitors are incapable of taking advantage of more pixels. If you use a higher resolution picture, all you'll do is produce a pixel-bloated picture that takes a looooong time to load online.

You don't need a million pixels, but here's what you really do need:

- **Quality lens:** I'm sure anyone who has worn glasses can tell the difference between a good lens and a cheap one. Really cheap cameras have plastic lenses, and the quality of the resulting pictures is accordingly lousy. You want to keep your camera as your workhorse for a while, so be sure to buy a camera from a company that's known for making quality products.

- **Removable media:** Taking the entire camera to your computer and using extra software to download pictures to your hard drive is pretty annoying. Removable media eliminates this annoyance. The most popular are Smart Media cards (black wafer-thin cards) and Compact Flash cards (in a plastic shell); both are about the size of a matchbook. You can insert these cards into floppy disk adapters that fit into the floppy disk drive on your computer, or you can get an adapter that connects to your computer through a USB or parallel port. You can get either at eBay for about $30.

- **Tripod/tripod mount:** Have you ever had a camera hanging around your neck while you're trying to repackage some eBay merchandise that you've just photographed? Or perhaps you've set down the camera for a minute and then can't find it? Avoid this hassle by using a tripod to hold your camera (a camera mounted on a tripod doesn't take blurry pictures because of shaking hands). To do so, you need a tripod mount, the little female screw hole that you see in the bottom of some cameras. See the following section where I give you some tips on finding the right tripod.

- **Macro Setting Capability or threading for a lens adapter:** If you're ever going to photograph coins, jewelry, or small detailed items, these tools will come in handy. A camera's macro setting enables you to get in really close to items while keeping them in focus. A *threaded lens mount* enables you to add different types of lenses to the camera for super macro (like coins and jewelry) or other uses.

- **Autofocus and zoom:** These options just make life easier when you want to take pictures. The ability to zoom in and keep things in focus should pretty much be standard features.

The bottom line here is to buy a brand name camera. I use an Olympus D-600L. It's outdated, but it's also loaded with all the bells and whistles I need for eBay photos. I bet you could find a camera that fits your needs right now at eBay for less than $200. Many professional camera stores also sell used equipment, where you might find a bargain.

Other studio equipment

Certain endeavors seem to be open pits that you throw money into. I promise that your eBay photo studio will not be one of these pits; and unlike some things, you won't have to spend much on it in the future.

Tripod

A tripod is an extendable aluminum stand that holds your camera. You should look for one that has a quick release so that if you want to take the camera off the tripod for a close-up, you don't have to unscrew it from the base and then screw it back on for the next picture.

The legs should extend to your desired height, should lock in place with clamp type locks, and should have a crank-style geared center column so that you can raise your camera up and down for different shots. Most tripods also have a panning head for shooting from different angles. You'll be glad you have one. You can purchase a tripod from a camera store or at eBay for as low as $25.

Power supplies

If you've ever used digital cameras, you know that they can blast through batteries faster than sugar through a five year old. A reliable power supply is a must. You can accomplish this in a coupla ways:

- ✔ **Rechargeable batteries:** Many specialists at eBay sell rechargeable batteries and chargers. Pick up the quality Ni-MH (nickel metal hydride) batteries because this kind has no memory effect. That means you don't have to totally discharge them the way you would the old style Ni-Cad (nickel cadmium) batteries.

- ✔ **Portable power:** If you're interested in a portable power supply, you can always use something like the Power Pak 6 from Battery Busters, which you can use with anything that requires a 6-volt power supply. It comes with an attractive case and can be recharged over 550 times; it has no charging memory. You can also use it for your video camera (up to 12 hours a charge) or other small electronic devices. Go to www. batterybusters.com to find it.

Because your eBay photo studio will have your camera on a tripod, you can also easily use the good, old-fashioned AC adapter (you know, it's the one that plugs into the wall) that comes with some digital cameras.

Lighting

Taking good pictures of your merchandise can be frustrating. If you try to do it in the kitchen, you don't have enough light. Add in the camera's flash? Now the image is all washed out. If you take the item outside, the sun might cast a shadow. Sometimes it may seem almost impossible to take a good picture.

I've seen eBay sellers using a flash and instructing their children to shine flashlights on the item to be photographed from a different angle, all the while hoping that the color doesn't totally wipe out. Some digital cameras have issues in low light, and the autofocus won't work very well. I finally gave up on this and went to an expert. You need to have proper lighting to take good, in-focus pictures with a digital camera because it can't focus properly without enough light.

I've contacted some specialists in the photo business, to solve the digital camera lighting problem. To solve it, I'm putting together a special, inexpensive (under $100) studio lighting set for online auction photography. Please check my Web site (www.coolebaytools.com) for information on how to obtain this package. It's the same one that I successfully use in my home photo studio; refer to Figure 11-1.

Professional studio lights can be expensive, but you might also be able to find a set — you need at least two lights: one for either side of the item so that you don't cast a nasty shadow — for around $150. Search eBay for used studio lighting; I'm sure you'll find a good deal.

Props

To take good photos, you're going to need some props. While you may think it strange that a line item in your accounting program will read "Props," props do qualify as a business expense. (Okay, you can put it under photography expense; *props* just sounds so Hollywood!) How often have you seen some clothing at eBay from a quality manufacturer, but you just couldn't bring yourself to bid more than $10 on it because it looked like it had been dragged behind a car for miles, squished up, and hung on a hanger before it was photographed? Could you really see how nice the outfit was? Could you see how the fabric would hang on a body? Of course not. Take a look at Figure 11-2; that dress looks simply fantastic, darling!

Diane Von Furstenberg BRAND NEW with tags!
100% Silk Jersey dress
Fits Size 6 or 8
This lovely silk number is THE sexiest dress! It's by hot designer Diane Von Furstenberg (who is featured in the new issue of Vogue). It's a fabulous silk jersey spaghetti strap dress, with a sexy cowl neckline. The original price of the dress is $220, and it can be yours for the highest bid. Draping beautifully on the body, it's got a sexy below the knee length and a very flattering cut.
Bid with confidence and bid whatever you feel this great dress is worth to you as it is selling with NO RESERVE! Winning bidder to pay shipping & handling of $5.25, and must submit payment within a week of winning the auction. Credit cards are accepted through Billpoint and PayPal.

GOOD LUCK, HAPPY BIDDING!

Click below to...
View my other auctions - Win more than one and $AVE on shipping!

Figure 11-2: A mannequin-modeled auction.

Mannequin

Don't recoil — and I hate to even say it — but if you're selling clothing, you'd better photograph it on a mannequin. If you don't want to dive right in and buy a mannequin, at least get yourself a body form to wear the outfit. Just search eBay for "mannequin" to find hundreds of hollow forms selling for less than $20. If you sell children's clothing, get a child's mannequin form as well. Same goes for men's clothes. If worse comes to worst, find a friend to model the clothes. There's just no excuse for hanger displayed merchandise in your auctions.

I got my mannequin (Midge) at a department store liquidation sale here in Los Angeles. I paid $25 for her. Her face is a little creepy, so I often crop her head out of the photos. She has a great body and everything she wears sells at a profit. Many stores upgrade their mannequins every few years or so. If you know people who work at a retail store, ask when they plan to sell their old mannequins; you may be able to pick one up at a reasonable price.

Steamer

Clothing is fairly crumpled when it comes out of a shipping box. It may also get crumpled lying around, waiting for you to photograph it and sell it at eBay. If the clothing isn't new but is clean, run it through your dryer with Dryel (the home dry cleaning product), which will take out any musty smells. There's nothing like old, musty-smelling clothes to sour a potentially happy customer.

The clothes you want to sell may be wrinkled, but ironing is a bear (and may damage the fabric), so do what the retail professionals do: use steamers to take the wrinkle out of freshly unpacked clothing. Get the kind of steamer that you use while the article of clothing is hanging up, so you can just run the steamer up and down and get the wrinkles out. The gold standard of steamers is the Jiffy Steamer. It holds a large bottle of water (distilled only), rolls on the floor, and steams from a hose wand. They sell for about $140, and I've seen some selling at eBay. Until you're ready to make an investment that big, get a small handheld version that removes wrinkles; search eBay for "garment steamer" to find some deals.

Display stands, risers, and more

Jewelry does not photograph well on most people's hands and actually looks a lot better when it's displayed on a stand (see Figure 11-3). If you're selling a necklace, display it on a necklace stand, not on a person. I bought my display stands from a manufacturer; I didn't receive the stands until several months after ordering them. Apparently, this type of quality display stand is made to order, so I recommend searching for them at eBay (you'll get them sooner).

Risers can be almost anything that you use to prop up your item to make it more attractive in a picture. Put riser pieces that aren't attractive under the cloth that you use as a background.

You wouldn't believe what the back of some professional photo setups look like. Photographers and photo stylists think resourcefully when it comes to making the merchandise look good — from the front of the picture, anyway! Throughout my years of working with professional photographers, I've seen the most creative things used to prop up items for photography:

Ralph Lauren Signed Silver 16' Necklace

This stunning, brand new designer necklace is just the right length, 16" – and adjustable for smaller necks. Signed on reverse of stirrup goldtone plate *(see photo below)*, also signed on the silver toggle. Your chance to get this retail $48 necklace for a fraction of the cost! The perfect gift for you or a friend.

Bid with confidence and bid whatever you feel this item is worth to you, as it is selling with *NO RESERVE*! I pack all my items carefully. Winning bidder to pay shipping & handling of $3, and must submit payment within a week of winning the auction. I will accept credit cards through BillPoint and PayPal - Good Luck, Happy Bidding!

Figure 11-3: Auction featuring a professional jewelry display.

- ✔ **Bottles of mercury:** Mercury is a heavy liquid metal. A photographer I once worked with used little bottles of this stuff to prop up small boxes and other items in a picture. But mercury is a poison, so I suggest you do the same with small bottles (prescription bottles work well) filled with sand.

- ✔ **Beeswax and clay:** To set up photos for catalogs, I've seen photographers prop up fine jewelry and collectible porcelain with beeswax (the kind you can get from the orthodontist works great) or clay. Beeswax is naturally a neutral color and doesn't usually show up in the photo. However, you must dispose of beeswax often because it picks up dirt from your hands and fuzz from fabric.

- ✔ **Metal clamps and duct tape:** These multipurpose items are used in many photo shoots in some of the strangest places. Your mannequin may be a few sizes too small for the dress you want to photograph. How do you fix that? Don't pad the mannequin; simply fold over the dress in the back and clamp the excess material with a metal clamp, or use a small piece of duct tape to hold the fabric taut.

Keep a collection of risers and propping materials in your photo area, so they're always close at hand.

Background fabric or paper

In professional photo-talk, *seamless* is a large roll of 6-foot (and wider) paper that comes in various colors and is suspended and draped behind the model and over the floor. (Ever wonder why you never see the floor and wall come together in professional photos?) Photographers also drape the seamless over tabletop shots and use fabrics in place of seamless; muslin is a popular choice.

I keep a selection of different fabrics on hand: velvet (be sure to clean black velvet with sticky tape before you use it in a picture — lint grows giant in pictures) and satin. Colors can clash with your items and distract from them, so I recommend selecting a few neutral fabrics for photographing your merchandise. Use only neutral colors (such as white, light gray, natural, and black) to eliminate the need to buy a bunch of different fabrics to go with different items.

Taking Good Pictures

If you have a small home photo studio setup (see the previous section) with a quality camera, tripod, props, and lights, you're well on your way to taking some quality shots for your auctions. A few things to remember:

- ✔ **Zoom in on your item:** Don't leave a bunch of extraneous background in your pictures. Crop out extra background in your photo editing program (see the section "Image Editing Software" a bit later in this chapter) before you upload the images to your image hosting service.

- ✔ **Watch out for distracting backgrounds:** If you don't have a studio tabletop, or if the item is something that won't fit on a table, try to make the background of the photo as simple as possible. If you're shooting the picture outside, shoot the picture away from chairs, tables, hoses — you get the idea. If you're shooting in your home, move the laundry basket out of the picture.

One of my favorite eBay pictures featured a piece of fine silver taken by the husband of the lady selling the piece at eBay. Silver and reflective items are hard to photograph because they pick up everything in the room in their reflection. In her description the lady explained that the man reflected in the silver coffeepot was her husband and not part of the auction. She handled that very well!

- ✔ **Be sure the items are clean:** Cellophane on boxes can get rather nasty-looking, clothing can get linty, and all merchandise can get dirt smudges. Not only will your items photograph better if they're clean, they'll sell better, too.

Clean cellophane with Goo Gone or even WD-40; both will take off any sticker residue and icky smudges. Un-Du is the best adhesive remover for paper, cardboard, clothing, and more, plus it comes with a handy plastic scraper. I also keep a clean eraser around to clean off small dirt smudges on paper items. Any cleaning solution helps your items (even a little 409), but use these chemicals with care so that you don't destroy the item while cleaning it.

✔ **Check the camera's focus:** Just because the cameras today come with the autofocus feature doesn't mean that the pictures automatically always come out crisp and clear. Low light, high moisture, and all kind of things can contribute to blurring your images. Double-check the picture before you use it.

Using a Scanner

Scanners have come a long way in the past few years. A once expensive item can now be purchased new for just over a hundred dollars. If you sell books, autographs, stamps, or documents, a scanner may be all you need to shoot your images for eBay.

When shopping for a scanner, don't pay too much attention to the resolution. As with digital cameras, images (JPEGs) for the Internet shouldn't be any higher than 72 dpi (dots per inch). Any quality scanner can get that resolution these days. Quality makes the difference in the manufacture of the scanner, so stick with brand names.

You should use a *flatbed* scanner, on which you're able to lay out your items and scan away. I replaced my old scanner with an HP OfficeJet, which is not only a scanner, but a printer and reducing/enlarging color copier, too — some even come with a fax! These nifty flatbed units are available brand new at eBay. I've seen the HP R40, new in box, sell for as low as $200.

A few tips on scanning images for eBay:

✔ If you're taking traditionally processed photographs and scanning them on a scanner, have them printed on glossy paper because they'll scan much better than those with a matte finish.

✔ You can scan 3D items, such as a doll, on your flatbed scanner and get some respectable-looking images. To eliminate harsh shadows, lay a black or white t-shirt over the doll or her box so that it completely covers the glass. This way you'll have a clean background and you'll get good light reflection from the scanner's light.

✔ If you want to scan an item that's too big for your scanner's glass, simply scan the item in pieces, and then re-assemble it to a single image in your photo editing program (see the following section).

✔ Boxed items are a natural for a flatbed scanner. Just set them on top of the glass, and scan away. You can crop out the shadowed background with your photo editing software (see the following section).

Image Editing Software

Lose the idea that the software that comes with your scanner is good enough. It may well be just fine for some uses, but the kind of control that you need is only available in *real* image editing software, not a mere e-mail picture generator.

I use — and recommend most highly — Adobe Photoshop. I realize that the program is a bit of overkill for online use only, but it processes and compresses absolutely beautiful images for the Internet. You don't have to pay a fortune for the product either; used versions are available at eBay (see Figure 11-4). I've seen brand new packages of Photoshop 5.5 sell for as low as $150 (if you're a good shopper, I know you *can* find these deals).

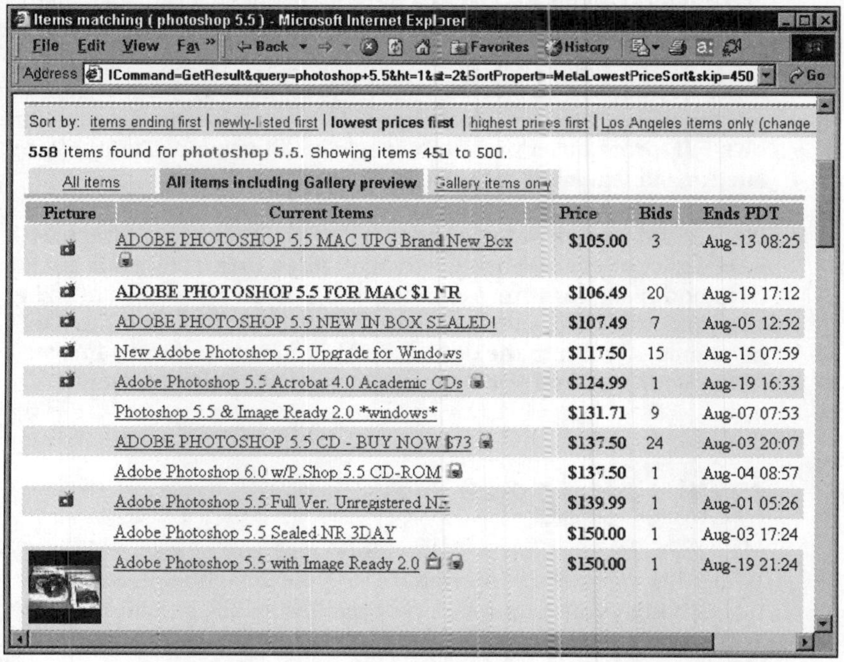

Figure 11-4: eBay completed auction search for Photoshop 5.5.

Picture	Current Items	Price	Bids	Ends PDT
	ADOBE PHOTOSHOP 5.5 MAC UPG Brand New Box	$105.00	3	Aug-13 08:25
	ADOBE PHOTOSHOP 5.5 FOR MAC $1 NR	$106.49	20	Aug-19 17:12
	ADOBE PHOTOSHOP 5.5 NEW IN BOX SEALED!	$107.49	7	Aug-05 12:52
	New Adobe Photoshop 5.5 Upgrade for Windows	$117.50	15	Aug-15 07:59
	Adobe Photoshop 5.5 Acrobat 4.0 Academic CDs	$124.99	1	Aug-19 16:33
	Photoshop 5.5 & Image Ready 2.0 *windows*	$131.71	9	Aug-07 07:53
	ADOBE PHOTOSHOP 5.5 CD - BUY NOW $73	$137.50	24	Aug-03 20:07
	Adobe Photoshop 6.0 w/P.Shop 5.5 CD-ROM	$137.50	1	Aug-04 08:57
	Adobe Photoshop 5.5 Full Ver. Unregistered NR	$139.99	1	Aug-01 05:26
	Adobe Photoshop 5.5 Sealed NR 3DAY	$150.00	1	Aug-03 17:24
	Adobe Photoshop 5.5 with Image Ready 2.0	$150.00	1	Aug-19 21:24

Photoshop 5.5 gives you control of the images and offers features that enable you to make a good picture out of a bad one. It also has an awesome export to Web feature that compresses the images so that they hold their quality while becoming smaller. Images compressed in this fashion download a lot quicker for dial-up customers.

You're going to be making graphics and images for your Web site as well; check out Chapter 8 for more about putting together a Web site. Figuring out just a little bit of Photoshop can take you a long way, so check out a copy of

Photoshop For Dummies, written by my buddy Deke McClelland (and published by Hungry Minds, Inc.). It's an excellent Photoshop primer and an entertaining read as well.

Here's a surprise: The photo editor that comes with the Auction Wizard 2000 software does a respectable job of editing your images. See Chapter 9 for more about this software.

A Home for Your Images

You need a professional and safe place to store your pictures for eBay. If your images don't appear when someone clicks your auction, or if your images take too long to load, a user might click off your auction and go to the next one. If you have more than one option, test each with a few pictures because you want one that's reliable.

If you use auction management software, you may not need an FTP program to upload your images. Most complete management programs integrate their own FTP program as part of the package. Check out Chapter 9 for more about auction management software packages.

You should always put your eBay images in a separate directory — not in an active part of your Web site. You may think that using your business Web site is a good place to store your images, but it isn't. If you want to keep track of your site statistics, such as number of visitors, hits, and the like, hosting your own images will ruin the data. A call for one of your eBay images counts as a hit on your site, and you'll never get accurate Web site stats.

Free ISP space

Most ISPs (Internet Service Providers) give you at least 5MB of storage space. While this space isn't appropriate for your final business site, it's a perfect place to host your pictures. Everyone has an ISP, and all ISPs give you space. You may have to use an FTP program to upload to your Web space, or your ISP may supply its own uploader. Check the home pages for your ISP (go to the member area) and check out what it offers. Visit Chapter 8 for more information on free ISP space.

AOL will try to get you to build some kind of hometown page, but here's what to do instead: Go to the Internet tab at the top of the AOL page frame and click FTP. When another screen appears, click the Go to FTP link. Whew, you're almost there. Now click the FTP site members.aol.com and you're taken to your FTP area. From there you can upload all your files to a maximum of 2MB per screen name. Remember which photos are stored in each screen name FTP space because the URL locator for each screen name is different.

Auction management sites

If you're using one of the auction management Web sites that I discuss in Chapter 9, you're covered. These Web sites supply enough Web space to hold all your eBay images. They also have their own one-click uploads from your hard drive; very convenient.

Paid image hosting

If you're running the auction business on your own, you're going to need a place to store your pictures. A few sites out there specialize in hosting images for online auctions.

MyAuctionPhotos.com is one such site. For a flat $26.95 a month, MyAuctionPhotos.com will host as many as 500 images for you on a private FTP site with unlimited downloads. If you have an item that you will repeat many times, you may have them host a minimal amount of items at $2.00 each. For more information on rates and services, visit its Web site.

eBay IPIX

You can also use the eBay IPIX service, but the quality of your photos is better if hosted directly from a site. Have you ever seen a really clear picture on IPIX? If you have, they're few and far between. The nature of IPIX is to reformat your photo to fit within the format (400 pixels wide by 300 pixels tall) and to compress the file for quick viewing. This process can destroy the quality of your carefully photographed images if you haven't saved them in a compatible size. If you're running a business, be businesslike and use the method that represents your photos in their best light.

To get the free title bar image that you see on many auctions, you must use the eBay picture service (see Figure 11-5). Use smaller, secondary images of your items and use the picture service. The first picture is free; all you have to do is click the box on the Sell Your Item page picture services area, next to Title Bar picture.

eBay may be improving IPIX, so don't give up on it. Use it as a secondary service, and see if the image you see in the auction is as crisp and clear as when you view it on your own computer. When it's ready for prime time, it may suit your needs for at least one of the pictures in your auction.

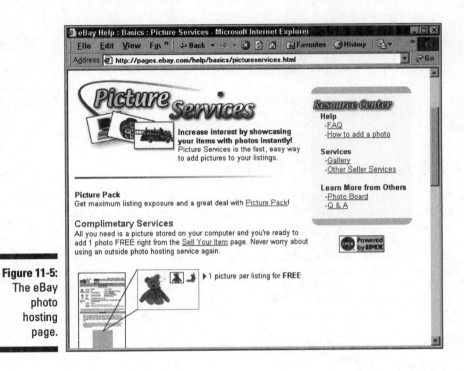

Figure 11-5:
The eBay
photo
hosting
page.

HTML and You

I am HTML-challenged. My small grasp of HTML gets me only so far. I must use my Web design program (or CuteHTML) to produce any kind of code for my Web site. Luckily, you don't have to know a lot of code to produce eBay auctions.

Go to my Web site (www.coolebaytools.com) and look for a couple of links. Click Virtual Auction Ad Pro to download a very simple program (see Figure 11-6) that will help you generate respectable looking eBay auctions. A product of Virtual Notions, Virtual Auction Ad Pro has been around for a few years. It's been around for a long time because it's easy to use.

For a quick and easy HTML fix, go to my Web site at www.coolebaytools.com and click where it says Click to JAZZ UP Your Auctions. You'll get a quick HTML generator; please feel free to use it as often as you like. There's no charge to use it, and it generates a nice, clean ad for you. You can select border colors and it will include an image in your description area. Nothing fancy, mind you, just nice clean HTML. I call it my *Cool FREE Ad Tool* (see Figure 11-7). On the page, just type in your information as indicated, select complementary colors to your photo, and click. On the next page, you'll see HTML code for your auction description that you can cut and paste into the auction description area of the Sell Your Item page. You can get to it from the link on the home page, or go directly to it at `www.collierad.com/coolebaytools/create_ad/free.pl`.

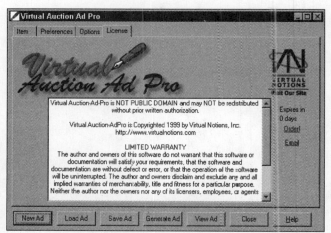

Figure 11-6:
Virtual
Auction Ad
Pro.

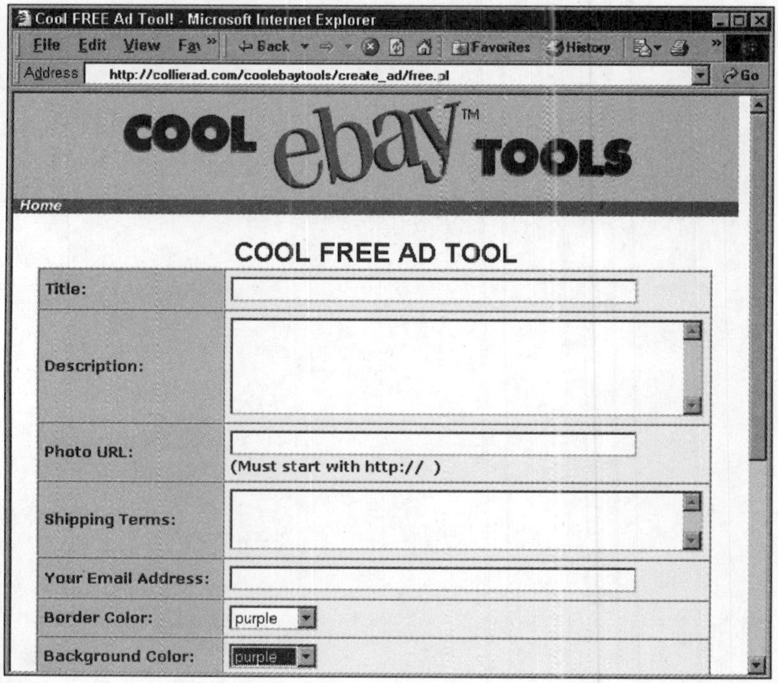

Figure 11-7:
The Cool
Free Ad Tool
page.

Chapter 12

Providing Excellent Customer Service

In This Chapter

▶ Making a good first impression

▶ Writing the perfect e-mail

*B*usiness, bah! eBay's supposed to be fun! But business is business and if you're in business, you must remember that your customers are number one. Many businesses have become successful — and even famous — in our country, and the way they got there (aside from selling incredible merchandise) is by providing fantastic customer service. You've got to move in the same direction. The image that you project through e-mails and ads identifies you to the bidders as a good guy or a bad guy. No kidding. Your e-mails should be polite and professional. Your ads shouldn't make prospective buyers feel like you're hustling them, sneaking in hidden fees, or being just plain pushy with several rules for bidding.

You don't have to have the most beautiful auctions on eBay to succeed, you need a product that sells and good customer relations! So in this chapter, I cover some ways — from writing effective auction descriptions to sending cordial e-mails — to let your customers know that they're number one in your book.

Meeting Your Customers

eBay is a person-to-person marketplace. Although many sellers are businesses (like you), the perception is that sellers at eBay are individuals earning a living. The homespun personal approach goes a long way to being successful at eBay.

After you've written a brilliant title for your auction, prospective buyers click your auction and scroll down to your description. Do they have to dodge through pointless verbiage, or do you get right down to business and state the facts about your item? If they have to dodge through pointless verbiage before getting the facts on the item, they often lose interest along the way.

Here are a few things to remember when writing your auction description:

- **Write a factual description.** Does it answer almost any question a potential buyer might ask? If not, do some revising.

- **Include some friendly banter to make the customer feel comfortable shopping with you.** Don't be afraid to let your personality show!

- **Update your My eBay page.** Let people know a little about you and who they're dealing with. When customers have to decide between two sellers selling the same item and all else is equal, they will place their bid (and their money) with the seller who makes them feel secure.

- **Limit the number of auction rules (the Terms of Sale, as some sellers call it) you include.** Some sellers actually include a list of rules that's longer than the item's description. Nothing will turn off a prospective bidder like paragraphs of regulations do — you may make a buyer feel like you're threatening them.

  If you really *must* put in a litany of rules, use a bit of HTML to take the type size down a size (so that your rules are in the auction, but aren't blaring at your readers):

  ```
  <font size=-1>
  ```

- **Choose a reasonable typeface size.** Many users are still looking at eBay through an 800 x 600 display. If you design your auctions at 1024 x 768, your typefaces will be way too large for the average user. Forcing a user to scroll and scroll to find the details only leads to frustrated customers.

- **Quote a shipping amount.** Many bidders pass up auctions that don't disclose the shipping charges in the auction description. If the item you're selling is common, many other sellers are selling it — and maybe quoting shipping costs.

  It's just plain bad taste to overcharge on shipping. Buyers at eBay expect that you'll pad up to a dollar for packing and shipping costs, but adding more than that can make you look like you're trying to squeeze every penny out of your bidder . . . not a good feeling when you're on the other end!

- **Keep photos a practical size.** Most users still connect with a dial-up Internet connection and if they have to wait for your large pictures to load, they may just go elsewhere for the item.

Figure 12-1 shows an excellent example from the eBay power seller bluemooncoins. As part of its descriptions, bluemooncoins leads in with a picture of kindly William Snyder, a published and nationally known numismatic expert in its employ. Bill gives a few tips, immediately giving you the down-home feeling that this seller really cares about you — which doesn't cost bluemooncoins an extra penny. This type of marketing works!

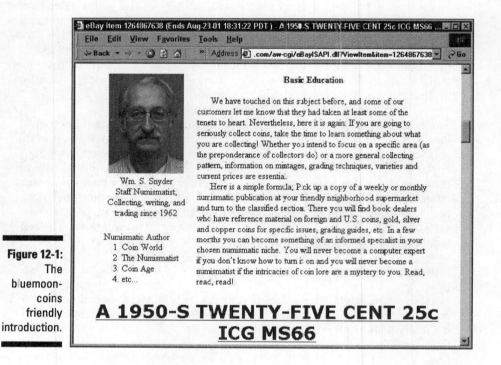

Figure 12-1:
The bluemooncoins friendly introduction.

Communicating with Your Customers

Perhaps English class wasn't your favorite, but when it comes to being a professional, incorporating good grammar, proper spelling, and punctuation in your communications portrays you as a real pro. Before writing this book, even I hooked up with some grammar and punctuation sites to brush up on my writing skills. (Okay, I also have three brilliant editors covering up my transgressions. . . .)

Throughout the rest of this section, I provide some examples of effective e-mails. Study these and also check out a couple of business letter books (for example, *Writing Business Letters For Dummies,* by Sheryl Lindsell-Roberts and published by Hungry Minds, Inc.). And don't forget good manners. You don't want to be too formal, but you do want to be personable and polite.

The initial inquiry

The first written communication you have with a prospective buyer is an inquiry e-mail. A bidder can ask you a question about your item by clicking the <u>ask the seller a question</u> link on the auction or sale page, which automatically generates an e-mail addressed to you. Often these questions are brief, but you must respond quickly, clearly, and politely — and with a sales pitch (see example following). At least 20 percent of the time that I send an inquiry, I don't even get a response — guaranteeing that I won't be buying that product. I refuse to buy from someone who doesn't even care to respond to a question. When I do get responses, more often than not I get terse, brusquely written notes. Many people choose not to use punctuation or capitalization in their e-mails. How professional looking is that? Not very.

The sellers who take the time to write out a short considerate reply that includes a salutation and a thank you for writing get my money. Remind the soon-to-be bidder that you can combine several wins to save on shipping costs; and yes — by all means — use this opportunity to point out other auctions you have that may also interest the writer. Now you've got some real customer service going. The letter doesn't have to be long and drawn out, just brief and straightforward. I wrote the following note in response to a question regarding the condition of the tree in one of my auctions. The reply is an example of a good, brief response:

Hello,

Yes, the aluminum Christmas tree in my auction is in excellent condition. The 58 branches are full and lush and will look great for the holidays. Please write again if you have any more questions or concerns.

Don't forget to check my other auctions for a color wheel and a revolving tree turner. They would look great with this tree, and I can combine them for shipping.

Thank you for writing,

Marsha

Isn't that nice? The note addresses the question in a respectful and personable manner. Writing a note like this doesn't take long. You should be doing it.

The winner's notification letter

Have you ever received a bulk-generated boilerplate winner's confirmation letter? The kind where the seller hasn't bothered to fill in half the blanks and it's so robotic that you're almost insulted just by reading it? If you have, did you feel like the seller cared about you and the money you've spent on the auction? Receiving a note like this after you've requested that the seller combine purchases (and the letter pays no attention to your request) is especially annoying. E-mails can cross, but a personal approach goes a long way with customers.

I'm not saying you shouldn't automate your eBay business. I'm merely suggesting — strongly recommending — that you take the time to personalize your e-mail responses. If you choose to send automated responses, choose a program that allows you to combine multiple wins in one letter and to apply the correct shipping costs the first time.

Here's the tried and true winner's notice that I send out:

Congratulations!

Yours was the winning bid on eBay item #122342911 for the Emilio Pucci book. You got a great deal! I am looking forward to a pleasant transaction and positive feedback for both of us.

Please include a copy of this e-mail with your name and shipping address along with your payment:

Winning Bid Amount	*$ 14.95*
Shipping and Handling	*2.50*
TOTAL Amount Due	*$ 17.45*

You may pay by money order, a personal check, or with a credit card through Billpoint or PayPal. If you are not set up with them, just e-mail me and I'll have them send you a request for payment.

A money order or online payment assures immediate shipping upon reciept of payment! If you pay by check, I will ship your item after a 14-day clearing period; be sure to include the item name and your e-mail address with payment. Please send your payment to the address shown below:

Marsha Collier

1234 Anywhere Street

Los Angeles, CA 91352

Your payment is expected on or before Monday, April 2, 2001. I look forward to receiving it. I will ship on receipt of payment in full, via U.S. priority mail with delivery confirmation.

Thank you for your Winning Bid! I am delighted to be dealing with you and know you will enjoy your purchase.

Marsha_c

At the end of a winner's notice letter, offer your winner some special discounts or other offers from your Web site. Include a couple of items this particular winner may be interested in (based on the current win) and include a link to your site. Also include the reminder that you can combine postage and that you look forward to a response.

The payment reminder

This type of correspondence can get sticky. You don't want to aggravate the buyer; yet time is wasting and you could spend this time reposting your item. When writing a payment reminder, you need to be firm but pleasant. Real things can happen in people's lives. Family members get sick, and people just plain forget things. Perhaps your payment fell between the seats of the winner's car on the way to the post office. (That's the excuse I used when I forgot to mail a payment — feel free to use it.)

When you honestly forget to send a payment, nothing is more humiliating than someone debasing you through e-mail. So remember that people do make mistakes and check the winner's feedback before you send the letter. If you can garner from the feedback that this winner has a habit of not following through on bids, you can definitely be a bit firmer in your wording. Always clearly set a deadline for receiving payment, as shown in the following letter:

Hello,

You won an auction of mine at eBay last week for the Emilio Pucci Book. Your payment was due yesterday and it still has not arrived. Perhaps sending payment has slipped your mind considering your busy schedule. I know it can easily happen.

Please e-mail back within 48 hours and let me know whether you want to go through with our transaction. I'd like to put the item back up for sale if you don't want it.

Thank you for your bid,

Marsha Collier

How firm you choose to get with a non-paying bidder is up to you. I've dealt with a few non-paying bidders at eBay, but I've left only two negative feedbacks. Some people who tend to overbid are indeed violating the contract to buy, but legitimate reasons might explain why someone hasn't followed through on an auction. You must decide which method to take and how far you want to stretch your karma (what goes around comes around). Assess each case individually, and don't be hasty in leaving negative feedback until you know the whole story.

The payment received/shipping notice

I know that you probably aren't going to send out a payment received letter for every transaction, but it would surely be nice if you did. Staying in constant communication with your buyers will make them feel more secure with you and with buying at eBay. You want them to come back, don't you?

When you receive payment and are ready to ship, sending a short note like the following helps to instill loyalty in your customer:

Hi there (insert name of winner),

Your payment was received and your item will ship tomorrow. Please e-mail me when it arrives so that I can hear how pleased you are with your purchase.

When the transaction is over, I hope you will leave positive feedback for me because building a good reputation at eBay is very important. I'd really appreciate it, and I'll be glad to do the same for you.

Thank you for bidding & winning,

Marsha Collier

Marsha_c

If you haven't heard from the buyer within a week, send another note.

Leaving feedback for buyers

After you leave feedback, you can't take it back and you can't repost to correct an erroneous evaluation of another user. I know that it's easier to leave feedback after you receive payment, but waiting to see how the transaction evolves afterwards is prudent — especially if the package gets lost in the mail, turning a previously kind and sweet buyer into a screaming nutcase. Same thing if the item is damaged. Evaluating a buyer is based on more than whether that buyer actually pays for an item. (Buyers are supposed to do that — it's a contract, remember?) When leaving feedback for buyers, consider the following:

- Did they return your communications quickly?
- Did they pay in a timely manner?
- If a problem occurred in shipping or with the item, did they handle it in a decent manner or did they try to make your life a living hell?

Remember that sellers are judged on communication, shipping time, the quality of packaging, and friendliness. As a seller, you have the duty of leaving quality feedback to set guidelines that all sellers use to rate buyers.

Chapter 13

When the Money Comes Rolling In

In This Chapter

▶ Money order, cash, or credit card: Finding the payment method that suits your needs

▶ Discovering the ins and outs of payment services

▶ Exploring merchant accounts

Your hard work finally pays off. The hours spent in selecting your items, photographing them, touching up the pictures, and writing brilliant auction copy all come down to one thing: getting paid. At first thought, you might be happy to take any form of negotiable paper, bonds, and stocks (okay, no dotcom stock). As you become more experienced and collect for more auctions, however, you'll decide which payment methods you prefer, and which are more heartache than they're worth.

Receiving and processing payments takes time and patience. The more payment methods that you accept, the more you have to keep track of. You can't accept all forms of payment, so narrow the payment choices you offer and you'll have less bookkeeping hassle. Throughout this chapter, I detail the various payment options (including how to handle payment from international buyers), and how each affects your business.

It Doesn't Get Any Simpler: Money Orders

I begin my discussion of payments with money orders and cashier's checks because I think they're just the greatest way to receive payment. Money orders and cashier's checks are fast, cheap, and negotiable (just like cash). Cashier's checks are purchased at a bank, and are generally debited immediately from the winner's checking account at purchase. For some unknown reason, banks take it upon themselves to charge a minimum of $5 to issue a cashier's check. This is a pretty steep charge to the winner, which is why I suggest money orders.

Money orders are available at almost every corner and cost less than a dollar. Your winners can get money orders almost anywhere. After a quick survey of my neighborhood, I found money order dealers galore. All the stores I spoke to charge 99 cents for a money order up to $500. In this section, I detail just four vendors (both online and off) that offer money order services. Table 13-1 shows a cost comparison of these vendors.

Table 13-1	Money Order Cost Comparison	
Vendor	*$25 Money Order*	*$110 Money Order*
7-Eleven	99 cents	99 cents
United States Post Office	90 cents	90 cents
BidPay.com	$5	$7.48
SendMoneyOrder.com	$3.34	$8.34

A growing group of online money order services enable your winners to send you money orders. If you want money orders, you should familiarize yourself with the various charges so that you can recommend the most reasonable amount to your auction winners. Asking buyers to pay a large fee to pay you is unfair — unless they're international. In that case, paying by money order through an online issuer such as SendMoneyOrder.com is the best way for them to pay you. International buyers deal in the currency of their own countries; when they purchase a money order and send it in dollars, you're paid with cash in good old American greenbacks.

7-Eleven

There are over 21,000 7-Eleven stores in the world. I'll bet there's one within driving distance of your house. For your customer, the best part about 7-Eleven is that each has an ATM to draw cash from credit cards with which to purchase a money order. 7-Eleven charges only 99 cents for money orders, certainly a real bargain! If you don't know where the closest 7-Eleven is, go to www.vicinity.com/a7eleven.startprx.hm.

7-Eleven has almost become a generic name for convenience stores. As everyone knows, you'll find several convenience store chains around the country that sell money orders, such as Circle K, Dairy Mart, AM/PM, and many local chains.

United States Postal Service

Most sellers especially love USPS money orders, which have all the benefits of a regular money order — plus, because the post office issues these money orders, the nice clerks at the post office will graciously cash them for you with proper identification. Postal money orders are safe, too, and are acceptable everywhere. The post office goes to great pains to ensure authenticity by including a Benjamin Franklin watermark, a metal security thread, and a double imprint of the dollar amount on the money order. (No more fears that you've received a color copy of a money order.)

Both domestic and international (for sending U.S. dollars to foreign countries) money orders are available at post offices in amounts up to $700 for 90 cents each. If the money order is lost or stolen (in eBay-speak, that usually means that the buyer hasn't sent it to you yet), buyers must present the receipt for a trace and back their money on a lost money order. For a small fee, buyers can also get a copy of a paid money order (as long as they have the receipt), for as many as two years after the date it has been paid.

SendMoneyOrder.com

In the battle for online money order services, SendMoneyOrder.com, a new site (see Figure 13-1), is a real contender. Primarily designed for auction payments, SendMoneyOrder.com cares about the seller and makes it easy for you to encourage its services as a money order vendor in your auctions. Winners from any part of the world can pay for their money orders by using credit cards from their PayPal accounts, and United States users can even pay from their checking accounts.

EnergyFlow, the owner of SendMoneyOrders.com, has an API (Applications Programming Interface) that you can integrate into your Web site (go to its home page, click the Web Tools tab, and then click the API link for more information). It also has a wizard that integrates the API into your Web site so that your winners can immediately click through and pay for their auctions. After your winners pay, SendMoneyOrder.com sends you a money order.

The site also hosts an API Wizard (from the Web Tools tab, click the Easy API Wizard link) that creates a template that you can insert onto your Web site for your customers to complete. When a payment is made, you're automatically sent an e-mail.

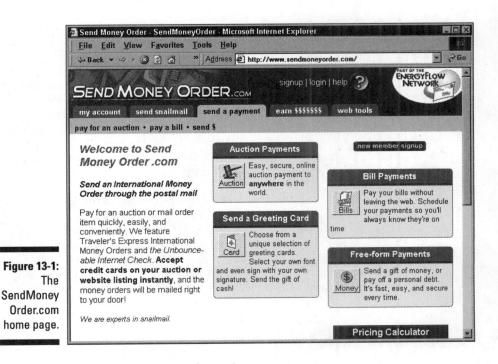

Figure 13-1: The SendMoney Order.com home page.

If your auction wins average less than $50, SendMoneyOrders.com can save your customers a little money. When sending a domestic or international money order, the charge is $3 for the first $25 and $1.25 for each $25 thereafter. To send you the money order via First Class Mail, the charge is 34 cents (what you'd expect to pay).

If you have questions about the SendMoneyOrder.com services, call them toll-free at 800-675-0702.

BidPay.com

BidPay (an affiliate of Western Union) is certainly the most popular money order seller, probably because it was the first or maybe because it promotes better than anyone else. BidPay accepts payments from any Visa, Mastercard, or Discover card, and sends payments in the United States and internationally. The site says it sends payments to any country that has a good postal system but not to countries with bad postal systems. Hmmm (see the sidebar "When good postal systems go bad" elsewhere in this chapter).

Luckily, the United States has a good postal system, so you can get your money orders from BidPay. If you're a high volume seller, BidPay is working on a way to send you a weekly deposit to cover all your weekly transactions.

BidPay charges your customers a flat rate of $5 for any money order amounting to less than $100. When you reach $100.01 and up (to $500 — the upper limit for a BidPay money order), it charges 2.25 percent plus $5 but mails the money order for free. 7-Eleven is sounding better all the time (see the section "7-Eleven" previously in this chapter).

To register with BidPay, go to www.bidpay.com (see Figure 13-2); under Seller Services, click the Register With Us button and provide your basic information so that you can begin to accept BidPay as payment for your auctions. After BidPay processes your application, you will receive a confirmation.

Figure 13-2: The BidPay.com home page.

When good postal systems go bad

BidPay mails payments only to countries with "good" postal systems. According to BidPay, these countries include Germany, Spain, France, Italy, Great Britain, Hong Kong, Japan, Singapore, Australia, Taiwan, Norway, Sweden, Denmark, and Holland. BidPay does *not* mail payments to countries with "bad" postal systems, which includes all of the Caribbean, Central and South America, and most African and Middle Eastern markets. Hey, I just found all that to be an interesting piece of trivia to share. After all, who knew BidPay was the arbiter of the world's postal systems?

Pay Me When You Get This: Cash On Delivery

I can't say enough about C.O.D. to discourage you from using this payment method. But I'm gonna try! You give your package to the post office, UPS, or FedEx, who collects the payment after delivering the package. Sound straightforward and easy? What happens when the carrier tries to deliver the package and the recipient isn't home? Your items can sit for a week or two, during which time buyers may decide that they don't want to pick up the items from the shipper. If you're lucky, you'll get items back in two to three weeks.

The cash on delivery service is expensive besides. In addition to postage, the post office charges $5.50 for C.O.D. service.

Another bad part of C.O.D.? You might wait a month to receive payment, even when the addressee is home the first time and accepts delivery. Do yourself a favor and don't offer it as a payment option. You're only asking for trouble. You're not a bank, and you're not in the finance business. Get your money up front.

The Check's in the Mail: Personal Checks

Personal checks are the easiest way for buyers to make payments. They can just dash off a check, put it in the mail, and bam, you're paid. It doesn't always work out so easy for the seller. You have to deposit the check into your bank account first and wait for the check to clear. Believe it or not, in these days of electronic transfers, wiring funds, and international money transfers, you still might wait more than two weeks for a check to clear.

Accepting cash payments

I'm sure you've received cash from some of your winners. I don't like cash. If the buyer doesn't send the exact amount due, you have to call the buyer, who may claim that the correct amount should be there. Mail can be stolen. We had a rash of mail thievery where I live; people were stealing envelopes right out of mailboxes. All of a sudden, *you* must have lost the difference — and you have no recourse with cash.

Postal inspectors are constantly battling this problem, but you won't know your mail is being stolen until you've missed enough mail — usually bills. Explaining to a buyer that the money never arrived is difficult. The thief has the cash while your reputation may be shot. You can e-mail, phone, and talk and discuss, but the bottom line is that you haven't received your money.

Paper checks

After you deposit a check, your bank sends it to a central clearinghouse, which then sends it to the signatory's bank clearinghouse. Then, the individual bank decides whether the check can be paid. You may think that a way around the system is to call the bank and see if the account currently has sufficient money in it. The account may have sufficient funds when you call, but the depositor can withdraw money before the check gets through the system and then the check bounces. And don't forget the 24-hour turnaround rule: Even if the bank has the money and you're standing there with the check, the bank can deny payment within 24 hours, leaving you with a bad check.

Bottom line? I warn all my winners that I may hold the check for over two weeks before I ship. I make exceptions for buyers I've successfully done business with before, who I know aren't a risk. Dealing with personal checks really isn't worth the potential grief they can cause. Try to get an e-check (an electronic funds transfer through Billpoint or PayPal; see the following section) or have your winners pay with credit cards through a payment service. For more on payment services, see the section "I Take Plastic: Credit Cards" later in this chapter.

Electronic checks

Despite attached fees and a short waiting period, accepting an e-check is a nice, clean transaction. After indicting that they want to pay with an e-check, buyers are presented with a screen similar to what's shown in Figure 13-3 featuring the Billpoint e-check. When a buyer pays with an electronic check, it will take as many as four days to clear. Table 13-2 shows costs for some popular electronic checks. See Figure 13-3 for an example of an electronic check.

Table 13-2		Costs for Electronic Checks	
Vendor	*Transaction Amount*	*Standard*	*Merchant Account*
Billpoint	1 cent–$15	35 cents + .5%	35 cents + .5%
Billpoint	$15.01–$200	35 cents +.75% +.5%	35 cents + 1.5% + .5%
PayPal	up to $10,000	30 cents + 2.9%	caps at $5

Maximum transaction amounts for electronic checks from Billpoint are $200 and from PayPal $10,000.

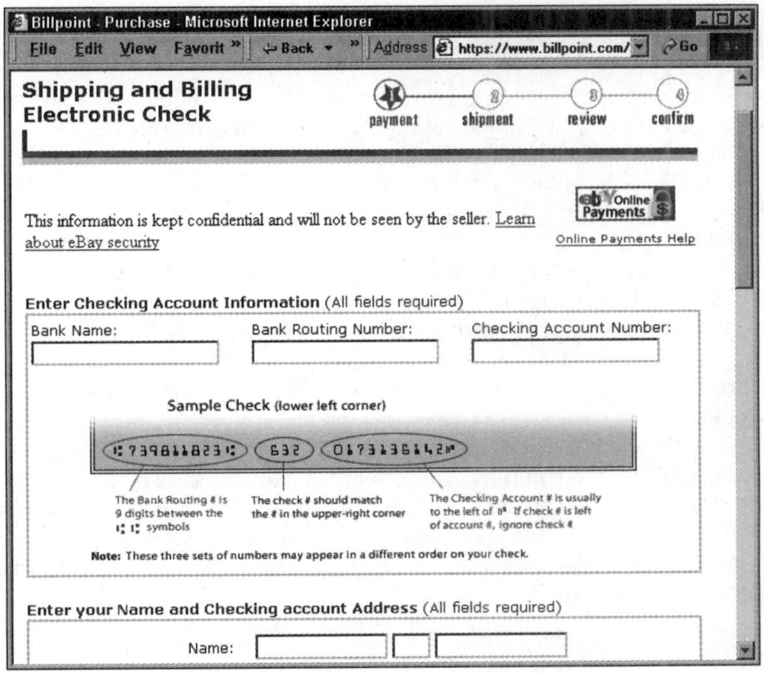

Figure 13-3: The Billpoint electronic check.

Hold This for Me: Tradenable Escrow Service

Tradenable.com (formerly i-Escrow.com) makes it more comfortable for the buyer to proceed with transactions over $200 (the upper limit for eBay fraud insurance). By using Tradenable, buyers gain peace of mind because they know the transaction will be completed securely and easily.

No membership is required; you just sign up and log on. Each escrow is considered a separate transaction. When you want to offer escrow as a payment option in one of your auctions, be sure to indicate such on the Sell Your Item form so that it appears on the auction page. After the auction, the seller should initiate the escrow by clicking the icon at the item page. If you've agreed with the buyer that you'll take escrow *after* you list the auction, you can initiate the escrow process by going to the SafeHarbor escrow page, and clicking Begin Escrow.

To proceed with escrow, the buyer must send payment to Tradenable, as shown in Figure 13-4. Tradenable accepts all credit cards (including American Express and Discover), cashier's checks, money orders, wire transfers, and personal or business checks. A check is subject to a 10-day delay.

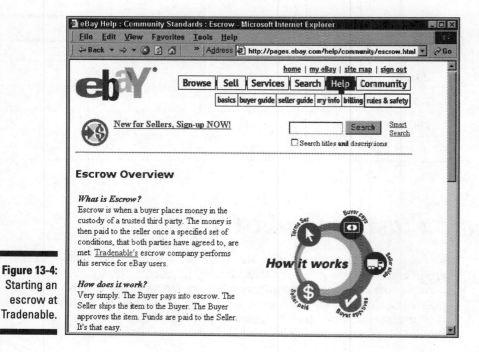

Figure 13-4:
Starting an
escrow at
Tradenable.

After the buyer makes the payment, Tradenable asks the seller to ship the item to the buyer. When the buyer receives the merchandise, the inspection period begins promptly at 12:01 a.m. the next weekday and continues for a time previously set by the buyer and seller.

The buyer notifies Tradenable that the merchandise is approved, and then Tradenable releases payment to the seller. If the buyer doesn't feel the merchandise is what was wanted, the buyer must return the item to the seller in its original condition, adhering to the Tradenable shipping requirements. The buyer also must log on to the Web site to input return shipping information.

In the event of a return, the seller has the same inspection period to ensure that the item was returned in its original condition. After that is confirmed, Tradenable will refund the buyer (less the escrow fee and, if agreed upon ahead of time, the shipping fee). Either the buyer or the seller can pay the escrow fee; the two can even split the cost. But you need to decide who will pay the fee up front and indicate this in your auction listing. The buyer is responsible for paying the escrow fee for all returns, no matter who had initially agreed to pay the fees. In Table 13-3, I include a listing of the Tradenable escrow fees.

Table 13-3	Tradeable Escrow Fees	
Transaction Amount	*Credit Card*	*Cash*
Up to $100	$2.50	$2.50
$100.01–$25,000	4%	2%
$25,000.01–$50,000	4%	1%
Over $50,000	Not accepted	1%

1 Take Plastic: Credit Cards

As people become more comfortable with using credit cards on the Internet, credit cards become more popular for eBay payments. Plus, major credit card payment services have insured eBay payments to registered users, making credit cards safe and easy: safe for the buyer and easy for you. Credit card transactions are instantaneous, and don't have to wait for a piece of paper to travel cross-country.

For all this instantaneous money transfer, however, you have to pay a price. Whether you have your own *merchant account* (a credit card acceptance account in your business' name) or take credit cards through a payment service (more on this in a minute), you pay a fee. Your fees can range from two to seven percent, depending on how you plan to accept cards and which ones you accept. Unfortunately, many states have made it illegal to charge a credit card surcharge to make up this difference. You've got to write off the expense of accepting credit cards as part of your business budget.

I have to explain the downside of accepting credit cards for your online sales. To protect yourself, please be sure to check the feedback — both feedback they've received and feedback they've left — of all bidders before accepting any form of credit card payment for a high-ticket item. Some buyers are chronic complainers and are rarely pleased with their purchases. They may not be satisfied with your item after it ships. In that case, they can simply call their credit card company and get credit for the payment; you'll be charged back (your account will be debited) the amount of the sale (see the sidebar "Forget the buyer: Seller beware!" elsewhere in this chapter).

Credit card payment services

Person-to-person payment systems, such as Billpoint, PayPal, and Yahoo PayDirect, allow buyers to authorize payments from their credit cards or checking accounts directly to the seller. These services make money by charging percentages and fees for each transaction. It's all done electronically through an automated clearinghouse — no fuss, no muss. The payment service only releases the buyer's shipping information to the seller; all personal credit card information is kept privy. This really speeds up the time it takes for the buyer to get merchandise because sellers are free to ship as soon as the service lets them know that the buyer has made payment and the payment has been processed.

From the seller's point of view, person-to-person payment service transaction fees are lower than the 2.5 to 3.5 percent (per transaction) that traditional credit card companies charge for merchant accounts (get the details in the section "Your very own merchant account," coming up). So even traditional retailers may switch their online business to these services to save money. The number of payment services seems to be growing daily with Ecount, Citibank's C2it, and Bank One joining the fray. Throughout this section, I discuss the top payment services and how each works.

Forget the buyer: Seller beware!

When a buyer disputes a sale, he can simply call his credit card company and refuse to pay for the item; you lose the sale and possibly won't be able to retrieve your merchandise. A payment service or merchant account will then *charge-back* your account without contacting you and without any negotiating. Technically, the buyer has made the purchase from the payment service — not from you — and the payment service won't defend you. I've heard of these charge-backs occurring as long as two months after the transaction. And no one is standing at your side, forcing the buyer to ship the merchandise back to you. Just like the eBay insurance (see Chapter 3), the credit card companies skew the rules to defend the consumer. As the seller, you have to fend for yourself; see Chapter 4 on how to report fraudulent buyers. You usually have no way to verify that the shipping address is actually the one the credit card bills to. So, to add to your problems, the card may actually be stolen.

PayPal confirms through AVS (Address Verification Service) that the buyer's credit card billing address matches the shipping address; PayPal gives you the option not to accept payments from buyers whose addresses don't match. Billpoint also confirms that the shipping address is one that matches the credit card and warns you not to ship to any other address than the one it sends to you in a confirmation e-mail.

If the issuing bank resolves a chargeback in the buyer's favor, Billpoint charges you a $10 investigation fee, along with the amount of the total transaction. Paypal charges you $10 if you are determined to be at fault, but will waive the fee if you meet all of the requirements of the PayPal Seller Protection Policy or participate in the PayPal Preferred program.

Here's some good news: Major credit card companies are trying to curb online fraud for their merchant accounts. Visa has the new Verified by Visa acceptance, which takes buyers to a Visa screen (through software installed on the merchant's server) and verifies their identity through a Visa-only password. Mastercard is coming out with SET (Secure Electronic Transactions), a similar encrypted transaction verification scheme. These systems are expected to substantially reduce fraud and chargebacks.

Before you decide which credit card payment service to use, get out your calculator and check out Web sites for current rates. Calculate your own estimates; don't rely on a site's advertised samples. I've found that the charts on the Web sites tend to leave out certain minor fees. I've also found that for promotional purposes (I assume), comparison charts quoting the competition's prices tend to include optional fees — beware and do your own math.

When you pay the fee to your payment service, realize that the total amount of your transaction, including shipping fees, handling charges, and any sales tax that you charge, incurs a fee. The payment service charges a percentage based on the total dollar amount that's run through its system.

PayPal

PayPal is the largest of the online person-to-person payment services. You can insert a link into your auction that your winners can click to go directly to the PayPal site (see Figure 13-5). From there, they log on and decide whether they want to pay with a credit card or with a debit from their checking account. Simple as that.

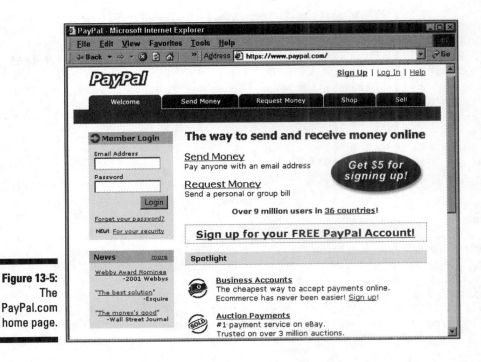

Figure 13-5:
The PayPal.com home page.

Because credit card and identity theft is so prevalent on the Internet — and such an expensive burden to e-commerce — PayPal uses the extra security measure provided by Visa and MasterCard called CVV2. These are three additional numbers listed on the back of most credit cards today, immediately following the regular 16-digit number (but not embossed). Because merchants aren't allowed to store these numbers, but merely use them for security/verification purposes, the numbers are presumably protected from hackers. However, in the unlikely event your credit card doesn't have these numbers yet, PayPal still allows you to use your card by verifying it through a procedure known as *random charge*. PayPal charges $1 to your card and asks you to disclose the pin number printed on your statement. Then PayPal knows that you control the card and didn't steal it.

Here are more than a few particulars about PayPal accounts:

- Auction payments are deposited into your PayPal account; choose one of several ways to get your money:

    - Have the money wired directly into your checking account.

    - Receive payment by check (PayPal charges $1.50 for the check).

    - Keep the money in your PayPal account for making payments to other sellers.

    - Withdraw the cash from an ATM with a PayPal debit card.

- PayPal accounts aren't insured by the government the way banks are, but PayPal insures them up to $100,000 against unauthorized withdrawals.

- PayPal has been integrated into QuickBooks, the Intuit accounting software, which is the perfect program to use with your eBay business. E-mail invoices or print them out to snail mail them to customers. More on QuickBooks in Chapter 16.

- PayPal has its own feedback system, the Buyer Community Participation Number. The number after a user's name reflects the number of unique PayPal Verified users this user has done business with. The higher the number, the more likely the user is experienced and trustworthy.

- As a seller with a Premier or Business account, you can choose to accept or deny a payment without a confirmed address. On the accept or deny page, information about the buyer is shown, including verification status, account creation date, and buyer number (see Figure 13-6).

    To specify whether you want to accept a credit card payment from a buyer without a confirmed address, log on, go to your account, and then click the Profile tab. Next, scroll down to preferences and click Payment Receiving Preferences. On the top of this page, you have the option of choosing to accept, not accept, or decide on a case-by-case basis, payments from users without confirmed addresses.

- PayPal assesses your account $10 for any chargeback. The fee is waived if you've fulfilled the requirements in the PayPal Seller Protection Policy (see next point).

✔ The PayPal Seller Protection policy protects you against chargebacks, unauthorized card use, and non-shipments. To comply with this policy, you must do the following:

• *Be a verified member of PayPal:* Allow PayPal to confirm with your bank that your checking account and address is your own.

• *Ship only to a confirmed address:* PayPal confirms that the buyer's ship to address coincides with the address that the credit company sends monthly bills to. Fraudulent shoppers often ask you to ship to another address — don't do it.

• *Keep proof of shipping that can be tracked online:* Here's where those delivery confirmation things really come in handy. See Chapter 14 to see how you can get them for free direct from post office servers.

• *Ship tangible goods:* PayPal doesn't cover goods that are transmitted electronically.

• *Accept only single payments from a single account:* Don't let a buyer try to pay portions of a purchase from different e-mail addresses. Someone who's trying to pay via several accounts may be attempting to defraud you.

• *Ship PayPal purchases only to United States buyers at United States addresses:* Seller protection isn't extended to international shipments.

For a rundown of PayPal fees at the time of writing, take a look at Table 13-4.

Table 13-4	PayPal Fees as of 7/14/2001	
Premier or Business	*Fee*	*PayPal Preferred**
Standard rate	2.9% + 30 cents	1.4% + 30 cents
Merchant rate**	2.2% + 30 cents	0.7% + 30 cents

*PayPal Preferred seller: A seller can accept Billpoint or other payment services but you can't advertise it in the listing and remain PayPal Preferred. The 1.5 percent discount reflected here can only be drawn from a PayPal credit card (not from a debit card).

**To get the Merchant rate: You must be a PayPal member in good standing for at least 90 days *and* you must have

✔ Received $3,000 in PayPal payments over the previous 90 days (an average of $1,000/month); or

✔ Received a competitive offer from an established merchant account provider, such as a Billpoint Merchant Account, First Data, M & I Data; or

✔ Proven to be a long-standing, high-volume eBay seller (eBay user ID and password must be provided on the Merchant Rate application)

Member Information

About **marshac@collierad.com:**

To protect your security, PayPal offers information on the status of this member.

Community Participation:	(58) Verified Buyers
Account Status:	Verified
Account Type:	Premier
Account Creation Date:	February 02, 2000
PayPal Member For:	1 year 5 months

• Member does not accept payments from international users
• Member may choose to deny payments without a Confirmed Address

Community Participation
A Seller's Community Participation measures the number of unique Verified PayPal members from whom a seller has received payments. To ensure that that the Participation Number reflects successful transactions over a period of time, buyers are added to a seller's number 30 days after the transaction is completed.

Account Status
Domestic Users are considered "Verified" if they maintain a confirmed bank account with their PayPal account. Verification is a positive signal to the Community that a user has complied with Community security measures.

Figure 13-6: A PayPal member information box.

Withdraw your funds from the PayPal account on a regular basis; you need that money to operate your business. Don't let it become a temporary savings account — unless you choose one of the PayPal interest-bearing accounts (check out www.PayPal.com for more details). Realize that any money you have in your account can be extricated for a chargeback. Chargebacks can be applied as many as 60 days after the transaction. For more about chargebacks, see the sidebar "Forget the buyer: Seller beware!" elsewhere in this chapter.

Billpoint

Using their stock as currency, eBay purchased Billpoint in May 1999 and fully launched Billpoint on the site in the spring of 2000 (after selling a 35 percent equity interest to banking giant Wells Fargo). Not surprisingly, Wells Fargo also then entered into a long-term payment processing and customer service contract with Billpoint. eBay entered into an agreement with Visa as well. With these big names involved, Billpoint had to come up with a great product, and it did.

Billpoint (see Figure 13-7) is a reliable payment service that allows buyers to click and buy with a credit card or e-check directly from the site after they've won an auction or made a purchase. It's conveniently integrated directly into eBay auctions, and if your auction uses the Buy It Now or Instant Purchase feature, you can have buyers immediately pay for their purchases with Billpoint payments.

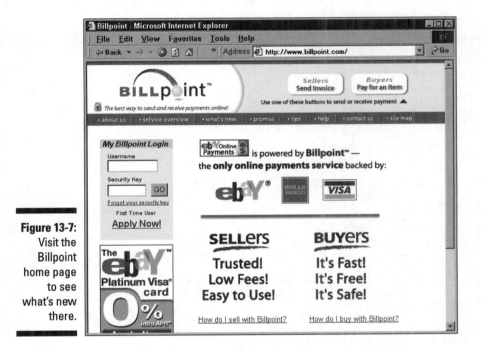

Figure 13-7: Visit the Billpoint home page to see what's new there.

You must register a separate account to get on Billpoint. Buyers may join when they win their first auctions and want to pay with Billpoint, or they can go to `pages.ebay.com/help/buyerguide/bp-buyerlogin.html`. The story's slightly different for the seller. You need to set up your Billpoint account *before* you choose to accept it in your auctions or sales.

One of the truly brilliant features of Billpoint is that you can download your sales history and your deposit history to your computer. Although PayPal integrates with QuickBooks, the Billpoint downloads are feature-rich. Rather than importing just sales figures, you see each and every detail of your transaction — dates, names, addresses, phone numbers, amounts, and more. Even fees and taxes (if you charge sales tax) are broken down separately, making your bookkeeping a breeze. The download imports into Microsoft Works (which comes on almost every new computer) and Excel. Downloading History will help you calculate income taxes and sales taxes, reconcile your accounts, predict sales trends, calculate total revenues, and perform other financial reporting tasks.

The deposits download will give you detailed information for all of the deposits that you receive: payments, Billpoint transaction and deposit fees, refunds, rebates, and any adjustments made to your account.

To download your Histories:

1. **On your My eBay page, go to your Billpoint summary on the Accounts tab.**

2. **On your My Billpoint page, click the <u>Sales History</u> link on the left side of the page.**

   For Deposits Download, click <u>Deposits</u>, and so on.

3. **Enter the time span, transaction, or buyer e-mail for the information that you want to view.**

4. **Click Search.**

   The basic information appears on-screen.

5. **When you're satisfied that you have all the right information, click the Download button.**

6. **Save the file in a directory that you can conveniently access for book-keeping purposes.**

Now you can just double-click the file to open it into your preferred program, either Excel or Works. You now have all the information you could ever possibly need to apply to your bookkeeping program.

If you aren't registered with Billpoint yet (what's holding you up??), you'll find a convenient link on the Sell Your Item page within the area where you indicated what sorts of payment you accept. To register, just click the <u>Apply now</u> link (see Figure 13-8). Or go to `pages.ebay.com/help/sellerguide/bp-sellers.html`; once there, click register (which takes you to a log-on page shown in Figure 13-9) and type in your eBay user ID and password to reach the application page, fill in the basic required information, and you're in.

Figure 13-8:
Billpoint
seller
registration.

The ultimate in payment convenience

eBay Online Payments by Billpoint

Accept credit cards (Visa, Mastercard, Discover) or electronic checks from winning bidders online. <u>Apply now</u>, if you have not registered as a seller with Billpoint.

☐ VISA ▭ ▭ Accept Credit Cards (available to buyers in these <u>countries</u>).

☐ ▭ Accept Electronic Checks (available to U.S. buyers only)

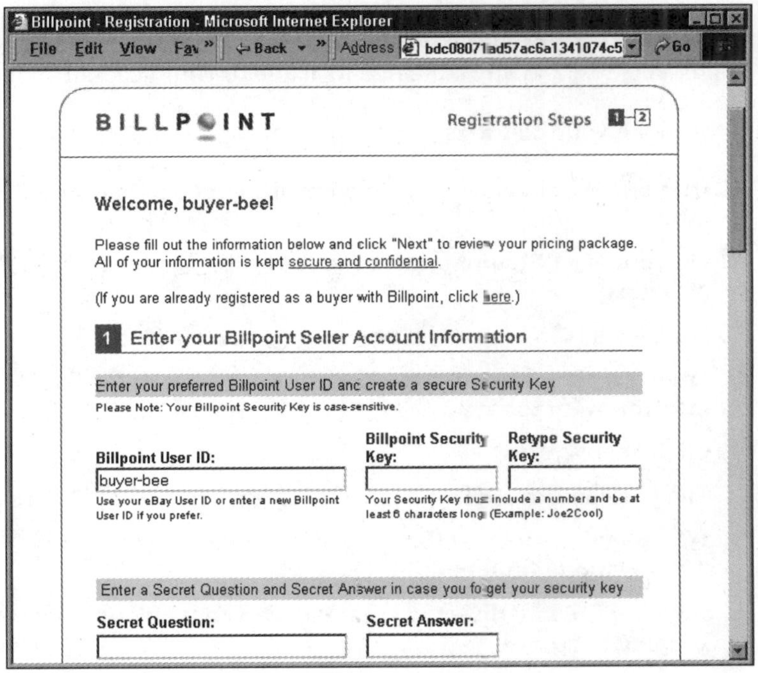

Figure 13-9:
The Billpoint
Registration
page.

If you have a buyer who wants to use Billpoint and you've forgotten to put a Billpoint link in your auctions (or you sell something from elsewhere on the Internet), you can always send a Billpoint Invoice.

The convenience of Billpoint integration into the eBay site really shines when you put the Instant Purchase option in your auctions. Winners just click a link that pops up on your auction page immediately after the auction closes. When you list auctions, you pre-set the shipping and handling charges that appear on the Billpoint payment page. When winners click the Pay Now button (see Figure 13-10), they're taken directly to a Billpoint payment page set up with your information. It's just as easy as when they purchase something through Buy It Now.

When a purchase is made and the payment is deposited in your Billpoint account, the system automatically sends the money to your bank account. For some reason, a credit card payment or electronic check payment usually takes about three days for the deposit to be made.

Billpoint accepts payments from about 46 foreign countries. It also charges you an additional one percent fee on any payments received from non-U.S. credit cards. For a current list of countries from which Billpoint accepts payments, go to www.billpoint.com/services/international.html.

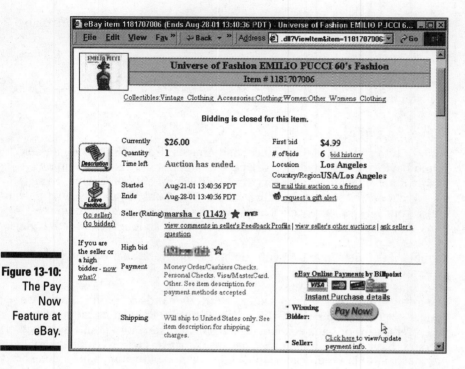

Figure 13-10:
The Pay
Now
Feature at
eBay.

Remember that Billpoint also charges you an additional 0.5 percent each and every time it deposits revenue into your account. That makes the Standard account 3 percent and the Merchant status account 2.25 percent. Remember that you have to watch for hidden charges when investigating the various choices for payment services, and you need to weigh the benefits of each. Check out Table 13-5 for the basic Billpoint fees.

Table 13-5	Billpoint Fees as of June 1, 2001	
Transactions Of	*$15 or less*	*Over $15*
Standard account	.5%* + 35 cents	2.5% + .5%* + 35 cents
Merchant account	.5%* + 35 cents	1.75% + .5%* + 35 cents

*The .5% fee is charged by Billpoint every time for depositing your transaction into your bank account.

To achieve merchant status at Billpoint, you must meet the following requirements:

✔ Your eBay sales volume must be big; you don't have to be a Power Seller, but you must gross at least $1,000 a month.

 ✔ You must have been a member of the eBay community for more than 6 months.

 ✔ You must have a positive feedback rating of 96 percent.

 ✔ Your eBay account (the money you owe eBay) must be kept in good standing.

Yahoo PayDirect

A new joint venture between Yahoo! and Amicus (from CIBC National Bank), Yahoo PayDirect is a payment service with a different twist. You can receive payment for any of your auctions through this new Yahoo! service. To sign up, go to www.yahoo.com and click the PayDirect link. To pay for auction winnings, your buyers simply click an HTML link that you insert into your auctions. As I write this, this service is free of charge, so it may be worth trying.

Yahoo! also offers a logo that you can insert into your auctions (via an HTML generator); see Figure 13-11.

Regarding chargebacks, Yahoo! keeps a strictly hands-off policy: There are none. Because Yahoo PayDirect first works by you depositing money from your credit card or bank account (electronic transfer) into your PayDirect account, buyers have no recourse because any transaction isn't an actual purchase on their credit cards. Also, moving money to start a balance in an account isn't a credit card debit, but is treated as a purchase transaction by Yahoo! and CIBC National Bank.

Your very own merchant account

If your eBay business is bringing in over $20,000 a month, a merchant account may be for you. At that level of sales, discounts kick in and your credit card processing becomes a savings to your business rather than an expense. Before setting up a merchant account, however, I recommend that you look at the costs carefully (check out Table 13-5). I get at least one e-mail each week begging me to set up my own merchant account, and each one offers lower fees than the last. But fees are often hard to calculate and even harder to compare. Charges are buried in the small print. Even those who advertise low fees often don't deliver. Be sure to look at the entire picture before you sign a contract.

The best place to begin looking for a merchant account may be your own bank because it knows you, your credit history, your business reputation, and has a vested interest in the success of your business. If, for whatever reason, your credit isn't up to snuff, I recommend building good credit before pursuing a merchant account because as your business grows, your credit rating is your feedback to the offline world.

If your bank doesn't offer merchant accounts for Internet-based businesses, find a broker to evaluate your credit history and hook you up with a bank that fits your needs and business style (or join Costco as a last resort; see following section). These brokers make their money from your application fee and/or from a finder's fee from the bank that you finally choose.

After you get a bank, you'll be connected to a *processor* (or transaction clearinghouse). Your bank merely handles the banking; the clearinghouse is on the other end of your Internet connection when you're processing transactions, checking whether the credit card you're taking is valid and not stolen or maxed out.

The next step is setting up your *gateway,* the software (ICVerify or PCAuthorize, for example) with which you transmit charges to the clearinghouse. Some gateways use HTML Web sites and take the transactions directly on Web-based forms (Cybercash or VeriFone, among others). Web-based gateways connect your Web forms to real-time credit card processing.

In Table 13-6, I highlight various possible costs associated with setting up and maintaining a merchant account.

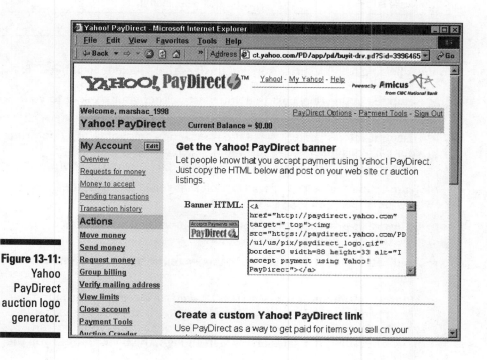

Figure 13-11:
Yahoo
PayDirect
auction logo
generator.

Table 13-6	Possible Internet Merchant Account Fees
Fee	**Average Amount**
Setup fee	$195–$300
Monthly processing fee to bank	2.5% (1.5%–5%)
Fee per transaction	20–50 cents
Processor's fee per transaction	35–50 cents
Internet discount rate	2%–4%
Monthly statement fees	$9–$15
Monthly minimum processing fee	$15–$30
Gateway processing monthly fee	$20–$40
Application fees	$50–$500
Software purchase	$350–$1000
Software lease	$25 per month
Possible chargeback fee	$15

In the following list, I describe some of the fees that I include in Table 13-6:

- **Setup fee:** A one-time cost that you pay to either your bank or to your broker.

- **Discount rate:** A percentage of the transaction amount (a discount from your earnings that goes to the bank), taken off the top along with the transaction fee before the money is deposited into your account.

- **Transaction fee:** A fee per transaction that's paid either to the bank or to your gateway and pays for the network.

- **Gateway or processing fee:** Your fee for processing credit cards in real time that's paid to the Internet gateway.

- **Application fee:** A one-time fee that goes to the broker or perhaps to the bank.

- **Monthly minimum processing fee:** If your bank's cut of your purchases doesn't add up to this amount, the bank takes it anyway. For example, if your bank charges a minimum monthly fee of $20, and you don't hit $20 in fees because your sales aren't high enough, the bank charges you the difference.

If you're comfortable with all the information in the preceding list and in Table 13-6, and you're looking for a broker, heed my advice and read everything a broker offers carefully. Be sure you aren't missing any hidden costs.

Costco member's credit card processing

Here's some true discount credit card processing: a one stop Merchant Account and Gateway in one! Not only can you buy tuna fish in bulk with a Costco membership, but you now can obtain a reasonably priced way to handle a merchant account (check out Table 13-7). Costco has gotten together with Nova Information Systems, one of the nation's largest processors of credit card transactions, to offer Costco Executive members a discounted Internet credit card processing service. They added Iongate to handle the Internet gateway in one neat package.

Table 13-7	**Fees for Costco Internet Credit Card Processing**
Type of Fee	*Amount*
Setup Fee to NOVA (Credit Card Processor)	$25
Discount Rate per transaction to NOVA	1.99%
Transaction fee to NOVA per transaction	28 cents
NOVA Monthly fees minimum	$20
Iongate (Gateway) one time Setup fee	$50
Iongate Transaction Fee (per transaction)	5 cents
Iongate Optional Web site shopping cart	$50
Iongate Optional shopping cart monthly fee	9.99

To begin the application process, go to www.costco.com and click the Apply Now link, input your Executive Membership number, and fill out the secure form. Filling out the form speeds up the application process. After sending your form, you'll receive a full application package via two-day air. A Costco representative will also contact you by telephone. For further information or to apply by phone, call Costco Member Services at 888-474-0500 or Iongate at 888-241-5099.

The VeriSign Payflow link service

If you have less than 1,000 transactions a month through eBay and your Web site, you may want to check out some of the services from VeriSign, a publicly traded company and the world's largest Internet trust service. A respected world-class company and the leader in its field, VeriSign offers gateway services at a reasonable price.

To participate, you must first sign up for a merchant account from your bank, and the VeriSign Payflow service picks it up from there. You can integrate the Payflow service directly into your Web site. When you send out your winner's congratulatory letter, include a link to the page on your site that links to VeriSign. When your orders are submitted to VeriSign for processing, both you and your customer receive a transaction receipt acknowledgement via e-mail when the transaction has been processed. VeriSign processes your transactions while you're online.

The cost is a $179 setup fee and $19.95 a month. For more information, go to www.verisign.com/products/payflow/link/index.html.

Chapter 14

Getting It from Your Place to Theirs

In This Chapter

▶ Examining shipping options and costs

▶ Finding out about free delivery confirmation

▶ Exploring private insurance

I think that the best part of eBay is making the sale and then receiving the payment. After that comes the depressing and tedious process of fulfilling your orders. You shouldn't feel bad if this is the point that makes you take pause and sigh. Order fulfillment is one of the biggest problems that face any mail order or online business. The onerous task of packing and mailing is the bane of almost all businesses.

But as an eBay businessperson, you must attend to these tasks, however much you'd rather not. So in Chapter 17, I detail what you need for packing (boxes, Bubble Wrap, and so on). And in this chapter, I explain just how your items will get to their destinations, exploring your shipping options, costs, and insurance coverage along the way.

Finding the Perfect Shipping Carrier: The Big Three

When you're considering shipping options, you must first determine what types of packages you'll generally be sending (small packages that weigh under two pounds or large and bulky packages) and then decide how you'll send your items. Planning this before listing the item is a good idea. Deciding on your carrier can be the most important decision in your eBay business. You need to decide which one is more convenient for you (is close to your home base, provides pick up service, gives better customer service) and which is the most economical (leverages your bottom line). Most eBay sellers send packages via ground service rather than airmail or overnight, but a shipper who can give you both options is offering you a good deal.

Settling on one main shipper to meet all your needs is important because all your records will be on one statement, or in one area. But depending on a secondary shipper for particular types of packages is a smart plan. One shipper can't be everything to every business, so having accounts with more than one can be to your advantage. Also, shippers may not sign up new accounts as readily in the middle of a strike or work slowdown. In Table 14-1, I provide a summary of shipping costs from the major carriers (The Big Three: FedEx, UPS, and the US Postal Service USPS). Throughout the following sections, I give you the lowdown on each of these carriers so that you can see who fits your requirements.

Table 14-1	Coast-to-Coast Drop-off to Residence (With Insured Value of $75)			
Delivery Service	*2 lbs.*	*5 lbs.*	*10 lbs.*	*15 lbs.*
FedEx Home Delivery (4 day)	$5.84	$6.73	$8.62	$11.53
UPS Residential (5 day)	$7.39	$9.01	$11.64	$15.69
USPS Priority Mail (2 day)*	$5.95	$9.70	$18.20	$25.45
USPS Media Mail (7 day)*	$3.78	$5.13	$6.93	$8.43
USPS Parcel Post (7 day)*	$5.45	$9.75	$17.26	$21.33

To add a delivery confirmation (included with FedEx and UPS), add 40 cents for Priority Mail and 50 cents for Media Mail and Parcel Post. To get free delivery confirmation, see the section on Shippertools.com later in this chapter.

Federal Express

Federal Express (FedEx) is world famous for its reliable service, the number-one choice for all major companies who "Absolutely, positively have to get it there on time." FedEx also has the reputation for some of the highest costs in the business — but only to the untrained eye. FedEx acquired Roadway Package Service (RPS) and formed FedEx Ground, which has a separate division that delivers to residences, FedEx Home Delivery. For the services these provide, you'll be happy to pay what you do. Read on.

FedEx Ground and Home Delivery service

Between its slogan ("The neighborhood friendly service that fits the way we live, work and shop today") and its logo (a puppy carrying a package in its mouth; see Figure 14-1), it doesn't get much warmer or fuzzier than FedEx Home Delivery. And the warm and fuzzy attitude carries over to low rates and quality of service. FedEx Home Delivery even offers a money-back guarantee on home service — the only shipper that does.

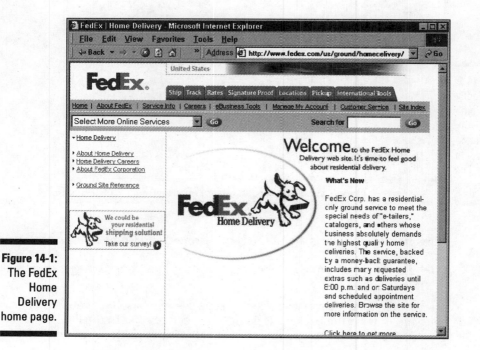

Figure 14-1:
The FedEx
Home
Delivery
home page.

Visit the FedEx Web site (www.fedex.com/us/ground/homedelivery/) to open an account. Even if you have a current Federal Express account, you need to sign on to add the ground service (which includes home delivery) to your account. Registering for ground service is even easier than registering at eBay, so give it a shot.

I opened my FedEx Home Delivery account through a link on the main FedEx home page, and got the skinny on how to use the service. FedEx Home Delivery is designed to deliver to residences. Because its online calculator allows you to choose the option of Home Delivery, you don't even have to look up alternative rates and charts. And just as other shippers do, FedEx Home Delivery gives you a service schedule to let you know how long it will take your package to arrive at its destination (see Figure 14-2).

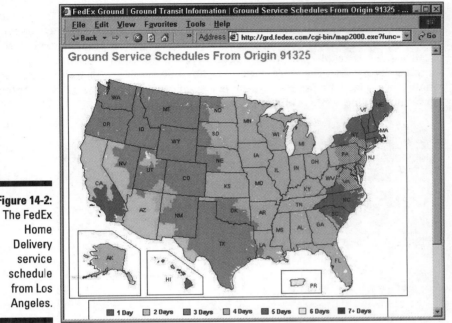

Figure 14-2:
The FedEx
Home
Delivery
service
schedule
from Los
Angeles.

Here are a few fast facts about the FedEx Ground and Home Delivery service:

✔ You print out your own labels and barcodes for your packages and track them online.

✔ FedEx Home delivery works on a zone system; based on your zip code and how far the package is going, you need to refer to the FedEx Home Delivery zone chart or get the cost online through the online calculator.

✔ Each shipment is covered for $100 in declared value. Additional insurance is 35 cents per $100 or a fraction thereof.

✔ You pay a $1.30 surcharge for residential deliveries (automatically calculated online).

✔ Residential deliveries are limited to 70-pound packages.

✔ Weekly pick-up service adds an additional weekly charge of $10 to your account.

✔ Dropping off packages at Federal Express counters incurs no additional charge.

✔ FedEx Home Delivery delivers Tuesday through Saturday.

✔ Currently FedEx Ground adds 1.25 percent to the rate. You must calculate this manually because the surcharge isn't reflected in the calculator.

FedEx Manager Software

Federal Express has one of the most intuitive desktop applications for shipping. FedEx Ship Manager Software will turn your computer into a one-person shipping shop. Generate labels for all forms of FedEx in one place. The software connects online to Federal Express to update itself, search for rate quotes, and track packages, and it includes a shipping notification option to send tracking information e-mail to your recipients.

Larger businesses can get the Ship Manager workstation, complete with PC and printers. It has the unique ability to choose from other carriers. Aside from FedEx Express and FedEx Ground, you can also access UPS shipping services, which allow you to rate, track, report, and ship for multiple carriers on one system.

United Parcel Service

Everyone's familiar with the big brown trucks that tool around town delivering packages here and yon. Those trucks belong to the United Parcel Service (UPS; see its home page in Figure 14-3), which offers three different levels of service based on your shipping needs:

- ✔ **Internet account:** Print your own barcoded labels so that you can drop off packages at the UPS counter (you can also do that without an account) or give packages to a UPS driver.

- ✔ **Occasional Shipper account:** Use UPS for the rare large box or heavy shipment. An occasional shipper is able to prepare packages one day and call UPS for a next day pick-up. You will also have to pay an additional $4 per package for the driver to pick up from you.

- ✔ **Pick-Up account:** When you hit the big time, you're able to get the lowest UPS rates and have a driver make daily stops to pick up your packages. Fees for a pick-up account can run from $7 to $16 per week over the cost of your package shipping.

For big shippers, UPS offers its Application Program Interface (API), which can be integrated into a company's home servers.

Go to www.ups.com/servlet/services?loc=en_US to first sign up for My UPS online (you have to do this to get to the Open An Account area), which allows you to track packages and more online. To set up an account, go to www.ups.com/using/custserv/index.html and sign in with your new User ID and password from My UPS. Based on your responses to some basic questions, *UPS* will decide what account is right for you.

Figure 14-3:
The UPS
hub.

Here are some quick facts about UPS:

- ✔ Shipping with UPS requires that you pay a different rate for different zones in the country (Zones 1–8). The cost of your package is based on its weight, your zip code (where there package ships from), and the addressee's zip code (where the package is going). To figure out your cost, use the handy UPS cost calculator shown in Figure 14-4.

- ✔ UPS offers a chart that defines the shipping time for your ground shipments.

- ✔ Each package has an individual tracking number that you can input online to verify location and time of delivery.

- ✔ Delivery to a residence costs over $1 more per pound than delivery to a commercial location.

- ✔ UPS delivers packages Monday through Friday.

- ✔ $100 in insurance is included with every shipment. For valuations over $100, insurance costs an additional 35 cents per $100.

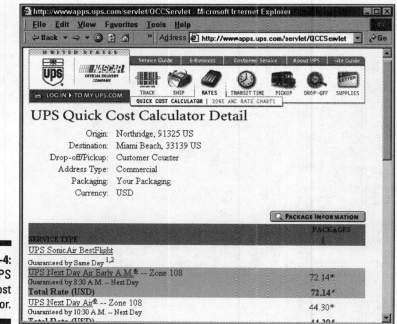

United States Postal Service

Whether you call it snail mail, pops (plain old postal service), or whatever nickname you like, the United States Postal Service (check out its Web site in Figure 14-5) has been delivering the mail since 1775, when our first postmaster (Benjamin Franklin) took the reigns. The USPS has attempted to get every piece of mail delivered to every part of our country.

The USPS is open to everyone. You don't have to set up an account to use its services. To get a basic idea of what you'll pay to send a package, you can access a rate calculator on the USPS Web site (www.usps.gov). The post office provides many services, so in this section, I simply go over the most popular forms of mail used by eBay sellers.

Priority Mail

The two to three day Priority Mail service is the most popular form of shipping eBay packages. You can get free cartons, mailing tape, and labels from the post office (see Chapter 17 for a complete list of what the USPS supplies for your mailing needs). Purchase and print postage online through stamps.com as you need it (Chapter 17 again).

The Priority Mail rates are perfect for one-pound packages ($3.50) and two-pound packages ($3.95). The rate (including free shipping materials) is attractive until you get into the heavier packages (refer to Table 14-1). Also, the post office charges an additional 40 cents for Priority Mail (for Parcel Post and Media Mail, you pay an extra 50 cents) for the use of tracking numbers, via delivery confirmation, that are included in FedEx Home Delivery and UPS costs. The delivery confirmation only tells you *if* the package has been delivered; it doesn't trace the package along its route.

Media Mail

To stay new and hip, the post office has renamed its old Book Rate to Media Mail, causing eBay sellers to miss out on this incredibly valuable mailing tool. The savings are immense (refer to Table 14-1). The only drawback is that you must mail only books, cassettes, videos, or computer readable media, which covers a whole lot of ground. Transit time on Media Mail is seven days, but the cost savings on heavy packages are worth it. Be sure to remember Media Mail when shipping one of those items.

Parcel Post

For heavy packages that don't fit into the requirements for Media Mail, use Parcel Post, a way of saving money when sending packages that weigh up to 70 pounds. Unfortunately, the USPS rates don't cut it when you compare them to the UPS or FedEx Ground rates.

The USPS Application Program Interface

If you want to print your own postage, use stamps.com or SimplyPostage (see Chapter 17) — that is, unless you're a large corporation. The USPS has an Application Program Interface (API; see Figure 14-6), which allows your Web site to interact with the USPS servers. With this software, big businesses can get delivery confirmation (among other services) at no charge and are able to print their own barcodes.

The integration of USPS APIs isn't for the meek and small (like me — and maybe you?), but you can go to someone who has done the work for us. The APIs are available through a reliable independent source for the little guy. See the following section on Shippertools.com.

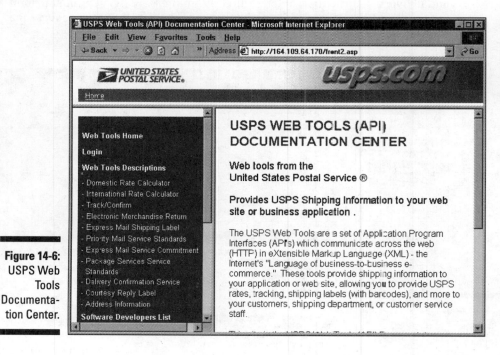

Figure 14-6: USPS Web Tools Documentation Center.

Getting Free Delivery Confirmation from Shippertools.com

A couple of pros that understand APIs and delivery confirmation stuff have licensed the post office API (see the previous section) and are offering its use through a simple Web interface. Shippertools.com has developed a site where you can get *free* (that's right — *FREE*) delivery confirmations on all of your USPS Priority Mail shipments. In addition, its system verifies shipping addresses through the post office servers, tracks your shipments in a handy online worksheet, and keeps an online address book for you. It even works when you're shipping from more than one location.

While the delivery confirmations are free, the nice folks at Shippertools.com do need a little something to cover server costs and their fine work, so you're going to fork over $6.95 a month for unlimited free delivery confirmations. You have to ship more than 18 packages per month for the service to pay for itself — but after you're through with this book, you'll be shipping at least 18 a week.

You don't have to purchase any fancy software or labels. After you sign up with Shippertools.com (see Figure 14-7), your computer receives a barcode and delivery confirmation number direct from the USPS servers. Just print it out on plain white paper and tape it to your package with clear packing tape. It's that easy!

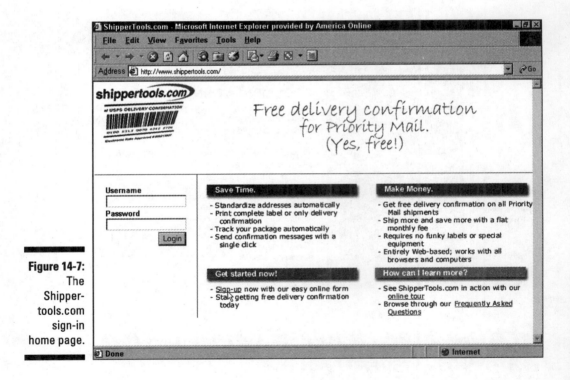

Figure 14-7:
The Shipper-tools.com sign-in home page.

Take a look at Table 14-2 to see how much this service can save you — not counting time you would have wasted in post office lines. . . .

Table 14-2	Shippertools.com Delivery Confirmation Savings per Month	
Packages Shipped per Month (At 40 Cents Per)	*Total USPS Charge*	*Shippertools.com (At $6.95 Monthly) Saves You*
25	$10	$3.05
50	$20	$13.05
100	$40	$33.05
200	$80	$73.05
300	$120	$113.05

Protecting Your Packages with Universal Parcel Insurance Coverage

If you think that printing your own postage is slick, you're gonna love the Universal Parcel Insurance Coverage (U-PIC), a service that automates the whole post office insurance hassle. U-PIC has been in the package insurance business since 1989, mainly insuring packages for large shippers. Recently U-PIC expanded its business to the online auction arena. By using its services, you can insure packages that you send through USPS, UPS, FedEx, and other major carriers. If you use its insurance on USPS-shipped packages, you can save as much as 80 percent on insurance rates.

The U-PIC service also enables you to package your items; you can print your postage through an online postage service, and, if you have just a few packages, give them directly to your USPS mail carrier. (You don't have to stand in line to get your insurance form stamped.) If you've got a ton of boxes, you'll need to drive them to the post office and shove them over the counter. No waiting in line, no hassle!

To apply for the U-PIC service, you must fill out a Request To Provide (RTP) form on its Web site (www.u-pic.com; see Figure 14-8). You must answer questions about who you are, how many packages you send, how many insurance claims you've filed in the past two years, and your average value per package. You must agree to the policy (Evidence of Insurance), and a U-PIC representative will contact you within 48 hours. You're basically applying for an insurance policy for your packages.

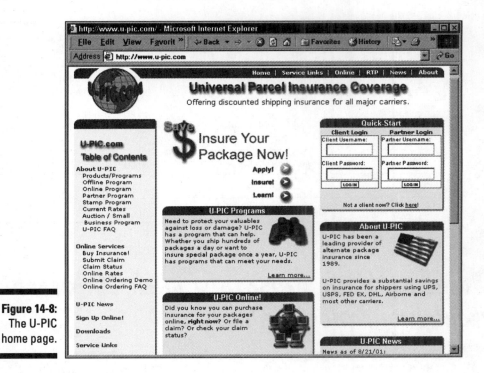

Figure 14-8:
The U-PIC
home page.

When you're approved, online auctioneers should select from two levels of service: the stamp program or the offline standard program (I give you some details about these in just a bit). After you begin using U-PIC, you can stop purchasing insurance for your packages with your carrier. Your U-PIC sales representative will explain to you exactly how to declare value with U-PIC based on your present system. At the end of each shipping month, you'll need to fax, e-mail, or snail mail your shipping reports to U-PIC. To place a claim with U-PIC on a USPS shipment, you must do so 30 days after the date of mailing and must also supply the following:

1. A signed letter, stating loss or damage from the consignee

2. A copy of the monthly insurance report you turned in to U-PIC reflecting insured value

3. A completed U-PIC claim form (one claim form per claim)

4. A copy of the original invoice or the End of Auction form

Because you're paying for private insurance, U-PIC suggests that you include a copy of your insurance policy in the box so that your buyer doesn't think you're overcharging (which makes some folks a bit cranky).

In Table 14-3, I provide you with a comparison of carriers' insurance rates.

Table 14-3		USPS and U-PIC Domestic Insurance Coverage Rate Comparison	
Coverage	*USPS*	*U-PIC Offline Standard*	*U-PIC Stamp Program*
1 cent to $50	$1.10	60 cents	60 cents
$50.01 to $100	$2	60 cents	$1
$100.01 to $200	$3	$1.20	$1.60
$200.01 to $300	$4	$1.80	$2.20
$300.01 to $400	$5	$2.40	$2.80

You can reach U-PIC by calling its toll-free number (800-955-4623) or by visiting its Web site (www.u-pic.com).

Stamp program

The stamp program is for the shipper who ships no more than one to five packages per day. You can purchase booklets of U-PIC stamps for USPS shipments, which come in 20-cent units. A new customer must initially purchase four booklets at $20 each.

Offline standard program

This is the service for eBay businesspeople who ship an average of 100 packages per month. If you reach that point, call U-PIC at 800-955-4623 for how to handle your shipping in a more streamlined manner. At the end of each shipping month, you generate an insurance report that you send in with your premium check or payment via PayPal. Calculate your premium by using the insurance report information. You can get a discount when shipping with the post office when you use a delivery confirmation.

Part IV
Your eBay Back Office

The 5th Wave   By Rich Tennant

"You've opened an insect-clothing shop at eBay? Neat! Where do you get buttons that small?"

In this part . . .

Setting up your eBay business as a real business entity involves doing some nasty paperwork and applying for licenses and organizing and record-keeping. Even though you should discuss your issues with a professional, I fill in the blanks and get you started on the right track. This part is where you find a checklist of the items that you'll need to run your business online.

Chapter 15

Going Legit

- -

In This Chapter
- ▶ Deciding your business format
- ▶ Covering the legalities

- -

*B*usiness format? You ask, "What's a business format?" I hate to be the one to tell you: You can't just say, "I'm in business," and be in business. When you started selling at eBay, maybe you were happy just adding a few dollars to your income. Now that the money is coming in faster, you have a few more details to attend to. Depending how far you're going to take your business, you have to worry about taxes, bookkeeping, and possible ramifications down the line.

I want to remind you that I am *not* a lawyer or an accountant. The facts I give you in this chapter are from what I've learned over the years. When you begin a formal business, it's best to involve an attorney and an accountant or a CPA. Visit www.nolo.com at the very least, a great Web site that offers some excellent business startup advice and forms.

A rule in numbered paragraph one of the eBay User Agreement reads ". . . your eBay account (including feedback) and User Id may not be transferred or sold to another party." This means that when you begin your business at eBay with another person, you'd better have some kind of agreement up front about who gets the user ID in case of a sale. If your business is sold, the person with the original ID had better be involved actively with the new company — as the rules say, your feedback can never be transferred or sold. A new owner would have to start a new account at eBay with a new name — unless the principal from the old company was contractually involved and was the actual eBay seller.

To my knowledge, this hasn't been tested in court, and I'll bet you don't want to be the first to face eBay's top-notch lawyers. Know that this is the rule and plan for it.

Types of Businesses

There are several forms of businesses, from a sole proprietorship all the way to a corporation. A corporation designation isn't as scary as it sounds. Yes, Microsoft, IBM, and eBay are corporations, but so are many individuals running businesses. Each form of business has its plusses and minuses. There are also costs involved. I go over some of the fees involved in incorporating later in this chapter. For now, I detail the various types of businesses, which I encourage you to weigh carefully.

Before embarking on any new business format, be sure to consult with a professional in the legal and financial fields.

Sole proprietorship

Even if you're running your business by yourself part-time or full-time, your business is a *sole proprietorship*. Yep, doesn't that sound official? A sole proprietorship is the simplest form of business that there is. Nothing is easier or cheaper, but believe it or not, being in business actually adds a few expenses to your lifestyle. But here's the bonus: Many things that you spend money on now (relating to your business) will be deductible from your state and federal taxes. It is the form of business that most use when they're first starting out. Many people often graduate to a more formal business form as things get bigger.

A husband and wife, if they file a joint tax return, *can* run a business as a sole proprietorship. If, however, both you and your spouse work equally in the business, running your business as a partnership — with a written Partnership agreement — is a much better idea. (See the next section, "Partnership," for more information.) This protects you in case of your partner's death: In the case of a sole proprietorship, the business ends with the death of the proprietor. There can be only one (sole — get it?) proprietor. If the business has been a sole proprietorship in your late spouse's name, you may be left out in the cold.

A sole proprietorship is a business owned by one person. The business can be run (although I don't advise it) out of your personal checking account. The profits of your business are taxed directly as part of your own income tax, and the profits and expenses are reported on Schedule C of your tax package. As a sole proprietor, you're at risk for the business liabilities. All outstanding debts are yours, and you could lose personal assets if you default.

Also, you must consider the liability of the products you sell at eBay. If you sell foodstuff of any kind — or vitamins or neutraceuticals (new age food supplements) — that makes someone ill, you may be personally liable for any court-awarded damages. If someone is hurt by something you sell, you may also be personally liable as the seller of the product.

Partnership

When two or more people are involved in a business, it is a *partnership*. A general partnership can be formed by an oral agreement. Each person in the partnership contributes capital or services and both share in the partnership's profits and losses. The income of a partnership is taxed to both partners, based on the percentage of the business that they own or upon the terms of a written agreement.

You'd better be sure that you're able to have a working relationship with your partner: This type of business relationship has broken up many a friendship. Writing up a formal agreement when forming your eBay business partnership is also not a bad idea. This agreement is useful in solving any disputes that may occur over time.

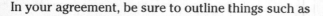

In your agreement, be sure to outline things such as

- ✔ How to divide the profit and/or loss
- ✔ Compensation
- ✔ Restrictions of authority and spending
- ✔ How disputes should be settled
- ✔ What happens if the partnership dissolves
- ✔ What happens to the partnership in case of death or disability

One more important thing to remember: As a partner, you're jointly and severally responsible for the business liabilities and actions of the other person or people in your partnership — as well as your own. Again, this is a personal liability arrangement. You are both personally open to any lawsuits that come your way through the business.

The partnership has to file an informational return with the IRS and the state, but the profits of the partnership are taxed to the partners on their personal individual returns.

Corporation

A *corporation* has a life of its own: its own name, its own bank account, and its own tax return. A corporation is a legal entity created for the sole purpose of doing business. One of the main problems a sole proprietor faces when incorporating is realizing that he or she cannot help themselves to the assets of the business. Yes, a corporation can have only one owner: the shareholder(s). If you can understand that you can't write yourself a check from your corporation, unless it's for salary or for reimbursement of legitimate expenses, you may be able to face the responsibility of running your own corporation.

The state in which you run your business sets up the rules for the corporations operating within its borders. You must apply to the Secretary of State of the state in which you want to incorporate. Federal taxes for corporations presently range from 15 to 35 percent, and they're generally based on your net profits. Often employee owners of corporations use the company to shelter income from tax by dividing the income between their personal and corporate tax returns. This is frequently called *income splitting* and involves setting salaries and bonuses so that any profits left in the company at the end of its tax year will only be taxed at the 15 percent rate. It's kind of fun to see how much the big guys pay, and how much you'll pay in taxes if you leave profits in a small corporation, so check out Table 15-1 for the rates.

Table 15-1	Representative Tax Rates for Corporations
Taxable Income	*Tax Rate*
$0–$50,000	15%
$50,001–$75,000	25%
$75,001–$100,000	34%
$100,001–$335,000	39%
$335,001–$10,000,000	34%
$10,000,001–$15,000,000	35%
$15,000,001–$18,333.333	38%
$18,333,334 and over	35%

Often in small corporations, most of the profits are paid out in tax-deductible salaries and benefits. The most important benefit for a business is that any liabilities belong to the corporation. Your personal assets remain your own, as they have no part in the corporation.

Taking Care of Regulatory Details

Letme give you some very important words to make your life easier in the long run: Don't ignore city, county, state, and federal regulatory details. Doing so may make life easier at the get-go, but if your business is successful, one day it will catch up with you. Ignorance is no excuse: To do business in this great country, you must comply with all the rules and regulations that are set up for your protection and benefit.

Fictitious business name statement

If you plan on running your business under a name different from your own, no matter what your business' legal format, you have to file a *fictitious name statement*. Every person who regularly transacts business for profit under a fictitious business name must file. Depending on where you live, you generally file this form with the county clerk. After a certain length of time after you file, your fictitious name will be published in a newspaper that has a section of fictitious names in its classified section. Usually the newspaper handles the filing with county agencies and publishing for you in one procedure.

If you have a small community or neighborhood newspaper, check with it to see if it files fictitious name statements. Many do and, as a matter of fact, these filings often reflect a large percentage of a newspaper's revenues. These types of newspapers also have the lowdown on all the licenses and certificates that you'll need for your locality. Choosing small newspapers to handle these issues for you is a smart idea because they tend to charge a lot less than big-city dailies; plus, you get to help another small business in your area.

Business license or city tax certificate

Business licenses are the official-looking pieces of paper you see behind the register at local stores. Every business must have one, and depending on your local laws, you may either have to have a *city license* or a *city tax registration certificate*. Yes, even if you're running a business out of your home and have no one coming to do business at your home, you may still need this. If you don't have one, the authorities may charge you a bunch of penalties if they ever find out. The risk isn't really worth avoiding this step.

To save you hanging on the phone, listening to elevator music, and being transferred and disconnected ad nauseam, I'm supplying you with the direct links to apply for your licenses. To find out how to apply in your state, go to the link for your state, which I supply in Table 15-2. (If no link appears next to your state, it may not have had a site set up to file for licenses at the time of this book's writing.) These URLs are accurate at the time of this writing, but as everybody knows, URLs change frequently. Check www.sba.gov/hotlist/license.html for updates.

Table 15-2:	Web Sites for Business License Information
State	**URL**
Alabama	www.ador.state.al.us/licenses/authrity.html
Alaska	www.state.ak.us/local/bus1.html
Arizona	www.revenue.state.az.us/609/licensingguide.htm
Arkansas	www.state.ar.us/business/newbus.html#run
California	www.calgold.ca.gov/
Colorado	www.state.co.us/gov_dir/oed/industry.html
Connecticut	www.state.ct.us/drs/
Delaware	www.state.de.us/revenue/obt/obtmain.htm
District of Columbia	www.dcra.org/main.shtm
Florida	sun6.dms.state.fl.us/dor/businesses/
Georgia	www.sos.state.ga.us/corporations/regforms.htm
Guam	www.admin.gov.gu
Hawaii	www.hawaii.gov/dbedt/start/index.html
Idaho	www.idoc.state.id.us/Pages/businesspage.html
Illinois	www.sos.state.il.us/depts/bus_serv/feature.html
Indiana	www.state.in.us/sic/owners/ia.html
Iowa	www.state.ia.us/sbro/blic/
Maine	www.business.mainetoday.com
Maryland	www.dllr.state.md.us/
Massachusetts	www.state.ma.us/sec/cor/coridx.htm
Michigan	medc.michigan.org
Minnesota	www.dted.state.mn.us/01x00f.asp
Mississippi	www.olemiss.edu/depts/mssbdc/going_intobus.html
Missouri	www.ecodev.state.mo.us/mbac/
Montana	www.state.mt.us/sos/biz.htm
Nevada	www.state.nv.us/binn/

State	URL
New Hampshire	www.nhsbdc.org/startup.htm
New Jersey	www.nj.com/njsbdc/skylands/0996regulations.html
New York	www.dos.state.ny.us/lcns/licensing.html
North Carolina	www.secretary.state.nc.us/blio/default.asp
North Dakota	www.state.nd.us/sec/
Ohio	www.state.oh.us/sos/info.html
Oregon	www.sos.state.or.us/corporation/corphp.htm
Rhode Island	www.state.ri.us/bus/frststp.htm
South Carolina	www.llr.state.sc.us/pol.asp
South Dakota	www.state.sd.us/STATE/sitecategory.cfm?mp=Licenses/Occupations
Texas	www.tded.state.tx.us/guide/
Utah	www.utah.gov/business.html
Vermont	www.sec.state.vt.us/
Virgin Islands	www.usvi.org/dlca/index.html
Virginia	www.dba.state.va.us/launchpad
Washington	www.wa.gov/dol/bpd/limsnet.htm
West Virginia	www.state.wv.us/taxrev/busreg.html
Wisconsin	www.wdfi.org/corporations/forms/
Wyoming	soswy.state.wy.us/corporat/corporat.htm

Sales tax number

If your state has a sales tax, a *sales tax number* (the number you use when you file your sales tax statement with your state) is required before you officially sell a thing. If sales tax applies, you may have to collect the appropriate sales tax for every sale that falls within the state that your business is in.

Some people also call this a *resale certificate* because when you want to purchase goods from a wholesaler within your state, you must produce this number (thereby certifying your legitimacy) so that the dealer can sell you the merchandise without charging you sales tax.

To find the regulations for your state, try a couple of terrific sites that supply links to every state's tax board, which should have the answers to your questions:

- www.mtc.gov/txpyrsvs/actualpage.htm
- www.kentis.com/siteseeker/taxusst.html

Don't withhold the withholding forms

Aye, caramba. I swear it feels like the rules and regulations are never going to end, but if you have regular employees, you need to file *withholding forms* in order to collect the necessary taxes that you must send to the state and the IRS on behalf of your employees. You're also expected to deposit those tax dollars with the IRS and your state on the date required, which may vary from business to business. Many enterprises go down because the owners just can't seem to keep their fingers out of the withheld taxes, which means the money isn't available to turn in when the taxes are due (another reason why you should have a separate bank account for your business).

When you have employees working for you, you more than likely have to file for the following:

- A **Federal Employee Tax ID number** by filing IRS form SS-4. To get the information you need, call 1-800-829-1040 or 1-800-829-3676 for forms.

- A **State Employer number** for withholding taxes if your state has an income tax. Check www.taxadmin.org/fta/forms.ssi for more information on your state.

Chapter 16

Practicing Safe and Smart Record-Keeping

. . . .

In This Chapter

▶ First things first: Bookkeeping basics

▶ Saving your records to save your bacon

▶ Bookkeeping software

▶ Using QuickBooks for your bookkeeping needs

▶ Navigating the QuickBooks Easy Step Interview

▶ Keeping your eBay business chart of accounts

. . . .

*B*ookkeeping, *bah!* You'll get no argument from me that bookkeeping can be the most boring and time-consuming task of your job. You may feel that you just need to add up your product costs, add up your gross sales, and bada-bing, you know where your business is. Sorry, not true. Did you add in that roll of tape that you picked up at the supermarket today? Although it cost only $1.29, it's a business expense. How about the mileage driving back and forth from garage sales and flea markets? Those are expenses, too. I suspect that you're also not counting quite a few other "small" items just like these in your expense column. But you should be.

Once I get into the task, I must confess that I actually enjoy posting my expenses and sales. It gives me the opportunity to know exactly where my business is at any given moment. Of course, I'm not using a pencil-entered ledger system (that I *really* wouldn't enjoy); I use a software program (it's easy and fun). Throughout this chapter, I give you the lowdown on the basics of bookkeeping, emphasize the importance of keeping records in case Uncle Sam comes calling, and explain why using QuickBooks is the smart software choice. Keep reading: This chapter is *required*.

Keeping the Books: Basics That Get You Started

Although posting bookkeeping can be boring, clicking a button to generate your tax information is a lot easier than manually going over pages of sales information on a pad of paper. That's why I like to use a software program, particularly QuickBooks (more about that in the section "QuickBooks: Making Bookkeeping Uncomplicated" later in this chapter).

I suppose that you *could* use plain ol' paper and a pencil to keep your books; if that works for you, great. I suspect, however, that while that may work now, it definitely won't in the future. Entering all your information into a software program now — while your books may still be fairly simple to handle — can save you a lot of time and frustration in the future, when your eBay business has grown beyond your wildest dreams and no amount of paper can keep it all straight and organized. I discuss alternative methods of bookkeeping in the section "Bookkeeping Software," also later in this chapter. For now, I focus on the basics of bookkeeping.

To effectively manage your business, you must keep track of *all* your expenses — down to the last roll of tape. You need to keep track of your inventory, how much you paid for the items, how much you paid in shipping, and how much you profited from your sales. If you use a van to pick up or deliver merchandise to the post office, you should keep track of this mileage as well. When you're running a business, every penny that goes in and out should be accounted for.

In bookkeeping, there are irrefutable standards. You've got Assets, Liabilities, Owner's Equity, Income, and Expenses. These are standard terms used over all forms of accounting to define profit, loss, and the fiscal health of your business. Every time you process a transaction, two things happen: one account is credited while another receives a debit (kind of like yin and yang). To get more familiar with these terms (and those in the following list), see the definitions in the chart of accounts later in this chapter and also in Appendix A (a mini glossary I've included for your convenience). Depending on the type of account, the account's balance either increases or decreases. One account increasing as another decreases is called *double-entry accounting:*

- When you post an expense, the debit *increases* your expenses, and *decreases* your bank account.

- When you purchase furniture or other assets, it *increases* your Asset account and *decreases* your bank account.

- When you make a sale and make the deposit, it *increases* your bank account and *decreases* your accounts receivable.

✔ When you purchase inventory, it *increases* your inventory and *decreases* your bank account.

✔ When a portion of a sale includes sales tax, it *decreases* your sales, and *increases* your Sales Tax account.

Manually performing double-entry accounting can be a bit taxing (no pun intended), but a software program will automatically adjust the accounts when you input a transaction. As a business owner, even if you're a sole proprietor (see Chapter 15 for information on business types), you should keep your business books separate from your personal expenses. (I recommend using a program like Quicken to keep track of your personal expenses for tax time.) By isolating the business records from the personal records, you're able to get a snapshot of what areas of your sales are doing well and which ones aren't carrying their weight. But that isn't the only reason keeping accurate records is smart; there's the IRS to think about, too. In the next section, I explain Uncle Sam's interest in your books.

Records Uncle Sam May Want to See

One of the reasons we can have a great business environment in the United States is because we all have a partner, Uncle Sam. Our government regulates business and sets the rules for us to transact our operations. To help you out with your business, the IRS maintains a business Web site at `www.irs.ustreas.gov/prod/smallbiz/index.htm` (see Figure 16-1). Throughout this section, I highlight what information you need to keep and for how long you should keep it (just in case you're chosen for an audit).

Hiring a professional to do your year-end taxes

When I say that you must hire a professional to prepare your taxes, I mean a certified public accountant (CPA) if your business format is a corporation, or an enrolled agent (EA) for a sole proprietorship or partnership. An *enrolled agent* is a tax professional who's licensed by the Federal Government. Enrolled agents must pass an annual two-day long exam (less than a third of the people who take the test actually pass it), and are required to fulfill continuing education requirements to maintain their standing. Just like a CPA or a tax attorney, EAs are authorized to appear before the IRS on your behalf in the event of an audit. Unlike a CPA or an attorney, however, EAs don't charge an arm and a leg.

Posting bookkeeping can be boring. At the end of the year when you have a professional do your taxes, however, you'll be a lot happier — and your tax preparation will cost you less — if you have all your information posted cleanly and in the proper order. That's why using QuickBooks (see the section "QuickBooks: Making Bookkeeping Uncomplicated" elsewhere in this chapter) is so essential to running your business.

Figure 16-1:
IRS Small
Business
Hub on the
Web.

Supporting information

Aside from needing to know how your business is going (which is really important), the main reason to keep clear and concise records is for the anticipation that Uncle Sam may one day come knocking. To stay on the good side of Uncle Sam, you must keep records. You never know when the IRS will pick *your* number and want to examine *your* records. In the following list, I highlight some of the important pieces of *supporting information* (things that support your expenses on your end-of-year tax return) that you should diligently keep track of:

✔ **Receipts:** Dear reader, read carefully and heed this advice: Save every receipt that you get. If you're out of town on a buying trip and have coffee at the airport, save that receipt — it's a deduction from your profits. Everything related to your business may be deductible, so you must save airport parking receipts, taxi receipts, receipts for a pen that you picked up on your way to a meeting, *everything* — if you don't have a receipt, you can't prove the write-off.

✔ **Merchandise invoices:** Saving all merchandise invoices is as important as — if not more than — saving all your receipts. If you want to prove that you actually paid $400 apiece for those PlayStation 2's that you sold at eBay for $500 apiece and not the $299 retail price, you'd *better* have an invoice of some kind. The same idea applies to most collectibles, in which case a retail price can't be fixed. Save all invoices!

- ✔ **Outside contractor invoices:** If you use outside contractors — even if you pay the college kid next door to go to the post office and bank for you — you should also get an invoice from them to document exactly what service you paid for and how much. This is supporting information that will save your bacon, should it ever need saving.

- ✔ **Business cards:** It may sound like I'm stretching things a bit, but if you use your car to look at some merchandise, pick up a business card from the vendor. If you're out of town and have a meeting with someone, take a card. Having these business cards can help substantiate your deductible comings and goings.

- ✔ **A daily calendar:** This is where your Palm Handheld comes in (if you use it for business, it's an expense). Every time you leave your house/office on a business-related task, make note of it in your Palm. Keep as much minutia as you can stand. Your Palm Desktop can print out a monthly calendar. At the end of the year, staple the pages together and include them in your files with your substantiating information.

- ✔ **Credit card statements:** You're already collecting the credit card receipts (although mine always seem to slip through the holes in my purse). If you have your statements, you have monthly proof of expenses. When you get your statement each month, post it into your bookkeeping program and itemize each and every charge, detailing where you spent the money and what for. (QuickBooks has a split feature that accommodates all your categories.) File these statements with your tax return at the end of the year in your year-end envelope (box?).

I know that all this stuff will pile up, but that's when you go to the store and buy some plastic file storage containers to organize it all. To check for new information and the lowdown on what you can and can't do, ask an accountant or a CPA. On your own, visit the IRS Tax Info for Business site, shown in Figure 16-2, at `www.irs.ustreas.gov/prod/bus_info/index.html`.

How long should you keep your records?

How long do you have to keep all this supporting information? I hate to tell you, but I think I've saved it all. I must have at least ten years of paperwork in big plastic boxes and old scary files in the garage. But you know, I'm not too extreme; the time period in which you can amend a return or in which the IRS can assess more tax is never less than three years from the date of filing — and can even be longer. As of my last visit to the IRS Web site, the information in Table 16-1 applied.

Figure 16-2:
IRS Tax Info
for Business
site.

Table 16-1	How Long to Keep Your Records
Circumstances	*Keep Records for This Long*
You owe additional tax (if the following three points don't apply)	3 years
You didn't report all your income and what you didn't report is more than 25% of the gross income shown on your return	6 years
You file a fraudulent tax return	No limit
You don't bother to file a return	No limit
You file a claim of refund or credit after you've filed after tax was paid (whichever is longer)	3 years or 2 years
Your claim is due to a bad debt deduction	7 years
Your claim is from worthless stock	7 years
You have information on assets	For the life of the asset

Even though I got this information directly from the IRS Web site and literature (Publication 583 "Starting a Business and Keeping Records"), it may change in the future. It doesn't hurt to store your information for as long as you can stand it and stay on top of any changes the IRS may implement.

Bookkeeping Software

If keeping track of your auctions is hard, keeping track of the dollars and cents is even harder (and more time consuming) without software. If using software to automate your auctions makes sense, so does using software to automate your bookkeeping. You can afford to make a mistake here and there within your own office, and no one will ever know. But if you make a mistake in the books, your partner (Uncle Sam) will notice — and be quite miffed. He may even charge you a penalty or two so that you'll remember not to make those mistakes again.

When I started my business, I used accounting ledger pads (which had just replaced the chisel and stone format). I soon found, even in the days of old, that I had way too much paper and ledgers to keep track of and cross reference with. A calculator was useful, based on the assumption that I typed in the correct figures to start with — and reconciling a checkbook was always an onerous task.

With bookkeeping software, reconciling a checkbook is a breeze, merely clicking off the deposits and checks. If I make a mistake in my inputting the data, the software (comparing my balance and my banks) lets me know that I made an error. This kind of efficiency would have put Bob Cratchit out of a job!

I researched various Web sites to find which software was the best selling and easiest to use. I had many discussions with CPAs, Enrolled Agents, and bookkeepers. I discovered from my research that the software that these professionals most recommend for business is Intuit's QuickBooks. (Thank goodness that's the one I use.) QuickBooks is considered the best and so that's why I devote so much of this chapter to it. Some people begin with Quicken and later move to QuickBooks when the business gets big or incorporates. My theory? Start with the best, it's not that much more expensive — I've seen the new, sealed software of QuickBooks Pro 2001 for as low as $120 and QuickBooks for as low as $65 — and it will see you directly to the big time. Interestingly, this is the first item that I've found it for less at sites other than eBay.

QuickBooks: Making Bookkeeping Uncomplicated

If you're wondering why you see two versions of QuickBooks, QuickBooks Pro and just QuickBooks, you'll want to know that there are a few significant differences between the two. QuickBooks Pro adds in job costing and time estimating features and the ability to use the program over a network. As I tell you in Appendix B, I'm a big fan of my home phone line network. Because I have a network, I use the networked version. You'll probably be networking down the line — something I highly recommend — so I give you the lowdown on QuickBooks Pro 2001 throughout the rest of this section.

Stephen L. Nelson wrote *QuickBooks 2001 For Dummies* (published by Hungry Minds, Inc.), an amazingly easy to understand book about QuickBooks. I swear that neither Steve nor my publisher gave me a nickel for recommending his book (I even had to pay for my copy); I recommend this book simply because it answers just about any question you'll have about using the program for your bookkeeping needs. Spend the money and get the book (it may be a tax write-off, just as this book may be). Any money spent on increasing your knowledge is money well spent.

I update my QuickBooks software every year, and every year (because of product improvements) it takes me less time to perform my bookkeeping tasks. As your business grows, you may find that you just don't have the time to input your own bookkeeping data, and you may have to hire a bookkeeper. The bonus is that professional bookkeepers probably already know QuickBooks, and the best part is that they can print out daily reports for you that keep you apprised of your business condition. Also, at the end of each year, QuickBooks will supply you with all the official reports your Enrolled Agent (EA) or Certified Public Accountant (CPA) will need to do your taxes. (Yes, you really do need an EA or a CPA; see the sidebar "Hiring a professional to do your year-end taxes" elsewhere in this chapter.) You can even send them a backup on a zip disk or a CD-ROM. See how simple bookkeeping can be?

QuickBooks 2001 integrates with PayPal

One other benefit of QuickBooks is that it integrates directly with PayPal. When you enable Online Billing within the program, you have the option of sending an invoice via e-mail. Customize the e-mail message that accompanies your invoice, select the Accept Online Payment for This Invoice check box, and then click Send Now. In QuickBooks 2001, an alert is displayed in your QuickBooks Company Page when your PayPal account receives an online payment. With one click in QuickBooks, the information will be recorded automatically in QuickBooks.

QuickBooks Pro 2001

Bookkeeping follows a universal format; when you first fire up QuickBooks Pro 2001, you must first answer a few questions to set up your account. A few things that you need to have ready before you even begin to mess with the software include some starting figures:

- **Cash balance:** This may be the amount in your checkbook (no personal money, please!) or it could be the amount of money from your eBay profits. Put these profits into a separate checking account to use for your business.

- **Accounts receivable balance:** Does anyone owe you money for some auctions? Outstanding payments comprise this total.

- **Account liability balance:** Do you owe some money? Are you being invoiced for some merchandise that you haven't paid for? Total it up and type it in when QuickBooks asks you.

If you're starting your business in the middle of the year, you should get any previous profits and expenses together that you want to include because you'll have to input those after you're set up as well. I can guarantee that this is going to take a while. But after you've organized your finances, even if it takes a little sweat to set it up initially, you'll be thanking me for insisting you get organized. It just makes everything work smoother in the long run.

QuickBooks EasyStep Interview

After you've organized all your finances, you can proceed with the QuickBooks EasyStep Interview (see Figure 16-3) to get you going. The EasyStep interview is designed to give those with "accountingphobia" and those using a bookkeeping program for the first time a comfort level. Don't get too scared when you do this. If you mess things up, you can always use the back arrow and change what you've input. If you need help, simply click the Help button and the program will answer many of your questions. Hey, if worse comes to worst, you can always delete the file from the root directory and start over.

For the whirlwind tour through the QuickBooks EasyStep Interview, just follow these steps (only a general guideline):

1. **Start QuickBooks.**

2. **On the first page of the interview, input your company name (this becomes the filename in your computer) and also the legal name of your company.**

    If you've filed a fictitious name statement (see Chapter 15), that's the legal name of your company.

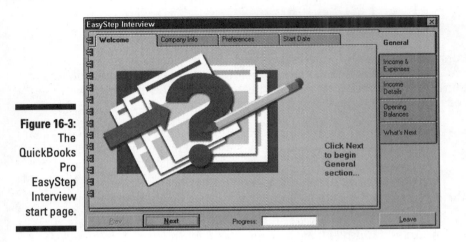

Figure 16-3:
The
QuickBooks
Pro
EasyStep
Interview
start page.

3. **Continue to follow the steps (answering other questions about your business, such as DBA and legal name), until QuickBooks finally asks what type of business you want to use.**

   Because QuickBooks doesn't offer an online sales business, choose Retail, which is the closest to what you need (see Figure 16-4). With the chart of accounts that I feature in the following section, you can make the appropriate changes to your accounts to adapt to your eBay business.

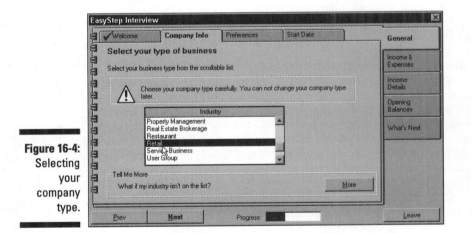

Figure 16-4:
Selecting
your
company
type.

4. **When QuickBooks asks whether you want to use its chosen chart of accounts, choose Yes (you can always change the accounts later); see Figure 16-5.**

   If you want to spend the time, you can input your custom chart of accounts manually (but I *really, really* don't recommend it).

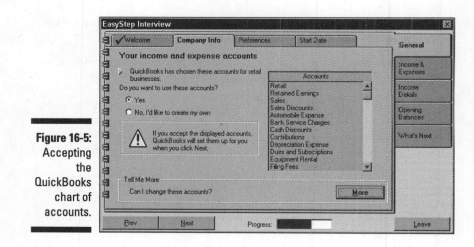

Figure 16-5:
Accepting
the
QuickBooks
chart of
accounts.

After answering more general questions that I'm sure you can handle with the aid of the incredibly intuitive QuickBooks help area, the preferences pages appear where you'll make some an important choice. I recommend that you select the option "Enter the bills first and then enter the payments later," because if you input your bills as they come in, you can get an exact idea of how much money you owe at any time by just starting the program.

5. **Next choose the type of invoice that you want to use.**

   You can customize your invoice with your logo later. I suggest that you select the *product* style of invoice (see Figure 16-6) because that's what you're selling!

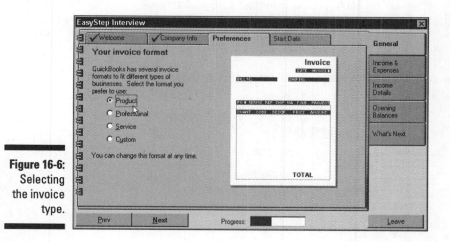

Figure 16-6:
Selecting
the invoice
type.

6. **Answer a few more questions including whether you want to use the Cash basis of accounting or the Accrual basis.**

   The *accrual* basis posts your sales the minute you write an invoice, and your expenses are posted as soon as you post the bills into the computer. Accrual basis accounting gives you a clearer picture of where your company is financially than cash basis accounting does. The *cash* basis is when you record bills by writing checks — expenses are posted only when you write the checks. This way of doing business may be simpler, but the only way you'll know how much money you owe is by looking at the pile of bills on your desk.

   If you're new to bookkeeping, you may want to go through the interview step-by-step. For more details, remember to check out *QuickBooks 2001 For Dummies* — this book can teach you almost everything you need to know about QuickBooks.

7. **If you're comfortable, just click Leave and input the balance of your required information directly into the program without using the interview.**

QuickBooks chart of accounts

After you've finished the EasyStep Interview and have successfully set yourself up in QuickBooks, the program presents a *chart of accounts.* Think of the chart of accounts as an organization system, like file folders. It keeps all related data in the proper area. When you write a check to pay a bill, it deducts the amount from your checking account, reduces your accounts payable, and perhaps increases your asset or expense accounts. You have a choice of giving each listing a number. These numbers, a kind of bookkeeping shorthand, are standardized throughout bookkeeping; believe it or not, everybody in the industry seems to know what number goes with what item. To keep things less confusing, I like to use numbers as well as titles.

To customize your chart of accounts, follow these steps:

1. **Choose Edit⇨Preferences.**

2. **When the box opens, click the Accounting icon on the left.**

3. **Go to the Company preferences tab and indicate that you'd like to use account numbers.**

   Figure 16-7 shows you the new numbered chart of accounts and where you go to add new items.

   An editable chart of accounts appears.

4. **Because QuickBooks doesn't have an Online Auction/Store as an option, you will need to edit.**

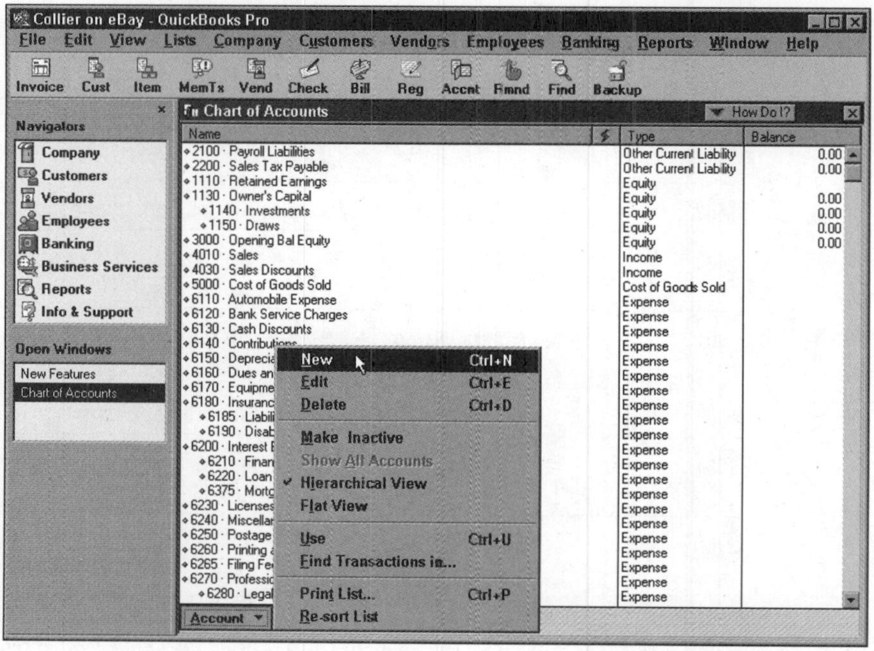

Figure 16-7:
Your chart
of accounts
now has
numbers
generated
by
QuickBooks.

In Table 16-2, I show you a chart of accounts that a CPA wrote for an
eBay business. Go through your QuickBooks chart of accounts and add
any missing categories. You may not need all these categories and you
can always add more later.

Table 16-2	eBay Business Chart of Accounts	
Account Number	*Account Name*	*What It Represents*
1001	Checking	All revenue deposited here and all checks drawn upon this account
1002	Money market account	Company savings account
1100	Accounts receivable	For customers to whom you extend credit
1201	Merchandise inventory	Charge to Cost of Sales as used, or take periodic inventories and adjust at that time
1202	Shipping Supplies	Boxes, tape, labels, and so forth. Charge these off to cost as used, or take an inventory at the end of the period and adjust to Cost of Sales.

(continued)

Table 16-2 *(continued)*

Account Number	Account Name	What It Represents
1401	Office Furniture & Equipment	Desk, computer, telephone
1402	Shipping Equipment	Scales, tape dispensers
1403	Vehicles	Your vehicle if it's owned by the company
1501	Accumulated Depreciation	For your accountant's use
1601	Deposits	Security deposits
2001	Accounts Payable	Amounts owed for the stuff you sell
2100	Payroll Liabilities	Taxes deducted from employees' checks and taxes paid by company on employee earnings.
2200	Sales Tax Payable	Sales tax collected at time of sale and owed to State.
2501	Equipment loans	
2502	Auto loans	
3000	Owner's capital	Your opening balance
3902	Owner's draw	Your withdrawals for the current year
4001	Merchandise sales	Revenue from sales of your products
4002	Shipping and handling	Paid by the customer
4009	Returns	Total dollar amount of returned merchandise
4101	Interest income	From your investments
4201	Other income	Income not otherwise classified
5001	Merchandise purchases	
5002	Freight in	Freight and shipping charges you pay for your inventory, not for shipments to customers
5003	Shipping	Shipping to your customers: USPS, FedEx, UPS, and so on

Account Number	Account Name	What It Represents
5004	Shipping Supplies	Boxes, labels, tape, Bubble Wrap
6110	Automobile expense	(when you use your car for work)
6111	Gas and oil	
6112	Repairs	(when your business owns the car)
6120	Bank service charges	Monthly service charges, NSF charges, and so forth
6140	Contributions	Charity
6142	Data services	
6143	Internet Service Provider	
6144	Web site hosting fees	
6150	Depreciation expense	(for your accountant's use)
6151	eBay fees	
6152	Discounts	Fees that you're charged for using eBay and accepting credit card payments; deducted from your revenue and reported to you on your eBay statement
6153	Other auction site fees (Yahoo! or Amazon.com or others give each auction site its own category and next following number)	
6156	PayPal fees	
6157	Billpoint fees	
6158	Credit card merchant account fees	
6160	Dues and subscriptions	
6161	Magazines and periodicals	
6162	User groups, organizations	
6170	Equipment rental	Postage meter, occasional van
6180	Insurance	

(continued)

Table 16-2 *(continued)*

Account Number	Account Name	What It Represents
6185	Liability Insurance	
6190	Disability Insurance	
6191	Health insurance	If provided for yourself, you may be required to provide it to employees
6200	Interest expense	Credit interest and interest on loans
6210	Finance charges	
6220	Loan interest	
6230	Licenses and permits	
6240	Miscellaneous	Whatever doesn't go anyplace else
6250	Postage and delivery	Stamps, e-stamps
6251	stamps.com fees	
6260	Printing	Your business cards, correspondence stationary, and so on
6265	Filing fees	
6270	Professional fees	
6280	Legal fees	
6650	Accounting and bookkeeping	
6290	Rent	Office, warehouse, and so on
6291	eBay online store rent	
6300	Repairs	
6310	Building repairs	
6320	Computer repairs	
6330	Equipment repairs	
6340	Telephone	Regular telephone, FAX lines
6350	Travel and entertainment	Business-related travel, business meals

Account Number	Account Name	What It Represents
6360	Entertainment	
6370	Meals	
6390	Utilities	
6391	Electricity and gas	
6392	Water	
6560	Payroll expenses	Wages paid to others
6770	Supplies	
6772	Computer	
6780	Marketing	
6790	Office	
6820	Taxes	
6830	Federal	
6840	Local	
6850	Property	
6860	State	

QuickBooks on the Web

If you want to handle everything on the Web, QuickBooks has an online service that you can use (see Figure 16-8). On the Web, the QuickBooks program is a bit less robust (offers less features) than the home version. If your accounting needs are simple, it may be a solution for you. Before you decide, however, consider that while your accounting needs may now be simple, they may not be so simple later.

Intuit charges $14.95 a month for the service, which is comparable to buying the QuickBooks Pro version. The online version also requires you to have a broadband connection to the Internet so that you're always online. The online edition doesn't include integrated payroll, purchase orders, online banking, and bill payments.

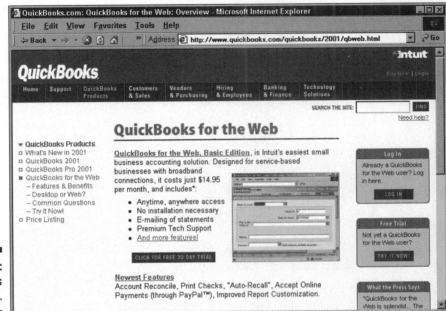

Figure 16-8:
QuickBooks
for the Web.

Chapter 17

Building an eBay Back Office

In This Chapter
▶ Organizing your stock
▶ Keeping inventory
▶ Exploring shipping materials
▶ Becoming your own post office

The more items you sell, the more confusing things can get. As you build your eBay business, that little side table that you use for storing eBay merchandise isn't going to work. You must think industrial. Even part-time sellers can benefit by adding a few professional touches to their business areas.

So here I emphasize the importance of setting up and organizing your back office. I cover everything from stacking your stock to keeping inventory to indispensable packing materials and online postage services. Organization will be your byword. Dive right in. The sooner you read this chapter, the sooner you can build your eBay back office and get down to business.

The Warehouse: Organizing Your Space

Whether you plan to sell large items or small items, you need storage space in which to store them. As you make savvy purchases, maintaining an item's mint condition will be one of your greatest challenges. Organized storage in itself is an art, so in this section, I cover the details of what you'll need to safeguard your precious stock.

Shelving your profits

Before you stock the shelves, it helps to have some! You also need a place to put the shelves, either your garage or in a spare room or somewhere. You have a choice between two basic kinds of shelves:

- **Plastic:** If you're just starting out, you can always go to the local closet and linen supply store to buy inexpensive plastic shelves. They're a bit bulky, but they're light and cheap — and will buckle in time.

- **Steel:** If you want to do it right the first time, buy steel shelving. The most versatile steel shelving is the wire kind, which is lighter and allows air to circulate around your items. Steel wire shelving assembles easily; I put mine together without help. They come with leveling feet and 4" casters, so should you need to move a shelf unit, you can. Installing the casters is up to you. You can combine steel wire shelving units to create a full wall of shelves. Each shelf safely holds as much as 600 pounds of merchandise.

    Search eBay for **shelving** to find sellers offering this kind of industrial shelving. The main problem with ordering this product online is that the shipping usually costs more than the shelving.

 To save you time, dear reader, I researched the subject and found some readily available, reasonably priced shelves. Just go to Sam's Club or Costco and look for Seville Classics Four shelf commercial shelving, sold in 48" and 36" wide units. These shelves are also available on the Costco Web site, but you have to pay for shipping.

Box 'em or bag 'em?

Packing your items for storage can be a challenge. As long as you're picking up your shelving (see previous section), pick up some sandwich baggies, and quart and gallon size plastic bags, too. These baggies are perfect for storing smaller items. In plastic, your items won't pick up any smell or become musty before you sell them. The plastic also protects the items from rubbing against each other and causing possible damage. If you package them one item to a bag, you can then just lift one off the shelf and put it directly into a shipping box when the auction is over.

Your bags of items will have to go into boxes for storage on the shelves. Clear plastic storage boxes, the kind you often find at superstores, are great for bulky items. They're usually 26 inches in size, so before you buy these big plastic containers, be sure that they'll fit on your shelving comfortably and that you'll have easy access to your items. Using the cardboard office-type file storage boxes from an office supply store is another option. These cardboard boxes are 10" x 12" x 16", which is a nice size for storing medium-size products. At around $1 each, they're the most economical choice. Smaller boxes with various compartments, such as the kind home improvement stores carry for storing tools, work great for storing very small items.

Inventory: Keeping Track of What You've Got and Where You Keep It

Savvy eBay sellers have different methods of handling home store inventory. They use everything from spiral-bound notebooks to sophisticated software programs. Although computerized inventory tracking can simplify this task, starting with a plain ol' handwritten ledger is fine, too. Choose whichever works best for you; keep in mind that as your eBay business grows, a software program that tracks inventory for you may become necessary.

Most of these systems seem rather basic, and wouldn't work for a company with a warehouse full of stock. Such basic systems, however, will work nicely in your eBay sales environment. Many sellers tape sheets of paper to their boxes to identify them by number, and use that as a reference to a simple Excel spreadsheet for selling purposes. Excel spreadsheets are perfect for keeping track of your auctions as well, but if you're using a management service or software, you don't need both. In Chapter 8, I detail a variety of auction management software and Web sites, many of which include inventory tracking features.

You may also want to use Excel spreadsheets for your downloaded Billpoint statements, to hold information waiting to transfer to your bookkeeping program.

Planning: The key to good organization

When it became time for me to put my eBay merchandise in order, I was busy with my regular business, and so I hired people to organize my eBay area. This decision turned out to be one massive mistake. They organized everything and put all my items in boxes — but didn't label the boxes to indicate what was stored in each. I still haven't recovered and don't know where a bunch of my stuff is! So a bit of advice: Think things out and plan where you'll put everything. Organize your items by theme, type, or size. If you organize before planning in advance, you might end up with organized disorganization.

The Shipping Department: Packin' It Up

If you've read *eBay For Dummies,* you know all about the various ways to pack your items; I hope you've become an expert! Throughout this section, I review some of the things that you must have for a complete, smooth-running shipping department: cleaning supplies, packing materials, and so on. The *handling fee* portion of your shipping charges pays for these kinds of items. Don't run low on them and pay attention to how you store shipping supplies. They must be kept in a clean environment. Plastic tends to pick up smells and dust doesn't help its appearance.

Pre-packaging clean up

Be sure the items you send out are in tip-top shape. Here are a few everyday chemicals that can gild the lily:

- **WD-40:** The decades-old lubricant works very well at getting price stickers off of plastic and glass without damaging the product. The plastic on a toy box may begin to look nasty, even when stored in a clean environment; a quick wipe with a paper towel with a dash of WD-40 will make it shine like new.

- **Goo Gone:** Goo Gone also works miracles in cleaning up gooey sticker residue from non-porous items.

- **un-du:** This amazing liquid easily takes stickers off cardboard without causing damage. It comes packaged with a mini scraper top that can be used in any of your sticker cleaning projects. If you can't find un-du, check out my Web site (www.coolebaytools.com) for places to purchase it or you can always just use lighter fluid (which is, of course, a bit more dangerous).

Packing materials

So that you can always be sure that your items will arrive at their destinations in one piece, you'll want to keep the following on hand at all times:

- **Bubble Wrap:** A clean, puffy product that comes in rolls, Bubble Wrap is available in several sizes. Depending on your product, you may have to carry two sizes of Bubble Wrap to properly protect the goods. Bubble Wrap can be somewhat expensive, but check out vendors at eBay; you'll find quite a lot of them there (and possibly find a deal). See Figure 17-1.

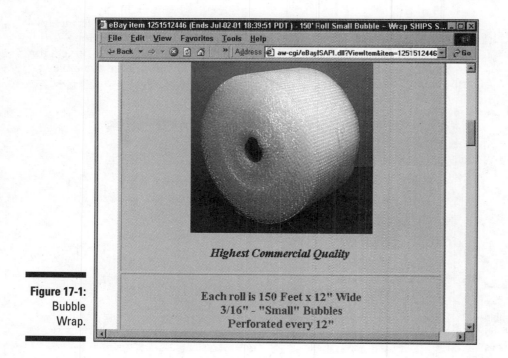

eBay item 1251512446 (Ends Jul 02 01 18:39:51 PDT) - 150' Roll Small Bubble ~ Wrap SHIPS S...

File   Edit   View   Favorites   Tools   Help

Back   ▼   →   ▼   ⊗   ↻   ⌂   »   Address   aw-cgi/eBayISAPI.dll?ViewItem&item=1251512446   ▼   →Go

Highest Commercial Quality

Figure 17-1:
Bubble
Wrap.

Each roll is 150 Feet x 12" Wide
3/16" - "Small" Bubbles
Perforated every 12"

- **Styrofoam peanuts:** Why they call them peanuts, I'll never know — I guess somebody thought they look like peanuts. Nonetheless, Styrofoam peanuts protect just about everything you ship. Storing them is the tricky part. One of the most unique storage solutions I've seen is putting the peanuts into 33-gallon plastic trash bags, and then hanging these bags on cup hooks (available at the hardware store) around the walls in a garage. When packing with peanuts, be sure that you place the item carefully and use enough peanuts to fill the box *completely;* leaving any airspace defeats the point of using the peanuts in the first place.

- **Plastic bags:** Buy plastic bags as cheaply as you can by buying in bulk. Buy various sizes and use them for shipping and storing. Even large kitchen or trash bags are good for wrapping up posters and large items; the plastic protects the item from inclement weather by waterproofing it.

- **Two- or three-inch shipping tape:** You'll need clear tape for finishing up packages that go any other way than USPS Priority. You'll also need the clear tape to place over address labels to protect them from scrapes and rain. I once got a package — just barely — with an address label soaked with rain and barely legible. Don't risk a lost package for want of a few inches of tape. If you're shipping via Priority Mail, the post office will supply you with free pre-printed tape. See the following section on boxes for more information.

✔ **Bubble envelopes** (see Figure 17-2): If you send out items that fit nicely into Bubble Wrap-lined envelopes, use them. This type of envelope — with paper on the outside and Bubble Wrap on the inside — is perfect for mailing small items via First class mail. These envelopes are available in quantity (an economical choice) and don't take up much storage space.

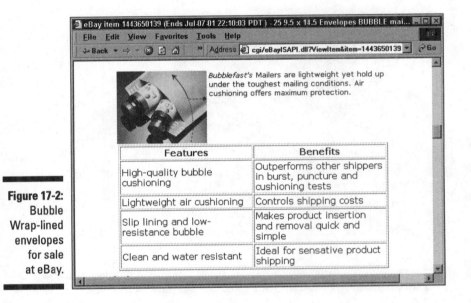

Figure 17-2:
Bubble
Wrap-lined
envelopes
for sale
at eBay.

Packaging — the heart of the matter

Depending on the size of the item you sell, you can purchase boxes in bulk at reliable sources. Because you have a resale number (see Chapter 15), look in your local yellow pages for boxes. You should find a large amount of box retailers. Try to purchase from a manufacturer that specializes in B2B (business to business) sales. Some box companies specialize in selling to the occasional box user. Knowing the size that you need enables you to buy by the case lot.

You can save big money if your items fit into boxes that the post office supplies and you plan on using Priority Mail. The USPS will give you all the boxes and mailing envelopes you need for free, and it offers plenty of sizes to choose from. Go to http://supplies.usps.gov/ (see Figure 17-3) to order your packing tape, labels, forms, and just about anything else that you'll need to ship Priority Mail. Be sure to order a month or so before you need the boxes so that you'll have the size you need when you need it. See the handy Table 17-1 for available sizes, so you can plan your order.

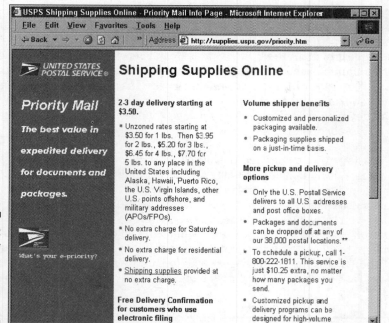

Figure 17-3:
Order
shipping
supplies
from the
USPS.

Table 17-1	Free Priority Mail Packaging	
Size	*Description*	*Minimum Quantity*
8⅝" x 5⅜" x 1⅝"	Small video box	25
9¼" x 6¼" x 2"	Large video box	25
11¼" x 14" x 2¼"	Medium	25
12¼" x 15½" x 3"	Large	25
6" x 38"	Triangle tube	10
7" x 7" x 6"	Small square	25
12" x 12" x 8"	Medium square	25
12½" x 15½"	Tyvek envelope	1
6" x 10"	Cardboard envelope	1
12½" x 9½"	2lb. Flat rate cardboard envelope	1
12½" x 9½"	1lb. Cardboard envelope	25
5" x 10"	Cardboard window envelope	1

The Mail Room: Sendin' It Out

In August of 1999, the United States Postal Service announced a new service: information-based Indicia (IBI). Targeted at the SOHO (small office/home office) market, IBI is USPS-certified postage that you can print on envelopes and sticker labels right from your PC. Throughout this section, I give you the lowdown on the main Internet postage vendors: Stamps.com, Pitney Bowes, and Simply Postage.

I'm a savvy consumer and businesswoman. I don't believe in paying for extras, nor do I believe in being a victim of hidden charges. The online postage arena — while providing helpful tools that make running your eBay business easier — is fraught with bargains, deals, and introductory offers. I urge you to read any of these offers carefully so that you know what you're getting yourself into: Evaluate how much it will cost you to start out, and how much it will cost you to maintain an ongoing relationship with the company. Although you may initially get some free hardware and pay a low introductory rate, in fine print, you may have agreed to pay unreasonably high

Clickstamp Online from Pitney Bowes

Pitney Bowes has just announced a new service, Clickstamp Online. Its functions are similar to the stamps.com functions, and it enables you to print postage directly from your computer. Register online at the Pitney Bowes Web site (www.pitneybowes.com/), and then you can download its software. Here's what you get:

✔ **Zip code check:** The software runs a check on your addresses and corrects any zip code errors you've made.

✔ **Weigh the package:** You must manually weigh your package with a separate postage scale (not attached to your computer) and input the weight amounts into the software. The scale is not integrated into the software.

✔ **Media mail:** None of the other Internet postage services currently support media mail postage. You need this rate of postage if you're mailing books, or selling items at Half.com.

✔ **Labels:** To use Clickstamp Online, you must print your package labels on 3.33" x 4" labels. (You aren't restricted to the pink-topped labels.)

✔ **Purchase postage online:** You can purchase postage with no surcharge, purchasing as little as $10 to a maximum of $500.

✔ **NO Delivery Confirmations:** You cannot print delivery confirmations with Clickstamp. An excellent workaround to this would be to use Clickstamp in conjunction with the free (covered by a monthly fee) delivery confirmations from Shippertools.com (see Chapter 14).

The best part? As I write this, Pitney Bowes offers a 30-day free trial period, and the total monthly fees are only $1.49 a month. Of course, this may be the big introductory bargain. Visit www.pitneyworks.com and click Internet postage to find out the current skinny on Clickstamp.

monthly prices six months down the line. I always double-check pricing before getting into anything, and I urge you to do the same.

Your old pal the United States Postal Service wants to help you grow online, too. The post office now has Web tools that enable you to file for delivery confirmations free of charge (that's right — no more 40 cents each). One caveat though: You have to install its API (or use the resources of Shippertools.com) to take advantage of this great service (see Chapter 14).

Stamps.com

Stamps.com (see Figure 17-4) recently purchased 31 Internet postage patents from e-stamp (which discontinued its online postage service late in 2000; I was a big fan of e-stamp), making its services a combination of the best of both sites. I moved my postage business over to Stamps.com and I like it.

Stamps.com works with software that you probably use every day, integrating itself into many programs, such as Microsoft Word, Outlook, and Office, Corel WordPerfect, Palm Desktop, Quicken, and more. Plus, I enjoy

- **Using my printer to print my postage:** If your printer allows it, you can even print your envelopes along with barcoded addresses, your return address, and postage. This saves quite a bit in label costs.

  The Stamps.com custom Envelope Wizard permits you to design your own envelopes, including your logo or graphics. You can purchase a box of 500 #10 envelopes for as little as $3.99 (available at office supply stores).

- **Having Stamps.com check to be sure that my addresses are valid:** Prior to printing any postage, the Stamps.com software contacts the USPS database of every valid mailing address in the United States. This Address Matching System (AMS) is updated monthly, so your addresses will always be valid and up to date.

- **Having Stamps.com add on the extra four digits to my addressee's zip codes:** A nifty feature that helps ensure delivery while freeing me of the hassle.

With Stamps.com, purchasing postage is as easy as clicking the mouse (go to www.stamps.com); your credit card information is secure on its site. It offers the following two plans:

- **Simple Plan:** The charges on the Simple Plan (for small users) are based on 10 percent of your postage printed each month. The minimum that your credit card is charged is $4.49 per month (in case you don't print that much postage).

- **Power Plan:** This plan is better suited to those who send out many packages a day, costs a flat rate of $18.99 per month, and includes a free four-pound digital postage scale.

Figure 17-4:
Stamps.com.

With Stamps.com, you don't *need* any extra fancy equipment, although it does offer an electronic scale that integrates with its software to calculate the correct postage for your item. The scale also functions on its own. Simple Plan users can actually get a better postage scale through the Stamps.com store, run online through Office Depot.

Office Depot also sells a digital scale that weighs packages up to ten pounds and works with the Stamps.com software. The software allows you to type in your postal class and any additional services (delivery confirmation, insurance, and so on) and add it to the postage amount. And in case you forget, you're reminded visually of which USPS form you need to attach to your package.

Because Office Depot delivers any order over $50 free the next day, it's a great place to get supplies. If you use the three-part Internet postage labels, you're given an address label, a return address label, and a pink-trimmed postage label set. You get 25 sheets to a package, giving you 150 label sets. The final cost per label set is .053 cents (that's little more than a nickel for 150 labels).

To find the Stamps.com deal of the month, visit its Web site. The site regularly offers sign-up bonuses that include as much as $20 free postage.

Simply Postage

Simply Postage has been actively promoting its services to attract eBay users. A division of Europe's largest mailroom equipment producer, Neopost, Inc. (in business for over 70 years, it knows quite a bit about the mailing business), Simply Postage conducts business online as Neopost Online, Inc. or as SimplyPostage.com (see Figure 17-5).

In the following list, I detail the highlights:

- **Integrated postage unit:** The Simply Postage way of putting a little post office in your eBay office is to supply you with an *integrated postage unit,* a mini postage meter/thermal printer/scale that fits in the palm of your hand. A hybrid system, it combines Internet postage and proprietary hardware (the integrated postage unit). The scale handles packages only up to 4.4 pounds.

  The integrated postage unit prints postage without needing you to input the addressee's address; it merely prints the postage indicia like the old-fashioned postage meter without the bar coded address label. A pre-bar coded address label goes through the post office somewhat quicker. Simply Postage has its own software, which allows you to purchase and download your postage from its servers by charging your debit or credit card. It will let you know how much is in your account at any time, and can print any amount of postage.

- **Create a Stamp software:** To help you become your own post office, Simply Postage sends you its Create a Stamp software on a CD that runs on your computer. The integrated postage unit hooks into your computer through a serial or USB connection to calculate the proper postage for your package. Should your package weigh over 4.4 pounds, you have to calculate the postage manually, and set the unit to print out the appropriate amount of postage.

- **Printing postage:** One of the benefits of the Simply Postage service is that you can print postage on your integrated unit — as long as you have postage money downloaded to your computer (whether you're online or offline). You can also disconnect the postage unit from your computer and print postage without the computer connection — just like the old postage meter. If you're a postage meter user, Simply Postage may be a good way to ease your shipping into the 21st century.

- **Competitive pricing:** The regular price for using the Simply Postage system is $14.95 per month, which covers the use of the integrated postage unit, plus the cost of your postage. There's no percentage surcharge on your purchases, so you can buy in any increment without additional cost. Should you decide to stop doing business with Simply Postage, you must return the integrated postage unit to them.

✔ **Thermal labels:** The only other cost is the cost of its proprietary thermal labels, which are available in rolls of 100, in units of 4 rolls at $18.49 (.0462 cents per label), 8 rolls at $32.79 (.0409 cents per label), and 16 rolls at $59 (.0368 cents per label). The site claims that if you download an average of $100 per month of postage, you go through approximately one roll (100 labels) per month.

Online postage introductory discounts can change monthly, so be sure to check www.simplypostage.com/ebay/default.asp for current offerings to eBay users. If you don't find any eBay user deals there, check out www.simplypostage.com.

Figure 17-5:
Simply
Postage.
com.

Part V
The Part of Tens

The 5th Wave   By Rich Tennant

"I think we ought to check first to see if eBay has a category for 'Fertility gods: Ancient.'"

In this part . . .

*N*ot everyone is a shooting star at eBay, but it's a good goal to reach for. So in this special part of tens (and for your inspiration), I've included profiles on some very interesting people — from all walks of life — who've turned eBay into a profitable enterprise, some working only part-time. You'll also find information on moving merchandise that you think you might never sell.

Chapter 18

Ten (Or So) Successful eBay Sellers and Their Stories

In This Chapter

▶ People who make their living selling at eBay . . .

▶ . . . and love it!

I really enjoy hearing stories about how much people like eBay. I enjoy it even more when I hear that they're doing something that they get pleasure from while earning a good living. One of the best parts of teaching at eBay University is talking to the sellers who attend. I get the opportunity to bounce ideas around with them, and learn about the creative ways they spend their time at eBay.

I thought you might like to know more about some of the people at eBay, so I interviewed them; it was so much fun getting to know about each of them. Everyone seems to be from a different background and lifestyle — but they all have one thing in common: eBay!

In favor of highlighting some regular folks at eBay, I dispensed with the customary writer thing (you know, finding the biggest sellers at eBay to interview). No one's a success overnight, and the people I discuss in this chapter certainly have been plugging away at eBay, growing their businesses and becoming quite successful. I dug through some old feedbacks (all the way back to 1997) and contacted sellers to see how they're doing these days. Here are their stories (and their advice). . . .

Ally-cat

Member since September 1997; Feedback: 8,118

Allison Morgan sells collectibles in Toy Shop Magazine and adds eBay (which she heard about early on) to her marketing mix (see Figure 18-1). Selling is a full-time job for Allison and her husband Craig, who work together on the auctions and finding merchandise. They once sold a car at eBay: a 1987 Camaro for $8500. Perhaps that isn't a toy to you and me, but I'm sure it is to someone.

Allison and Craig visit yard sales, shows, and other places to find unique items to sell. They once bought a Batman Pez dispenser at a yard sale for a dime; they sold it at eBay for $170. They also bought a 1970s classic Blythe doll at another sale for just fifty cents; they turned it around at eBay for $175. Now that's smart yard sale shopping. (Check out Chapter 6 for ideas on finding merchandise to sell at eBay.)

Their full-time eBay work takes up about 40–50 hours a week, which includes shopping for merchandise, shipping, posting auctions, and answering e-mails. They try to run 200 to 300 auctions per week, depending on merchandise flow. If they've found no collectibles to sell, they also sell software and electronics. Even though they spend a lot of hours working their eBay business, they enjoy setting their own hours and working on their own schedule.

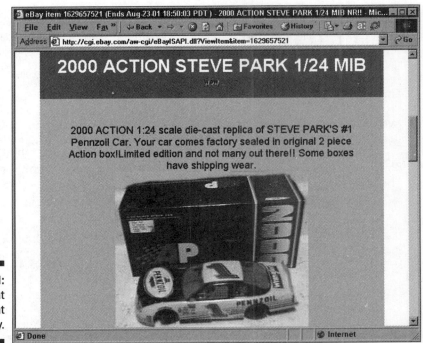

Figure 18-1: An Ally-cat auction at eBay.

Ally-cat's #1 tip for new eBay businesses: If eBay becomes your full-time job, "be prepared for a lot of long hours!"

BobMill

Member since November 1997; Feedback: 13,992

When you take a look at Bob Miller's feedback, you can see that he has a mass of repeat customers. Although his feedback rating is over 14,000, he has over 28,000 positives. Pretty impressive. Bob collects stamps, and that's how he found his way to eBay, purchasing stamps for his own collection. Boy does he collect stamps! In his collection, he has almost all of the 3, 4, 5, 6, and 8 cent stamp sheets and first-day covers — and that's only part of his collection.

He's a pretty funny guy: I recommend checking out his Web site at `www.xmission.com/~emailbox/bob.htm`. His full-time (90 hours a week, no kidding) work is at eBay; he sells stamps, first-day covers, and postcards in his auctions and from his eBay store (see Figure 18-2).

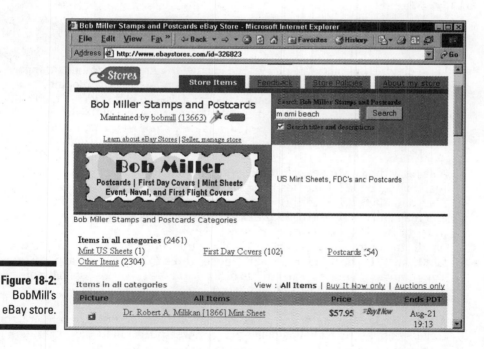

Figure 18-2: BobMill's eBay store.

Bob told me an amazing story about selling a mint sheet of stamps that featured the Final Reunion of the Grand Army of the Republic. The buyer asked him to mail it to a lady recovering from hip surgery. A few days later, he got a handwritten, seven-page letter of thanks. The lady said it brought back such good memories. At age 96, this lady is the only surviving daughter of the last surviving member of the Union Army. She remembered her father's stories of the heat, the noise, and the fear as he and his comrades faced the charge of General Pickett at the Battle of Gettysburg. Selling an item that gets a response like that can make you feel glad to be alive.

Before I get too warm and fuzzy here, however, I'll say that Bob's a serious seller who's aware of his business and the competition at eBay, especially the amateurs who sell valuables at whatever price they can get. He uses software to run his business: AuctionSubmit, Mister Lister for his eBay Store, and eBud for auction management.

Bob's #1 tip for new sellers at eBay: "Listen to your customers. Nothing is more important, but fast shipping is a close second."

Bubblefast

Member since May 1999; Feedback: 6,180

I first met the Bubblefast family when I needed to move my mother's things from Florida to California. When I got the price quote from the moving company for rolls of cushioning, I nearly fell over it was so high! I knew that I could find a better price at eBay and I did. Bubblefast prices were 50 percent less than the moving company had quoted, and they shipped the wrap directly to my mom's house so that I could meet it there to wrap her valuables.

A seller with many repeat customers (nearly 10,000 positives; repeat customers help build businesses!), the Mann Family — Robin, Alan, Jenny, son Alan, and Michelle — work closely together, putting in 70 to 80 hours a week. Son Alan and Jenny (the night owl) help post auctions each night. Jenny also posts the feedback several times a week. Seventeen-year-old Michelle helps handle the order entry system and answers the phone and e-mail. The entire family helps in the packing and shipping for three to four hours each Saturday. They ship anywhere from 100 to 200 orders a day — their postage bill runs $15,000 per month and UPS often $10,000.

Alan, a CPA by training, is now an eBay seller at heart, getting two semi-tractor trailers of bubble cushioning delivered each week. The family has customers from around the world — they've shipped to every state in the U.S. and internationally as far as Japan — who buy from their auctions (see Figure 18-3), eBay store, and Web site (www.bubblefast.com). Last year their business grossed $500,000. The profit margin in the Bubblefast products is low, so they have to make it up in volume.

The Manns' first transaction at eBay took place in early 1999, when Alan bought a Macintosh computer. When it came to finally selling, Alan figured that all eBay sellers would need shipping supplies. At first, they sold just one product, a 150' roll of ³⁄₁₆" (small size) bubble cushioning. Now they sell over 65 variations of 8 or 9 products: bubble cushioning (Bubble Wrap is a registered trademark like Kleenex), anti-static bubble, bubble bags, bubble lined mailers, rolled shipping foam, boxes, sealing tape, and stretch film.

eBay has totally changed this family's lives. "Our family is together all the time now," says Alan. "We've learned to pull together for a common goal." How amazing is that?

The Mann family's tip for eBay sellers: "If you want to create a thriving eBay business and are willing to put the time and energy into it, the possibilities are endless. With minimal investment of money, you have the potential to reach the world! Treat every customer like you want to be treated. After all this time, the customer is still always right."

---

eBay item 1625508774 (Ends Aug-15-01 20:40:35 PDT) - 250 6 x 10 Envelopes BUBBLE mailers F...

File　Edit　View　Fav »　← Back ▾ → ▾ ⊗ ▣ ⚐ ▣ Favorites ☺ History ▤ ▾ ⊿ »

Address ▣ http://cgi.ebay.com/aw-cgi/eBayISAPI.dll?ViewItem&item=1625508774 　 ▾ ⟳ Go

Case of 250 6" x 10" (size #0)
Minimal Internal Dimensions 6" x 8 1/2"
Self-Sealing Bubble Mailers

See our about me Page	
For fixed price items identical to the ones in this auction ready to ship today, and for our complete selection of everything else we sell click now to visit our eBay store-->	The Bubblefast Store!
To see all our other auctions, click here-->	ALL Bubblefast auctions

Bubblefast's Mailers are lightweight yet hold up under the toughest mailing conditions. Air cushioning offers maximum protection.

Features	Benefits
High-quality bubble cushioning	Outperforms other shippers in burst, puncture and

Figure 18-3:
A
Bubblefast
auction.

A community pulls together

Shortly before this book went to press, tragedy struck the Mann family. On August 11th, 2001, Alan Mann was running in a community 10K race when he suffered a massive heart attack. After lingering in a coma, he died on August 28th without ever regaining consciousness. The loss was devastating and unexpected, but the Mann family's close-knit group of relatives and friends banded together to help out. Robin says this of their efforts: "While Alan was in the hospital, some amazing things happened here [at Bubblefast]. We have an incredible group of friends, relatives, and community volunteers (organized by the superintendent of the school

district where Alan was board president) who came in and figured out how to run our business for us virtually uninstructed. System documentation was never a high priority for either of us, so the fact that the business was somehow able to keep running was just unbelievable. It was like something you would see in a movie."

Thanks to the unstinting support she received from a caring group of people, Robin and her children expect to be able to carry on the business that Alan gave so much of his time and energy to create. She knows he would have wanted it that way.

CaliforniaMagic

Member since October 1999; Feedback: 423

An eBay part-time seller, CaliforniaMagic (a.k.a. John Parnell) just loves the contacts he has made and the people he has met at eBay. He never wanted to get involved in selling online until his boss at the largest family-owned camera store chain in Los Angeles (Hooper Camera) roped him into it. John now runs the eBay business for Hooper Camera (eBay user ID HooperCamera, feedback 245), along with his other duties as Industrial Sales Manager for the company. In his spare time, John runs his own general merchandise auctions at eBay (see Figure 18-4).

He started by selling the excess from his home, but John Parnell always wanted to grow up and be a magician who owned a magic store. So when he ran out of excess household stuff, John began to sell specialized magic tricks. He and his fiancée love animals, so they also sell animal-related gifts at eBay. Quite a combination!

In the evenings after work, John spends about 20 hours a week working on his eBay endeavors. He uses Microsoft Excel to keep his records and posts his auctions manually. eBay has enabled him to enjoy a few of life's luxuries: After eight months of selling, he bought a diamond ring for his fiancée.

Figure 18-4:
California
Magic
auction.

John's tip for sellers: "Research! There is nothing worse than posting something for sale without researching it first, only to find that you are one out of a hundred sellers offering the same item for sale, and you are asking more than everyone else."

Cardking4

Member since September 1998; Feedback: 1,609

This seller is one of my favorite people in the world. I knew Ken Tate long before he discovered eBay. He was the sports card king of the San Fernando Valley (a suburb of Los Angeles), selling cards wholesale to various sports card shops in the area, which is his retirement dream job. After years of working with Caltech, Fairchild, and JPL (deep space networks), this renowned engineer settled down to selling baseball cards in 1986 and found an outlet at eBay over a decade later. Ken is 78.

A visit to Ken's warehouse is a collector's dream come true. He has all the real stuff, and things signed by all the greats: Mantle, Williams, Cobb, Ali — you name the sports memorabilia, he either owns it or has seen it. This man knows his stuff. Check out Figure 18-5 for an example of one of Ken's auctions. From his ever-growing stock and collection of hockey sticks, signed bats, tobacco cards, and cases and cases of sports cards come his eBay sales — his full-time work. He's an expert when it comes to his collectibles, and he has an entire room of reference books on almost any collectible item you can imagine. His place is part museum, part library, and part Disneyland all rolled into one.

Ken collects and sells coins, too. He has currency and coins from all over, mostly uncirculated American coins. His is the first place that I ever saw an ancient Sassanian coin from AD 459. He part-times at local coin shows, evaluating coins for the participants.

eBay has changed Ken's life for the better. He no longer has time to watch TV because he's always busy studying the market, seeing what the new trends are, and making deals for new merchandise. He's constantly learning and studies eBay the way some people study the stock market. His lovely wife Dot is a painter, and he has convinced her to dabble a bit at eBay as well.

Ken is an eBay Power Seller and uses software from AuctionHelper to post his auctions and Quicken to keep his books.

Ken's tip for sellers: "Start off slowly, study your market, and see what's selling."

Figure 18-5:
A Cardking4
auction.

CharmsandChains

Member since May 2000; Feedback: 3,855

Sheila Goff Wooden once owned a successful company that produced videos for lawsuits: depositions, accident sites, and settlement tapes. During the traditional holiday season lull in her business, Sheila listed a few items at eBay. Within a month, she decided that she would take eBay on full-time. She saw a couple of big clients through their cases, and then CharmsandChains was born.

By becoming an online entrepreneur, Sheila is able to sell merchandise all over the world. Her most memorable moment was the first time she shipped an order to Japan; very heady — all of a sudden, she's an international business. Now she ships internationally every week.

Sheila's international online business sells over 3,500 different sterling silver charms and accessories. She's expanded past eBay auctions to her own Web site (www.charmsandchains.com) and runs an eBay store (see Figure 18-6) in which she's currently listing 834 items. She spends at least 50 hours a week fulfilling all those eBay duties, and answers e-mails as quickly as she can.

Her biggest challenge is trying to find management software that will fit her varied needs.

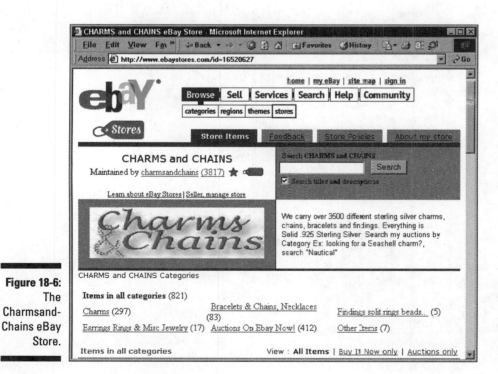

Figure 18-6:
The CharmsandChains eBay Store.

A tip from CharmsandChains to eBay sellers everywhere: "Be accessible and answer your e-mail; buyers just want to know that you really exist." Her customers know she really exists. She has a ton of repeat business at eBay; her positive rating is over 7,000.

CoinsByHucky.com

Member since August 1999; Feedback: 5,245

I bought some of my first coins from Hucky (Mike Hakala's nickname). I easily found his auctions again because his savvy marketing ploy is putting his nickname Hucky in the title of all his auctions. So even if you forget his user ID, you can always search for **Hucky** and find his auctions.

Mike sold coins for a living before he ever knew about eBay. He's now a gold-level power seller selling over $20,000 a month. At one time, he sold wholesale coins to other dealers, but now sells all his wholesale stock to eBay buyers (see Figure 18-7) who are grateful to get their hands on quality coins while getting a good deal. He's opened his own Web site, `www.coinsbyhucky.com`, and sells from there as well.

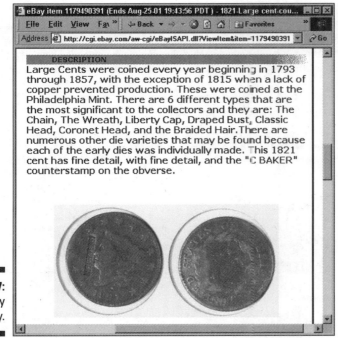

Figure 18-7:
CoinsBy
Hucky.

At one time, Hucky had only one computer, and his wife Linda supplemented their income with a full-time job. Now they have several computers (networked together in the basement of their home), Linda works with Mike, and they have a full-time employee. Hucky's eBay business has really taken off.

He estimates that he spends as many as 80 hours a week on his eBay business — but he loves it. He says that eBay has given him the opportunity to meet people from all over the world. Hucky has a customer in Guam who calls at 3:45 in the morning, and another customer in his own hometown whom he's never met. The best part of eBay for him is that everyone has a common goal — to collect something. He loves talking to people about their collections, sharing stories, and at the same time, making money.

Hucky uses AuctionHelper for listing his auctions, and has a tip for new sellers: "Realize that eBay is going to be twice as hard as the job you left behind; then again, the rewards are twice as great! Because, if you think you are going to do something, you are halfway to achieving it!"

Dollectibles

Member since August 1997; Feedback: 2,156

Dollectibles is a doll shop: a real brick-and-mortar store with walk-in, live customers and lots of merchandise. Robin Hornsby runs the store and one day heard from one of her customers about a Web site called eBay where you could buy dolls online. Her gears started turning, and Robin immediately jumped at the idea of expanding her marketplace at eBay.

Robin has now cut back her hours in her brick-and-mortar shop to spend 25 to 30 hours a week selling online. Her sales are pretty regular, and she always has a lovely group of popular dolls up for sale. I've bought some dolls from Robin, and I have to add that her packaging is second to none. She not only wraps the packages carefully, but settles each doll box in a load of Styrofoam peanuts. She really cares about her customers, and answering e-mail is a number one priority to her.

Robin has taught herself HTML and enjoys designing her own ads; she feels that it adds a personal touch that sets her auctions apart from others (see Figure 18-8). She is also currently stocking her eBay store with the hottest dolls today, mostly Barbie and character dolls.

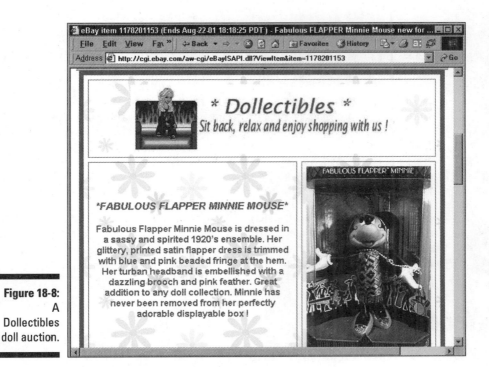

* Dollectibles *
Sit back, relax and enjoy shopping with us !

FABULOUS FLAPPER" MINNIE

FABULOUS FLAPPER MINNIE MOUSE

Fabulous Flapper Minnie Mouse is dressed in a sassy and spirited 1920's ensemble. Her glittery, printed satin flapper dress is trimmed with blue and pink beaded fringe at the hem. Her turban headband is embellished with a dazzling brooch and pink feather. Great addition to any doll collection. Minnie has never been removed from her perfectly adorable displayable box !

Figure 18-8: A Dollectibles doll auction.

A gentleman purchasing a very hard-to-find doll from her is Robin's most memorable sale. He wanted a quick delivery because this doll was the final piece to a collection that his wife — then terminally ill — had started; he wanted her to see her collection complete. Robin stayed in touch with him throughout the stages of his wife's illness to the end. She glows at the memory of that transaction because she was able to make this woman happy at the end. It was more worthwhile than any other transaction she's ever completed.

Robin's tip for sellers: "Customer satisfaction and honesty. Make sure your descriptions are 100 percent accurate, and give a lot of personal attention to your customers. It may take you a little more time, but the personal contact from the beginning to the end of the transaction will reap its rewards."

Propigate@home.com

Member since December 1999; Feedback: 922

Rick Jarrett loves gardening and loves to collect rare and special plants. He found eBay while looking for some new and exotic plants for his collection. After a while, he began propagating his plants, and ended up with more plants than he knew what to do with. He shared them with friends and co-workers, but still had too many plants. The thought hit him that because he had bought his parent plants at eBay, why couldn't he sell his babies on the site as well?

He currently has over 400 plant species in his yard; eBay is a part-time job and a way to finance his gardening habit. Rick is a registered nurse in a local hospital's emergency room. While at work, Rick takes care of people; during his off hours, he takes care of plants. Check out Figure 18-9 for a sampling.

Repeat customers are common for Rick (I bought four plants from him and my neighbor bought three), and his positive rating is over 1,385. His biggest sale to date is 27 plants to one eBay bidder. Even though this is only a part-time business, Rick finds that he spends 18 to 20 hours a week on it; that's 18 to 20 hours spending time on something he truly enjoys.

Shipping is his biggest challenge because of the perishable nature of his merchandise. He really puts a lot of effort into seeing that his plants stay healthy and don't spend a weekend at the post office.

Rick has a Web site (`tipsfromrick.homestead.com/tipsfromrick.html`) not for selling plants, but for sharing gardening tips and tricks. It's full of good information.

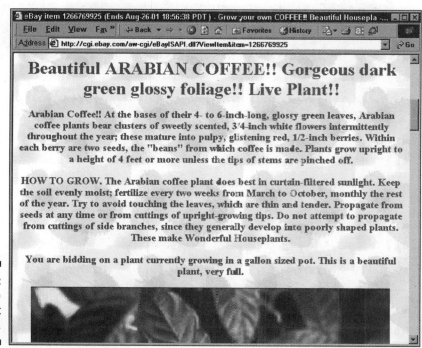

Figure 18-9:
A Propigate
plant
auction.

Rick's tip for new eBay sellers: "Go the one extra step when it comes to customer relations and service. It is very hard for many people still to order online, and give someone your credit card, or money order when they don't have a clue who you are, or how trustworthy you are. Feedback is EVERYTHING!"

SallyJo

Member since January 1998; Feedback: 2,925

Sally Severance is an eBay power seller, a mother of four valedictorians, a rancher specializing in purebred Charolais cattle, and a North Dakota farmer with her husband. She gave up a successful ten-year banking career to stay home with her family, and by the way, she buys and sells at eBay.

From her ranch in North Dakota, Sally sells collectibles (see Figure 18-10) and general merchandise at eBay to supplement her income. Her 25 to 30 hours a week that she spends at eBay earn her the money to buy things that she and her kids want.

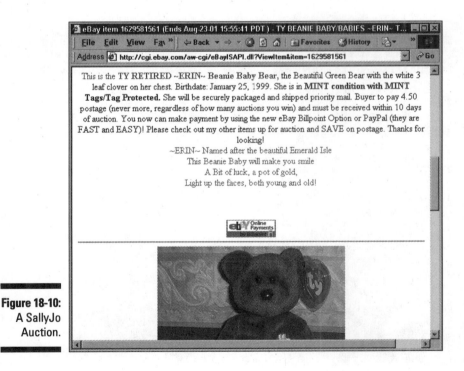

Figure 18-10:
A SallyJo
Auction.

Sally also shops for her family at eBay, and considers that part of her business. She can save money by finding some special things for her kids (three are in college, one is in high school). She has made many friends at eBay and really enjoys personal contact with customers.

Her new eBay store is slowly filling with items. She lists all her auctions without software because she feels her auctions are more personal when she does them herself.

Sally's tip for eBay sellers: "My #1 tip on setting up a business on eBay is to be HONEST, especially when writing up a description of what you are selling!"

www.nelson.hm

Member since January 1999; Feedback: 118

Perhaps they're not the most prolific eBay sellers, but that's because the Nelson Brothers — Gunnar and Matthew — are busy making music and touring. www.nelson.hm is their user ID. Matthew and Gunnar are the third generation in their family of hitmakers, starting with Ozzie Nelson (their grandfather) and Rick Nelson (their father).

I first met Gunnar and Matthew in the green room prior to appearing on a Los Angeles morning show. As guests do, we began chatting, and when they found out that I had written *eBay For Dummies,* I actually felt like a celebrity. They loved talking about eBay. The Nelsons are involved with eBay to ensure that their fans get authentic merchandise. Check out their About Me page, an official VeRO page. They're members of the VeRO (Verified Rights Owner; see Chapter 4) program to prevent online sales of bootlegged products and items that infringe on the Nelson family trademarks.

Gunnar is really hooked on eBay. When he and I talked, he was sitting on a Herman Miller Aeron chair that he had purchased just a few days before at eBay. He personally spends a lot of time at eBay, searching auctions for bargains. Their Webmistress Tana runs the Nelson Brothers' eBay store and auctions; she also runs their fan Web site and online store at www. thenelsonbrothers.com.

The Nelson Brothers sell their regular merchandise on their Web site, but put special rare items up for sale at eBay (see Figure 18-11). Gunnar comments, "Fans of my band's music are ravenous, and they're always looking for special/rare items. It's these special items that we offer exclusively at eBay, and our fans have come to know that. If they want a rarity, they search us out on eBay."

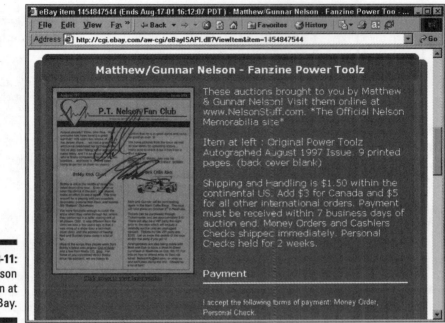

Figure 18-11:
A Nelson
Auction at
eBay.

About selling at eBay? "It's like having the world's most efficient store, that has the most effective advertising campaign behind it, that gets the highest price possible for each sale."

Gunnar's tips for eBay sellers: "Start yesterday, be ethical and honest when describing your items, and follow through completely with every single sale."

Chapter 19

Ten Other Places to Move Merchandise

● ●

In This Chapter

▶ Giving it away: Charitable donations

▶ Garage sales, swap meets, the local antique mall, and community events

▶ Unloading on other eBay sellers

▶ Going, going, gone: Turning over your goods to a live auctioneer

▶ Finding a place that specializes

▶ Placing a classified ad

▶ Selling it cheap: A last-ditch effort

● ●

*W*hen a corner of your eBay storage area becomes the graveyard of unsold stuff (at some point it will — believe me), whatcha gonna do? Inevitably, you'll find yourself holding onto some merchandise that you feel may never scrape together a profit and you'll become sick of looking at it. Whether thousands of those salad spinners that you bought to sell at eBay are suddenly appearing in multiple auctions or you jumped on the opportunity to buy a truckload (literally) of bargain-priced cat scratching posts, you've got to make room for this stuff immediately or sell it fast.

You've got to make some quick decisions and plan on getting rid of your excess inventory. Every business has this problem, so don't feel bad about it. You can't expect to bat .300 every time you pick a product to sell. The key is getting rid of the excess products while hopefully losing nothing on your investment. None of your merchandise is trash — I hope — so someone out there may want it and will pay *something* for it. If not, you can always give it away. So throughout this chapter, I highlight the top ten ways to move that superfluous merchandise and still save your investment.

Donate to Charitable Organizations

Charitable donating is my personal favorite way of unloading unwanted items. Not only are you doing something good for someone else, but your donation may be a 100 percent business write-off. Many private schools, churches, and synagogues are in my community. What these places all have in common is putting on fundraisers (auctions, raffles, tournaments, bingo) and loving donations. You have to give the best stuff to your schools or churches — especially if your item is meant as some sort of prize. Many charities often gratefully take your boxes of miscellaneous stuff (think Salvation Army and Goodwill).

Classy gifting

Something I like to do is put together little gift baskets for charity auctions. I'll take a bunch of female-related, male-related, or kids items and put them in a basket on a base of shredded Sunday comics. I keep a roll of clear cellophane on hand to wrap up the entire thing. I then top it off with a nice big bow. It's always an appreciated donation and, wrapped up this way, it always gets a higher price at bazaars or silent auctions.

Online charities

One of my favorite Web sites, MissionFish.com (see Figure 19-1), is a rare Web site that holds online charity auctions. (I must confess that I've bought some items here that I've then sold at eBay.) MissionFish helps non-profit organizations support their missions by teaching them to fish (to paraphrase the parable) and also by teaching them to build their own fisheries. You just register on the site, select your charity, and MissionFish does the rest.

When an item sells, you (the donor) are responsible for shipping the item. You must use a shipping company that supplies a tracking number, which you submit to MissionFish. (The entire cost of shipping is tax-deductible along with the item.) After the winner receives the item, all proceeds are sent from MissionFish to the designated non-profit. You then receive a thank you letter as proof of your gift to the charity for IRS tax purposes. You'll have a write-off and you'll feel good about what you've done to help others.

Figure 19-1:
The
MissionFish.
com charity
auctions
home page.

Have a Garage Sale

Sell your items to other eBay sellers. Hee hee, only kidding! Perhaps some of the stuff you have may appeal to the locals (some of whom probably do sell at eBay). Garage sales draw big crowds when promoted properly, and you'll be surprised at the amount of stuff you'll unload. An especially good time to have a garage sale is late fall, early winter — just in time for the holidays.

Because you've probably been to a bunch of garage sales but maybe haven't given one in a long, long time, here are a few reminders:

- ✔ **Plan the sale at least three weeks in advance:** Decide on the weekend of your sale well beforehand and be sure to set a specific opening time. If you welcome *early birds* (people who like to show up at 6 or 7 a.m.), be sure to put that in your ad and flyers.

- ✔ **Invite neighbors to participate:** The more the merrier, right? Also, the bigger the sale, the more customers you're likely to entice. Everyone can drum up at least a few items for a garage sale.

- ✔ **Gather and price items to go in the sale:** After you set a date, immediately start putting things aside and pricing them with sticky tags. This way, you won't have to scramble the day before to find things.

✔ **Place a classified ad:** Call your local newspaper a week before the sale and ask the friendly classified department people when the best time is to run an ad. Take their advice — they know what they're talking about!

✔ **Make flyers to post around the neighborhood:** Fire up your computer and make a flyer; include your address, a map, the date, and the starting time. Be sure to mention special items that you've thrown into the sale to bring 'em in. If two or three families are participating in the sale, mention that too. If you have small throwaway types of items, include the line "Prices start at 25 cents." Hang the flyer in conspicuous places around your neighborhood.

✔ **Post large signs on nearby corners:** The day before the sale, put up *large* posters (you can pick up 22 x 28 poster board from an art store or Office Depot) advertising the sale. When you make them, use thick black shipping markers on a light board. Use very few words, including only the basic details: "Garage Sale June 22-24, 8 a.m., Tons of Stuff, 1234 Extra Cash Blvd." Also make a sign to hang at the sale location "Sale Continues tomorrow, New Items will be Added!"

✔ **Clean up any dusty or dirty items:** If you want someone to buy it, you've got to make it look good.

✔ **Gather supplies:** Get lots of change; make sure you have plenty of tens, fives, a ton of singles, and several rolls of change. Get several calculators for everyone who will be taking money. Set aside a box to use as the cash box. Collect all the supermarket shopping bags that you can for those with multiple purchases.

✔ **Hang helium balloons to draw attention to your signs:** The day of the sale, go to the busiest corner near your sale and tie some helium balloons to your sign — that's sure to attract attention. Do the same thing at the corner near your sale and also at the curb of the sale.

✔ **Display everything in an orderly fashion:** Pull out your old card tables and arrange items so that people can easily see what's there; they will be turned off by a literal pile of junk. Hang clothes on a temporary rack (or use a clothesline on the day of the sale).

✔ **Get ready to negotiate!:** Talk to people when they approach and *make that sale!*

Rent a Table at the Local Swap Meet

Local *swap meets* (regularly scheduled events where you can rent space for a token fee and sell your wares) can be a great place to meet other eBay sellers. But whatever you do, don't mention that you sell at eBay. Let the customers think you're a rube, and that they can get the best of you. Offer great deals; give 'em a discount if they buy a ton of stuff. Just like the garage sale (see previous section), you can move lots of merchandise here. Don't forget to try to unload your goods to other sellers; perhaps they can do with a little extra inventory. Check the classifieds of local newspapers for swap meets; you should be able to find ads listing these types of sales, which often occur once a month in some towns.

Consign Merchandise to the Local Antique Mall

An antique mall is a retail store that's often run by several people who take your merchandise on consignment. You can probably find several in your area. Your items are sold in the store (good for you), and the storeowners take a commission on each sale (good for them). They take your items, tag them with your own identifying tag, and display them for sale. Antique malls usually see an enormous amount of foot traffic, and this may be as close to having a retail store that you'll ever get.

Take a Booth at a Community Event

Where I live, the local business community often holds special events: street fairs, Fourth of July extravaganzas, pumpkin festivals, and others I can't think of right now. As a vendor, you can buy a booth at such events to peddle your wares. For seasonal events, purchasing a bunch of holiday-related items to make your table match the festivities is a savvy marketing idea. Your excess eBay inventory will just be part of the display — and a big part of your sales.

If the event is in the evening, purchase a few hundred glow-in-the-dark bracelets at eBay (you can often get 100 for $20). The kids love them and they'll drag their parents to your booth. Be creative and think of other ways to make your booth stand out. Support your community, have a barrel of fun, and make some money!

Resell to Sellers at eBay

Package up your items into related lots that will appeal to sellers who are looking for merchandise online. Take a tip from the very successful eBay seller — the Post Office Mail Recovery Center — that often combines many lost packages into single lots to sale at eBay. If you're overstocked with stuffed animals, put together a lot of a dozen. If you don't have a dozen of any one item, make the lots of related items that will appeal to a certain type of seller.

Be sure to use the words *liquidation* and *resale* in your description. There's an entire world of savvy sellers out there looking for items to sell. Perhaps it's just not the right time for your items to sell and you don't want to store them. Maybe another seller can move the items at a later date or in a different venue.

Visit a Local Auctioneer

Yes, I mean a real live auctioneer, one who actually holds live auctions at real auction houses that real people attend. There's a whole world out there of people who enjoy going to live auctions. (I recommend that you go once in a while to acquire unique items to resell at eBay.) Shopping at auctions can be addictive (duh) and live auctions attract an elite group of knowledgeable buyers. The basic idea is to bring your stuff to an auctioneer, who auctions off lots for you. A good auctioneer — like those at the Los Angeles Butterfields (www.butterfields.com); see Figure 19-2 — can get a crowd going, bidding far more than an item is expected to sell for.

Here are a few facts about real live auctioneers and some pointers to keep in mind when looking for one:

- ✔ **Make sure that the auction house you choose is licensed (also insured and bonded) to hold auctions in your state.** You don't want to leave your fine merchandise with someone who will pack up and disappear with your stuff before the auction.

- ✔ **Get the details before agreeing to the consignment.** Many auction houses give you at least 75 percent of the final hammer price. Be sure to ask the auctioneer's representative about all the details before you consign your items to them, including the following questions:

    When will the auction be held?

    How often are the auctions held?

    Have you sold items like this before? If so, how much have they sold for in the past?

    Will there be a printed catalog for the sale, and will my piece be shown in it?

  Get the terms and conditions in writing and have the rep walk you through each and every point so that you thoroughly understand each.

- ✔ **Search the Internet.** Type in **licensed auctions** and see what you come up with; it can't hurt.

- ✔ **Contact local auctioneers.** If your items are of good quality, a local auction house may be interested in taking your items on consignment.

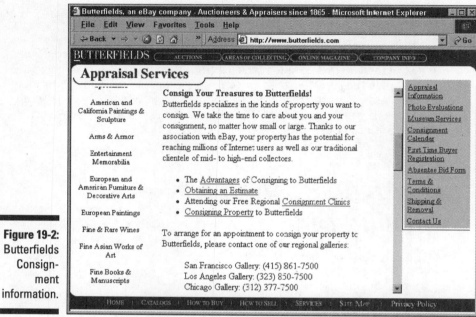

Figure 19-2:
Butterfields
Consign-
ment
information.

Find Specialty Auction Sites

If you have some specialized items that just don't sell very well at eBay, you might look for a different venue. While eBay is the best all-purpose selling site in the world, you may have an item that only a specialist in the field can appreciate.

For example, I've seen some fine works of art not sell at eBay. But don't fret, you'll find many other places online where you can sell these items. I searched Yahoo! for **art auctions**; the results filled an entire page. I clicked the Web sites link at the bottom of the page so that I could see the online Web sites only. I found 205 different Web sites that auction off artwork.

You may find an online auctioneer who specializes in the particular item you have for sale, something too esoteric for the eBay crowd. I've gotten some incredible bargains for myself on elegant brand new sunglasses made by a company in Italy called Persol, a company world famous for crystal lenses and ultra-fine quality. The super-famous wear these sunglasses: Robert De Niro, Tom Cruise, Donald Trump, Sharon Stone, Mel Gibson, and Cindy Crawford. These sunglasses normally retail from $150–$300 a pair, but you can sometimes find them at eBay for as low as $40. Unless you're buying them dirt cheap, you're not making your profits at eBay. Maybe the crowd just doesn't know about them.

Run a Classified Liquidation Ad

Sell your special items in the appropriate categories of the classifieds. Sell the rest of them in pre-assigned bulk lots for other sellers to "make big $$" with! It's all in the ad copy when you write a newspaper ad. Make your lots sound fantastic; give the reader a reason to call you. When they call, get all excited about your merchandise. But be honest and tell them you're just selling the stuff to raise cash.

Sell Everything at eBay for a $1 Opening Bid . . .

. . . and take what you get.

Part VI

Appendixes

The 5th Wave — By Rich Tennant

"How many times have I told you that you can't sell your brother at eBay?"

In this part . . .

Appendix A is my random glossary of words that may be new to you, but will soon become part of your day-to-day vocabulary; refer to it often as you peruse other parts of the book. In Appendix B, I briefly discuss home networking: what it is, the benefits, and how to set one up.

Appendix A

Glossary of Auction and Accounting Terms

• •

1099: An end-of-year form that you file with the IRS to record your payments to outside contractors. A 1099 must be filed for anyone to whom you pay over $600 in a calendar year.

absentee bid: A bid that an auction house employee places on a lot (or lots) — up to a maximum amount that you designate — in your absence. When you want to participate in a live auction but can't attend it physically, you can pre-arrange to have the auction house place absentee bids for you.

accounts payable: The amount your business owes to vendors, office supply stores, your credit card charges; this includes any and all money your business owes.

accounts receivable: The money people owe you: the checks and money orders that you're expecting in the mail; the money sitting in your Paypal account that you haven't transferred to your checking; and outstanding Billpoint money that hasn't been deposited.

announcements pages: eBay has announcements pages that you need to check periodically to get all the latest eBay information. eBay links can be misleading:

> If you follow the link at the bottom of every eBay page, you end up at the *Community* announcements page at `pages.ebay.com/community/news/index.html`.

> If you're wondering whether it's your computer's problem or an eBay problem when the search engine isn't working. check out the *System Status Announcements Board* at `www2.ebay.com/aw/announce.shtml`.

> Another well-hidden announcement board shows TOS (Terms of Service) and educational announcements at `www2.ebay.com/aw/marketing.shtml`.

as is/where is: An item that comes with no warranty, implied or otherwise, speaking to the merchantability of the product.

bid increment: The amount that a bid must advance, based on the auction's high bid. See Chapter 2 for a chart.

bid retraction: A cancelled auction bid. eBay denies spurious bid retractions within the last twelve hours of an auction. Retractions in the last 12 hours can only occur under extreme (like you typed in the wrong numerals) circumstances, and *only* until one hour before the auction's close. In the last hour, be darn sure that you don't make a mistake.

bid shielding: An illegal process wherein two bidders work together to defraud a seller out of high bids by retracting a bid at the last minute and granting a confederate's low bid the win. Not as much of an issue anymore due to eBay's new bid retraction policy; *see also* bid retraction.

card not present: Credit card services use this term to describe transactions that typically happen over the Internet or by mail order. It means that the seller hasn't seen the actual card.

caveat emptor: Latin for *let the buyer beware.* If you see this posted anywhere, proceed cautiously — you're responsible for the outcome of any transaction you take part in.

chargeback: When someone calls his or her credit card company and refuses to pay for a transaction. The credit card company will credit the card in question while making you pay back the amount.

consignment: When someone hands over merchandise to you, which you then auction at eBay; you make a little commission and this other person sells something without the hassle. *See* Chapter 6.

cookie: A small text file that may be left on your computer to personalize your experience on a particular Web site. When you sign on to eBay, a cookie is placed on your computer that keeps your User ID and password active for as long as you're on the site.

corporation: A separate entity set up for the purpose of doing business.

CPA: *Certified Public Accountant.* A CPA is someone who has been educated in accounting and has passed a certification test. CPAs are at the top of the accounting professional heap.

DBA: *Doing Business As.* These letters appear next to the common name of a business entity, sole proprietorship, partnership, or corporation that conducts business under a fictitious name.

DOA: *Dead on Arrival.* The product you purchased doesn't work at all from the moment you opened the package.

DUNS Number: *Data Universal Numbering System number.* An identification number issued to businesses from a database maintained by the great and powerful Dun and Bradstreet. These numbers are issued to allow your business to register with more than 50 global, industry, and trade associations, including the United Nations, the U.S. Federal Government, the Australian Government, and the European Commission. My business has had a DUNS number for years. You can get yours at no cost by calling Dun and Bradstreet at 800-333-0505 (www.dnb.com.au/dunshow.htm).

EIN: *Employer Identification Number.* If you run your business as a partnership or a corporation, you need an EIN number from the IRS. If you're a sole proprietor, your Social Security number is your EIN because you file all your business in your personal tax return.

Entrepreneur: That's you! An entrepreneur is someone who takes the financial risk to start a business. Even if you're buying and reselling garage sale items, you're still an entrepreneur.

FOB: *Free on Board.* When you begin purchasing large lots of merchandise to sell, you'll encounter this term. The FOB location technically means the place where the seller delivers the goods. If the price you're quoted is FOB Chicago, you're responsible for all shipping costs to get the goods from Chicago to your home city.

hammer fee: A fee that the auction house charges at a live auction. Be sure to read the information package *before* you bid on an item in a live auction. Hammer fees usually add 10–15 percent to the amount of your bid.

HTF: *Hard to Find.* An abbreviation that commonly appears in eBay auction titles to describe items that are, uh, hard to find.

keystone: In the brick-and-mortar retailing world, 100 percent markup. A product sells for keystone if it sells for twice the wholesale price. Products that you can sell at keystone are very nice to find.

live auctions: Auctions held online in real time. Check out www.ebayliveauctions.com.

MIB: *Mint in Box.* Okay, the item inside the box is mint, but the box looks like a sixteen-wheeler ran over it.

MIMB: *Mint in Mint Box.* Not only is the item in mint condition, but it's in an absolutely perfect box as well.

mint: An item in perfect condition is described as mint. This is truly a subjective opinion, usually based on individual standards.

NARU: *Not a Registered User.* A user of eBay or other online community who has been suspended for any number of reasons.

OOP: *Out of Print.* When a book or CD is being published, it usually has its own lifetime in the manufacturing process. When it is no longer being made, it's Out Of Print or OOP.

provenance: The story behind an item, including who owned it and where it came from. If you have an interesting provenance for one of your items, be sure to put it in the auction description because it adds considerable value to the item.

QuickBooks: A top-of-the-heap accounting program that helps you keep your records straight.

register: Similar to a checkbook account listing, QuickBooks keeps *registers* that go up and down depending on the amount of flow in an account balance.

ROI: *Return on Investment.* A figure expressed as a percentage that stands for your net profit after taxes and your own equity.

sole proprietorship: A business that's owned by only one person, and the profits and losses are recorded on that person's personal tax return.

split transaction: A transaction that you must assign to more than one category. If you pay a credit card bill and a portion of the bill went to purchased merchandise, a portion to gas for business-related outings, and yet another portion to eBay fees, you must post each amount to its own category.

tax deduction: An expenditure on your part that represents a normal and necessary expense for your business. Before you get carried away and assume that *every* penny you spend is a write-off (deduction), check with your tax professional to outline exactly what *is* and what *isn't*.

TOS: *Terms of Service.* eBay has a TOS agreement; check it out at `pages. ebay.com/help/community/png-user.html`.

W-9: A form that must be filled out by any outside contractor that you pay for services. This form includes the contractor's Social Security number and address. Your outside contractors must give you an invoice for each payment that you make to them. You use the information from this form to issue your 1099s at the end of the year. *See also* 1099.

wholesale: Products sold to retailers (that's you) at a price above the manufacturer's cost, allowing for a mark-up to retail. Hopefully, you'll buy most of your merchandise at wholesale costs. Stores such as Costco or Sam's Club sell items in bulk at prices marginally over wholesale. You must get a resale number from your state to buy at true wholesale.

Appendix B

The Hows and Whys of a Home Network

· ·

*W*hat is a network? A *network* is a way to connect all the computers at your business so that they can communicate with each other — as if they were one giant computer with different terminals. The best part is that it enables high-speed Internet connection sharing, as well as the sharing of printers and other peripherals. By setting up a computer network, a particular computer may run bookkeeping, another may be a graphics server, and others might serve as personal PCs for different users; from each networked computer, it's possible to access programs and files on all other networked computers.

When you have an office at home, today's technologies allow you to perform this same miracle on the *home network*. You can connect as many computers as you like, and run your business from anywhere in your home. You can have several computers in your office; by installing a network, you can also hook up your laptop from the bedroom if you don't feel like getting out of bed one day.

Now for the *whys* of a home network. A network is a very convenient way to run a business. All big business companies use them, and so should you: You can print out your PC postage on one printer — from any computer in your home or office. You can extend your DSL line or Internet cable connection (high-speed broadband) so that you can use it anywhere in your home — as well as your office. You also save money because a network is efficient and you don't need a printer at every computer.

In a network, you can set certain directories of each computer to be *shared;* that is, other computers on the network can access certain directories (all networked computers share those directories). You're able to prevent other users from accessing your personal files by password-protecting certain files and directories. Password protection prevents unauthorized access of your files by employees and/or your children.

You have your choice of three different types of home networks (see Table B-1 for a quick rundown of some pros/cons of each): an Ethernet, a home phone-line, or a wireless network. The *wireless network* is currently the new and highly touted kid on the block; because I have an aversion to being a guinea pig, I haven't used it myself. There are indeed issues with this technology because it runs with the same 2.4 GHz technology as some home wireless telephones. *Home phoneline networks* are the tried and true version of home networks, and I swear by them.

Table B-1	Types of Networks Pros and Cons	
Type	*Pros*	*Cons*
Traditional Ethernet*	Fast, cheap, and easy setup	Computers and printers must be hardwired; cables run everywhere
Home phoneline	Fast; your home is prewired with phonelines	Midrange cost; may not always work due to old wiring
Wireless network	Pretty fast; wireless (no ugly cords to deal with)	Expensive; may not be reliable because of interference from home electrical devices

Connects computers with high quality cable over a maximum of 328 feet of cabling.

So now you know why I've devoted the rest of this appendix to a quick and dirty discussion of the home phoneline network (installed on Windows-based PCs). Throughout the next few pages, I give you a lesson on what I know works for most people. (Hey, if it doesn't work, don't e-mail me — head back to the store and get your money back!)

At this point, I want to remind you that I'm not a techno-whiz (just like I'm not a lawyer nor an accountant). For more information about anything you'd think to ask about home networking, I defer you to Kathy Ivens, author of *Home Networking For Dummies* (published by Hungry Minds, Inc.).

What I know about home networks, I've learned the hard way — from the school of hard knocks. Okay, a lot of research went into this appendix as well, so humor me and read on.

Home Phoneline Network

Home phoneline networks have been around for a while and are in the second round of technology, growing in popularity by leaps and bounds. An ingenious invention, a phoneline network uses your existing home phonelines to carry your network and your high-speed connection (or dial-up connection if that's all you can have at this time). You access your network by plugging a phone-line from your computer into a phone jack on the wall. The wall telephone cabling contains four wires, and your telephone only uses a portion of two. There's plenty more room in the cable for your network.

If you have broadband, you don't even need to have a main computer turned on to access the connection anywhere else in the house. If you keep a printer turned on, you can also connect that to your router (gadget that enables multiple PCs to share an Internet connection; for further details, see Table B-2) and print on it from your laptop in another room — right through the network. Best of all, you can talk on the same phoneline without causing any interference.

The phoneline network sends data at a speedy 10MB per second (the same speed as a regular Ethernet network) and can operate with computers or other equipment placed as far as 1,000 feet apart and will work in homes as large as 10,000 square feet.

Preparing to install your home phoneline network

According to the Home Phoneline Networking Alliance (the association that works with hardware companies to develop a single networking standard), tests indicate that phoneline network technology can be successfully installed and operational in 99 percent of today's homes. In real life, how your home is wired and the quality of those wires dictates that success. I can hook up to my network successfully from 90 percent of the phone jacks in my house.

Take a look at the jacks at the end of all your phone cords; if you see only two copper-colored wires in the plastic jack, toss the cord. The ones that you need to carry your full load must have *four* wires visible in the clear plastic end of the jack.

I've been told the reason that I can't connect to some jacks is that they aren't *home run jacks* (jacks that go directly from the electrical connection box). The techs say whether a jack is a home run or not makes no difference, but they also say that some jacks may be wired incorrectly. If you get your network functioning, and one of your jacks won't carry the connection, try this: Unscrew the jack that works and make note of the wiring. Now unscrew the jack that doesn't work and see that it's wired *exactly* the same as the other jack. If it isn't, rewire the colored wires to match the working jack. (Or ask a friendly handyman to do it for you.)

To set up your network to carry files and your high-speed connection throughout your house, you need several pieces of hardware. (See Table B-2 for a list of hardware you must have.) I use products from a company called NETGEAR (www.netgear.com), which have worked for me right out of the box (see

Figure B-1 for a sample network). Netgear has 24/7 tech support on the Web and via telephone at 1-888-NETGEAR. On its Web site, you'll find a support area featuring a valuable cable ISP router configuration chart for individual ISPs around the country. All NETGEAR products come with a 100 percent satisfaction guarantee. Please realize that, always being cost-conscious, I've used the least expensive method (not with the highest level of bells and whistles) to accomplish my goals.

Suppose that you have four desktop computers that you want networked (three in your office and your teenager's computer to share the broadband connection), plus a laptop that you use in different places of your home. You need hardware and drivers for each computer that you plan to install on the network. When you install new software and your computer makes a demand for a disk, it's asking for the drivers. You can also download current drivers from the Internet. A *driver* is the software that enables your computer to understand what the network cards are doing. That means that each computer needs its own network card or network USB adapter. Study Table B-2 for the rundown of the necessary hardware.

Table B-2	Hardware Needed for Sharing on a Home Phoneline Network
Hardware	**What It Does**
Modem	For Internet connection sharing; comes from your cable or phone company and plugs into an outlet with cable (just like your TV) or Ethernet for DSL, and connects to your router with an Ethernet cable.
Router	The gizmo that allows multiple PCs to share an Internet connection; performs rudimentary firewall protection (available for as little as $99). You still need firewall software (see the section "Firewall software").
Bridge	A device that connects your Ethernet (router connection) with your home phoneline network. You can get a device that combines the router and the bridge (adds $100 to the setup cost).
Phoneline network card	For a desktop computer, you need a card that enables your computer to become one with other computers on the network; available for about $30 each.
USB Adapter	USB adapters are used instead of installing a phoneline network card and are particularly easy to use with laptops; function just as well as cards and can be hot-swapped (plugged in while your computer is on); and are available for less than $30 each.

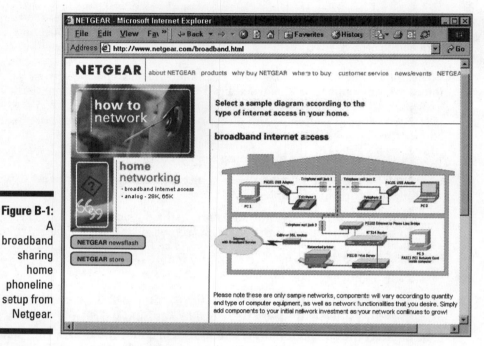

Figure B-1:
A
broadband
sharing
home
phoneline
setup from
Netgear.

Windows Me works flawlessly on my network. I can view files, pass documents, and, of course, share an Internet connection. I recommend using Windows Me (and later versions of Windows) for setting up a home network; it just does a great job of handling networks and seems to integrate the network much better than Windows 98 SE. (You *can* network Windows 98 SE, but not without effort.)

Installing your home phoneline network

Modern technology makes installing a home phoneline network a fairly simple procedure. If you have a broadband connection, there's a chance that your ISP will send out a professional to install the Internet connection to one computer. If you can set your network up first, get it up and running before you get your high-speed connection; doing so enables you to work out any file transfer and printing issues.

Before opening your computer, be sure to touch a grounded metal object to free yourself of static electricity before touching your network card; a spark could go from your hand to the delicate components in the phoneline network card, thereby rendering the card useless. Go to an electronics store and purchase a wrist strap that has a cord with a gator clip (which you clip to a metal part of the computer before touching anything inside for safety).

If you're installing a USB (Universal Serial Bus) adapter, don't bother trying to open your computer. Just plug in the adapter to an available USB port and proceed to Step 5.

To install a home phoneline network, just follow these steps (be sure to follow your manufacturer's instructions if they vary from this information):

1. **Turn off your computer and disconnect the power cord from the back of the computer.**

2. **Open your computer by opening the PC cover.**

3. **Look for a free slot that matches your type of network card, and install it into an available slot.**

   Touch the card only by the metal part on the outside edge of the card. To be safe, do not touch the chips on the board with your fingers. When installing the card, merely press firmly down on the top of the card with your thumb to properly seat it into the slot. Fasten the card to the chassis by tightening the screw on the metal edge.

4. **After the card is firmly seated into the slot, replace the cover to your PC and reconnect the power cord.**

5. **Connect the supplied (RJ-11) telephone cord that came with your network card to the port labeled *To Wall* on the phoneline network card, and plug the other end into a convenient wall telephone jack.**

   If you have a telephone that needs to use that wall jack, connect it to the port labeled *To Phone;* your telephone will work through the network card.

6. **After you connect everything, power up your computer.**

   Hopefully, your computer will see the new hardware and ask you to install the driver. If it doesn't, check the instructions (as a last ditch effort, you can always read the instructions!) for troubleshooting tips.

7. **Insert the CD or the disk that came with the card (containing those tricky drivers) when asked and follow the on-screen instructions.**

   As you go through the instructions, decide on a name for each computer that you want to install so that each has an identifying name on the network.

8. **Set up directories that you want shared on the network.**

   Go to My Computer, select (highlight) the directories (denoted by folder icons) that you want to share, and right-click to indicate that you want to share these directories with other computers on the network. Do the same with your local printers.

9. **Repeat Steps 1–8 on each computer.**

   As you add a computer, double-check that it can communicate with the other computers that you've already installed on the network by trying to open a shared directory on a remote computer or by printing a test page on a remote printer.

10. **If your network is not functioning properly after you complete all recommended steps, be sure to call tech support as many times as necessary to get your network up and running.**

    When your network connection is flying and working flawlessly, it's time to add your broadband.

11. **To install the broadband connection, it's recommended that you take the Ethernet cable from the modem and connect it to the back of your router. Then take the supplied Ethernet cable and connect that to the phoneline network bridge.**

    Your bridge comes with a phoneline. Connect that phoneline from the bridge to a telephone wall jack and voilà — you should be good to go with your Internet connection on all the computers in your network.

    The connectors each have an outlet for a telephone cord that you plug into your wall jack. (I cheated in one room and connected two computers to one phone jack with a splitter that makes two jacks out of one.)

    You can connect to the high-speed connection on any networked computer without having to keep a computer on all the time as a server with this setup; just be sure that you're plugged into the proper phone jack.

Internet Security and Your Home Network

A dial-up connection exposes your computer to the Internet only when you dial up and get connected. Most broadband Internet connections are always on — which means your computer is always exposed. You should shield your computer with a strong firewall and an antivirus program.

Firewall software

When you're connected to the Internet, not only are you exposed to hackers, but you're wide open to threats such as *Trojan horses,* programs that can get into your computer when you innocently view an infected Web site. Once inside your computer, the Trojan horse, like ET, phones home. From there, an evil deed-doer may be able to wreak havoc with a direct line to your computer with all your precious data.

If you're technically inclined — and even if you're not — visit the Web site for Gibson Research Corporation (`www.grc.com`). Gibson Research is the brainchild of an early PC pioneer, Steve Gibson, who's renowned as a genius in the world of codes and programming. Steve is *the* expert when it comes to exposing the vulnerabilities of systems over the Internet. A few free diagnostic programs that you'll find on this site will check your computer's vulnerability to Internet threats.

Shields Up and LeakTest are programs that test your computer and terrify you with results that expose the vulnerability of your Internet connection. I learned about ZoneAlarm Pro on Steve's site. This program (which costs just $39.95) has won every major award in the industry as the most secure current software firewall. If your main concern is safety, visit `www.zonelabs.com` for a free 30-day trial download of ZoneAlarm Pro.

For more information about protecting your computer from potential Internet threats, check out *Firewalls For Dummies,* written by Brian Komar, Ronald Beekelaar, and Joern Wettern, PhD (published by Hungry Minds, Inc.). Although much of this book is geared to corporate users, a great deal of the information it contains applies to small businesses and home networks as well. One chapter is specifically devoted to an in-depth tutorial on ZoneAlarm and another popular personal firewall, BlackICE.

Antivirus software

You're still going to need an antivirus software to protect you from the idiots who think it's fun to send destructive code along the Internet through e-mail. The leading programs in this area are Norton AntiVirus and McAfee. One of the problems inherent in buying software is that you might be urged to load much more than you need onto your computer. If all you need is an antivirus software, then only purchase an antivirus software. But don't delay. Purchase it now — and be sure to update the antivirus files each week so that you're fully protected from the latest and greatest viruses.

Index

• A •

AAPro's Template, 189
About Me page, 28, 53, 57, 69–72, 112–113
About the Store page, 71, 107
absentee bid, 337
accounting. *See* bookkeeping
Accounts page, 69
accounts payable, 337
accounts receivable, 337
Accredited Registrar Directory, 164
accrual basis, 290
Adobe Photoshop, 217–218
Adult Only area, 48
advanced searches, 143–144
Advanced Selling Tips course, 81
advertising. *See* marketing auctions
agreement, business, 273
alcohol, 86
All tab, 60
Alley-cat, 312–313
Amazon.com, 105–106
America Online (AOL), 154–155, 218
ampersand, 143
announcements page, 337
antique mall, 331
antivirus software, 348
AOL. *See* America Online (AOL)
API, USPS, 263–265
API Wizard, 233
appraisals, 150
art. *See* fine art
articles, 143
as is/where is item, 337
auction management software. *See also*
    software
  Auction Wizard, 175, 187–188
  automatic e-mail, 175
  cost of, 179–180
  HTML templates, 176
  inventory tracking, 175
  listing merchandise, 176–177

Mister Lister, 190–191
  overview, 26, 186
  Seller's Assistant, 175, 189–190
  templates, 186–187
Auction Wizard, 187–188
auctioneer, 332–333
AuctionHelper.com Web site, 53
AuctionLynxx, 181–182
auctions. *See also* bidder; marketing
    auctions
  About Me page, 53, 57
  bonuses, 56, 85
  Buy It Now feature, 51, 202–203
  canceling, 73
  charity auction, 58, 129
  choice, 54
  closing time, 52, 67
  color coding, 62–63
  duplicate auction, 55
  Dutch auction, 45–46
  eBay Live Auctions, 37–38, 339
  estate, 129
  five-day auction, 51
  home page featured auction, 196–197
  keyword spamming, 56, 87–89
  length of, 51–52
  linking from, 53, 56–57
  liquidation, 129
  live, 37–38, 339
  optional listing features, 196–203
  Personal Offer feature, 53–54
  policies, 54–57, 84
  pre-sale listing, 55–56
  Private auction, 48–49
  prizes, 56
  raffles, 56
  removing, 62
  Reserve Price auction, 47–48
  Restricted Access auction, 48
  searches of, 147
  seven-day auction, 51
  silent, 129
  specialty, 333–334

auctions *(continued)*
  ten-day auction, 52
  three-day auction, 51
  tracking, 63–66
  traditional auction, 45
  types, 45–49
Auctionworks, 182–183
authentication services, 151–152
autofocus, 210, 216
automation of tasks, 171–178

• B •

back office, 297–299
background fabric or paper, 214–215
bags, 298, 301
Ballista template listing system, 183
banks, 27, 28, 231, 250–251
banner ad, 165–166
Basic Selling course, 80
battery, 211
Battery Busters Web site, 211
bCentral Banner Network, 166
Beekelaar, R., 348
beeswax, 214
bid
  absentee bid, 337
  canceling, 72–73
  color coding, 62–63
  Dutch auction, 45–46
  Items I've Bid On page, 62
  proxy bidding system, 50–51
  Reserve Price auction, 47
  shill bidding, 91
  starting, 50–51
  tracking, 62–63
  traditional auction, 45
bid increment, 51, 338
bid retraction, 338
bid shielding, 93, 338
bidder. *See also* auctions
  bid shielding, 93, 338
  blocking, 74
  communication with, 94
  eBay employee as, 97
  non-paying bidders, 94–96, 228
  preapproved, 74
  underage, 96
  unwelcome, 93–94

bidder-management tools, 72–74
Bidding/Watching page, 61–64
BidPay.com, 234–235
Big Lots company, 124
Billpoint Instant Payment, 27, 66, 178, 237, 245–250
binoculars icon, 64
BlackICE, 348
blocking bidders, 74
BobMill, 313–314
boldface option, 199
bonuses, 56, 85
book condition rating, 43
bookkeeping
  accounts payable, 291, 337
  accounts receivable, 291, 337
  accrual basis, 290
  Billpoint, 246–247
  cash basis, 290
  certified public accountant (CPA), 281
  chart of accounts, 290–295
  overview, 279–281
  records, 281–285
  software for, 26, 281, 285–295
books, 18, 42–43
booth, community event, 331
boxes, 298–299, 302
Broker Spotlight, 39
Bronze level Power Seller, 12
Browsing and Buying course, 80
Bubble envelope, 302
Bubble Wrap, 300
Bubblefast, 314–316
budget, 10–12, 193, 196
business. *See* eBay business
business cards, 283
business to business transactions, 136
Butterfields, 332, 333
Buy It Now feature, 51, 116–117, 202–203
buyer information, 178, 241
buyer's premium, 129

• C •

cable connection, 22–23
calendar, 283
CaliforniaMagic, 316–317
canceling
  auctions, 73
  bid, 72–73

car parts, 33
card not present, 338
Cardking4, 317–318
Cardservice, 161
cars, 34–36
cash basis, 290
cash on delivery, 236
cashier's check, 231
categories
  choosing, 110, 194–195
  custom, 110
  eBay stores, 110
  favorites, 67
  Motors category, 33–36
  overview, 31–33
  real estate, 205
  research of, 33
  searches of, 145, 194–195
Category Overview page, 32
caveat emptor, 338
CDs, 18
cell phone, 70
certified public accountant (CPA), 281, 338
changing user ID, 23–24
chargeback, 241, 243, 250, 338
charitable organizations, 328
charity auction, 58, 129
CharmsandChains, 319–320
chart of accounts, 290–295
check, cashier's, 231
check, personal, 236–237
checkout, 178
children, 16–17, 96
children's clothing, 18
choice auction, 54
choosing
  categories, 110, 194–195
  merchandise, 13–20
  shipping carriers, 255–256
  user ID, 23–24
city tax certifcate, 275–276
clamps, 214
classified liquidation ad, 334
clay, 214
cleaning merchandise, 215, 300
ClickLaunch Single Step Launcher, 182
Clickstamp Online, 304
closing time, auction, 52, 67
clothing, 15, 18, 212–213

CoinsByHucky.com, 320–321
collectibles, 14–15, 141
collecting payment, 27–28, 43
color coding, 62–63
color scheme, eBay store, 113
commission, Half.com, 43
communication with bidder, 94
Compact Flash card, 209
computer hardware, 20, 343–344
confirmation of sale, 117, 119, 226–228
conjunctions, 143
consignment fees, 36–37, 139
consignment sales, 137, 139, 331–332, 338
consumer reviews, 21
Contact Info form, 97
contractor invoice, 283
cookie, 338
Cool eBay Tools Web site, 5
copyright, 87–89
corporation, 273–274, 338
Costco, 125, 126, 253
costs. *See also* fees
  auction management software, 179–180
  BidPay.com, 235
  boldface option, 199
  Buy It Now feature, 203
  digital cable connection, 23
  disclosing, 224
  DSL connection, 22
  eBay store, 106
  electronic check, 237
  Featured Plus option, 198
  gallery, 173, 200
  highlight option, 199
  home page featured auction, 197
  insurance, 267
  ManageAuctions.com, 184
  mediation, 101
  merchant accounts, 28
  of money orders, 232
  online auction management service, 179–180
  online store, 106
  paid image hosting, 219
  postage vendors, 305, 307
  real estate category, 205
  search engine listings, 167
  SendMoneyOrder.com, 234
  shipping, 13, 35–36, 224, 256, 258, 260, 262
  SquareTrade Seal, 102

counter, 199–200
courses, eBay, 80–81
Create a Stamp software, 307
creating
  About Me page, 71–72, 112–113
  eBay store, 107–114
  full-time business, 12
  gallery, 173–175
  office space, 29
credit cards. *See also* payments
  Adult Only area, 48
  BidPay.com, 234
  buyer information, 241
  Cardservice, 161
  chargeback, 241, 243, 250, 338
  Costco processing service, 253
  disadvantages of, 240
  fees, 240–242, 244, 249, 253–254
  fraud, 241–243
  ID Verify feature, 75
  insurance, 243
  merchant account, 250–253
  numbers on, 242–243
  online payment services, 27
  overview, 27, 240
  payment services, 240–250
  random charge, 243
  statements, 283
  VeriSign, 254
custom categories, 110
customer service, 112, 223–229
CuteFTP, 155, 173
CuteHTML, 26

• D •

dash in user ID, 109
Data Transfer limit, 158
DBA (Doing Business As), 338
dealers, art, 36
dedicated hosting, 160
Delete Selected Ended Items button, 62
delivery confirmation, 263–265
description, writing, 110, 207–208, 224–225
designing graphics, 114, 165
dial-up connection, 21–22
digital cable connection, 22–23
digital camera, 209–210

Digital Subscriber Line (DSL). *See* DSL
  connection
discipline for eBay business, 9
discount club stores, 125–126
display stands, 213
dispute resolution, 98–102
DOA (Dead on Arrival), 338
dollar stores, 124
Dollectibles, 321–322
domain name, 163–164
donations to charity, 328
Dornfest, A., 155
double-entry accounting, 280–281
Downloading History feature,
  Billpoint, 246–247
driver, 344
drop-ship service, 134
DSL connection, 22
DSL Reports Web site, 21
duct tape, 214
DUNS Number, 339
duplicate auction, 55
Dutch auction, 45–46, 63, 96

• E •

e-mail
  America Online (AOL), 155
  automatic, 175
  confirmation of sale, 226–228
  inquiry, 226
  notice of receipt, 229
  payment reminder, 228
  wireless, 70
e-mail address, 24, 56, 69, 96, 154
e-mail alert, 67–68
earnings, eBay seller, 9–10, 12, 78
eBay Auction Web history, 10
eBay Billpoint. *See* Billpoint Instant
  Payment
eBay business
  agreements, 273
  business cards, 283
  business to business transactions, 136
  children in, 16–17
  choosing merchandise, 13–20
  communication, 94
  computer hardware, 20–23, 343–344
  customer service, 112, 223–229

discipline for, 9
families in, 16–17
fictitious name statement, 275
full-time, 12
hobby as, 14–16
Internet connection, 20–23
liabilities, 272–273
license for, 275
versus mail order sales, 19
naming, 24, 107, 110, 275
office space, 28–29, 297–299
real estate sales, 19
required tasks for, 11–12
resale license, 136
sales tax number, 277–278
seller services, 72–81
software for, 25–26
tax certificate, 275–276
technology for, 20–23, 343–344
types, 272–274
eBay employee, 97
eBay home page, 13
eBay ID card, 24–25
eBay Live Auctions, 37–38
eBay Online Payments, 178
eBay Power Seller, 12, 78–79
eBay Premier, 36–37
eBay seller
    characteristics, 9
    earnings, 9, 12
    favorites, 68
    fee avoidance, 92
    non-selling, 92
    reselling to, 331–332
    seller services, 72–81
    shill bidding, 91
    SquareTrade Seal, 101–102
    tracking, 68
    transaction interception, 92
    transaction interference, 91–92
eBay store
    About the Store page, 71, 107
    categories, 110
    color scheme, 113
    commitment to, 108
    costs, 106
    creating, 107–114
    customer service, 112
    description, 110

fees, 44, 116
fixed price sales, 40
graphics for, 114
listing merchandise, 114–116
location, 105
marketing, 116
number of visitors, 105–106
optional features, 116
overview, 18–19, 44
payment information, 110
payment methods, 111
and personal Web site, 28
return policy, 112
sales tax, 112
searches for merchandise, 116
selling merchandise, 116–119
shipping locations, 111
eBay store, stocking. *See* merchandise,
    stocking
eBay University, 80–81
education, eBay, 80–81
electronic check, 237–238
employees, 97, 278
Employer identification number, 339
entrepreneur, 339
escrow service, 238–240
estate auction, 129
Excel (Microsoft), 26, 246
extend auction listing fee, 38

• F •

fabric, background, 214–215
families, 16–17, 128
fashion. *See* clothing
favorite categories, 67
Favorites page, 67–68
featured auction fee, 37
Featured Plus option, 198
Federal Express (FedEx), 256–259
Federal Trade Commission Web site, 56
Federal Wirefraud statute, 91
FedEx Ship Manager Software, 259
fee avoidance, 92
feedback rating
    Buy It Now feature, 203
    negative, 76, 77, 102
    overview, 24–25, 75
    Power Sellers program, 78

feedback rating *(continued)*
  responding to, 77–78
  SquareTrade Seal, 102
  star icons, 75
  submitting, 76–77, 178–179, 229
fees. *See also* costs
  Billpoint, 249
  for car sales, 34–35
  consignment, 36–37, 139
  Costco credit card processing, 253
  credit cards, 240–242, 244, 249, 253–254
  domain name registration, 164
  Dutch auction, 45
  eBay Premier, 36, 37
  eBay store, 44, 116
  escrow service, 239–240
  featured auction fee, 37
  final value fee, 35, 37–38, 95–96, 196, 205
  Half.com, 43
  hammer fee, 129, 339
  ID Verify feature, 75
  insertion fee, 35, 37–38, 196, 203–204
  listing fees, 203–204
  merchant account, 252
  PayPal, 244
  Personal Offer feature, 53
  Priority Mail, 303
  real estate sales, 38
  Reserve fee, 37
  Reserve over $25 fee, 35, 38
  Reserve Price auction, 48
  VeriSign, 254
fictitious name statement, 275
File Transfer Protocol (FTP), 155,
      172–173, 218
final value fee, 35, 37–38, 196, 205
final value fee credit, 95–96
fine art, selling, 36–37
firewall, 347–348
Firewalls For Dummies, 348
fixed price sales, 40
forwarding, URL, 164
fraud, credit card, 241–243
Fraud Protection Program, 79–80
freebies, 131–132
Front Runner, 181

FrontPage 2002 For Dummies, 155
FrontPage (Microsoft), 26, 155
FTP. *See* File Transfer Protocol (FTP)
full-time business, 12

• *G* •

gallery, photo, 173–175, 200–202
garage sales, 127–128, 329–330
gateway, 251–252
Gibson, S., 348
Gibson Research Corporation, 348
gift baskets, 328
giveaways, 56
GlobalSCAPE Web site, 26
going-out-of-business sales, 127–128
Gold-level Power Seller, 78
Gomez Associates Web site, 106
Goodwill, 130–131
graphics, 114, 165. *See also* images
Griffith, J., 80
guarantee, satisfaction, 78–79

• *H* •

Hakala, M., 320–321
Half.com, 40–44
hammer fee, 129, 339
hard drive, 20
hard goods, 13
highlight option, 198–199
history, viewing, 61
hobby, 14–16
home network, 341–348
Home Networking For Dummies, 342
home page featured auction, 196–197
home phoneline network, 342–347
Hooper Camera, 316
Hornsby, R., 321–322
hot item stage, 50
HTF item, 339
HTML, 11, 26, 167, 174–176, 220

• *I* •

ID Verify feature, 75
image editing software, 217–218
image hosting, 219

images. *See also* graphics
  America Online (AOL), 155
  automatic upload, 172–173
  gallery pictures, 200–202
  at Half.com, 42
  photo studio, 208–215
  pixels, 209
  scanning, 216
  storage, 20, 218–220
  taking pictures, 215–216
  title bar, 219
Improving Your Listing with Photos and
    HTML course, 80
income tax, 272–274
indefinite suspension, 94
Indicia (IBI), 304
infringing items, potentially, 87–89
inquiry e-mail, 226
insertion fee, 35, 37–38, 196, 203–204
installing home phoneline
    network, 345–347
Instant Purchase option, 248
insurance, 79–80, 243, 260, 265–267
Interland.com, 160–161
Internal Revenue Service (IRS), 278, 281–285
International Standard Book Number
    (ISBN), 41
Internet connection, 20–23
Internet security, 347–348
Internet Service Provider (ISP), 154–156, 218
inventory, 26, 175, 299
invoice, 282–283
IPIX service, 219–220
Ipswitch Web site, 155
ISBN, 41
ISP Menu Web site, 21
Items I'm Selling page, 65–66
Items I'm Watching page, 63–64
Items I've Bid On page, 62
Items I've Sold area, 66
Items I've Won page, 63
Ivens, K., 342

• J •

jacks, phone, 343
Jarrett, R., 322–324

jewelry, 213–214
job lots, 135–136

• K–L •

keystone, 339
keyword spamming, 56, 87–89
Komar, B., 348
law enforcement, 98
laws. *See* policies
LeakTest, 348
Leave Feedback link, 77
Leave Response button, 77
leaving feedback, 76–77, 178–179, 229
Legal Buddy program, 89
lens, camera, 209
letter, notification, 226
liabilities, business, 272–273
license, business, 275
lighting, 211
Lindsell-Roberts, S., 225
link buttons, 52–53
LinkExchange, 166
linking
  to About Me page, 57
  from auctions, 53, 56–57
  to e-mail, 56
  to vendor, 57
liquidation ad, 334
liquidation auction, 129
liquidation merchandise, 132–136
liquidators, 68, 133–137
listing merchandise. *See* merchandise,
    listing
listing policies, 54–57, 84
live auction, 37–38, 339
Lloyd's of London insurance, 79–80
locations, searches of, 145
logo, 79, 114

• M •

mail order sales, 19
ManageAuctions.com, 184–186
Mann family, 314–316
mannequin, 212–213
marketing, eBay store, 116

marketing auctions. *See also* auctions
  About Me page, 53, 57
  budget, 193, 196
  Items I'm Watching page, 64
  listing techniques, 194–203
  optional listing features, 196–203
  overview, 52–53
  writing descriptions, 110,
      207–208, 224–225
marketing Web sites, 164–168
matchstick icon, 50
McAfee, 348
McClelland, D., 218
Me icon, 72
Media Mail, 262
mediation, 101
mega pixels, 209
Member search, 96
merchandise
  alcohol, 86
  as is/where is item, 337
  auction management software, 176–177
  books, 18
  car parts, 33
  CDs, 18
  choosing, 13–20
  cleaning, 215, 300
  clothing, 15, 18, 212–213
  collectibles, 14–15
  hard goods, 13
  jewelry, 213–214
  liquidation, 132–136
  packaging, 302–303
  popular, 143
  potentially infringing items, 87–89
  prohibited, 85–86
  questionable items, 86–87
  searching for, 116, 134–137, 143
  selling in eBay store, 116–119
  shipping, 13
  soft goods, 13
  sports equipment, 15–16
  storage, 13, 132
  toys, 18
  tracking, 65–66
  unsold, 327–336
  videos, 18

merchandise, listing
  in eBay store, 114–116
  fees, 203–204
  listing policies, 54–57, 84
  marketing techniques, 194–203
  optional features, 196–203
  pre-sale listing, 55–56
  Relisting feature, 11, 176
  synonyms, 89
  using automatic management
      software, 176–177
merchandise, stocking
  auctions, 128–129
  consignment sales, 137, 139
  disount club stores, 125–126
  dollar stores, 124
  freebies, 131–132
  garage sales, 127–128
  going-out-of-business sales, 127–128
  Goodwill, 130–131
  job lots, 135–136
  pallets, 134–135
  resale merchandise, 137–138
  resale shops, 130–131
  salvage merchandise, 132–136
  Salvation Army, 130
  wholesalers, 136–137
merchandise invoice, 282
merchandise value
  authentication services, 151–152
  collectibles, 141
  eBay searches for, 142–147
  online appraisals, 150
  publications of, 148–149
  Web sites, 149–150
merchant account, 27–28, 250–252
mercury, bottled, 214
meta tags, 167
MIB item, 339
Microsoft bCentral, 161–162, 185–186
Microsoft Passport sign-in service, 70
Microsoft Works, 246
Miller, B., 313–314
MIMB item, 339
mint condition, 339
MissionFish.com, 328–329
Mister Lister program, 11, 79, 183, 190–191
modem, 21–22
money order, 231–235

Morgan, A., 312–313
Morgan, C., 312–313
Motors category, 33–36
Mr. Lister Twister, 183
MSN LookSmart, 167
My Auction Photos Web site, 114, 219
My eBay page
  Accounts page, 69
  Bidding/Watching page, 61–64
  Favorites page, 67–68
  as home page, 61
  links at, 60
  navigation bar, 60
  overview, 60
  pages in, 60
  Preferences/Set-up page, 69–70
  Selling page, 64–66
  Shortcut to Desktop option, 61
  viewing history, 61
My Max Bid column, 62

• *N* •

name. *See* user ID
NameProtect Web site, 163
naming
  eBay business, 24, 107, 110, 275
  Web sites, 163
NARU user, 340
National Fraud Information Center, 98
navigation bar, My eBay, 60
negative feedback, 76–77, 102
Nelson, G., 325–326
Nelson, M., 325–326
Nelson, S. L., 286
Neopost Online, Inc., 307–308
NETGEAR, 343–344
network, computer, 341–348
Network Solutions, 164
99¢ Only store, 124
Nolo Web site, 271
non-paying bidder, 94–96, 228
non-selling eBay seller, 92
Norton Antivirus, 348
notification letter, 226–228
numbers, credit card, 242–243

• *O* •

office space, 28–29, 297–299
offline standard program, 267
Omidyar, P., 10, 14
online appraisals, 150
online auction management service
  AuctionHelper, 180–181
  Auctionworks, 182–183
  checkout area, 178
  cost of, 179–180
  ManageAuctions.com, 184–185
  Microsoft bCentral commerce
    manager, 185–186
  specific providers, 180–185
  storing images, 219
  tracking buyer information, 178
online charity, 328–329
online dispute resolution, 100
online payment services, 27
online seminars, 81
OOP book, 340
Open Store Now button, 109
optional listing features, 196–203
organizing the back office, 297–299

• *P* •

packaging merchandise, 302–303
packing materials, 300–302
pallets of merchandise, 134–135
paper, background, 214–215
Parcel Post, 262
Parnell, J., 316–317
partnership, 273
password, 59, 69–70
payments. *See also* credit cards
  Accounts page, 69
  cash on delivery, 236
  collecting, 27–28, 43
  eBay store information, 110
  escrow service, 238–240
  Half.com, 43
  merchant account, 27–28
  methods of, 111
  money order, 231–235
  non-paying bidder, 94–96, 228
  notice of receipt, 229

payments *(continued)*
  online payment services, 27
  personal checks, 236–237
  refusing, 92
  reminders, 66, 228
  Review Payments page, 116–117
  split transaction, 340
Paypal, 27, 178, 237, 242–245, 286
penalties for violations, 90–91, 94
personal check, 236–237
Personal Offer feature, 53–54
Personal Shopper tool, 67–68
phone jacks, 343
phone number, 96
photo studio, 208–215
photos. *See* images
Photoshop (Adobe), 217
Photoshop For Dummies, 218
pictures. *See* images
Pitney Bowes, 304
pixels, 209
plastic bags, 298, 301
policies
  auctions, 54–57, 84
  notification of change, 84
  reporting violations, 97–99, 103
  resolving disputes, 98–102
  return, 112
  trading violations, 89–97
postage, 304–308
potentially infringing items, 87–89
Power Pak 6 (Battery Busters), 211
Power Seller Satisfaction Guarantee, 78–79
power supply, 211
pre-sale listing, 55–56
preapproved bidders, 74
Preferences/Set-up page, 69–70
Preservation Publishing, 112–113
printing
  postage, 305, 307
  shipping labels, 178
Priority Mail, 261, 303
Private auction, 48–49
prizes, 56

prohibited items, 85–86
Propigate@home.com, 322–324
props, 212–215
provenance, 340
proxy bidding system, 50–51
publications, 148–149

• *Q–R* •

questionable items, 86–87
QuickBooks, 243, 340
QuickBooks 2001 For Dummies, 286
Quicken, 281
raffles, 56
random charge, 243
ReadyHosting.com, 159–160
real estate sales, 19, 38–39, 205
receipts, 282
rechargeable battery, 211
registers, 340
registration, domain name, 163–164
Relisting feature, 11, 176
reminder, payment, 66, 228
removable media, 209
removing auctions, 62
reports, generating, 178
resale certificate, 277–278
resale license, 136
resale shops, 130–131
research, business, 11, 33, 148–150
reselling to eBay sellers, 331–332
Reserve fee, 37
Reserve over $25 fee, 35, 38
Reserve Price auction, 47–48
Restricted Access auction, 48
return policy, 112
returns, 133
Review Payments page, 116–117
risers, 213
Road Runner Web site, 155
Roadway Package Service (RPS), 256
ROI (Return on Investment), 340
rules. *See* policies
Rules & Safety report form, 98

• S •

SafeHarbor, 98, 103
sales tax, 112
sales tax number, 277–278
SallyJo, 324–325
Salvation Army, 130
Sam's Club, 125, 126
satisfaction guarantee, 78–79
scale, postage, 306
scams. *See* trading violations
scanners, 216
search engines, 166
Search Results by Category link, 145
searches, eBay
  advanced, 143–144
  ampersand, 143
  articles, 143
  of categories, 145, 194–195
  for completed auctions, 147
  conjunctions, 143
  e-mail alerts, 67–68
  for eBay store merchandise, 116
  favorites, 67–68
  keyword spamming, 56, 87–89
  of locations, 145
  Member search, 96
  for merchandise value, 142–147
  for popular merchandise, 143
  for resale merchandise, 137–138
  Smart Search, 144–147
  sorting results, 145
  tips, 142–143
  title versus seller, 116
  wild cards, 67
seasonal overstock, 133
security, Internet, 347–348
selecting. *See* choosing
Sell Your Item form, 38–39
seller. *See* eBay seller
Seller Assistant Pro Software course, 81
seller services, 72–81
Seller's Assistant, 175, 189–190
selling
  car parts, 33
  cars, 34–36
  fine art, 36–37
  merchandise in eBay store, 116–119
  real estate, 38–39
  user ID, 271
Selling page, 64–66
Sellphone account, 41
seminars, online, 81
SendMoneyOrder.com, 233–234
seven-day auction, 51
7-Eleven, 232
Severance, S., 324–325
shared hosting, 160
shelf-pulls, 133
shelves, 298
Shields Up, 348
shill bidding, 91
Shippertools.com, 263–265
shipping labels, 178, 306
shipping merchandise
  boxes, 302
  carriers, 255–263
  cars, 35–36
  costs, 13, 35–36, 256, 258, 260, 262
  delivery confirmation, 263–265
  disclosing costs, 224
  FedEx Ship Manager Software, 259
  Half.com, 43
  insurance, 260, 265–267
  liquidation merchandise, 134–135
  locations, 111
  notice of shipment, 229
  packaging merchandise, 302–303
  packing materials, 300–302
  postage, 304–308
  Shippertools.com, 263–265
  soft goods versus hard goods, 13
  stamps, U-PIC, 267
shipping tape, 301
Shop eBay With Me link buttons, 53
shopping cart, 158–159, 161
Shortcut to Desktop option, 61
Sign In activities, 70
signing out, 59
silent auction, 129
Silver-level Power Seller, 78
Simply Postage, 307–308
skeletons, 86
Skoll, J., 10

skulls, 86
Smart Media card, 209
Smart Search, 144–147
Snyder, W., 225
soft goods, 13
software. *See also* auction management
    software
  antivirus, 348
  bookkeeping, 26, 281, 285–295
  courses in, 81
  Create a Stamp, 307
  driver, 344
  for eBay business, 25–26
  FedEx Ship Manager Software, 259
  firewall, 347–348
  FTP, 172–173
  gateway, 251–252
  image editing, 217–218
  inventory tracking, 26, 299
  merchant account, 27–28
  Mister Lister program, 79
  online management software, 26
  QuickBooks, 285–295, 340
  Quicken, 281
sole proprietorship, 272, 340
sorting search results, 145
spam, keyword, 56, 87–89
specialty auction, 333–334
speed
  of digital cable connection, 23
  of DSL connection, 22
  home phoneline network, 343
  of modem, 21–22
split transaction, 340
sports equipment, 15–16
spreadsheet program, 26
SquareTrade, 98–102
stamps, 304–308
Stamps.com, 305–306
star icon, 75
starting bid, 50–51
state employer number, 278
statistics, Web site, 158, 218
steamer, 213
stock certificates, 86
stocking merchandise. *See* merchandise,
    stocking

storage
  America Online (AOL), 155
  bags, 298, 301
  boxes, 298–299
  hard drive, 20
  of images, 20, 218–220
  organizing, 297–299
  physical space, 28–29
  problems, 13
  for salvage merchandise, 132
  shelves, 298
store. *See* eBay store
Store Content page, 109
Styrofoam peanuts, 301
Submit It, 167–168
submitting feedback, 76–77, 178–179, 229
swap meet, 330–331
synonyms, 89

• T •

taking pictures, 215–216
tasks, business, 11–12, 171–178
Tate, K., 317–318
tax
  city tax certificate, 275–276
  income, 272–274
  IRS Tax Info for Business site, 283
  records, 281–285
  sales, 112
  sales tax number, 277–278
  withholding forms, 278
tax deduction, 340
tax ID number, 278
technology for eBay business, 20–23,
    343–344
telephone company, 22
ten-day auction, 52
1099 form, 337
thermal labels, 308
threaded lens mount, 210
three-day auction, 51
time
  budgeting, 10–12
  for business research, 11
  and earnings, 10
  length for auctions, 51–52
  minimum required, 12
  for shopping, 11

time-saving tips, 11
title bar image, 219
TOS (Terms of Service, 340
toys, 18
tracking
  auctions, 63–66
  bids, 62–63
  buyer information, 178
  inventory, 26, 175, 299
  sellers, 68
  sold merchandise, 65–66
trademark, 87–89, 163
Tradenable, 238–240
trading violations, 89–99, 103
traditional auction, 45
transaction interception, 92
transaction interference, 91–92
transferring user ID, 271
tripod, 210

• U •

unclaimed freight, 132
underage bidder, 96
underscore in user ID, 23, 109
Uniform Resource Locator (URL). *See* URL
United Parcel Service (UPS), 259–261
United States Postal Service (USPS),
    233, 236, 261–265
Universal Parcel Insurance Coverage
    (U-PIC), 265–267
Universal Product Code (UPC), 41
Universal Serial Bus (USB) adapter, 346
unsold merchandise, 327–336
unwelcome bidders, 93–94
UPC, 41
uploading, automatic, 172, 177
URL, 23, 164, 166–168
USB adapter, 346
User Agreement, eBay, 54, 84, 271
user ID
  changing, 23–24
  choosing, 23–24
  dash in, 109
  e-mail address as, 24
  guidelines, 23
  multiple, 59
  preferences, 69
  selling, 271

and signing out, 59
transferring, 271
underscore, 23, 109
URL as, 23
USPS, 233, 236, 261–265

• V •

values, eBay, 83–84
values, merchandise. *See* merchandise
    value
Vehicle Identification Number (VIN), 35
vehicles. *See* cars
vendor, linking to, 57
Verified Rights Owners (VeRO) program, 89
VeriSign, 254
videos, 18
view counter, 199–200
viewing history, 61
VIN, 35
violations, trading, 89–99, 103
Virtual Auction Ad Pro, 220–221
visitors to online stores, 105–106

• W •

W-9 form, 340
Watch This Item function, 64
Web hosts, 157–162, 184
Web page editors, 157
Web sites
  Accredited Registrar Directory, 164
  API Wizard, 233
  AuctionHelper.com, 53
  banner ad, 165–166
  Battery Busters, 211
  Big Lots company, 124
  Cool eBay Tools, 5
  Data Transfer limit, 158
  domain name registration, 163–164
  DSL Reports, 21
  versus eBay store, 28
  Federal Trade Commission Web site, 56
  FedEx, 257
  File Transfer Protocol (FTP), 155
  forwarding feature, 164
  free space for, 154–156, 218
  GlobalSCAPE, 26

Web sites *(continued)*
  Gomez Associates, 106
  Goodwill, 130–131
  Ipswitch, 155
  IRS Tax Info for Business site, 283
  ISP Menu, 21
  job lots, 135–136
  link buttons for, 52–53
  links to auctions, 53
  of liquidators, 133, 135–136
  marketing, 164–168
  of merchandise value, 149–150
  My Auction Photos, 114
  NameProtect, 163
  naming, 163
  99¢ Only store, 124
  Nolo, 271
  online auction management services,
    180–185
  paying for space, 157–162
  questionable items, 86–87
  Road Runner, 155
  SafeHarbor, 103
  Sellphone account, 41
  shopping cart, 158–161
  statistics, 158, 218
  submitting to search engines, 166–168
  trademark name, 163
  WebTrends, 158
  WholesaleCentral.com, 137
WebTrends Web site, 158
Wettern, J., 348
wholesale products, 340
WholesaleCentral.com, 137
wholesalers, 68, 136–137
wild card searches, 67
Windows Me (Microsoft), 345
wireless e-mail, 70
wireless network, 341–342
withholding forms, 278
Wooden, S. G., 319–320
wrinkles in clothing, 213
Writing Business Letters For Dummies, 225
writing description, 110, 207–208, 224–225
WS_FTP Pro, 155

• X-Y-Z •

Yahoo!, 105–106, 162, 167
Yahoo PayDirect, 250
ZoneAlarm Pro, 348
zoom, 210, 215

Notes

Notes